Albert Forbes Sieveking

**Gardens Ancient and Modern**

An Epitome of the Literature of the Garden-Art

Albert Forbes Sieveking

**Gardens Ancient and Modern**
*An Epitome of the Literature of the Garden-Art*

ISBN/EAN: 9783337068189

Printed in Europe, USA, Canada, Australia, Japan

Cover: Foto ©Andreas Hilbeck / pixelio.de

More available books at **www.hansebooks.com**

# GARDENS
# ANCIENT AND MODERN

AN EPITOME OF THE LITERATURE OF
THE GARDEN-ART

WITH AN
HISTORICAL EPILOGUE

BY
ALBERT FORBES SIEVEKING, F.S.A.

WITH ILLUSTRATIONS

LONDON
J. M. DENT & CO.
ALDINE HOUSE, 29 & 30 BEDFORD STREET, W.C.
1899

Cross in the Church at Wishball, Roxburgh

To
MARGARET AND MARGOT

# PROLOGUE

I SHOULD not perhaps venture now for the first time to set adrift upon the flowing tide of garden literature, old and new, a volume such as this; but when the first edition of 'The Praise of Gardens' made its appearance fourteen years ago, it might almost have claimed to be a pioneer in the revival of old garden books. Imperfect as it was in execution, it sought to bring together a series of prose passages giving an historical survey of their delightful subject; to show lovers of gardens and literature alike that the title of the volume was meant in the good old wide-embracing sense of Elizabethan days, when to praise a subject was also to appraise and appreciate it. If that aim more nearly hits the mark in the present edition, by means of the many passages omitted and added, which fourteen years' further familiarity with the sources have suggested, the collection may better deserve the eulogy, 'a scholarly little book,' passed upon its infancy in all too indulgent and encouraging conversation by my friend and master, Walter Pater. At least I trust that the unity of its subject, garden-art or design, will in some degree fuse and harmonise the variety of voices joining in the choir of praise.

It is vain to expect that everyone will be satisfied with the choice, and that all will find their favourite authors quoted or their favourite gardens mentioned. Many will wonder why poetry is so poorly represented, one reason perhaps being that poetry is richer in flowers than in gardens, and it is with gardens as a whole, rather than their contents, that this book is busy. Besides, in a garden everyone is his or her own poet. Moreover, are

## PROLOGUE

there not verse Anthologies enough and to spare? Of the gaps in my garden-hedges I am only too conscious, marvelling how I can have overlooked such obvious and striking claims. Where are the Garland and Plant lore of Athenæus and Theophrastus, and the Garden 'Points' of old Thomas Tusser? Where are Bulleyn's 'Bulwarks of Defence,' Andrew Borde's 'Dyetary of Health,' and Bishop Grossteste's 'Boke of Husbandry'? Where are the lines of the Poet-King James I. of Scotland on Windsor Garden? And why is Gerarde preferred to his predecessor, Dr Wm. Turner? Why find we no mention of Raleigh's Gardens at Beddington, or at Sherborne, described by Pope? Where are Ralph Austen and Sir Hugh Platt, John de Garlande (1081), Jon Gardener (1440), John Rea, John Rose, John Tradescant, John Reid (author of the 'Scots' Gard'ner,' 1683, the earliest Scotch garden-book), John Dalrymple (are all gardeners Johns?), James Justice, and Gibson's 'Gardens about London,' 1691?

Well, some are to be found in the Epilogue, some are perhaps too exclusively technical, and the absence of the others can only be explained by the short word, Space!

And now to the real purpose of this Prologue, that of most Prologues, Thanks!

Where all is borrowed it seems invidious to make distinctions in gratitude. And so 'to the Great Men of the Past' who unconsciously lend their names and writings to the following pages I offer my deepest and most reverent thanks. To the living writers (and their publishers) who in this edition or the last have allowed me to quote from their works, I repeat my sense of their kindness and my obligation.

In regard to the Art contributions, first and foremost to Mr George S. Elgood, R.I., for his liberality in allowing me to make

# PROLOGUE

a selection from many of his beautiful and famous drawings, I am most sincerely grateful.

To Mrs William Graham I am indebted for permission to copy her lovely water-colour of 'The Lady in the Garden,' by Frederick Walker, which makes so poetical a frontispiece, and Walker's own comment strikes an admirable key-note to the book : 'The Garden is the perfection of Peace and Loveliness.'

To Miss Ella Sykes, author of 'Through Persia on a Side-Saddle,' I owe my thanks for leave to use 'the Garden of Fin, at Kashan'; and for the sixth photogravure, 'In a Scotch Walled Garden,' I am indebted to the photographic skill of my brother-in-law, Mr A. G. Campbell, as well as for the view of the Inn Garden at Nara, Japan, taken upon his travels.

To Professor Brinckmann, Director of the Arts and Crafts Museum at Hamburg, I am under deep obligation for the artistic and altruistic impulse which prompted him to place at my disposal and send to England a large case of rare engravings selected by himself, at a sacrifice of great labour and time, from the fine and perhaps unique historical collection of Garden Prints, which he has formed for the Museum, and exhibited at the great Gardening Exhibition in Hamburg, 1897.

I must further thank Mrs W. A. Wills for her photograph of the Pond Garden, at Hampton Court; and Mr George Clausen, A.R.A., for procuring me the photograph of the Pompeian Garden.

To the three chief Histories of Gardening in English, viz. :—

(i) The general one prefixed to J. C. Loudon's 'Encyclopædia of Gardening' (1834), a masterly and exhaustive treatise, which only requires to be brought down to date:

(ii) George W. Johnson's 'History of English Gardening' (1829), which also strongly merits the honour of a second edition : and

# PROLOGUE

(iii) Hon. Alicia Amherst's 'History of Gardening in England' (1895)—my obligations are none the less great that it is impossible to express them every time they are incurred.

Finally, to my old friend Francis Henry Cripps-Day for general and generous assistance given me unstintingly in revising the book, as well as for the labour of preparing the Index (*non solum verborum, sed amicitiæ*), I am heartily grateful.

And now a last word of egoistic reverie. Where may one indulge in day-dreams, if not in a garden? My dream is of a Library in a Garden! In the very centre of the garden away from house or cottage, but united to it by a pleached alley or pergola of vines or roses, an octagonal book-tower like Montaigne's rises upon arches forming an arbour of scented shade. Between the bookshelves, windows at every angle, as in Pliny's Villa library, opening upon a broad gallery supported by pillars of 'faire carpenter's work,' around which cluster flowering creepers, follow the course of the sun in its play upon the landscape. 'Last stage of all,' a glass dome gives gaze upon the stars by night, and the clouds by day: 'les nuages... les nuages qui passent... là bas... les merveilleux nuages!' And in this ΒΙΒΛΙΟΚΗΠΟΣ—this Garden of Books—*Sui et Amicorum*, would pass the coloured days and the white nights, 'not in quite blank forgetfulness, but in continuous dreaming, only half-veiled by sleep.'

A. FORBES SIEVEKING.

12 Seymour Street, Portman Square,
*November* 1899.

# TABLE OF CONTENTS

|  | PAGE |
|---|---|
| PROLOGUE | vii |
| LIST OF ILLUSTRATIONS | xiv |
| *Hortorum Laudes* | xvi |

### CHAPTER I
#### ANCIENT EGYPTIAN, HEBREW, PERSIAN, SYRIAN, GREEK AND ROMAN GARDENS

Egyptian MS. (19*th Dynasty*)—Solomon—Homer—Xenophon—Plato—Aristotle—Theophrastus—Epicurus—Theocritus—Cato—Cicero—Varro—Diodorus Siculus—Pliny *the elder*—Pliny *the younger*—Plutarch—Columella—Tacitus—Seneca—Quintilian—Lucian—Palladius. . . . . . . . . 1-22

### CHAPTER II
#### SOME EARLY CHRISTIAN AND LATE PAGAN WRITERS ON THE GARDEN

St Jerome—T'Ao Yüan-ming—Longus—Tatius—Mohammad—Chou-tun-i—Lien-tschen—William of Malmesbury . . . 23-29

### CHAPTER III
#### MEDIÆVAL, RENAISSANCE AND TUDOR GARDENS

Neckham—Petrarch—St Bernard—Brunetto Latini—Maundeville—Boccaccio—Machiavelli—Erasmus—More—Luther—Gawen Douglas—Baber—Fitzherbarde—Polydore Vergil—C. Estienne—Palissy—Du Cerceau—Heresbach—Googe—Montaigne—Tasso—Treveris—Leland—Cœsalpinus—De Serres . . . . . 30-61

### CHAPTER IV
#### ELIZABETHAN AND STUART GARDENS

Gerarde—Lyly—Sidney—Bacon—Hentzner—Drayton—Parkinson—Hill (*Dydymus Mountaine*)—Maschal—Lawson—Laneham—Wotton—Bishop Hall—Burton—Taylor (*the Water Poet*)—Comenius—Harrison—George Herbert—Gassendi—Howell—Sir W. Waller . . 62-93

xii        TABLE OF CONTENTS

PAGE

CHAPTER V

THE FORMAL GARDEN IN THE SEVENTEENTH CENTURY UNDER FRENCH AND DUTCH INFLUENCE : ORIENTAL TRAVELLERS ON PERSIAN AND JAPANESE GARDENS

Sir T. Browne—Milton—Fuller—Cowley—Hartlib—Le Nôtre—Evelyn—Shaftesbury—De la Quintinye—De Sévigné—Bunyan—Ray—Meager—Temple—Huet—Pepys—London and Wise — Mandelslo—Chardin—Dufresny—Kaempfer—Worlidge     .     .     .     .     .    94-130

CHAPTER VI

DECLINE OF THE FORMAL AND INDICATIONS OF THE NATURAL OR LANDSCAPE GARDEN IN THE FIRST HALF OF THE EIGHTEENTH CENTURY

Defoe—Switzer—Swift—Addison—St Simon—Bolingbroke—Kent—Pope Montesquieu—Miller—Voltaire—Chesterfield—Batty Langley     .    131-153

CHAPTER VII

THE SENTIMENTAL, LANDSCAPE, AND PARK SCHOOLS OF GARDENING, FOUNDED UPON PAINTING; AND THE CHINESE AND ENGLISH 'NATURAL' STYLES, AT THE END OF THE EIGHTEENTH CENTURY

Kames—Spence—Chatham—Johnson—De Brosses—Rousseau—Sterne—Diderot—Shenstone—Brown (*Capability*)—Gray—Horace Walpole—Watelet—Gilbert White—Adam Smith—W. Mason and Burgh—Sir W. Chambers — Wilkes — Goldsmith — Kant — Bradley — Erasmus Darwin—Cowper     .     .     .     .     .     .     .    154-193

CHAPTER VIII

GARDEN DESIGN AS A LIBERAL OR FINE ART: THE 'COMPOSITION' OF NATURE OR LANDSCAPE—REACTION OF THE 'PICTURESQUE' WRITERS—ECLECTICISM, COSMOPOLITANISM AND ROMANTICISM IN GARDEN LITERATURE.

Whately — Prince de Ligne — Girardin—G. Mason—Gibbon—L'Abbé Delille—Young—Uvedale Price—Goethe—Payne Knight—Windham—Repton—Joubert—Alison—Schiller—Beckford—Cobbett—de Staël—Maine de Biran—Isaac Disraeli—Alex. von Humboldt     .     .    194-232

# TABLE OF CONTENTS xiii

## CHAPTER IX

### THE GARDEN IN THE NINETEENTH CENTURY

Wordsworth—Scott—Southey—Sydney Smith—Lamb—Landor—Hallam—Lord Campbell—Humphry Davy—Washington Irving—Leigh Hunt—John Wilson (*Chris. North*)—Thomas Love Peacock—Byron—Schopenhauer—Lamartine—Shelley—Thomas Arnold—Whewell—Heine—Alcott—Newman—Victor Hugo—Bulwer Lytton—Douglas Jerrold—George Sand—Benjamin Disraeli—Hawthorne—Alphonse Karr—O. W. Holmes—Poe—Maurice de Guérin—Gautier—Kinglake—Thoreau—Baudelaire—Amiel—de Goncourt—Renan—Mortimer Collins—James ('*Carthusian* ')—'*Quarterly Review*'—Helps—Stirling Maxwell—Watson—Ruskin—Matthew Arnold—William Morris—Walter Pater—'Vernon Lee'—Mrs Meynell—Henry Bright—George Milner—Alfred Austin—Zola—R. Blomfield and Inigo Thomas—Mrs J. F. Foster—William Robinson—Phil Robinson—Charles Dudley Warner—D'Annunzio—' E. V. B.' . . . . 233-313

HISTORICAL EPILOGUE . . . . . . 315

INDEX . . . . . . . . . 415

# LIST OF ILLUSTRATIONS

1. The Lady in the Garden, Stobhall, Perthshire. Fred Walker, A.R.A. . . . . . *Frontispiece*

                                        PAGE

2. An Ancient Egyptian Garden (*after Rosellini*) . . 2
3. Generalife, Granada, Spain. George S. Elgood, R.I. *To face* 86
4. The Garden of Fin, Kashan, Persia . . *To face* 127
5. Villa Muti, Frascati, Italy. George S. Elgood, R.I. *To face* 161
6. Brockenhurst, Hampshire. George S. Elgood, R.I. *To face* 212
7. In a Scotch Walled Garden (*from a Photograph by A. G. Campbell*) . . . . . . *To face* 289
8. Inner Garden of the House of Aulus Vettius, recently excavated at Pompeii . . . . . 323
9. Plan of the Abbey Garden of St Gall, by a Monk of the Ninth Century . . . . . . 325
10. 'The Garden of Love.' From the earliest known Flemish engraving (*circa* 1450), by 'Der Meister der Liebesgärten' . . . . . 329
11. The Terraced Gardens of St Germain-en-Laye, 1523. From G. Braun's 'Civitates orbis Terrarum.' . 333
12. The Tudor 'Pond Yard' or Garden, Hampton Court, in its Present State (*from a Photograph by Mrs W. A. Wills*) . . . . . . . 335
13. The Villa d'Este, Tivoli. After Piranesi, 1765 . . 339
14. 'Hortus Penbrochianus.' From 'Le Jardin de Wilton,' by Isaac de Caus, 1640 . . . . . 344
15. A Garden, engraved by Crispin de Pass. From the 'Hortus Floridus,' Arnheim, 1614 . . . 347
16. The Title-Page of Gerarde's 'Herball,' 1st Edition, 1597 349

# LIST OF ILLUSTRATIONS

|  | PAGE |
|---|---|
| 17. PORTRAIT OF SIR PHILIP SIDNEY IN THE GARDEN AT PENSHURST | 353 |
| 18. PORTRAIT OF LE NÔTRE. AFTER CARLO MARATTI | 355 |
| 19. PERSPECTIVE VIEW OF THE CHÂTEAU AND GARDENS OF VERSAILLES. ENGRAVED BY A. PERELLE, AFTER ISRAËL SYLVESTRE (*circa* 1688) | 359 |
| 20. 'LE THÉÂTRE D'EAU,' VERSAILLES. FROM AN ENGRAVING BY PERELLE (*circa* 1660) | 361 |
| 21. 'LES BAINS D'APOLLON,' VERSAILLES. FROM AN ENGRAVING BY J. RIGAUD | 365 |
| 22. 'LA SALLE DE BAL,' VERSAILLES. AFTER COTTEL, 1688 | 367 |
| 23. PORTRAIT OF JOHN EVELYN. AFTER NANTEÜIL (WITH AUTOGRAPH) | 371 |
| 24. VIEW OF THE DUTCH GARDEN AT JACOBSDAHL | 376 |
| 25. BIRD'S-EYE VIEW OF HAMPTON COURT AND GARDENS. FROM KIP'S 'BRITANNIA ILLUSTRATA' (1706-1710) | 379 |
| 26. PARTERRE FROM PORTICO OF HOUSE AT STOWE, BUCKS, AS DESIGNED BY BRIDGMAN, 1714-1739 | 381 |
| 27. PLAN OF POPE'S GARDEN AT TWICKENHAM AT THE TIME OF HIS DEATH, BY HIS GARDENER, JOHN SERLE | 385 |
| 28. THE GARDENS OF TRINITY COLLEGE, OXFORD. FROM WILLIAMS' 'OXONIA DEPICTA,' 1732-3 | 387 |
| 29. 'THE GARDEN OF GARDENS', PEKIN, BEGUN 1723 | 391 |
| 30. ESHER, AS LAID OUT BY KENT FOR HENRY PELHAM (1725-1735). FROM A DRAWING BY WOOLLET (1801) | 395 |
| 31. VIEW OF THE PAVILION AND 'JEU DE BAGUE' IN THE GARDEN OF MONCEAU(X), AS LAID OUT BY CARMONTELLE | 400 |
| 32. JAPANESE MOUNTAIN GARDEN IN THE 'SHIN' OR 'FINISHED STYLE' | 406 |
| 33. INN GARDEN AT NARA, JAPAN (*from a Photograph by A. G. Campbell*) | 408 |
| 34. 'LE BOSQUET DE BACCHUS.' ENGRAVED BY C. N. COCHIN, AFTER A PAINTING BY WATTEAU | 411 |

# HORTORUM LAUDES.

## ΤΟΙΣ 'ΑΠΟ ΤΩΝ ΚΗΠΩΝ ΤΑΥΤΑ ΧΑΡΙΖΟΜΑΙ.

"Σὺ τοῦτο πρὸς ἐμὲ ἐν τῷ κήπῳ ὑπὸ ταῖς δάφναις αὐτὸς ἔφησθα ἐννενοηκέναι."
—*Plato to Dionysius.*

"Cogito trans Tiberim hortos aliquos parare, et quidem ob hanc causam maxime: nihil enim video quod tam celebre esse possit."—*Cicero ad Atticum.*

"Hic mihi magis arridet, ut est sua cuique sententia, etiam in Hortis."—*Erasmus.*

"Adsis, nam Laudes nostri cantabimus Horti."—*Gilbert Cousin,* 1552.

"Mio picciol orto,
A me sei vigna, e campo, e silva, e prato."—*Baldi.*

"In garden delights 'tis not easy to hold a mediocrity; that insinuating pleasure is seldom without some extremity."—*Sir Thomas Browne.*

"And I beseech you, forget not to informe yourselfe as dilligently as may be, in things that belong to Gardening."—*John Evelyn.*

"My Garden painted o'er
With Nature's hand, not Art's."—*Cowley.*

"Consult the Genius of the Place in all."—*Pope.*

"Il faut cultiver notre Jardin."—*Voltaire.*

"Les Jardins appelaient les champs dans leur séjour;
Les Jardins dans les champs vont entrer à leur tour:

Chacun d'eux a ses droits; n'excluons l'un ni l'autre
Je ne décide point entre Kent, et Le Nôtre."—*L'Abbé De Lille.*

"Pères de famille, inspirez le *jardinomanie* à vos enfants."—*Prince de Ligne.*

„Eine mit Geist beseelte und durch Kunst eraltierte Natur."—*Schiller.*

"Nothing is more completely the child of Art than a Garden."—*Sir Walter Scott.*

"Laying out grounds may be considered as a Liberal Art."—*Wordsworth.*

"Exclusiveness in a garden is a mistake as great as it is in society."—*Alfred Austin.*

"What may be called the literary history of gardening shall be succinctly and impartially attempted."—*Dallaway.*

"It is a natural consequence that those who cannot taste the actual fruition of a garden should take the greater delight in reading about one. But the enjoyment next below actual possession seems to be derived from writing on the topic."—*Quarterly Review,* 1851.

"Any book I see advertised that treats of Gardens I immediately buy."
"*The Solitary Summer,*" 1899.

# THE PRAISE OF GARDENS

## CHAPTER I

ANCIENT EGYPTIAN, HEBREW, PERSIAN, SYRIAN, GREEK AND
ROMAN GARDENS

SHE led me, hand in hand, and we went into her garden to **EGYPTIAN**
converse together. **MS.**
There she made me taste of excellent honey. (19*th Dynasty*,
The rushes of the garden were verdant, and all its bushes flourishing. B.C. 1300).
There were currant trees and cherries redder than the ruby.[1]
The ripe peaches[2] of the garden resembled bronze,
and the groves had the lustre of the stone *nashem*.[3]
The *menni*[4] unshelled like cocoa-nuts they brought to us,
its shade was fresh and airy, and soft for the repose of love ;
' Come to me,' she called unto me,
' and enjoy thyself a day in the room of
a young girl who belongs to me,
the garden is to-day in its glory ;
there is a terrace and a parlour.'

> ' *The Tale of the Garden of Flowers*,' *translated by M. François Chabas* ('*Records of the Past*,' *Egyptian Texts*).

Gardens are frequently represented in the tombs of Thebes and other parts of Egypt, many of which are remarkable for their extent. The one here introduced is shown to have been surrounded by an embattled wall, with a canal of water passing in front of it, connected with the river. Between the canal and the wall, and parallel to them both, was a shady avenue of various trees ; and about the centre was the entrance, through a lofty door

[1] Fruits termed *Kaion* and *Tipau*, which probably had nothing in common with cherries and currants except their colour.
[2] The Persea fruit, a species of sacred almond.
[3] Green felspar, or Amazon stone.         [4] An unknown fruit.

## THE PRAISE OF GARDENS

whose lintel and jambs were decorated with hieroglyphic inscriptions, containing the name of the owner of the grounds, who in this instance was the King himself.

The vines were traced on a trellis-work, supported by transverse

An Ancient Egyptian Garden (after Rosellini).

rafters resting on pillars; and a wall extending round it separated this part from the rest of the garden. At the upper end were suites of rooms on three different storeys, looking upon green trees, and affording a pleasant retreat in the heat of summer

On the outside of the vineyard wall were planted rows of palms, which occurred again with the *dôm* and other trees, along the whole length of the exterior wall: four tanks of water, bordered by a grass plot, where geese were kept, and the delicate flower of the lotus was encouraged to grow, served for the irrigation of the grounds; and small kiosks, or summer-houses, shaded with trees, stood near the water, and overlooked beds of flowers.—*Sir J. Gardner Wilkinson*, '*The Ancient Egyptians.*'[1]

—∿∿∿—

A GARDEN enclosed is my sister, my spouse; a spring shut up, a fountain sealed. **SOLOMON**
(B.C. 1033-975).
Thy plants are an orchard of pomegranates, with pleasant fruits;
camphire, with spikenard,
Spikenard and saffron; calamus and cinnamon, with all trees of frankincense; myrrh and aloes, with all the chief spices.
A fountain of gardens, a well of living waters, and streams from Lebanon.
Awake, O north wind: and come, thou south; blow upon my garden, that the spices thereof may flow out. Let my beloved come into his garden, and eat his pleasant fruits.—*The Song of Solomon.*

—∿∿∿—

AND without the court-yard hard by the door is a great garden, of four plough-gates, and a hedge runs round on either side. **HOMER** (B.C. 962-927).
And there grow tall trees blossoming, pear-trees and pomegranates, and apple-trees with bright fruit, and sweet figs, and olives in their bloom. The fruit of these trees never perisheth, neither faileth winter or summer, enduring through all the year. Evermore the West Wind blowing brings some fruits to birth and

[1] From an interesting paper in the *Morning Post* by Mr Percy E. Newberry, I gather, while correcting these proof sheets, that there is a Tomb at Thebes of a man named Nekht, who, under Thotmes III. (about 1500 B.C.), held the office of Head Gardener of the Gardens attached to the Temple of Karnak, which there is good reason to suppose were designed by him as represented in our illustration. This tomb was discovered first by Mr Robert Hay early in the century, during a residence of thirteen years in the Nile Valley, and has now been re-explored and excavated afresh by Mr Newberry, Lord Northampton, and Dr Spiegelberg.

ripens others. Pear upon pear waxes old, and apple on apple, yea, and cluster ripens upon cluster of the grape, and fig upon fig. There too hath he a fruitful vineyard planted, whereof the one part is being dried by the heat, a sunny plot on level ground, while other grapes men are gathering, and yet others they are treading in the wine-press. In the foremost row are unripe grapes that cast the blossom, and others there be that are growing black to vintaging. There too, skirting the furthest line, are all manner of garden beds, planted trimly, that are perpetually fresh, and therein are two fountains of water, whereof one scatters his streams all about the garden, and the other runs over against it beneath the threshold of the court-yard, and issues by the lofty house, and thence did the townsfolk draw water.—These were the splendid gifts of the gods in the palace of Alcinöus.—*Odyssey, VII.* (*Done into English Prose by S. H. Butcher and A. Lang.*)

—―⋀⋁⋀⋁—―

**XENOPHON** (B.C. 444-359). *SOCRATES.*—But in some part of Persia there is a great prince called Satrapa, who takes upon him the office both of soldiery and husbandry.

*Critobulus.*—If the king acts as you inform me, he seems to take as much delight in husbandry as he does in war.

*Soc.*—I have not yet done concerning him; for in every country where he resides, or passes a little time, he takes care to have excellent gardens (such as are called Paradeisioi),[1] filled with every kind of flower or plant that can by any means be collected, and in these places are his chief delight.

*Crit.*—By your discourse it appears also, that he has a great

---

[1] 'A Paradise seems to have been a large Space of Ground, adorned and beautified with all Sorts of Trees, both of Fruits and of Forest, either found there before it was inclosed, or planted after; either cultivated like Gardens, for Shades and for Walks, with Fountains or Streams, and all Sorts of Plants usual in the Climate, and pleasant to the Eye, the Smell or the Taste; or else employed like our Parks for Inclosure and Harbour of all Sorts of Wild Beasts, as well as for the Pleasure of Riding and Walking: And so they were of more or less extent, and of differing Entertainment, according to the several Humours of the Princes that ordered and inclosed them.'—(*Sir William Temple: Upon the Gardens of Epicurus.*)

delight in gardening; for, as you intimate, his gardens are furnished with every tree and plant that the ground is capable of bringing forth. . . .

When Lysander brought presents to Cyrus from the cities of Greece, that were his confederates, he received him with the greatest humanity, and amongst other things showed him his garden, which was called 'The Paradise of Sardis'; which when Lysander beheld he was struck with admiration of the beauty of the trees, the regularity of their planting, the evenness of their rows, and their making regular angles one to another; or, in a word, the beauty of the quincunx order in which they were planted, and the delightful odours which issued from them. Lysander could no longer refrain from extolling the beauty of their order, but more particularly admired the excellent skill of the hand that had so curiously disposed them; which Cyrus perceiving, answered him: 'All the trees which you here behold are of my own appointment; I it was that contrived, measured, laid out the ground for planting these trees, and I can even show you some of them that I planted with my own hands.'—'Œconomicus,' *translated by R. Bradley, F.R.S.*

**PLATO**
(B.C. 427-347).

*SOCRATES.* Lead on then, and at the same time look out for a place where we may sit down.

*Phædrus.* Do you see that lofty plane-tree?

*Socr.* How should I not.

*Phæ.* There, there is both shade and a gentle breeze, and grass to sit down upon, or, if we prefer it, to lie down on.

*Socr.* Lead on, then.

*Socr.* By Juno, a beautiful retreat. For this plane-tree is very wide-spreading and lofty, and the height and shadiness of this agnus castus are very beautiful, and as it is now at the perfection of its flowering, it makes the spot as fragrant as possible. Moreover, a most agreeable fountain flows under the plane tree, of very cold water, to judge from its effect on the foot. It appears from these images and statues to be sacred to certain nymphs and to Achelous. Observe again the freshness of the spot, how charming and very delightful it is, and how summer-like and shrill it sounds from the choir of grasshoppers. But the most delightful of all is the grass, which with its gentle slope is naturally adapted to give an easy support to the head, as one reclines. So that, my dear Phædrus, you make an admirable stranger's guide.— '*Phædrus,*' translated by *H. Carey.*[1]

Would a husbandman, who is a man of sense, take the seeds, which he values and which he wishes to be fruitful, and in sober earnest plant them during the heat of summer, in some garden of Adonis,[2] that he may rejoice when he sees them in eight days appearing in beauty?—*Phædrus (Jowett).*

*Socrates.* Of whom then are the writings and institutes relating to gardening?

*Friend.* Of gardeners.

*Soc.* Of those who know how to manage gardens?

*Fr.* How not?—*Minos.*

[1] Popular tradition gives the name of Academy (Kathemnia) to a place about three-quarters of a mile north-west of the Dipylum, in the broad belt of olive-wood which stretches along both Banks of the Cephisus from its source at the western foot of Mt. Pentelicus, nearly to the sea. Thus, though no remains of buildings belonging to it have as yet come to light, the situation of the Academy may be regarded as approximately ascertained. 'It is on the lowest level, where some water courses from the ridges of Lycabettus are consumed in gardens and olive plantations. These were the waters which, while they nourished the shady groves of the Academy and its plane trees remarkable for their luxuriant growth, made the air unhealthy. They still cause the spot to be one of the most advantageous situations near Athens for the growth of fruit and pot-herbs, and maintain a certain degree of verdure when all the surrounding plain is parched with the heat of summer.' (Leake, 'Athens.') It is said that Plato taught at first in the Academy, but afterwards in a garden of his own adjoining it, near Colonus Hippius. His house was in the garden, and for house and garden he seems to have paid 3000 drachms. He was so much attached to the place that though it was said to be unhealthy and the doctors advised him to shift his quarters to the Lyceum he positively refused to do so.—*J. T. Frazer. Pausanias's ' Description of Greece.'*

[2] The *Adonis gardens* (κῆποι Ἀδώνιδος), so indicative of the meaning of the festival of Adonis, consisted, according to Böckh, of plants in small pots, which were no doubt intended to represent the garden, where Aphrodite met Adonis. The Ancients frequently used the term *Adonis gardens* proverbially, to indicate something which had shot up rapidly, such as lettuce, fennel, barley, wheat.—*Humboldt's ' Kosmos.'*

# ARISTOTLE 7

SOME plants are born and grow by means of nutriment well **ARISTOTLE** digested; and others, on the contrary, spring from residues, (B.C. 384-322). and materials quite different. Cultivation causes the nutriment to digest, and fertilises it; this it is which produces fruits good to eat. The plants which arise from this tempering, are called tame plants, because the art of cultivation has been profitable to them, and has effected, to some extent, their education. Those, on the contrary, which art has not been able to direct, and which are derived from materials of which the conditions are contrary, remain wild and cannot shoot in a cultivated ground. For Nature tames plants in rearing them; but these other plants can only come from corruption. The caper-tree is one of the plants of this sort. . . .

Why is thyme in Attica so bitter, whilst all the other fruits are so sweet? Is it not because the soil of Attica is light and dry, so that plants do not find in it much moisture? . . .

Why do myrtles rubbed between the fingers seem to produce a better scent, than when not rubbed? Is it not the same as with grapes, of which the bunches submitted to the vintage seem sweeter than the ones gathered from the stock?—'*The Problems*': *from the French of Barthélemy Saint-Hilaire.*

—⋘—

*Theophrastus attached himself to Plato and then to Aristotle, and was the* **THEO-** *master of the comic poet Menander: his true name of Tyrtamus, Aristotle* **PHRASTUS** *exchanged for Theophrastus, in allusion to the divine grace of his speech: after* (4th Cent. B.C.). *the death of Aristotle, Theophrastus possessed a garden of his own, in the acquisition of which he was aided by Demetrius of Phalerus, whose friendship he enjoyed: he died at the age of eighty-five.*

*Diogenes Laertius gives an enormous list of works, all of which have perished except his 'Characters' (translated by La Bruyère), the History and Causes of Plants, on Stones, the Senses, and several fragments: the Lyceum, under his guidance, was attended by 2000 disciples.*

*There is no complete English translation of his work on Plants.*

I GIVE to Callinus the land which I possess at Stagira, and all my books to Neleus. As to my garden, the walk, and the houses adjacent to the garden, I give them in perpetuity to those of my friends mentioned below, who desire to devote themselves in common to study and philosophy therein, for everyone cannot always travel: provided that they shall not be able to alienate this property; it shall not belong to any of them individually; but they shall own it in common as a sacred possession, and shall enjoy it peaceably and amicably as is just and fitting. I admit to this common enjoyment Hipparchus, Neleus, Straton, Callinus, Demotimus, Democrates, Callisthenes, Melantus, Pancreon and Nicippus. Aristotle, son of Metrodorus and of Pythias, shall enjoy the same rights, and shall share them with these, if he desire to devote himself to philosophy; in this case the eldest shall take every possible care of him, to the end that he may make progress in science. I desire to be buried in the part of the garden judged to be most fitting, and no excessive expense shall be incurred for my funeral or my tomb. After the last rites have been paid me according to my will, and the temple, my tomb, my garden, and the walk have been provided for, I direct that Pompylus, who inhabits the garden, shall keep the custody of it, as before, and that he shall likewise have the superintendence of all the rest.—*Will of Theophrastus, preserved by Diogenes Laërtius.*

—⁂—

**EPICURUS** (B.C. 342-270). AS for myself, truly (I speak modestly, and therefore may be permitted) I am not only well content, but highly pleased with the Plants and Fruits growing in these my own little Gardens; and have this Inscription over the door, 'Stranger, Here, if you please, you may abide in a good condition; Here, the Supreme Good is Pleasure; the Steward of this homely Cottage is hospitable, humane, and ready to receive you; He shall afford you Barley-broth, and pure water of the Spring, and say, Friend, are you not well entertained? For, these Gardens do not invite hunger, but satisfie it; nor encrease your thirst with drinks, while they should extinguish it, but wholly overcome it with a Natural and Grateful Liquor.'— *Epicurus's Morals, Englished by W. Charelton, M.D.,* 1655.

## THEOCRITUS

SO, I and Eucritus and the fair Amyntichus, turned aside into the house of Phrasidamus, and lay down with delight in beds of sweet tamarisk and fresh cuttings from the vines, strewn on the ground. Many poplars and elm-trees were waving over our heads, and not far off the running of the sacred water from the cave of the nymphs warbled to us: in the shimmering branches the sun-burnt grasshoppers were busy with their talk, and from afar the little owl cried softly out of the tangled thorns of the blackberry; the larks were singing and the hedge-birds, and the turtle-dove moaned; the bees flew round and round the fountains, murmuring softly; the scent of late summer and of the fall of the year was everywhere; the pears fell from the trees at our feet, and apples in number rolled down at our sides, and the young plum-trees were bent to the earth with the weight of their fruit.—*Idyll VII.,* '*Thalysia,*' *translated by Walter Pater.*

**THEOCRITU** (3*rd Cent.* B.C.).

———∿∿∿———

*Marcus Porcius Cato the Censor, called by Livy* '*a man of almost iron body and soul*'—*originally a Sabine farmer, he fought against Hannibal at the battle of Metaurus: as* '*a plant that deserved a better soil*' *he was transplanted to Rome and became Quæstor, Consul and Censor. A great orator, more than* 150 *of his orations having been long preserved, and one of the first Roman writers* '*De Re Rustica,*' *or Farm Management—fragments of his* '*Origines*' *remain. At the age of eighty-four he conducted a law suit of his own.*

**M. PORCIUS CATO** (B.C. 234-149).

PLANT the Mariscan Fig in a chalky and exposed soil: put, on the contrary, into a rich and sheltered earth the sorts from Africa, Cadiz, Sagonta, the black Telanus, with long stalks. If you have a water-meadow, you will not want hay. If you have it not, smoke the field, to have hay.

Near the city, you will have gardens in all styles, every kind of ornamental trees, bulbs from Megara, myrtle on palisades, both white and black, the Delphic and Cyprian laurel, the forest kind, hairless nuts, filberts from Prœneste and Greece. A city garden, especially of one who has no other, ought to be planted and ornamented with all possible care.—*De Re Rustica.* § *VIII.*

## THE PRAISE OF GARDENS

Who is there (says Atticus) Marcus, that, looking at these natural falls, and these two rivers, which form so fine a contrast, would not learn to despise our pompous follies, and laugh at artificial Niles, and seas in marble; for, as in our late argument you referred all to Nature, so more especially in things which relate to the imagination, is she our sovereign mistress.—*De Legibus.* (*Introduction to 2nd Dialogue.*)

---

**CICERO**
(B.C. 106-43).

NOR husbandry is onely pleasant and plenteous by reason of corne and medowes and vyneyardes and trees joyned with vynes: but also by reason of orchardes, gardynes, also fedynge of cattell, and hyves of been: also the diversite of all maner of floures. Nor the plantynge and settyng of trees delyteth a man: but also graffynges than the which the husbande man never invented thynge more crafty and excellent. . . .

And for as moche as some men desyre these thynges, let us come in favour withe pleasure. For the wyne celler of the good man of the house diligent is couched full; also his oyle celler, and his pantry, and all his house is full of rychesse, it hath abundance of hogges, kydde, lambe, pultry ware, mylke, chese and hony. Now husbandmen call their garden a seconde larder. Also fowlyng, and huntyng, an exercyse at ydle tymes, maketh these thinges more savouryng. That whiche I wyll speke of the greennes of medowes, or the ordre of trees, or of the vyneyardes, or of the maner of olyve trees I shall declare brevely. The grounde well tylled and ordred, nothing may be more plenteous in profyte, nor more clenly and comly in syght: to the whiche grounde to be well cherysshed, olde age not onely dothe not let a man, but also moveth hym and allureth hym. For where may that olde age waxe so warme: or more warme by reason of sonnynge place or fyre: or upon the other parte by reason of covert, or waters be refresshed or cooled more holsom.—' *Tullius de Senectute, bothe in Latyn and Englysshe tonge. Translated by Robert Whitinson, Poete-Laureate,*' 1535.

## M. TERENTIUS VARRO

*M. T. Varro, the most learned of the Romans, historian, philosopher, naturalist, grammarian and poet, was entrusted by Cæsar to purchase the books for, and to manage all the Greek and Latin Libraries at Rome. Later, Augustus made him superintendent of the Library founded by Asinius Pollio: he was a friend of Cicero, to whom he dedicated ' De Lingua Latina,' his only extant work besides ' De Re Rusticâ,' written at the age of eighty. His Villa at Casinum was destroyed by Antony.*

M. TERENTIUS VARRO (B.C. 116-27).

YOU know that I have in my villa of Casinum a deep and clear stream, which threads its way between two stone margins. Its breadth is 57 feet, and bridges must be crossed to communicate from one part of my property to the other. My study (Museum) is situated at the spot where the stream springs; and from this point as far as an island formed by its junction with another water-course, is a distance of 850 feet. Along its banks a walk is laid out 10 feet broad, open to the sky; between this walk and the country my aviary is placed, closed in left and right by high walls. The external lines of the building give it some resemblance to writing tablets, surmounted by a Capitol. On the rectangular side its breadth is 48 feet, and its length 72, not including the semi-circular Capitol, which is of a diameter of 27 feet. Between the aviary and the walk which marks the lower margin of the tablets, opens a vaulted passage leading to an esplanade (*ambulatio*). On each side is a regular portico upheld by stone columns, the intervals between which are occupied by dwarf shrubs. A network of hemp stretches from the top of the outside walk to the architrave, and a similar trellis joins the architrave to the pedestal. The interior is filled with birds of every species, which receive their food through the net. A little stream supplies them with its water. Beyond the pedestal run to left and right along the porticos two rather narrow fish-ponds, which, separated by a small path, extend to the extremity of the esplanade. This path leads to a *tholus*, a kind of Rotunda, surrounded by two rows of isolated columns. There is a similar one in the house of Catulus, except that complete walls replace the colonnade. Beyond is a grove of tall brushwood encompassed with walls, of which the thick growth only allows the light to penetrate below.—' *Of Agriculture,*' *Book III.*

**DIODORUS SICULUS**
(*About* B.C. 50).

THE Hanging Garden of Babylon was not built by Semiramis who founded the city,[1] but by a later prince called Cyrus, for the sake of a courtezan, who being a Persian, as they say, by birth, and creating meadows on mountain tops, desired the king, by an artificial plantation, to imitate the land in Persia. This garden was 400 feet square, and the ascent up to it was to the top of a mountain, and had buildings and apartments out of one into another, like a theatre. Under the steps to the ascent were built arches one above another, rising gently by degrees, which supported the whole plantation. The highest arch, upon which the platform of the garden was laid, was 50 cubits high, and the garden itself was surrounded with battlements and bulwarks. The walls were made very strong, built at no small charge and expense, being 22 feet thick, and every sally port 10 feet wide. Over the several storeys of this fabric were laid beams, and summers of large massy stones, each 16 feet long and 4 broad. The roof over all these was first covered with reeds daubed with abundance of brimstone (or bitumen), then upon them were laid double tiles, joined with a hard and durable mortar, and over them all was a covering with sheets of lead, that the wet, which drained through the earth, might not rot the foundation. Upon all these was laid earth, of a convenient depth, sufficient for the growth of the greatest trees. When the soil was laid even and smooth, it was planted with all sorts of trees, which both for beauty and size might delight the spectators. The arches, which stood one above the other had in them many stately rooms of all kinds, and for all purposes. There was one that had in it certain engines, whereby it drew plenty of water out of the river Euphrates, through certain conduits hid from the spectators, which supplied it to the platform of the garden.

[1] The Syrians are great Gardiners, they take exceeding paines, and bee most curious in gardening; whereupon arose the proverb in Greeke to this effect, 'Many Woorts and Pot-hearbs in Syria.'—*Pliny's* '*Natural History*' (*P. Holland*).

# PLINY THE ELDER

*The elder Pliny perished in the eruption of Vesuvius, a martyr to scientific curiosity. Cuvier says of his 'Natural History': "Pliny's great work is at the same time one of the most precious monuments left us by antiquity, and a proof of the astonishing learning of a warrior and a statesman." Whewell writes: 'His work has, with great propriety, been called the Encyclopædia of Antiquity.'*

**PLINY THE ELDER**
*(Caius Plinius Secundus,*
A.D. 23-79).

IN all the twelve tables throughout which containe our ancient lawes of Rome, there is no mention made so much as once of a Grange or Ferme-house, but evermore a Garden is taken in that signification, and under the name of Hortus (*i.e.* Garden) is comprised Hœredium, that is to say, an Heritage or Domaine; and hereupon grew by consequence, a certain religious or ridiculous superstition rather, of some, whom we see ceremoniously to sacre and bless their garden and hortyard dores onely, for to preserve them against the witchcraft and sorcerie of spightfull and envious persons. And therefore they use to set up in gardens, ridiculous and foolish images of Satyres, Antiques, and such like, as good keepers and remedies against envie and witchcraft; howsoever *Plautus* assigneth the custodie of gardens to the protection of the goddesse *Venus*. And even in these our daies, under the name of Gardens and Hortyards, there goe many daintie places of pleasure within the very citie; and under the colour also and title of them men are possessed of faire closes and pleasant fields, yea, and of proper houses with a good circuit of ground lying to them, like pretie fermes and graunges in the countrey: all which, they tearme by the name of Gardens. The invention to have gardens within a citie came up first by *Epicurus*, the Doctor and master of all voluptuous idlenes, who devised such gardens of pleasance in Athens: for before his time, the manner was not in my citie, to dwell (as it were) in the countrey, and so to make citie and countrey all one, but all their gardens were in the villages without. Certes at Rome, a good garden and no more was thought a poor man's chievance; it went (I say) for land and living. The Garden was the poore commoner's shambles, it was all the market-place he had for to provide himselfe of victuals....

Certaine it is, that in old time, there was no market-place at

## THE PRAISE OF GARDENS

Rome yeelded greater impost unto the State than the Hearberie. . . . *Cato* highly commendeth the garden Coules or Cabbages, whereby we may know, that in his daies Gardens were in some respect. . . . And hereupon it came, that Salads of hearbs were called Acedaria,[1] so little care and trouble went to the provision and making of them. . . . That quarter of the Garden which serveth an house with poignant hearbs instead of sauce, to give a commendable tast and seasoning to our meat, sheweth plainly that the master and mistresse thereof were not woont to run in the Merchants bookes for Spicerie, but chaunged the Grocer or Apothecaries shop, for the Garden. . . . And as for the other quarters set out with beds of floures and sweet smelling hearbs, what reckoning was made of them in old time may appear by this, That a man could not heretofore come by a commoner's house within the citie, but he should see the windowes beautified with greene quishins (cushions), wrought and tapissed with floures of all colours; resembling daily to their view the Gardens indeed which were in outvillages, as being in the very heart of the citie, they might think themselves in the countrey. . . . Let us give therfore to Gardens their due honor; and let us not (I say) deprive things of their credit and authoritie, because they are common and nothing costly: for I may tell you, some of our nobilitie, yea, and the best of the citie, have not disdained to take their surnames from thence . . . in the noble house and lineage of the *Valerii*, some were not abashed nor ashamed to be called *Lactucini* in regard of the best kind of Lectuce that they either had in their gardens or affected most. And here I cannot chuse but mention by the way, the grace that hath growne to our name by occasion of some diligence employed and paines taken this way; whereby certain cherries beare our name and are called *Pliniana*, in testimonie of our affection and love to that fruit.—*Plinie's 'Naturall Historie,' Book XIX., chap. iv. Translated by Philemon Holland, Doctor in Physicke* (1551-1636).

[1] *i.e.* a sinecure: from ἀ, not, and κῆδος, care. "Acetaria" was the title chosen by John Evelyn for his 'Discourse on Sallets.'

# PLINY THE YOUNGER

**PLINY THE YOUNGER**
—*Nephew of the elder Pliny*
(A.D. 62-116).

MY villa¹ is so advantageously situated, that it commands a full view of all the country round; yet you approach it by so insensible a rise that you find yourself upon an eminence, without perceiving you ascended. Behind, but at a great distance, stand the Apennine Mountains. In the calmest days we are refreshed by the winds that blow from thence, but so spent, as it were, by the long tract of land they travel over, that they are entirely divested of all their strength and violence before they reach us. The exposition of the principal front of the house is full south, and seems to invite the afternoon sun in summer (but somewhat earlier in winter) into a spacious and well-proportioned portico, consisting of several members, particularly a porch built in the ancient manner. In the front of the portico is a sort of terrace, embellished with various figures and bounded with a box-hedge, from whence you descend by an easy slope, adorned with the representation of divers animals in box, answering alternately to each other, into a lawn overspread with the soft—I had almost said the liquid—Acanthus:² this is surrounded by a walk enclosed with tonsile evergreens, shaped into a variety of forms. Beyond it is the Gestatio,³ laid out in the form of a circus,⁴ ornamented in the middle with box cut in numberless different figures, together with a plantation of shrubs, prevented by the shears from shooting up too high; the whole is fenced in by a wall covered by box, rising by different ranges to the top. On the outside of the wall lies a meadow that owes as many beauties to nature, as all I have been describing *within* does to art; at the end of which are several other meadows and fields interspersed with thickets. At the extremity of this portico stands a

---

¹ Pliny's favourite villa in Tuscany, known as the Tusculan, about 150 miles from Rome; his Laurentine Villa is also described in his letters. Both have been the subject of learned disquisition and restoration by Scamozzi, Félibien, Schinkel and R. Castell in 'Villas of the Ancients.'
² Sir William Temple supposes the '*Acanthus*' of the ancients to be what we call '*Pericanthe*'; Mr Castell imagines it resembles moss.
³ *Gestatio*, a place for exercises in vehicles: 'the Row.'
⁴ *Circus*, set apart for public games.

grand dining-room, which opens upon one end of the terrace;[1] as from the windows there is a very extensive prospect over the meadows up into the country, from whence you also have a view of the terrace and such parts of the house which project forward, together with the woods enclosing the adjacent hippodrome. Opposite almost to the centre of the portico stands a square edifice, which encompasses a small area, shaded by four plane-trees, in the midst of which a fountain rises, from whence the water, running over the edges of a marble basin, gently refreshes the surrounding plane-trees and the verdure underneath them. . . . In the front of these agreeable buildings lies a very spacious hippodrome, entirely open in the middle, by which means the eye, upon your first entrance, takes in its whole extent at one glance. It is encompassed on every side with plane-trees covered with ivy, so that while their heads flourish with their own foliage, their bodies enjoy a borrowed verdure; and thus the ivy, twining round the trunk and branches, spreads from tree to tree, and connects them together.

Between each plane-tree are planted box-trees, and behind these, bay-trees, which blend their shade with that of the planes. This plantation, forming a straight boundary on both sides of the hippodrome, bends at the farther end into a semicircle, which, being set round and sheltered with cypress-trees, varies the prospect, and casts a deeper gloom; while the inward circular walks (for there are several), enjoying an open exposure, are perfumed with roses, and correct, by a very pleasing contrast, the coolness of the shade with the warmth of the sun. Having passed through these several winding alleys, you enter a straight walk, which breaks out into a variety of others, divided by box-hedges. In one place you have a little meadow, in another the box is cut into a thousand different forms:[2] sometimes into letters expressing the name of the master; sometimes that of the artificer; whilst here and there little obelisks rise, intermixed

[1] *Xystus*, terrace (properly a large portico for athletic exercises).
[2] *Matius* is said to have introduced the fashion of 'shaping' trees, the *ars topiaria*.

alternately with fruit-trees: when, on a sudden, in the midst of this elegant regularity, you are surprised with an imitation of the negligent beauties of rural nature: in the centre of which lies a spot surrounded with a knot of dwarf plane-trees.[1]

Beyond these is a walk planted with the smooth and twining Acanthus, where the trees are also cut into a variety of names and shapes. At the upper end is an alcove of white marble, shaded by vines, supported by four small Carystian pillars. From this bench, the water, gushing through several little pipes, as if it were pressed out by the weight of the persons who repose themselves upon it, falls into a stone cistern underneath, from whence it is received into a fine polished marble basin, so artfully contrived that it is always full without ever overflowing.

When I sup here, this basin serves for a table, the larger sort of dishes being placed round the margin, while the smaller ones swim about in the form of little vessels and water-fowl. Corresponding to this, is a fountain which is incessantly emptying and filling; for the water, which it throws up a great height, falling back into it, is by means of two openings, returned as fast as it is received. Fronting the alcove (reflecting as great an ornament to it, as it borrows from it) stands a summer-house of exquisite marble, the doors whereof project and open into a green enclosure; as from its upper and lower windows the eye is presented with a variety of different verdures. Next to this is a little private recess (which, though it seems distinct, may be laid into the same room) furnished with a couch; and notwithstanding it has windows on every side, yet it enjoys a very agreeable gloominess, by means of a spreading vine which climbs to the top and entirely overshades it. Here you may recline and fancy yourself in a wood; with this difference only—that you are not exposed to the weather. In this place a fountain also rises and instantly disappears; in different quarters are disposed marble seats, which serve, no less than the summer-house, as so many reliefs after one is wearied with walking. Near each seat is a little fountain; and, throughout the whole hippodrome, several

[1] *The plane-tree* was nourished on wine by the Romans.

small rills run murmuring along, wheresoever the hand of art thought proper to conduct them; watering here and there different spots of verdure, and in their progress refreshing the whole.—'*Letter to Apollinaris*,' *translated by William Melmoth.*

—∞—

**PLUTARCH**
(1st Cent. A.D.).

TISSAPHERNES, in all other cases savage in his temper, and the bitterest enemy that Greece experienced among the Persians, gave himself up, notwithstanding, to the flatteries of Alcibiades, insomuch that he even vied with and exceeded him in address. For of all his gardens that which excelled in beauty, which was remarkable for the salubrity of its streams and the freshness of its meadows, which was set off with pavillions royally adorned and retirements finished in the most elegant taste, he distinguished by the name of ALCIBIADES; and every one continued to give it that appellation.—'*Life of Alcibiades*.' *Langhorne's translation.*

Cimon, too, first adorned the city with those elegant and noble places for exercise and disputation, which a little after came to be so much admired. He planted the forum with plane-trees; and whereas the Academy before was a dry and unsightly plat, he brought water to it, and sheltered it with groves, so that it abounded with clean alleys and shady walks.—'*Life of Cimon.*'

Beside these, Lucullus had the most superb pleasure-houses in the country near Tusculum, adorned with grand galleries and open saloons, as well for the prospect as for walks.[1] Pompey, on a visit there, blamed Lucullus for having made the villa commodious only for the summer, and absolutely uninhabitable in the winter. Lucullus answered with a smile, 'What then, do you think I have not so much sense as the cranes and storks, which change their habitations with the seasons?'—*Life of Lucullus.*

For as these connynge gardiners thynke to make rosis and

[1] Hortus Luculli, cujus villa erat in Tusculano, non floribus fructibusque, sed *tabulis* fuisse insignis.—*Varro.*

violettis the better, if they sowe oynyons and garlyke nere by them, that what so ever sower savour be in them, it may be purged into the tother: so an enmye receyvynge in to him our envie and waywardnes, shal make us better and lesse grevous to our frendis that have good fortune.—'*Howe one may take profette of his Enmyes.*' (*De capienda ex inimicis utilitate.*) Sir Thomas Elyot (d. 1546).

*Columella, native of Gades (Cadiz), wrote a voluminous and valuable work on* **COLUMELLA** *Roman Agriculture, in twelve books, of which the tenth is a poem on the vegetable* (1st Cent. A.D.). *and flower garden, meant as a supplement to the Georgics of Virgil. Columella makes use of the work of his predecessors, Cato the Censor, Varro, Celsus and Atticus, Græcinus, and Mago the Carthaginian. He is quoted by Pliny the Elder, Vegetius, and Palladius, the work of the latter superseding Columella's. The writings of these three with Varro are generally found together as 'Scriptores de Re Rustica.' (English translation by Owen, 1803).*

THERE remains, therefore, the culture of gardens, notably neglected formerly by ancient Husbandmen, but now in very great request. Though it is true, indeed, that, among the ancients there was greater parsimony and frugality, nevertheless the poor were wont to fare better, and to be frequently admitted to public feasts.... Wherefore we must be more careful and diligent than our ancestors were in delivering precepts and directions for the cultivation of gardens, because the fruit of them is now more in use; and I would have subjoined them in prose to the preceding books, as I had resolved, unless your frequent and earnest demand had overcome my purpose, and prevailed with me to fill up, with poetical numbers, those parts of the *Georgic* poem, which were omitted, and which even Virgil himself intimated, that he left to be treated of by those that should come after him.—'*Of the Culture of Gardens*' (*Preface*).

MOREOVER, Nero turned the ruins of his country to his **TACITUS** private advantage, and built a house, the ornaments of (A.D. 61-117). which were not miracles of gems and gold, now usual in vulgar luxuries, but lawns and lakes, and after the manner of a desert;

here groves, and there open spaces and prospects; the masters and centurions being Severus and Celer, whose genius and boldness could attempt by art what Nature had denied, and deceive with princely force.[1]—*Annals, lib. XV.*

—vvv—

**SENECA**
(*d*. A.D. 65).

LIVE they not against nature that in winter long for a Rose, and by the nourishment of warme waters, and the fit change of heat in winter time, cause a lily, a spring flower, to bloom? Live not they against nature that plant orchards on their highest towers, that have whole forests shaking upon the tops and turrets of their houses, spreading their roots in such places where it should suffice them that the tops of their branches should touch. *Epistle* 122. (*Lodge's translation and L'Estrange.*)

A shrub, although it be old, may be translated into another place. This is necessarie for us to learne, who bee old men, of whom there is none but planteth an Orchard of Olives for another man. That which I have seene, this I speak; namely, that an Orchard of three or foure years old will, with a plentifull fall of the leafe, yeeld forth fruit; yea, also that tree will cover thee: which

> Hath been slow to make a shade before
> To yong nephewes and those that were unbore:

As our Virgil saith, (who beheld not what might be spoken most truly, but most seemely; neither desired he to teach husbandmen, but to delight those that read.—*Epistle* 86 : *Of the Country House of Africanus.* (*T. Lodge.*)

Why now, Gardens and houses of pleasure? he had divers, and differently bewtified. *Juvenall* toucheth it, 'The Gardens of most wealthy Seneca.' Hee himselfe likewise maketh mention of his houses: Nomentanum, Albanum and Baianum, and without question hee had manie.—'*Life of L. A. Seneca*,' by *Justus Lipsius.*

[1] The striking similarity of this description to that of a modern park is too obvious to escape notice.—(*Loudon.*)

BUT is the garden that is for use to avail of no ornament? **QUINTILIAN** by all manner of means let these trees be planted in a (1st Cent. A.D.). regular order, and at certain distances. Observe that quincunx, how beautiful it is; view it on every side; what can you observe more straight, or more graceful? Regularity and arrangement even improves the soil, because the juices rise more regularly to nourish what it bears. Should I observe the branches of yonder Olive Tree shooting into luxuriancy, I instantly should lop it; the effect is, it would form itself into a horizontal circle, which at once adds to its beauty and improves its bearing. '*Institutes of Eloquence,*' *Book VIII. Wm. Guthrie's translation*, 1756.

—∿∿∿—

IN the Island of the Blessed they have no night nor bright day, **LUCIAN** but a perpetual twilight; one equal season reigns throughout (A.D. 120-200). the year: it is always Spring with them, and no wind blows but Zephyrus; the whole region abounds in sweet flowers, and shrubs of every kind; their vines bear twelve times in the year, yielding fruit every month, their apples, pomegranates, and the rest of our autumnal produce, thirteen times, bearing twice in the month of Minos: instead of corn, the fields bring forth loaves of ready made bread, like mushrooms; there are three hundred and sixty-five fountains of water round the city, as many of honey, and five hundred rather smaller, of sweet scented oil, besides seven rivers of milk, and eight of wine.

Their Symposia are held in a place without the city, which they call the Elysian Field; this is a most beautiful meadow, skirted by a large and thick wood, affording an agreeable shade to the guests, who repose on couches of flowers; the winds attend upon, and bring them everything necessary, except wine, which is otherwise provided, for there are large trees on every side, made of the finest glass, the fruit of which are cups of various shapes and sizes; whoever comes to the entertainment gathers one or more of these cups, which immediately becomes full of wine, and so they drink of it, whilst the nightingales, and other birds of song, with their bills peck the flowers out of the neighbouring fields, and drop them on their heads; thus are they crowned with perpetual garlands; their manner of perfuming them is this; the clouds suck up the scented oils from the fountains and rivers, and the winds gently fanning them, distil it like soft dew on those who are assembled there; at supper they have music also, and singing, particularly the verses of Homer, who is himself generally at the feast, and sits next above Ulysses, with a chorus of youths and virgins: he is led in, accompanied by Eunomus the Locrian, Arion of Lesbos, Anacreon and Stesichorus, whom I saw there along with them, and who at length is reconciled to Helen: when they have finished their songs, another chorus begins of swans, swallows, and nightingales; and to these succeeds the sweet rustling of the Zephyrs, that whistle through the woods, and close the concert. What most contributes to their happiness is, that near the symposium are two fountains, the one of milk, the other of pleasure; from the first they drink at the beginning of the feast, there is nothing afterwards but joy and festivity.[1]—' *True History*' (*Dr Francklin's Translation*).

—ww—

**PALLADIUS RUTILIUS** (4th or 5th Cent. A.D.).

*Palladius lived about time of Theodosius, wrote ' De Re Rustica' in fourteen books, a compilation from writers like Columella or Gargilius: Book I. contains general rules about Agriculture—the next twelve are devoted to agricultural work of each month—Book XIV. in elegiac verse, on grafting trees: much used in Middle Ages, and the 'Speculum' of Vincent de Beauvais borrows largely from it.*

WITH orchard, and with gardeyne, or with mede,
　　Se that thyne hous with hem be umviroune;
The side in longe upon the south thou sprede,
The cornel ryse upon the wynter sonne,
And gire it from the cold West yf thou conne.

*The Middle English translation, 'Palladius on Husbondrie,' from the unique MS. of about* 1420 A.D. *in Colchester Castle. English Text Society.*

[1] Böttiger sees in this hyperbole a parody on the prodigies of Homer's Garden of Alcinous ('*Racemazionen zur Gartenkunst der Alten*').

# CHAPTER II

### THE GARDEN IN SOME EARLY CHRISTIAN AND LATE
### PAGAN WRITERS

IN those days, through the vast and horrible solitude, Hilarion **ST JEROME** at length came to a very high mountain, having found there (A.D. 345-420). two monks, Isaac and Pelusianus, of whom Isaac had been the interpreter of Anthony. And because the occasion presents itself and we have reached that place, it appears worthy of our subject to describe in a short account the dwelling of so great a man.

A rocky and high mountain presses forth its waters at its foot for about a mile, of which waters the sands absorb some, and others flowing to the lower regions make a river, over which on both banks innumerable palm trees give much both of beauty and convenience to the place. Here you might see the old man going up and down with the disciples of the blessed Anthony. Here, they said, he (Anthony) was accustomed to sing psalms; here to pray; here to work; here, when tired, to sit down. He himself planted those vines, those shrubs. He settled this little garden-bed. He it was who made with much labour this pond for watering the little garden. He had for many years this little rake for digging the earth.—*The Life of St Hilarion: his visit to the cell of St Anthony.*

—ww—

HOMEWARDS I bend my steps. My fields, my gardens, are **T'AO** choked with weeds: should I not go? My soul has led a **YÜAN-** bondsman's life: why should I remain to pine? But I will waste **MING—** no grief upon the past: I will devote my energies to the future. *Chinese* I have not wandered far astray. I feel that I am on the right *Writer* (A.D. track once again. 365-427).

# THE PRAISE OF GARDENS

Lightly, lightly speeds my boat along, my garments fluttering to the gentle breeze. I inquire my route as I go. I grudge the slowness of the dawning day. From afar I descry my old home, and joyfully press onwards in my haste. The servants rush forth to meet me: my children cluster at the gate. The place is a wilderness; but there is the old pine-tree and my chrysanthemums. Wine is brought in full bottles, and I pour out in brimming cups. I gaze out at my favourite branches. I loll against the window in my new-found freedom. I look at the sweet children on my knee.

And now I take my pleasure in my garden. I lean on my staff as I wander about, or sit down to rest. I raise my head and contemplate the lovely scene. Clouds rise, unwilling from the bottom of the hills: the weary bird seeks its nest again. Shadows vanish, but still I linger round my lonely pine. Home once more! I'll have no friendships to distract me hence. The times are out of joint for me; and what have I to seek from men? In the pure enjoyment of the family circle I will pass my days, cheering my idle hours with lute and book. My husbandmen will tell me when spring-time is nigh, and when there will be work in the furrowed fields. Thither I shall repair by cart or by boat, through the deep gorge, over the dizzy cliff, trees bursting merrily into leaf, the streamlet swelling from its tiny source. Glad is this renewal of life in due season: but, for me, I rejoice that my journey is over. Ah, how short a time it is that we are here! Why then not set our hearts at rest, ceasing to trouble whether we remain or go? What boots it to wear out the soul with anxious thoughts? I want not wealth: I want not power: heaven is beyond my hopes. Then let me stroll through the bright hours as they pass, in my garden among my flowers; or I will mount the hill and sing my song, or weave my verse beside the limpid brook.

Thus will I work out my allotted span, content with appointments of fate, my spirit free from care.—*Herbert A. Giles,* '*Gems of Chinese Literature.*'

I (*Daphnis* and *Chloe*) am that old Philetas, who have often **LONGUS** sung to these Nymphs; and often pip't to yonder *Pan*; and (4*th or* 5*th Cent.* A.D.). have led many great herds, by the art of musick alone; and I come to shew you what I have seen, and to tell you what I have heard. I have a Garden which my own hands and labour planted; and ever since by my old age I gave over fields and herds to dresse and trim it, has been my care and entertainment; what flowers or fruits the season of the year teems, there they are at every season. In the Spring there are Roses, and Lilies, the Hyacinths, and both the forms of Violets. In the Summer, Poppies, Pears, and all sorts of Apples. And now in the Autumne, Vines and Fig trees, Pomegranats, Oranges, Limons, and the green myrtles. Into this Garden, flocks of birds come every morning; some to feed, some to sing. For it is thick, spacious, and shady; and watered all by three fountains; and if you took the wall away, you would think you saw a Wood. As I went in there yesterday about noon, a boy appear'd in the Pomgranate and Myrtle grove, with myrtles and Pomgranats in his hand; white as milk, and shining with the glance of fire; clean and bright, as if he had newly washt himself in all the three transparent Fountains. Naked he was, alone he was; he play'd and wanton'd it about, and cull'd and pull'd, as if it had been his own garden.—*Daphnis and Chloe. A most Sweet and Pleasant Pastorall Romance for Young Ladies, by Geo. Thornley, Gent,* 1657.

—ᴡᴡᴡ—

AFTER we had dispatcht his funerall rites, I ranne straightway **ACHILLES** to *Leucippe*, who was then in our garden. There was **TATIUS** (5*th Cent.* A.D.) a grove of a most pleasant aspect, environed with a row of trees thinly set, and all of one height; whose foure sides, for there were so many in all, were covered with a shelter, which stood on foure pillars, the inner part was planted with all sorts of trees, whose boughes flourisht, and mutually embrac'd each other, growing so thicke, that their leaves and fruit were promiscuously mingled; upon the bigger trees grew ivie, some of it on the soft plane trees, other some sticking to the pitch tree made it tenderer by its embracements; so by this meanes the tree served to beare up the ivie, and the ivie was a crowne to the tree; on both sides many fruitfull Vines bound with reeds spread forth their branches, which displaying their seasonable blossomes through the bands, seemed like the curled lockes of some young lover. The walkes which the trees hanging over shaded, were here and there enlightened, whilst the leaves driven this way and that way with the winde, made roome for the sunne to shine through. Moreover, divers flowers strived as it were to shew their beauty; the daffadilly and the rose, whose beauties were equal, made the earth of a purple colour, the upper part of the rose-leaves was of the colour of blood and violets, the lower part white as milk; the daffadilly differed not at all from the lower part of the rose; the violets were of the colour of the sea when it is calm; in the midst of the flowers sprang up a fountaine, which was first received in a foure square bason, and running from thence it fed a little rivulet made with hand: in the grove were birds, some used to the house, and to bee fed by the hands of men, others more free sported on the tops of trees, some of them being eminent for their singing, as the grass-hopper and the swallow, some of them againe for their painted wings, as the peacocke, the swanne and the parrot. The grasshopper sang of *Aurora's* bed, the swallow of *Tereus* table; the swan was feeding near the head of the fountaine; the parrot hung on the bough of a tree in a cage: the peacocke stretching forth his golden plumes seemed to contend in beautie not onely with the rest of the birds, but even with the flowers themselves, for to say truth, his feathers were flowers: wherefore willing to give her a hint of my intended love, I fell in talke with *Satyrus* my Father's man (who was at that time in the garden) taking the argument of my speech from the peacocke, which by some chance spread her wings just over against him. . . .

Concerning trees, now that they are in love one with another, it is the common received opinion of Philosophers, which I should think fabulous, did not the experience of an husbandman subscribe unto it that the palm trees are distinguished by sexes. . . . While these love-stories were a-telling, I narrowly observed how *Leucippe* was affected with them, who seemed to me to heare them gladly; but let them say what they will *Leucippe's* countenance farre surpassed the rare and exquisite splendour of the peacocke, nay the whole garden, for in her forehead were daffadillies, in her cheekes roses, in her eyes violets, her locks were more curled than the twining Ivie, and every part held such correspondence with the Garden, that I may truly say the best flowers were in her face. Not long after she departed, being called to her Lute.—*The Loves of Clitophon and Leucippe. Englished from the Greeke by Anthony Hodges, Oxford,* 1638.

—⋀⋁⋀—

BUT for him who feareth the majesty of his Lord shall be **MOHAMMAD**
two gardens: (A.D. 571-632).
With trees branched over:
And therein two flowing wells:
And therein of every fruit two kinds:
Reclining on couches with linings of brocade and the fruit of the
 gardens to their hand:
Therein the shy-eyed maidens neither man nor Jinn hath touched
 before:
Like rubies and pearls:
Shall the reward of good be aught but good?
And beside these shall be two other gardens:
Dark green in hue:
With gushing wells therein:
Therein fruit and palm and pomegranate:
Therein the best and comeliest maids:
Bright-eyed, kept in tents:
Man hath not touched them before, nor Jinn:
Reclining on green cushions and fine carpets:
Blessed be the name of thy Lord endued with majesty and honour.
 '*The Speeches of Mohammad*,' *by Stanley Lane Poole.*

## THE PRAISE OF GARDENS

**CHOU TUN-I—**
*Chinese Writer*
(1017-1073).

LOVERS of flowering plants and shrubs we have had by scores, but T'ao Yüan-ming alone devoted himself to the chrysanthemum.

Since the opening days of the T'ang dynasty, it has been fashionable to admire the peony; but my favourite is the water-lily. How stainless it rises from its slimy bed! How modestly it reposes on the clear pool—an emblem of purity and truth! Symmetrically perfect, its subtle perfume is wafted far and wide; while there it rests in spotless state, something to be regarded reverently from a distance, and not to be profaned by familiar approach.

In my opinion, the chrysanthemum is the flower of retirement and culture; the peony, the flower of rank and wealth; the water-lily, the Lady Virtue *sans pareille*.

Alas! few have loved the chrysanthemum since T'ao Yüan-ming; and none like the water-lily like myself; *whereas the peony is a general favourite with all mankind.—Herbert A. Giles,* 'Gems of Chinese Literature.'

—ww—

**LIEN-TSCHEN.**

THE art of laying out gardens consists in an endeavour to combine cheerfulness of aspect, luxuriance of growth, shade, solitude and repose, in such a manner that the senses may be deluded by an imitation of rural nature. Diversity, which is the main advantage of free landscape, must, therefore, be sought in a judicious choice of soil, an alternation of chains of hills and valleys, gorges, brooks, and lakes covered with aquatic plants. Symmetry is wearying, and ennui and disgust will soon be excited in a garden where every part betrays constraint and art.—*Quoted by A. von Humboldt.*

—ww—

**WILLIAM OF MALMESBURY**
(1095-1143).

IT (Thorney Abbey) represents a very Paradise, for that in pleasure and delight it resembles Heaven itself. These marshes abound in trees, whose length without a knot doth emulate the stars. The plain there is as level as the sea, which with green grass allures the eye, and so smooth that there is nought to hinder him who runs through it. Neither is therein any waste place: for in some parts are apple trees, in other vines, which are either spread on the ground or raised on poles. A mutual strife is there between nature and art; so that what one produces not, the other supplies.

# CHAPTER III

## MEDIAEVAL, RENAISSANCE AND TUDOR GARDENS

**ALEXANDER NECKAM (1157-1217).**   *Alexander Neckam, the earliest Englishman to write on Gardens, was born at St Albans, 1157, being the foster-brother of Richard Cœur de Lion —his mother "fovit Ricardum ex mamilla dextra, sed Alexandrum fovit ex mamilla sua sinistrâ"—at the age of twenty-three he became a professor at the University of Paris, 1180-1186. Hurt at the pun on his name by the Benedictine Abbot of St Albans " Si bonus es venias ; si nequam, nequaquam" (" Come if you are good, if naughty, by no means ") he became an Augustinian monk at Cirencester, and Abbot 1213. Died 1217 near Worcester and was buried in Cathedral. Author of a Latin poem, " De Laudibus Divinæ Sapientiæ," a metrical paraphrase of his own prose treatise " De Naturis rerum" which was meant to be a manual of the scientific knowledge of the time, with contemporary anecdotes and stories.*—Thomas Wright, M.A. Preface to Neckam's Works.

HERE the garden should be adorned with roses and lilies, the turnsole (heliotrope), violets, and mandrake; there you should have parsley, cost, fennel, southern-wood, coriander, sage, savery, hyssop, mint, rue, ditanny, smallage, pellitory, lettuces, garden-cress, and peonies.

There should also be beds planted with onions, leeks, garlic, pumpkins and shalots. The cucumber growing in its lap, the drowsy poppy, the daffodil and brank-ursine (acanthus) ennoble a garden. Nor are there wanting, if occasion furnish thee, pottage-herbs, beets, herb-mercury, orache, sorrel and mallows. Anise, mustard, white pepper and wormwood (absynth) do good service to the gardenlet.

A noble garden will give thee also medlars, quinces, warden-trees, peaches, pears of St Riole, pomegranates, lemons (citron apples), oranges (golden apples), almonds, dates, which are the fruits of palms, and figs. I make no mention of ginger and *gariofiliæ*, cinnamon, liquorice, and *zituala*, and *Virgæ Sabeæ* distilling incense, myrrh, aloe and lavender, resin, storax and balsaam, and Indian laburnum.

Saffron and sandyx will not be absent, if thou wilt follow our counsel. Who has not experienced the virtues of thyme and pennyroyal? Who is ignorant that borage and purslain are devoted to uses of diet? ... The myrtle, too, is the friend of temperance; whence it comes that it is wont to be offered to the goddess who is named Cypris, for the same reason that the tufted bird is slain to Nux, the goddess of night, that the goat is devoted to Bacchus, and the swine to Ceres.

But those, whom such toil interests, distinguish between heliotrope (*solsequium*) and our heliotrope, which is called marigold (*calendula*); and between wormwood, (*artemisia*) and our wormwood, which is called centaury (*febrifugium*).

It is agreed, too, that the beard of Jove (*Jovis barba*) is one grass, and Jove's beard (*barba Jovis*) is another.

The iris bears a purple flower, the marsh elder a white one; the gladiolus a yellow one; but the fœtid palm (*Spatula fœtida*) has none.

The horehound, hound's tongue, the Macedonian rock, parsley, the hoop withe (snakewood), groundsel, ground ash, which is also the queen, three kinds of milk-vetch (*astrologia*) are well-known herbs. But Macer and Dioscorides and many others make diligent inquiries into the properties of herbs. Whence let us now pass to other matters. — *Of the Natures of Things.* (*On herbs, trees, and flowers which grow in the garden.*)[1]

—⁓⁓⁓—

I HAVE made two gardens that please me wonderfully. I do not think they are to be equalled in all the world. And I must confess to you a more than female weakness with which I am haunted. I am positively angry that there is anything so beautiful out of Italy.

PETRARCH
(1304-1374).

[1] Mr T. Hudson Turner, in his "Observations on the State of Horticulture in England in Early Times" (*Archæological Journal*, vol. v.), a paper full of antiquarian research and of great interest, regards Neckam's description of a "noble garden" as in a great degree rhetorical and untrustworthy.

## THE PRAISE OF GARDENS

One of these gardens is shady, formed for contemplation, and sacred to Apollo. It overhangs the source of the river, and is terminated by rocks, and by places accessible only to birds. The other is nearer my cottage, of an aspect less severe, and devoted to Bacchus; and, what is extremely singular, it is in the midst of a rapid river. The approach to it is over a bridge of rocks; and there is a natural grotto under the rocks; which gives them the appearance of a rustic bridge. Into this grotto the rays of the sun never penetrate. I am confident that it much resembles the place where Cicero sometimes went to declaim. It invites to study. Hither I retreat during the noontide hours; my mornings are engaged upon the hills, or in the garden sacred to Apollo. Here I would most willingly pass my days, were I not too near Avignon, and too far from Italy. For why should I conceal this weakness of my soul? I love Italy, and I hate Avignon. The pestilential influence of this horrid place impoisons the pure air of Vaucluse, and will compel me to quit my retirement.—*Letter from Vaucluse,* 1336.—'*Life of Petrarch,*' *by Thomas Campbell.*

—∽∧∧∽—

ST BERNARD OF CLAIRVAUX (1091-1153).

IF thou desire to know the situation of Clairvaux, let those writings be to thee as a mirror. . . . Then the back part of the Abbey terminates in a broad plain, no small portion of which a wall occupies, which surrounds the Abbey with its extended circuit. Within the enclosure of this wall many and various trees, prolific in various fruits constitute an orchard resembling a wood. Which, being near the cell of the sick, lightens the infirmities of the brethren with no moderate solace, while it affords a spacious walking place to those who walk and a sweet place for reclining to those who are overheated. The sick man sits upon the green sod, and while the inclemency of Sirius burns up the Earth with his pitiless star, and dries up the rivers, he (the sick man) tempers the glowing stars, under leaves of the trees, into security, and concealment, and shade from the heat of the day; and for the comfort of his pain, the various kinds of grass are fragrant to his nostrils, the pleasant verdure of the herbs and trees gratifies

# BRUNETTO LATINI 33

his eyes, and their immense delights are present, hanging and growing before him, so that he may say, not without reason: I sat under the shade of that tree, which I had longed for, and its fruit was sweet to my throat.[1] The concert of the coloured birds soothes his ears with their soft melody; and for the cure of our illness, the Divine tenderness provides many consolations, while the air smiles with bright serenity, the earth breathes with fruitfulness, and he himself drinks in with eyes, ears, and nostrils, the delights of colours, songs and odours.

Where the orchard terminates, the garden begins, distributed into separate plots, or rather, divided by intersecting rivulets; for although the water appears stagnant, it flows nevertheless with a slow gliding. Here also a beautiful spectacle is exhibited to the infirm brethren: while they sit upon the green margin of the huge basin, they see the little fishes playing under the water, and representing a military encounter, by swimming to meet each other. This water serves the double duty of supporting the fish and watering the vegetables,—to which water, Alba, a river of famous name, supplies nourishment by its unwearied wandering.—*Description of Clairvaux by a Contemporary of St Bernard.*

---

**BRUNETTO LATINI (1230-1294).**

MAIS les Français ont maisons granz, et plenières et peintes, et belles chambres pour avoir joie et delit sans guerre et sans noise et pour ce savent ils mieux faire preaux et vergiers et pommiers entre la manoir car ce est une chose qui molt vaut à delit d'ome.—Libre I., pt. iv., chap. cxxx. *Li Livres dou Tresor.* P. Chabaille.

---

**SIR JOHN MAUNDEVILLE (1300-1372).**

*Maundeville was an early and imaginative traveller in Palestine, Egypt and China, and resided three years at Pekin. His work is a pot-pourri of fact, fiction, chronicle, legend and romance.*

NEAR the isle of Peutexoire, which is the land of Prester John, is a great isle, long and broad, called Milsterak, which is in the lordship of Prester John. That isle is very

[1] See extract from Burton's 'Anatomy of Melancholy.'

rich. There was dwelling not long since a rich man, named Gatholonabes, who was full of tricks and subtle deceits. He had a fair and strong castle in a mountain, so strong and noble that no man could devise a fairer or a stronger. And he had caused the mountain to be all walled about with a strong and fair wall, within which walls he had the fairest garden that might be imagined; and therein were trees bearing all manner of fruits, all kinds of herbs of virtue and of good smell, and all other herbs also that bear fair flowers. And he had also in that garden many fair wells, and by them he had made fair halls and fair chambers, painted all with gold and azure, representing many divers things and many divers stories.

There were also beasts and birds which sang full delectably, and moved by craft, that it seemed they were alive.

And he had also in his garden all kinds of birds and beasts, that men might have play or sport to behold them. And he had also in that place the fairest damsels that might be found under the age of fifteen years, and the fairest young striplings that men might get of that same age; and they were all clothed full richly in clothes of gold; and he said they were angels. And he had also caused to be made three fair and noble wells, all surrounded with stone of jasper and crystal, diapered with gold, and set with precious stones and great Orient pearls. And he had made a conduit under the earth, so that the three wells, at his will, should run one with milk, another with wine, and another with honey. And that place he called Paradise. And when any good Knight, who was hardy and noble, came to see this royalty, he would lead him into Paradise, and show him these wonderful things for his sport, and the marvellous and delicious song of divers birds, and the fair damsels, and the fair wells of milk, wine, and honey, running plentifully.—*The Voyages and Travels of Sir J. M.* (*The first English Edition was printed by Winkyn de Worde,* 1499.)

## BOCCACCIO

BOOKES (Courteous Reader) may rightly be compared to **BOCCACCIO** *Gardens*; wherein, let the painfull Gardiner expresse never (1313-1375). so much care and diligent endeavour; yet among the very fairest, sweetest, and freshest Flowers, as also Plants of most precious Vertue; ill savouring and stinking Weeds, fit for no use but the fire or mucke-hill, will spring and sprout up. So fareth it with Bookes of the very best quality; let the Author bee never so indulgent, and the Printer vigilant: yet both may misse their ayme, by the escape of Errors and Mistakes, either in sense or matter, the one fault ensuing by a ragged Written Copy; and the other thorough want of wary Correction.—*The Decameron (containing a hundred pleasant Novels.) (Preface to the last five days),* 1620.

On the morrow, being Wednesday, about breake of day, the Ladies, with certaine of their attending Gentlewomen, and the three Gentlemen, having three servants to waite on them, left the City to beginne their journey, and having travelled about a league's distance, arrived at the place of their first purpose of stay; which was seated on a little hill, distant (on all sides) from any highway, plentifully stored with faire spreading Trees, affording no meane delight to the eye. On the top of all stood a stately Pallace, having a large and spacious Court in the middest, round engirt with galleries, hals and chambers, every one separate alone by themselves, and beautified with pictures of admirable Cunning. Nor was there any want of Gardens, Meadowes, and other pleasant walkes, with welles and springs of faire running waters, all encompassed with branching vines, fitter for curious and quaffing bidders, then women sober and singularly modest.—*Ibid.*

—⁂—

TO be as brief as I can then, Fabrizio was regaled there with **MACHIAVELLI** all possible demonstrations of honour and respect: but (1469-1527). after the entertainment and usual formalities were over (which generally are few and short amongst men of sense, who are more desirous of gratifying the rational appetite), the days being long, and the weather intensely hot, Cosimo, under a pretence of avoiding the heat, took his guests into the most retired and shady part of the gardens; and being all sat down, some upon the grass (which is very green and pleasant there), and some upon seats placed under the trees, Fabrizio said it was a most delightful garden, and, looking earnestly at some of the trees, seemed not to know the names of them; but Cosimo, being aware of it, immediately said, perhaps you may not be acquainted with this sort of trees; and, indeed, I am not at all surprised at it, for they are very old ones, and were much more in vogue amongst our ancestors than they are at present. Having then told him the names of them, and that they were planted by his grandfather Bernardo, who was fond of such amusements: I thought so, replied Fabrizio; and both the place and the trees put me in mind of some Princes in the Kingdom of Naples, who took much delight in planting groves and shady arbours to shelter them from the heat.—*The Art of War.*

—∿∿—

**ERASMUS** *E*USEBIUS.—But what if we should take the Cool of the Morning
(1467-1536). now to see the Gardens, while the Wench in the Kitchen provides us a Sallad? *Timotheus.* Never was anything in better order. The very Design of this Garden bids a Man welcome to't. . . . *Eu.* Strangers are generally pleased with this Garden; and hardly a Man that passes by the place without an Ejaculation. Instead of the Infamous *Priapus*, I have committed not only my Gardens, but all my Possessions, both of Body and Mind, to the protection of my *Saviour.* . . . You are loth, I perceive to leave this Place; but let's go on, and I'll show you a square wall'd Garden here beyond, that's better worth your seeing . . . this Garden was design'd for Pleasure; but for honest Pleasure, the Entertainment of the Sight, the Smell, and the Refreshment of the very Mind. To have nothing here but sweet Herbs, and those only choice ones too; and every kind has its bed by itself. *Ti.* I am now convinc'd that the Plants are not mute, as you were saying e'en

now. *Eu.* You're in the right: as I have rang'd my several Plants into several Troops, so every Troop has its Standard to itself with a peculiar *Motto.* The *Marjoram's* Word is *Abstine Sus, non tibi spiro: My perfume was never made for the Snout of a Sow;* being a Fragrancy to which the Sow has a natural Aversion. And so every other Herb has something in the Title to denote the particular Virtue of the Plant. *Ti.* I have seen nothing yet that pleases me better than this Fountain. It is the Ornament, the Relief, and Security of the whole Garden. But for this *Cistern* (Bason) here, that with so much satisfaction to the Eye, waters the whole Ground in Chanels, at such equal Distances, that it shows all the Flowers over again, as in a Looking-Glass; this *Cistern,* I say, is it of *Marble*? *Eu.* Not a word of that, I prithee. How should *Marble* come hither? 'tis only a *Paste* that's covered over with an artificial Counterfeit. . . . *Ti.* But how comes it that all your *Made-Hedges* are Green too? *Eu.* Because I would have everything Green here. Some are for a Mixture of Red to set off the other. But I am still for Green; as every Man has his Fancy, though it be but in a Garden. *Ti.* The Garden is very fine of itself, but these three Walks, methinks, take off very much from the Lightsomness and Pleasure of it. *Eu.* There do I either Study, or Walk, or Talk with a Friend, or Eat a Dish of Meat, according as the Humour takes me. *Ti.* And could you not content yourself with so neat and well-finish'd a Garden in *Substance,* without more Gardens in *Picture* over and above. *Eu.* First, one piece of Ground will not hold all sorts of Plants. Secondly, 'tis a double Pleasure to compare painted Flowers with the Life . . . and lastly, the Painting holds fresh and green all the Winter, when the Flowers are dead and wither'd. . . . *Eu.* These Walks serve me so many Purposes. But if you please we'll take a View of 'em nearer Hand. See how green 'tis under Foot; and ye have the Beauty of painted Flowers in the very Chequering of the Pavement. Here's a Wood now in *Fresco*; there's a strange Variety of Matter in't; so many Trees, and but one of a sort; and all exprest to the

Life: and so for the Birds too, especially if any way remarkable. . . . *Eu.* Here's an indifferent fair Garden cut into two: the one's for the Kitchin, and that's my Wife's; the other is a *Physick Garden.* Upon the left hand, you have an open green Meadow enclosed with a Quickset-Hedge, (septum est sepe perpetuâ è spinis implexis, sed vivis contextâ). There do I take the Air sometimes, and divert myself with good Company. Upon the right hand there's a Nursery (Orchard) of foreign Plants, which I have brought by degrees to endure this Climate. At the end of the upper Walk, there's an *Aviary*: at the further end of the Orchard, I have my *Bees*, which is a sight worth your Curiosity.

This *Summer Hall*, I suppose, you have had enough of. It looks three ways, you see; and which way soever you turn your Eye, you have a most delicate Green before ye. . . . Here do I eat in my House, as if I were in my Garden; for the very Walls have their Greens and their Flowers intermixt, and 'tis no ill Painting. . . . You shall now see my Library: 'tis no large one, but furnish'd with very good Books. . . . To my Library there belongs a Gallery, that looks into the Garden. Let's go those three Walks now above the other, that I told you look'd into the *Kitchen-Garden.* These upper Walks have a Prospect into both Gardens, but only through Windows with Shutters. . . . At each Corner there's a Lodging-Chamber, where I can repose myself, within sight of my Orchard, and my little Birds.— *Colloquia:* ' *Convivium Religiosum.*' (*Translated by Sir Roger L'Estrange, Kt.*)

—ww—

**SIR THOMAS MORE** (1480-1535).

THEY set great store by their gardeins. In them they have vineyardes, all manner of fruite, herbes and flowres, so pleasaunt, so well furnished, and so fynely kepte, that I never sawe thynge more frutefull, nor better trimmed in anye place. Their studie and deligence herein commeth not onely of pleasure, but also of a certen strife and contention that is between strete and strete, concerning the trimming, husbanding, and furnishing

# MARTIN LUTHER

of their gardens : everye man for his owne parte. And verelye you shall not lightelye finde in all the citie anyethinge, that is more commodious, eyther for the profite of the Citizens or for pleasure. And therefore it maye seme that the first founder of the citie mynded nothing so much as these gardens. For they saye that Kinge Utopus himselfe, even at the first beginning, appointed, and drewe furth the plattefourme of the city into this fashion and figure that it hath nowe, but the gallant garnishinge, and the beautifull setting furth of it, whereunto he saw that one mannes age would not suffice : that he left to his posteritie.—*Utopia (Of the cities and namely of Amaurote), translated by Ralph Robinson.*

—∿∿∿—

I HOLD that the whole world was named a Paradise. Moses describes it according to Adam's sight, so far as hee could see; but it was called Paradise by reason it was all over so sweet and pleasant. Adam was, and dwelled towards the East in Syria and Arabia, when hee was created : but after hee had sinned, then it was no more so delightful and pleasant.

Even so in our time hath God cursed likewise fruitful lands, and hath caused them to bee barren and unfruitful by reason of our sins : for where God gives not His blessing, there grows nothing that is good and profitable ; but where He blesseth, there all things grow plentifully, and are fruitful.[1]—*Colloquia (Table Talk).*

**MARTIN LUTHER**
(1483-1546).

—∿∿∿—

AND blissful blossoms in the blooming yard
Submit their heads to the young sun's safe-guard.
Ivy leaves rank o'erspread the barmkin wall,
The blooming hawthorn clad his pikis all.

**GAWEN DOUGLAS—**
*Bishop of Dunkeld*
(1474-1522).

[1] In the spring of 1538, Luther writes to Jonas that, instead of being forced to carry on tedious and often fruitless business, he would much rather, as an old and worn-out man, be delighting himself in his gardens with the wonders of God—trees, plants, flowers, and birds ; but that he was fully conscious of having deserved these burdens by past sins.—*Julius Koestlin's 'Martin Luther.'*

# 40 THE PRAISE OF GARDENS

Forth from fresh burgeons the wine-grapes ying
End-long the trellises did in clusters hing.
The locked buttons on the gemmed trees,
O'erspreading leaves of Nature's tapestries.
Soft gresy verdure after balmy showers
On curling stalk(y)s smiling to their flowers.
Beholding them so many diverse new
Some pers, some paille, some burnet, and some blue,
Some grey, some gules, some purple, some sanguine,
Blanched, or brown, some fawch, yallow many a one,
Some heavenly coloured in celestial (de)gree,
Some watery-hued as the deep wavy sea,
And some depart in freckles red and white,
Some bright as gold with aureate leavys light;
The daisy spread abroad her crownet small,
And every flower onlappit in the dale.
In battle gear burgeons the banewort wild,
The clover, catcluke, and the cammamyld;
The flower-de-luce forth spread his heavenly hue,
Flower Damasks, and Columbine white and blue,
Seyr downye small on Dent-de-lion sprang,
The young green blooming strawberry-leaves amang.

—*Prologue to Twelfth Book of Æneid*
(*slightly modernised*).

---

**ZEHIR-ED-DIN MUHAMMED**
—*surnamed Baber or the Tiger*
(1482-1530).

*Emperor of Hindustan, one of the descendants of Zengiskhan and of Tamerlane, extended his dominions by conquest to Delhi and the greater part of Hindustan; and transmitted to his famous descendants, Akber and Aurengzebe, the magnificent Empire of the Moguls. A desperate warrior, an elegant poet, a great admirer of beautiful prospects and fine flowers, a very resolute and jovial drinker of wine. The following extracts are from a faithful translation of his Journal and Narrative of his life and transactions.*—(Lord Jeffrey's Review of 'Memoirs of Baber,' by Leyland & Erskine, 1827).

OPPOSITE to the fort of Adînaphûr (south of the Kâbul river), to the south on a rising ground, I formed a charbagh (great garden), in the year 914 (=1508). It is called

## ZEHIR-ED-DIN MUHAMMED 41

Bagh-e Vafá (the Garden of Fidelity). It overlooks the river, which flows between the fort and the palace. In the year in which I defeated Behâr Khan, and conquered Lahore and Dibâlpûr, I brought plantains and planted them here. They grew and thrived. The year before I had also planted the Sugarcane in it, which throve remarkably well. I sent some of them to Badakshân and Bokhâra. It is on an elevated site, enjoys running water, and the climate in the winter season is temperate. In the garden there is a small hillock, from which a stream of water, sufficient to drive a mill, incessantly flows into the garden below. The four-fold field plot of this garden is situated on this eminence. On the south-west part of this garden is a reservoir of water ten gaz square, which is wholly planted round with orange trees; there are likewise pomegranates. All around the piece of water the ground is quite covered with clover. This spot is the very eye of the beauty of the garden. At the time when the orange becomes yellow, the prospect is delightful. Indeed the garden is charmingly laid out. To the south of the garden lies the Koh-é-Sefîd (the White Mountain) of Nangenhâr, which separates Bengash from Nangenhâr. There is no road by which one can pass it on horseback. Nine streams descend from this mountain. The snow on its summit never diminishes, whence probably comes the name of Kok-é-Sefîd. No snow ever falls in the dales at its foot. . . .

Few quarters possess a district that can rival Istâlif. A large river runs through it, and on either side of it are gardens, green, gay, and beautiful. Its water is so cold that there is no need of icing it; and it is particularly pure. In this district is a garden called Bagh-e-Kilân (the Great Garden), which Ulugh Beg Mirza seized upon. I paid the price of the garden to the proprietors, and received from them a grant of it. On the outside of the garden are large and beautiful spreading plane-trees, under the shade of which there are agreeable spots finely sheltered. A perennial stream, large enough to turn a mill, runs through the garden; and on its banks are planted plane and other trees. Formerly this stream flowed in a winding and crooked course, but

42        THE PRAISE OF GARDENS

I ordered its course to be altered according to a regular plan, which added greatly to the beauty of the place.

—ww—

**MAYSTER FITZHER-BARDE**  *Fitzherbarde is either Sir Anthony Fitzherbert, Judge of the Common Pleas and author of the 'Grand Abridgment of the Common Law,' or his brother John Fitzherbert (d. 1538).*

OF bees is lyttell charge but good attendaunce; at the time that they shall cast the swarme, it is convenient that the hyve be set in a garden, or an orchyarde, where as they maye be kepte from the northe wynde, and the mouthe of the hyve towarde the sonne.

*To plasshe or pleche a hedge.*

If the hedge be of x or xii yeres growing sythe it was first set, thanne take a sharpe hatchet, or a handbyll and cutte the settes in a playne place, nyghe unto the erthe, the more halve a-sonder; and bend it downe towarde the erthe, and wrappe and wynde them together, but alwaye so that the toppe lye hyer than the rote a good quantytie, for elles the sappe wyll not runne in-to the toppe kyndely, but in processe the toppe wyll dye; and than set a lyttel hedge on the backe-syde, and it shall need noo more mendynge manye yeres after. *The Boke of Husbandry*, 1534 (*edited by Skeat*, 1882).

—ww—

**POLYDORE VERGIL** (d. 1555).  *In 1498, Polydore Vergil published 'Adagia' before Erasmus, who was and remained his friend; 1499, De Rerum Inventoribus; 1503, sent to England by Pope Alexander VI. to collect Peter-pence and stayed fifty years there; Rector of Church Langton, Leicestershire, and Archdeacon of Wells; his History of England in Latin finished 1533.*

I HAVE diligentlie noted at London, a cittie in the south partes of the riolme, that the nighte is scarslie v houres in length in soommer when as the sonne is at his highest reache. . . . The grownde is luxurient and frutefull; besides corne and pulse, of the owne accorde bringing forthe all kinde of matter, saving firre and (as Cæsar saithe) beeche trees, with diverse other, as olives

# CHARLES ESTIENNE 43

which are woonte to growe in whotter soyles; but yt is well known that nowe there are beeches eche where in the londe. Thei plante vines in their gardins, rather for covert and commoditee of shaddowe then for the fruite, for the grape seldom commeth to ripenes excepte an hotte summer ensewe.—*English History, edited by Sir Henry Ellis, for Camden Society.*

---

*Son of Henri Estienne; Doctor of Medicine, Royal Printer and author of* **CHARLES**
*several treatises on Medicine, Natural History, and Agriculture—'De re* **ESTIENNE**
*Hortensi Libellus,' 1545, on the Antiquities of Gardening.* **(STEPHENS)**
*Collaborated with Jean Liébault, Médicin (d. 1596), to produce 'La Maison* (1504-1564).
*Rustique' (Prædium Rusticum), translated into English by R. Surflet (1600), and reprinted with additions from Olivier de Serres, Vinet and others, by Gervase Markham in 1616.*

THE most pleasant and Delectable thing for recreation belong- *Surflet's* ing unto our French Fermes, is our Flower Gardens, as well *translation.* in respect that it serveth for the chiefe Lord, whose the inheritance is, to solace himselfe therein, as also in respect of their service, for to set Bee-hives in. It is a commendable and seemely thing to behold out at a window manie acres of ground well tilled and husbanded, whether it be a Medow, a Plot for planting of Willowes, or arable ground, as we have stood upon heretofore: but yet it is much more to behold faire and comely Proportions, handsome and pleasant Arbors, and, as it were, Closets, delightfull borders of Lavender, Rosemarie, Boxe, and other such like: to heare the ravishing musicke of an infinite number of pretie small Birds, which continually, day and night, doe chatter, and chant their proper and naturall branch-songs upon the Hedges and Trees of the Garden; and to smell so sweet a Nose-gay so neere at hand; seeing that this so fragrant a smell cannot but refresh the Lord of the Farme exceedingly, when going out of his bed-chamber in the morning after the Sunne-rise, and whiles as yet the cleare and pearle-like dew doth pearche unto the grasse, he giveth himself to heare the melodious musicke of the Bees; which busying themselves in gathering of the same, doe also fill the ayre with a most acceptable sweet and pleasant harmonie: besides, the Borders and continued Rowes of soveraigne Thyme, Balme, Rosemarie, Marierome (Marjoram), Cypers, Soothernwood, and other fragrant hearbes, the sight and view whereof cannot but give great contentment unto the beholder.

*This section is not in Surflet's translation of 1600, and is due to G. Markham.*

And in this Garden of Pleasure you are verie much to respect the forme and proportion of the same: wherein, according to the opinion of *Serres* and Uniett (Vinet), you must be much ruled by the nature of the Soyle: which albeit you may, in part, by your industrie and cost helpe, as touching the levelling, raysing, abating, or enriching of the same; yet, for the most part, and especially touching the ayre, temperature, and clyme, you must be governed by the Soyle in which you live. Now for the general proportions of Gardens, they may at your pleasure carrie anie of these foure shapes, that is to say, either Square, Round, Ovall or Diamond. As for that which is more long than broad, or more broad than long (neither of which are uncomely), they are contained under the titles of Squares. This is but the outward proportion; or the Verge and Girdle of your Garden. As for the inward proportions and shapes of the Quarters, Beds, Bankes, Mounts and such like, they are to be divided by Alleyes, Hedges, Borders, Rayles, Pillars, and such like, and by these you may draw your Garden into what form soever you please, not respecting what shape soever the outward Verge carrieth; for you may make that Garden which is square without, to be round within; and that which is round, either square or ovall; that which is ovall, either of the former and that which is diamond, anie shape at all: and yet all exceedingly comely. You may also, if your ground be naturally so seated, or if your industrie please so to bring it to passe, make your Garden rise and mount by severall degrees, one levell ascending above another, in such sort as if you had divers gardens one above another, which is exceeding beautifull to the eie, and very beneficiall to your flowers and fruit trees, especially if such ascents have the benefit of the Sun-rising upon them: and thus, if you please, you may have in one levell

## BERNARD PALISSY 45

a square plot, in another a round, in a third a diamond, and in the fourth an ovall, then alongst the ascending bankes which are on either side the staires, you mount into your severall gardens, you shall make your physicke garden or places to plant your physicke hearbes upon, according as the modell is most bravely set forth by *Oliver de Serres*, and as the late King of France caused his physicke garden to be made in the Universitie of Montpellier,[1] being all raised upon bankes or heights one above another, some round, some square, in the manner of a goodly, large, and well-trimmed Theatre as may be seene at this day to the great admiration thereof.—*Maison Rustique, or, the Countrey Farme. Compyled in the French Tongue by Charles Stevens, and John Liébault, Doctors of Physicke. And translated into English by Richard Surflet, Practitioner in Physicke. Now newly Reviewed, Corrected, and Augmented, with divers large Additions, out of the Works of* { *Serres, his Agriculture,* / *Vinet, his Maison Champestre,* / *Albyterio, in Spanish,* / *Grilli, in Italian, and other Authors.* } *French. And the Husbandrie of France, Italie, and Spaine, reconciled and made to agree with ours here in England. By Gervase Markham, London. Printed by Adam Islip for John Bill,* 1616.

—⁂—

*Potter, Glass-Painter, Chemist, Agriculturist and Engineer.* **BERNARD**
*He designed the rustic grotto for the Gardens of the Constable Montmorency* **PALISSY**
*at the Château d'Écouen: was employed at the founding of the Tuileries by* (1508-1589).
*Queen Catherine de Médicis in* 1566, *Philibert de l'Orme being the Architect.*
*In the Gardens here, of which the design by Androuet du Cerceau is in existence, Palissy constructed his famous Grotto, as described in the following extract. The Park at Chaulnes was laid out after a plan resembling the 'delectable Garden': Palissy was also employed at the Château de Nesle in Picardy, Reux in Normandy, and possibly the Château de Madrid, in the Bois de Boulogne. In the dedication of his book, 'Recepte Véritable,' to the Queen Mother, he wrote: 'Il y a des choses escrites en ce livre qui pourront beaucoup servir à l'édification de vostre jardin de Chenonceux.'*

[1] *See* illustration in de Serres's *Théâtre d'Agriculture.*

*John Evelyn wrote of him in the Preface to his 'Sylva':—'It was indeed a plain man (a Potter by trade), but let no one despise him because a Potter (Agathocles and a King was of that craft), who, in my opinion has given us the true reason why Husbandry and particularly Planting is no more improved in this age of ours—especially where persons are Lords and owners of much land.'*

ALSO, because you are a puissant and magnanimous Lord, and of good judgment, I have found it good to design for you the plan of a garden as beautiful as the world ever held, except that of the Earthly Paradise, which design of a garden I am assured you will find of good invention. . . . I have not put the portrait of the said garden in this book, because several are unworthy to see it, and singularly enemies to virtue and good *engin*; also my poverty and occupation in my art would not permit it. I know that some ignorant people—enemies to virtue and calumniators—will say that the design of this garden is only a dream, and will perhaps compare it to the 'Dream of Polyphilus,'[1] or say that it will be too costly, and that a suitable place could not be found for the erection of the said garden, according to the design. To this I answer that there are more than four thousand noble houses in France, in the neighbourhood of which are several suitable spots to erect the said garden, according to the tenour of my design.—*Dedication to the Mareschal de Montmorency of the 'Recepte Véritable.'*

*Question.*—I prythee discourse to me on the plan of the garden thou desirest to build.

*Answer.*—It is impossible to have a spot proper for a garden, unless there be some fountain or stream passing through it: and for this reason I wish to choose a level spot at the foot of some

[1] The 'Hypnerotomachia Polyphili' of Fra Francesco Colonna, (Aldus, 1499), and better known in its French translation of 'Le Songe de Polyphile' by Beroalde de Verville, Paris, fol., 1600, of which the designs are said to be by Jean Goujon; there are numerous lovely woodcuts illustrating arbors, fountains, trellises and garden scenes. Facsimiles of the woodcuts of the Venice edition of 1499 have been reproduced, 1888.

# BERNARD PALISSY

mountain or highland, with a view to take some spring of water from the said land, to make it course at my pleasure through all the parts of my garden.

*Question.*—Tell me, then, how you propose to adorn your garden, after you have bought the ground.

*Answer.*—In the first place, I shall mark out the square of my garden, of such length and breadth as I shall hold to be requisite, and I shall form the said square in some plain which may be encompassed by mountains, burrows or rocks, towards the side of the North wind and of the West wind, in order that the said mountains, burrows or rocks may serve me for the purposes which I shall presently tell you. I shall be careful, too, to place my garden near some spring of water issuing from the said rocks, and coming from high ground, and, this done, I shall make my said square; but, wherever it may be, I mean to set up my garden in a place where there may be a meadow beyond, to issue sometimes from the garden into the meadow; and this for the reasons which shall be presently given. And having thus established the situation of the garden, I shall next proceed to divide it into four equal parts; and, for the separation of the said parts, there will be a long alley, which shall cross the said garden, and at the four ends of the said cross-way there will be at each end an arbour (*cabinet*), and in the middle of the garden and cross-way there will be an amphitheatre such as I shall presently describe to you. At each of the four corners of the said garden there will be an arbour, making eight arbours in all and one amphitheatre, which will be set up in the garden; but you must understand that all the eight arbours will be differently filled, and of such invention as has never yet been seen or heard tell of. That is why I mean to found my garden upon the Psalm civ., the one wherein the prophet describes the excellent and wonderful works of God, and in their contemplation he humbles himself before Him, and bids his friend to praise the Lord in all His wonders.

I intend also to set up this admirable garden in order to give men an opportunity to make themselves lovers of the cultivation of the earth, and to leave all vicious occupations or delights, and evil commerce, to amuse themselves by cultivation of the earth.

*Question.*—I prithee, discourse to me of those beautiful cabinets, which thou proposest thus to raise.

*Answer.*—In the first place, thou must understand that I shall conduct the stream of water, or part of that from the rock, to the eight cabinets aforesaid. This will be easy enough to do; for as soon as the water distils from the mountain or rock, I shall lead its spring through all parts of the garden, as shall seem good; and give a portion to each cabinet, as I shall find necessary, and shall build my cabinets with such invention that from each shall issue more than a hundred jets of water, and this by the means I shall discover to you, in discoursing of the beauty of the cabinets. Let us now come to the description of all my cabinets in turn.

### OF THE FIRST CABINET.

The first, which shall face the North wind at the corner and anglet of the garden, at the bottom and adjoining the foot of the mountain or rock, I shall build of terra cotta (*briques cuites*), but they shall be formed in such a way that the cabinet shall resemble the form of a rock hollowed out upon the very spot, having inside several hollow seats within the wall, and between every two seats there will be a column, and below this a pedestal, and above the capitals to the columns there will be an architrave, frieze and cornice, which shall prevail round the said cabinet, and along the frieze will be certain antique letters adorning the said frieze, and along it shall be written, *Dieu n'a prins plaisir en rien, sinon en l'homme, auquel habite Sapience* (God has taken no pleasure in aught, save in Man, in whom dwelleth Wisdom): and thus my cabinet will have its windows towards the South, and the said windows and entrance to the

## BERNARD PALISSY 49

cabinet shall be in the shape of a rock: therefore the said cabinet shall be on the sides of the North and West masoned against the *terriers* or rocks, so that in descending from the high land, one can come upon the said cabinet without knowing there is any building below; and to make the cabinet pleasanter, I shall plant upon its vault several bushes bearing fruits good to nourish birds, and also certain herbs, whose seeds they love, to accustom the said birds to repose and utter their songlets on the said bushes, to give pleasure to those within the cabinet and garden, and on its outside will be masonry of great stones of rocks, unpolished and rough-hewn, in order that the outside of the cabinet may represent no shape of building: and with the masonry I shall introduce a canal of water, which I shall cause to pass within the wall, and thus masoned in the wall, I shall distribute it in several directions by jets, in such a way as shall appear that they issued from the rock like water-falls . . . when the cabinet is thus masoned I shall cover it with various colours of enamels from the top of the vaults to the foot; this done I shall make a great fire within the cabinet, until the said enamels are melted or liquified on the masonry—and the enamels liquifying will run and fuse, and in fusing will form very pleasant figures and ideas, and the fire being put out, the enamels will be found to have covered the joints of the bricks in such a way that the cabinet will appear all of one piece— and the cabinet will glow with such a lustre that the lizards and *langrottes* entering will behold themselves as in a mirror, and will admire the statues; and if any one surprises them, they will not be able to ascend the wall of the cabinet because of its polish, and in this way the cabinet will last for ever, and will require no tapestry, for its decoration will be of such beauty as if it were jasper or porphyry or well-polished calcedony.

I have not found in this world a greater source of delight than to possess a beautiful garden; thus God, having created the earth for the service of man, placed him in a garden in which were several kinds of fruits, which was the cause why, when meditating the sense of Psalm civ., as I have told you above, straightway there took hold of me so great a desire to set up my said garden, that since that time I have done nought but dream about the erection thereof, and very often in my sleep me-seemed that my garden was already made in the same shape as I have told you, and that I was already beginning to eat the fruits, and to recreate myself therein, and methought that passing in the morning through the said garden, I came to consider the wonderful actions which the Sovereign has commanded Nature to perform, and amongst other things I gazed upon the branches of the vines, peas, and gourds which seemed to have some feeling and knowledge of their weakly nature; for being unable to support themselves, they threw out certain small arms, like threads, into the air, and finding some small branch or bough, proceeded to bind and attach themselves to it, without separating from it again, in order to support the parts of their weakly nature.—'*Jardin Delectable.*'

'The Archives of the History of Switzerland' (Zurich, 1864) give an account of a visit of the Swiss Ambassadors to the Tuileries, 11th May 1555:—

'In the morning the Ambassadors set out for the garden of the Queen, called the Tuillerie. The garden is very large and very pleasant. A broad path divides it into two parts, planted on each side with tall trees, elms and sycamores, which afford shade to the walkers. There is a labyrinth designed with such art, that, once inside, the exit is difficult. There are tables made of branches and leaves, beds, etc. The astonishing thing is that this labyrinth is almost entirely formed of bent cherry trees. There are several fountains with nymphs and fauns, holding urns from which the water flows. One is especially remarkable. It is a rock over which run various reptiles, serpents, snails, tortoises, lizards, frogs, and every kind of aquatic animal. They also poured water—one would have said the rock itself exuded water.'

M. Anatole de Montaiglon sees in this description the Grotto

## ANDROUET DU CERCEAU

of Palissy, but M. Louis Audiat disagrees, and points out it is a fountain not a grotto.

—ᏕᎳᏂᏁ—

*A great French Architect, whose book of Designs is invaluable: he began building the Pont Neuf in* 1578, *and the Gallery of the Louvre in* 1596: *being a Protestant, he died in exile.*

ANDROUET DU CERCEAU (*d.* 1592).

BEHIND the seignorial mansion of Anet there is a terrace from which you descend into the garden. Beneath the terrace is a long vaulted gallery. The garden is of great size, and richly girt with galleries all round about, the three sides of which are as often with arched as with square openings; the whole rustic. The garden is ornamented with two fountains. Behind it are two large places serving as parks, separated and shut in. These places are fitted as enclosures (*parquets*), some with meadows, others with clipped trees (*taillis*) others with warrens, fruit-trees, fish-ponds, and those are separated by alleys and canals.

Anet.

Gaillon is fitted with two gardens—one of which is on a level with the Castle, and between the two is a place in the manner of a terrace. Now this garden is adorned (*accompli*) with a beautiful and agreeable gallery, worthy to be so called on account of its length, and of the manner in which it is erected, with a view over the garden on one side, and on the other over the said valley, towards the river. In the midst of the garden is a pavilion, in which is seen a fountain in white marble. As to the other garden, it is contained in this valley, over which the gallery has a marvellously wide prospect, adjoining which is a park of vines, dependent on the house—not enclosed. Beyond, in the same valley, in the direction of the river, the Cardinal de Bourbon has erected and built a *lieu de Chartreuse*, abounding with every pleasure. Moreover there is in this place a Park, which, if you wish to enter, either from the house or from the garden above, you must often ascend, as well by alleys covered with trees, as by terraces always looking over the valley; and

Gaillon.

continuing you reach a spot wherein is built a little chapel, and a little house with a hermitage rock, situated in the middle of a lake, with a square margin, and round this are little alleys for walking, to enter which you must pass a small swing-gate. Near to this is a small garden, and therein many pedestals, on which are placed whole figures 3 or 4 feet high, and of every kind of device; therewith, some alleys (*Bercées*), covered with hazel-trees.
—'*Les plus excellents Bastiments de France*,' 1576-9.

—ww—

**CONRAD HERESBACH** (1509-1576) and **BARNABY GOOGE** (1540-1594).

NOW when Thrasybulus, travailing in the affayres of his prince, chaunced to come to the house of Marius, and carried by him into a Garden that he had, which was very beautifull, being led about among the sweet smelling flowres, and under the pleasant Arbours, what a goodly sight (quoth Thrasybulus) is heere: how excellently have you garnished this paradise of yours with all kinde of pleasures: your Parlers, and your banketting houses both within and without, as all bedecked with pictures of beautifull Flowres and Trees, that you may not onely feede your eyes with the beholding of the true and lively Flower, but also delight yourselfe with the counterfait in the midst of winter, seeing in the one, the painted flower to contend in beautie with the very flower; in the other, the wonderfull worke of Nature, and in both the passing goodness of God. Moreover, your pleasant Arbours to walke in, whose shaddowes keepe off the heate of the sunne, and if it fortune to raine, the cloisters are hard by. But specially this little River, with most cleere water, encompassing the garden, doth wonderfully set it forth, and herewithall the greene and goodly quickset hedges, no chargeable kinde of enclosures, differeth it both from Man and Beast. I speake nothing of the well ordered quarters, whereas the Hearbes and Trees are severed every sort in their due place, the Pot-hearbes by themselves, the flowers in another place, the Trees and Impes[1] in another quarter, all in just square and proportion, with Alleis and walkes among them.

[1] *Imp*, a graft or shoot.

Among these goodly sights, I pray you, remember according to your promise (for so the time requireth) to shew mee some part of your great knowledge in Garden matters, sith you have upon this condition heard me heretofore grabling, or rather wearying you with the declaiming of my poore skill in the tilling of the field. . . .

*Marius.*—Nature hath appointed remedies in a readinesse for all diseases, but the craft and subtiltie of man, for gaine, hath devised Apothecaries shops, in which a man's life is to be sold and bought; where for a little byle, they fetch their medicines from Hierusalem, and out of Turkie, while in the meane time every poore man hath the right remedies growing in his Garden: for if men would make their Gardens their Phisitians, the Phisitians craft would soone decay. You know what your olde friend Cato saith, and what a deale of Phisicke he fetched out of a poore Colwort. . . .

*Thrasybulus.*—Every thing liketh me passing well: Good Lord what a pleasant ground, what a Paradise is this: methinks I see the Orchards of Alcinous, the Trees are set Checkerwise, and so catred, as looke which way you will, they lie levell: King Cyrus himselfve never had better. If Lysander had ever seene this Orchard, he would have wondred a great deal more than he did at Cyrus his orchard.—' *The whole Art and Trade of Husbandry* ' (*Of Gardens, Orchards, and Woods*), enlarged by *Barnaby Googe.*

—◊◊◊—

HUSBANDRY is otherwise a very Servile Employment, as Salust tells us; though some parts of it are more excusable than the rest, as the Care of Gardens, which *Zenophon* attributes to *Cyrus*, and a mean may be found out betwixt Sordid and Homely Affection, so full of perpetual Solitude, which is seen in Men who make it their entire Business and Study, and that stupid and extream Negligence, letting all things go at Random, we see in others.—' *Of Solitude.*'

**MONTAIGNE** (1533-1592).

When at home, I a little more frequent my library, from whence I at once survey all the whole concerns of my Family: 'tis situated at the Entrance into my House, and I thence under me see my Garden, Court and base Court, and into all the parts of the building. Then I turn over now one Book and then another, of various subjects, without method or design: one while I meditate, another I record, and dictate as I walk to and fro, such whimsies as these I present you here.—*Essays: Charles Cotton's Translation.*

The house (of the Duke Cosimo, at Castello near Florence) is nothing to speak of; but these different pieces of gardenage, the whole situated on the slope of a hill, in such a way that the straight alleys are all on a gentle and easy decline; the cross-alleys are straight and close. There are several galleries (berceaux) to be seen very thickly interwoven and covered with all kinds of aromatic trees, like cedars, cypresses, orange, lemon and olive trees, the branches so mingled and interlaced, that it is easy to see the sun at its greatest strength could not penetrate them. The trunks of the cypresses and of those other trees are planted in rows so close to one another, that only three or four people could walk abreast. There is a large basin amongst others, in the midst of which is to be seen a natural or artificial rock, which seems all frozen over the top, by means of the same material with which the Duke has covered his grottos at Pratolino; and above the rock is a great copper medallion, representing a very old hairy man sitting down, his arms crossed, from whose beard, forehead and skin, drips water incessantly drop by drop, representing sweat and tears, and the fountain has no other conduit but this. Elsewhere they had an amusing experience—for walking through the Garden, and looking at its singularities, the gardener having left them for the purpose, as they were standing at a certain spot looking at the marble figures, there issued under their feet and between their legs through infinite small holes, jets of water so fine as to be almost invisible, and representing sovereignly well the distillation of fine rain, with which they were all spirted by means of some subterranean spring, which the gardener turned on more than 200 paces off, with such art that he raised and depressed these ejaculations at pleasure. . . . They saw too the head fountain issuing from the Canal by two great bronze figures . . . there is also an arbour (Cabinet) amid the branches of an ever-green tree, but richer than any other they had seen—for it is all filled with the living green branches of the tree, and all round the arbour is so enclosed with this verdure that there is no view except through certain openings, which must be made by separating the branches here and there; and in the middle, through a concealed pipe, mounts a stream of water through the arbour, in the centre of a small marble basin. There is heard too the water music. . . . A beautiful grotto is also to be seen, where every kind of animal is represented materially, emitting either by the beak, the wing, the claw, the ear or the nostril, the water of those fountains.

At Rome I had always some occupation, if not so agreeable as I could wish, at least sufficient to stave off ennui: such as visiting the Antiquities, the Vines, which are the Gardens and pleasure-resorts, of singular beauty; and then I learnt how far art could turn to advantage a woody, mountainous, and uneven spot, for they draw inimitable graces from our levels, and elude very artistically this diversity. Among the most beautiful are those of the Cardinals d'Este at Monte Cavallo; Farnese on the Palatine; Ursino, Sforza, Medicis; that of Pope Julius, that of Madama (Marguerite, Duchess of Parma); the Gardens of Farnese, and of Cardinal Riario at Transtevere, of Cesio, outside the People's Gate.—*Travels of Montaigne in Germany and Italy.*

FORTHWITH was the Table furnished with Fruits, as Mellons, Cytrons, and such like, which at the end of Supper were, at a wincke of his, reserved and set up; and then he began thus. The good old man Coricius, the Gardener of whom I remember I have reade in Virgill:

**TORQUATO TASSO** (1544-1595).

'Nocte domum dapibus mensas onerabat inemptis.'
Hyed home at night and fild his bord with delicats unbought;

and in imitation whereof Petrarch speaketh, reasoning of his Plowman :

> ' Epoi la mensa ingombra
> Di povere vivande,
> Simili a quelle ghiande
> Le quai fuggendo tutto 'l mondo honora.'
>
> And then he decks his boord about
> With meats of meane esteeme,
> Like to those Jayes whose flight contents
> The world, cause faire they seeme.

So that you neede not mervaile if I after their fashion, fill your Table with unbought viands, which, though they bee not such as you are used to taste elsewhere, remember you are in a Country town, and lodged in the house of a poore Host. I hold it (quoth I) a happy thing to have no neede to send for necessaries to the Cittie for the supply of good manners—I meane not of good meate, for thereof, sir, me seemes heere wants no store. It lightlie happeneth not (quoth hee) that I send to $y^e$ Cittie for any thing necessarie or fit for the life of a poore Gentleman, for (God be praised) I have aboundaunce of every thing ministred unto me upon myne owne ground, $y^e$ which I have devided into foure parts or formes, call them what you will. The first and greatest part I plow and sowe with wheate and all kind of graine. The seconde part I leave for Trees and plants, which are also necessarie either for fire, the use of Architecture, and other instruments of household, as also in those places that are sowne are manie rewes of Trees, whereupon the Vines, after the manner of our *petit* Countries, are laid and fastened. The third is Medowe ground, whereon the Heards and little flocks I have are wont to graze. The fourth I have reserved for hearbes, flowers, and rootes, where also are some store of hyves for Bees, because beyond this Orchard, wherein you see that I have gryft so many fruitfull Plants, and which you see is somewhat separat from my possessions, there is an other Garden, full of all sorts of sallet

## PETER TREVERIS

hearbes and other rootes.—'*The Householder's Philosophie, first written in Italian by that excellent orator and poet, Signior Torquato Tasso, and now translated by T. K.*' London, 1588.

—⁂—

WHEREFORE brotherly love compelleth me to wryte thrugh **PETER** ye gyftes of the holy gost, shewynge and enformynge how **TREVERIS** man may be holpen to grene herbes of the gardyn, and wedys of *(circa 1516).* ye feldys as well as by costly receptes of the potycarys prepayred. *The grete herball whiche geveth parfyt knowledge, and understandyng of all maner of herbes & theyre gracyous vertues whiche god hath ordeyned for our prosperous welfare and helth, for they hele and cure all manner of dyseases and sekenesses that fall or mysfortune to all manner of creatours of god created, practysed by many expert and wyse maysters as Avicenna & other etc. Also it geveth full parfyte understandynge of the booke lately printed by me (Peter Treveris) named the noble experiens of the vertuous hand warke of surgery.—Imprinted at London in Southwarke.* MDXXVI.

—⁂—

*Famous Antiquary to Henry VIII, who commissioned him to search after* **JOHN** *England's antiquities and peruse the libraries of cathedrals, abbeys, colleges* **LELAND**— *and other places, 'where records and the secrets of antiquity were deposited' or Laylonde —travelled through England and Wales for six or seven years and embodied* (1506-1552). *the results in his 'New Year's Gift' to the King. His 'Itinerary' was published by Thomas Hearne in nine vols., at Oxford* 1710-12.

THE Gardens within the mote, and the orchardes without, were exceeding fair. And yn the orchardes were mounts, *opere topiario*,[1] writhen about with degrees like the turnings in

[1] According to Mr Hudson Turner, 'mounts' in English gardens date from the period of the connexion of England with Burgundy in the 15th century. They were contrived to enable persons in the orchard to look over the enclosure wall, and were formed of stone, or wood 'curiously wrought within and without, or of earth covered with fruit trees,' as Lawson, 'the Isaac Walton of gardeners,' tells us.

The topiary art (*opus topiarium*) came into practice in this country at the beginning of the 16th century.—*Archæological Journal*, Vol. V.

cokil shelles, to come to the top without payn.—'*Itinerary*,' 1540 A.D. (*Of Wressel Castle, near Howden, Yorkshire.*)

—∞∞—

**ANDREAS CŒSALPINUS OF AREZZO** (1519-1603).
*Cæsalpinus called by Linnæus 'Primus Verus Systematicus'; author of 'De Plantis Libri XVI.' Florence, 1583.*

IN this immense multitude of plants, I see that want which is most felt in any other unordered crowd if such an assemblage be not arranged into brigades like an army, all must be tumult and fluctuation: for the mind is overwhelmed by the confused accumulation of things, and thus arise endless mistake and altercation. . . . For many years I have been pursuing my researches in various regions, habitually visiting the places in which grew the various kinds of herbs, shrubs and trees; I have been assisted by the labours of many friends, and by gardens established for the public benefit,[1] and containing foreign plants collected from the most remote regions.—*Whewell's History of the Inductive Sciences.*

—∞∞—

**OLIVIER DE SERRES, SEIGNEUR DU PRADEL** (1539-1619).
*Agronome, called 'The Father of Agriculture'—he planted white mulberry trees in the Tuileries Gardens under Henry IV., and throughout France, and practically re-introduced its silk industry. 1599, published 'Treatise on the Silk-worm,' and 1600, 'Théâtre d'Agriculture.'*[2]

I regarded the residence of the great parent of French agriculture (at Pradel), who was undoubtedly one of the first writers on the subject that had then appeared in the world, with that sort of veneration, which those only can feel who have addicted themselves strongly to some predominant pursuit, and

---

[1] One of the first gardens directed to the public study of Botany was that of Pisa, in 1543, by order of the Grand Duke Cosmo I.: of this Cœsalpinus was the second Director.

[2] For Flemish Garden-design contemporary with De Serres, the plates in 'Hortorum Vividariorumque elegantes Formae' by Jan Vrederman de Vries, Antwerp, 1583, 4to, are worth consulting.

## OLIVIER DE SERRES

find it in such moments indulged in its most exquisite feelings. Two hundred years after his exertions, let me do honour to his memory; he was an excellent farmer and a true patriot, and would not have been fixed on by Henry IV. as his chief agent in the great project of introducing the culture of silk in France, if he had not possessed a considerable reputation; a reputation well earned since posterity has confirmed it. The period of his practice is too remote to gain any thing more than a general outline of what may now be supposed to have been his farm. The basis of it is limestone; there is a great oak wood near the Château, and many vines, with plenty of mulberries, some apparently old enough to have been planted by the hand of the venerable genius that has rendered the ground classic. The estate of Pradel belongs at present to the Marquis of Mirabel, who inherits it in right of his wife, as the descendant of De Serres. *Arthur Young, ' Travels in France,' August* 1789.

CE sont les Jardinages, qui fournissent à l'ornement utile de nostre Mesnage, innumerables especes de racines, d'herbes, de fleurs, de fruit avec beaucoup de merveille. Aussi merveilleux en est le Createur, donnant à l'homme tant de sortes de viandes differentes en matière, figure, capacité, couleur, saveur, propriété, qu'impossible est de les pouvoir toutes discerner ni comprendre . . . Le Jardin excelle toute autre partie de terre labourable, mesmes en cette particulière propriété, qu'il rend du fruit chacun an et à toutes heures: là ou en quelque autre endroit que ce soit, le fonds ne rapporte qu'une seule fois l'annee; ou si deux, c'est tant rarement, que cela ne doit estre mis en ligne de compte. . . .

A l'imitation de telles Nations, des plus excellentes du monde toutes sortes de gens ont honoré les jardinages. Empereurs Rois, princes et autres grands seigneurs ont esté veus travailler à ordonner de leurs propres mains, leurs jardinages, eslisans telles peines pour soulagement en leurs grandes affaires. Leurs noms qu'ils ont engravés en plusieurs herbes et fruicts, pour en perpétuer la mémoire monstrent combien agréables leur ont esté tels exercises. Nous les lisons en l'herbe dicte lysimachie, du roi Lysimachus: en la gentiane, du Gentius, roi d'Illyrie: en l'armoise, d'Artemisia, roine de Carie: en l'achilleia, d'Achilles: en l'eupatoire, du roi Eupator: en scordium, autrement dicte l'herbe mithridates, de Mithridates roi de Pont et de Bithinie, et en plusieurs autres. Dont est venu, qu'aujourd'hui les jardinages sont en autant grand credit que jamais part oute l'Europe mesme en France, Alemagne, Angleterre, Italie, Espaigne, sont-ils cultivé avec beaucoup d'art et de diligence. . . .

Le jardinage se distingue en quatre espèces, assavoir, en potager, bouquetier, médecinal fruictier. Le Potager fournit toutes sortes de racines, herbes, fruicts rempans sur terre destinés à la cuisine, et autrement bons à manger, cruds et cuits. Le bouquetier est composé de toutes sortes de plantes, herbes, fleurs, arbustes, ageancés par compartiments ès parterres, et eslevés en vouçeures et cabinets, selon les inventions et fantasies des seigneurs, plus pour plaisir que pour profit. Pour la necessité est inventé le médecinal, encores que plusieurs herbes et racines pour remède aux maladies se cueillent indifféremment sur toutes sortes de possessions. . . . Le fruictier, autrement appellé, verger, est celui qui estant complanté de toutes sortes d'arbres, rapporte richement avec grande délectation, des fruicts d'infinies espèces. . . . Tous lesquels jardins, contigus et mis ensemble, seront enfermés dans un clos, entr'eux divisés par allées descouvertes ou couvertes en treillages, plats ou voutoyés, ou autrement, ainsi qu'on les voudra disposer. . . . Plus grand sera le seul jardin potager que les bouquetier et médicinal ensemble, estant en cet endroit plus requis le profit, que la simple délectation. . . . En sa figure n'y a aucune subjection car toutes sont agréables, pourveu que le jardin soit profitable : voire la plus bigearre (bizarre) est la plus souhaittable pour le plaisir comme ceux qui estans en pente, et retenus par bancs et murailles traversantes, sont fort prisés, ainsi qu'avec beaucoup de lustre, paroissent les jardins du roi à Sainct-Germain en Laie. . . . Le bouquetier se taillera aux revenus et plaisirs du seigneur, car puisqu'il est destiné pour le seul contentement, est raisonnable que ce soyent ces deux là, que y plantent les limites. . . .

Et à ce que la Jardinier n' aille rechercher loin des desseins pour ses Parterres, j'ai mis ici quelque nombre de Compartiments de diverses façons d'entre lesquels, y en a de ceux que la Roi a fait faire à Sainct-Germain en Laie et en ses nouveaux Jardins des Tuilleries, et de Fontainebleau au dresser desquels M. Claude

# OLIVIER DE SERRES

Mollet, Jardinier de sa Majesté, a fait preuve de sa dexterité.[1]—
*Le Théâtre d'Agriculture.* 1600.

[1] Claude Mollet, Head Gardener to Henri IV. and Louis XIII,—predecessor of Le Nôtre and de la Quintinye—was son of the Chief Gardener of Château d'Anet, where he collected rare flowers and medical herbs and enjoyed the confidence of its owner the Duc d'Aumale.

Claude Mollet was the first, in 1582, in France to create the 'parterres à compartiments et broderie,' after the designs of the Sieur du Perac, architect to the King, of which Olivier de Serres gives examples.

In 1595, he laid out the gardens of Saint Germain-en-Laye,[1] of Monceaux and of Fontainebleau, where by 1607 he had planted 7000 feet of fruit trees, bearing fruit existing half a century later. In the Tuileries he made fine plantations of Cypresses, destroyed in the winter of 1608, when the hardier box and yew were substituted.

His work 'Théâtre des Plans et Jardinages' appeared in 1652 at Paris, with twenty-two plates of designs of parterres, bosquets, labyrinths and palisades, invented by himself and his sons André, Jacques and Noel, and was several times re-printed and translated at Stockholm and London. The translation is sometimes attributed to his son André, who helped him. Mollet was the first to apply meteorology, which he calls 'Astrology,' to gardening. Near the Hôtel de Matignon, where Claude Mollet lived, behind St Thomas of the Louvre, he had raised white Mulberries, producing in 1606 12 lbs of silk, which he sold at 4 crowns (40 francs) the lb.

[1] See Illustration in Appendix.

# CHAPTER IV

ELIZABETHAN AND STUART GARDENS

JOHN
GERARDE
(1545-1607).
*Educated as a surgeon—superintended Lord Burghley's garden for twenty years—lived in Holborn, where he had a large physic garden—in his youth took a voyage to the Baltic—he drew up letter for Lord Burleigh to University of Cambridge, recommending that a physic garden be established there, with himself at its head, to encourage 'the facultie of simpling.' 1596, published catalogue of his garden in Holborn, and in 1597, his 'Herbal,' the woodcuts from Frankfurt, having served for the 'Kreuterbuch' of Tabernæmontanus (folio, 1588).*[1]

AMONG the manifold creatures of God (right Honorable and my singular good Lord) that have in all ages diversly entertained many excellent wits, and drawn them to the contemplation of the divine wisedome, none hath provoked mens studies more, or satisfied their desires so much, as plants have done, and that upon just and woorthie causes: For if delight may provoke mens labour, what greater delight is there than to behold the earth apparelled with plants, as with a robe of imbroidered worke, set with orient pearles, and garnished with great diversitie of rare and costlie jewels? If this varietie and perfection of colours may affect the eie, it is such in herbes and flowers, that no Apelles, no Zeuxis ever could by any art express the like: if odours, or if taste may worke satisfaction, they are both so soveraigne in plants, and so comfortable, that no confection of the Apothecaries can equall their excellent vertue. But these delights are in the outward senses: the principal delight is in the minde, singularly enriched with the knowledge of these visible things, setting foorth to us the invisible wisedome and admirable workmanship of almightie God. The delight is great, but the use greater, and joyned often

[1] See Illustration in Appendix.

with necessitie. In the first ages of the world they were the ordinarie meate of men, and have continued ever since of necessarie use both for meates to maintaine life, and for medicine to recover health. The hidden vertue of them is such, that (as Plinie noteth)[1] the very brute beasts have found it out: and (which is another use that he observeth) from thence the Diars took the beginning of their art.

Furthermore, the necessarie use of these fruits of the Earth doth plainly appeere by the great charge and care of almost all men in planting and maintaining of gardens, not as ornaments onely, but as a necessarie provision also to their houses. And here beside the fruit, to speake againe in a word of delight; gardens, especially such as your Honor hath, furnished with many rare simples, do singularly delight, when in them a man doth behold a flourishing shew of sommer beauties in the middest of winters force, and a goodly spring of Flowers, when abroade a leafe is not to be seene.

Beside these and other causes, there are many examples of those that have honored this science: for to passe by a multitude of the philosophers, it may please your Honor to call to remembrance that which you knowe of some noble Princes that have joyned this studie with their most important matters of state: Mithridates the great was famous for his knowledge herein, as Plutarch noteth: Euan also king of Arabia, the happie garden of the world for principall simples, wrote of this argument, as Plinie sheweth: Diocletian might he have his praise, had he not drowned all his honor in the blood of his persecution. To conclude this point, the example of Salomon is before the rest and greater, whose wisedome and knowledge was such, that he was able to set out the nature of all plantes, from the highest Cedar to the lowest Mosse.—*The Herball, or Generall Historie of Plantes, gathered by John Gerarde of London, Master in Chirurgie.* 1597. (*Dedication to Sir William Cecill Knight, Baron of Burgleih.*)

---

[1] Pliny, lib. 8, cap. 27; and lib. 22, cap. 2.

I list not seeke the common colours of antiquitie; when not withstanding the world can brag of no more ancient monument than Paradise, and the garden of Eden: and the fruits of the Earth may contend for seignioritie, seeing their mother was the first creature that conceived, and they themselves the first fruit she brought foorth. Talke of perfect happinesse or pleasure, and what place was so fit for that, as the garden place, wherein *Adam* was set, to be the Herbarist? Whither did the poets hunt for their syncere delights, but into the gardens of *Alcinous*, of *Adonis*, and the orchards of *Hesperides*? Where did they dreame that heaven should be, but in the pleasant garden of *Elysium*? Whither do all men walke for their honest recreation but thither, where the Earth hath most beneficially painted her face with flourishing colours? And what season of the yeere more longed for than the Spring, whose gentle breath inticeth foorth the kindly sweetes, and makes them yeeld their fragrant smells?—*Ibid. Preface 'to the courteous and well-willing Readers.'*

—⁂—

JOHN LYLY—
"*the Euphuist*"
(1554-1606).

ONE of the Ladies who delighted much in mirth, seeing *Philautus* behold *Camilla* so stedfastly, saide unto him: Gentleman, what floure like you best in all this border, heere be faire Roses, sweete Violets, fragrant primroses, heere wil be Jilly-floures, Carnations, sops in wine, sweet Johns, and what may either please you for sight, or delight you with savour: loth we are you should have a Posie of all, yet willing to give you one, not yat which shal looke best, but such a one as you shal lyke best.

Philautus omitting no opportunitie, yat might either manifest his affection, or commend his wit, answered hir thus:

Lady, of so many sweet floures to chuse the best, it is harde, seeing they be all so good. If I shoulde preferre the fairest before the sweetest, you would happely imagine that either I were stopped in the nose, or wanton in the eyes; if the sweetnesse before the beautie, then would you gesse me either to lyve with sauours, or to have no judgement in colours; but to tell my minde (upon correction be it spoken), of all flowers, I love a faire woman.

In deede, quoth Flavia (for so was she named), faire women are set thicke, but they come up thinne; and when they begin to budde, they are gathered as though they wer blowne. Of such men as you are, Gentleman, who thinke greene grasse will never be drye Hay, but when ye flower of their youth (being slipped too young) shall fade before they be olde, then I dare saye, you would chaunge your faire flower for a weede, and the woman you loved then, for the worst violet you refuse now.

Lady, aunswered Philautus, it is a signe that beautie was no niggard of hir slippes in this gardein, and very enuious to other grounds, seing heere are so many in one Plot, as I shall neuer finde more in all *Italy*, whether the reason be the heate which killeth them, or the country that cannot beare them. As for plucking them up soone, in yat we shew the desire we have to them, not the malyce. Where you conjecture that men haue no respect to things when they be olde, I cannot consent to your saying; for well do they know that it fareth with women as it doth with the Mulbery tree, which the elder it is, the younger it seemeth; and therefore hath it growen to a Prouerb in *Italy*, where one seeth a woman striken in age to looke amiable, he saith she hath eaten a Snake: so that I must of force follow mine olde opinion, that I love fresh flowers well, but faire women better. —'*Euphues and his England.*'

—⁓⁓⁓—

BUT *Palladius* having gotten his health, and only staying there to be in place, where he might hear answer of the ships set forth: *Kalander* one afternoon let him abroad to a well-arrayed ground he had behind his house, which he thought to show him before his going, as the place himself more than in any other, delighted in. The backside of the house was neither field, garden, nor orchard; or, rather, it was both field, garden, and orchard: for as soon as the descending of the stairs had delivered

SIR PHILIP SIDNEY (1554-1586).

them down, they came into a place cunningly set with trees of the most taste-pleasing fruits; but scarcely they had taken that into their consideration, but that they were suddenly stept into a delicate Green; of each side of the Green a Thicket, and behind the Thickets again new Beds of Flowers, which being under the Trees, the Trees were to them a Pavilion, and they to the Trees a Mosaïcal floor; so that it seemed that Art therein would needs be delightful, by counterfeiting his enemy Error, and making order in confusion.

In the midst of all the place was a fair Pond, whose shaking Crystal was a perfect Mirror to all the other beauties, so that it bare shew of two Gardens; one indeed, the other in shadows; and in one of the Thickets was a fine Fountain made thus: a naked Venus of white Marble, wherein the Graver had used such cunning, that the natural blue veins of the Marble were framed in fit places, to set forth the beautiful veins of her body. At her breast she had her Babe Æneas, who seemed (having begun to suck) to leave that, to look upon her fair Eyes, which smiled at the Babe's folly, meanwhile the breast running. Hard by was a house of Pleasure, built for a Summer retiring-place; whither *Kalander* leading him, he found a square room full of delightful Pictures, made by the most excellent Workmen of Greece.

\* \* \* \* \* \* \*

So *Gynecia* herself, bringing me to my Lodging, anon after I was invited and brought down to sup with them in the Garden, a place not fairer in natural ornaments than artificial inventions; where, in a Banquetting house, among certain pleasant Trees, whose heads seemed curled with the wrappings about of Vine-branches, the Table was set near to an excellent Water-work; for, by the Casting of the Water in most cunning manner, it makes (with the shining of the Sun upon it) a perfect Rain-bow, not more pleasant to the Eye than to the Minde, so sensible to see the proof of the Heavenly Iris. There were Birds also made so finely, that they did not only deceive the sight with their figure, but the hearing with their Songs, which the watry Instruments did make their Gorge deliver. The Table at which we sate was round, which being fast to the Floor whereon we sate, and that divided from the rest of the Buildings, with turning a Vice (which *Basilius* at first did to make me sport), the Table, and we about the Table, did all turn round, by means of Water which ran under, and carried it about as a mill.—' *The Countess of Pembroke's Arcadia*,' Book I.

—ww—

GOD Almighty first planted a Garden; and indeed it is the purest of humane pleasure. It is the greatest refreshment to the Spirits of Man, without which Buildings and Palaces are but gross Handy-works. And a Man shall ever see, that when Ages grow to Civility and Elegancy, Men come to build stately, sooner than to garden finely: as if Gardening were the Greater Perfection. I do hold it in the Royal Ordering of Gardens, there ought to be Gardens for all the Months in the Year, in which, severally, things of Beauty may be then in season.

**FRANCIS BACON—**
*Lord Verulam*
(1561-1626).

For December and January, and the latter part of November, you must take such things as are green all Winter: Holly, Ivy, Bays, Juniper, Cypress-Trees, Yews, Pine-Apple Trees, Fir-Trees, Rosemary, Lavender, Periwinckle, the White, the Purple, and the Blue, Germander, Flags, Orange-Trees, Limon-Trees, and Myrtles, if they be stirred, and Sweet Marjoram warm set.

There followeth, for the latter part of January and February, the Mezerion Tree, which then blossoms, Crocus Vernus, both the Yellow and the Grey, Prim-Roses, Anemones, the Early Tulippa, Hiacynthus Orientalis, Chamaïris, Frettellaria.

For March, there come Violets, specially the Single Blue, which are the Earliest, the yellow Daffadil, the Daisy, the Almond-Tree in blossom, the Peach-Tree in blossom, the Cornelian-Tree in blossom, Sweet Briar.

In April follow the double White Violet, the Wall-Flower, the Stock-Gilly-Flower, the Cowslip, Flower-de-Lices, and Lilies of all natures, Rosemary-Flowers, the Tulippa, the Double Piony, the pale Daffadill, the French Honey-Suckle, the Cherry-Tree

## 68  THE PRAISE OF GARDENS

in blossom, the Dammasin and Plum-Trees in blossom, the White Thorn in leaf, the Lelack Tree.

In May and June, come Pinks of all Sorts, specially the Blush-Pink, Roses of all kinds (except the Musk, which comes later), Honey-Suckles, Strawberries, Bugloss, Columbine, the French Marygold, Flos Africanus, Cherry-Tree in fruit, Ribes, Figs in fruit, Rasps, Vine-Flowers, Lavender in Flowers, the Sweet Satyrion with the White Flower, Herba Muscaria, Lillium Convallium, the Apple-Tree in blossom.

In July come Gilly-Flowers of all Varieties, Musk-Roses, and the Lime-Tree in blossom, Early Pears and Plumbs in fruit, Ginnitings, Quodlings.

In August, come Plumbs of all sorts in Fruit, Pears, Apricocks, Barberries, Filberds, Musk-Melons, Monkshoods of all Colours.

In September come Grapes, Apples, Poppies of all Colours, Peaches, Melo-Cotones, Nectarines, Cornellians, Wardens, Quinces.

In October and the beginning of November come Servises, Medlars, Bullaces; Roses Cut or Removed to come late, Hollyoaks, and such like.

These particulars are for the climate of London: But my meaning is perceived, that you may have *Ver Perpetuum*, as the place affords.

And because the Breath of Flowers is far Sweeter in the Air (where it comes and goes, like the Warbling of Musick) than in the Hand, therefore nothing is more fit for that Delight, than to know what be the Flowers and Plants that do best perfume the Air. Roses, Damask and Red, are fast Flowers of their Smells, so that you may walk by a whole Row of them, and find nothing of their Sweetness; yea, though it be in a morning Dew. Bays likewise yield no Smell as they grow, Rosemary little, nor Sweet-Marjoram. That, which above all others, yields the sweetest smell in the Air, is the Violet, specially the White double Violet, which comes twice a year, about the middle of April, and about Bartholomew-tide. Next to that is the Musk Rose, then the Strawberry Leaves dying with a most excellent Cordial Smell. Then the Flower of the Vines; it is a little

Dust, like the Dust of a Bent, which grows upon the Cluster in the first coming forth. Then Sweet-Briar, then Wall-Flowers, which are very delightful to be set under a Parlour, or lower Chamber Window. · Then Pinks, especially the Matted Pink, and Clove Gilly-Flower. Then the Flowers of the Lime-Tree. Then the Honey-Suckles, so they be somewhat afar off. Of Bean-Flowers I speak not, because they are Field-Flowers. But those which perfume the Air most delightfully, not passed by as the rest, but being Trodden upon and Crushed, are three: that is Burnet, Wild-Time, and Water-Mints. Therefore you are to set whole Alleys of them, to have the Pleasure when you walk or tread.

For Gardens (speaking of those which are indeed Prince-like, as we have done of Buildings), the Contents ought not well to be under thirty Acres of Ground, and to be divided into three parts; a Green in the entrance, a Heath or Desart in the going forth, and the Garden in the midst, besides Alleys on both sides. And I like well, that four Acres of Ground be assigned to the Green, six to the Heath, four and four to either Side, and twelve to the Main Garden. The Green hath two pleasures; the one because nothing is more pleasant to the Eye than Green Grass kept finely shorn; the other because it will give you a fair Alley in the midst, by which you may go in front upon a Stately Hedge, which is to enclose the Garden. But because the Alley will be long, and in great Heat of the Year or Day, you ought not to buy the shade in the Garden, by going in the Sun through the Green; therefore you are, of either Side the Green, to plant a Covert Alley upon Carpenter's Work, about twelve foot in Height, by which you may go in shade into the Garden. As for the making of Knots or Figures, with Divers Coloured Earths, that they may lie under the Windows of the House, on that Side which the Garden stands, they be but Toys, you may see as good sights many times in Tarts. The Garden is best to be Square, Encompassed on all the four Sides, with a Stately Arched Hedge: the Arches to be upon Pillars of Carpenter's Work, of some ten foot high, and six foot broad, and the Spaces between of the same Dimension with the Breadth of the Arch. Over the Arches let there be an Entire Hedge, of some four foot high, framed also upon Carpenter's Work, and upon the Upper Hedge, over every Arch, a little Turret with a Belly, enough to receive a Cage of Birds; and over every Space between the Arches some other little Figure, with broad Plates of Round Coloured Glass, gilt, for the Sun to play upon. But this Hedge, I intend to be raised upon a Bank, not steep, but gently slope, of some six foot, set all with Flowers. Also I understand, that this Square of the Garden should not be the whole breadth of the Ground, but to leave on either side Ground enough for diversity of Side Alleys unto which the two Covert Alleys of the Green may deliver you, but there must be no Alleys with Hedges at either End of this Great Inclosure: not at the Hither End, for letting your Prospect upon this fair Hedge from the Green; nor at the Further End for letting your Prospect from the Hedge through the Arches upon the Heath.

For the ordering of the Ground within the Great Hedge, I leave it to Variety of Device. Advising nevertheless, that whatsoever form you cast it into; first it be not too busie, or full of Work; wherein I, for my part, do not like Images cut out in Juniper, or other Garden-stuff; they are for Children. Little low Hedges, round like Welts, with some pretty Pyramids, I like well; and in some places, Fair Columns upon Frames of Carpenter's Work. I would also have the Alleys spacious and fair. You may have closer Alleys upon the Side Grounds, but none in the Main Garden.

I wish also in the very middle a fair Mount, with three Ascents and Alleys, enough for four to walk abreast, which I would have to be perfect Circles, without any Bulwarks or Imbossments, and the whole Mount to be thirty foot high, and some fine Banquetting House, with some Chimneys neatly cast, and without too much Glass.

For Fountains, they are a Great Beauty and Refreshment, but Pools mar all, and make the Garden unwholesome, and full of

Flies and Frogs. Fountains I intend to be of two Natures: the one that sprinkleth or spouteth Water, the other a fair Receipt of Water, of some thirty or forty foot square, but without Fish, or Slime, or Mud. For the first, the Ornaments of Images Gilt, or of Marble, which are in use, do well; but the main matter is, so to convey the Water, as it never stay, either in the Bowls, or in the Cistern, that the Water be never by rest discoloured, Green, or Red, or the like; or gather any Mossiness or Putrefaction. Besides that, it is to be cleansed every day by the hand; also some steps up to it, and some Fine Pavement about it, doth well. As for the other kind of Fountain, which we may call a Bathing Pool, it may admit much Curiosity and Beauty, wherewith we will not trouble ourselves, as, that the Bottom be finely paved, and with Images, the Sides likewise; and withal Embellished with coloured Glass, and such things of Lustre; Encompassed also with fine Rails of low Statua's. But the main point is the same, which we mentioned in the former kind of Fountain, which is, that the Water be in perpetual Motion, fed by a Water higher than the Pool, and delivered into it by fair Spouts, and then discharged away under Ground by some Equality of Bores, that it stay little. And for fine Devices, of Arching Water without spilling, and making it rise in Several forms (of Feathers, Drinking Glasses, Canopies, and the like) they be pretty things to look on, but nothing to Health and Sweetness.

For the Heath, which was the third part of our Plot, I wish it to be framed, as much as may be, to a Natural Wildness. Trees I would have none in it, but some Thickets, made only of Sweet-Briar and Honey-suckle, and some Wild-Vine amongst; and the Ground set with Violets, Strawberries and Primroses: for these are Sweet, and prosper in the Shade. And these to be in the Heath, here and there, not in any Order. I like also little Heaps, in the Nature of Mole-Hills (such as are in Wild-Heaths) to be set, some with Wild-Thyme, some with Pinks, some with Germander, that gives a good Flower to the Eye; some with Periwinkle, some with Violets, some with Strawberries, some with Cowslips, some with Daisies, some with Red-Roses, some with

Lilium Convallium, some with Sweet-Williams Red, some with Bear's-Foot, and the like Low Flowers, being withall Sweet and Sightly. Part of which Heaps, to be with Standards, of little Bushes prickt upon their top, and part without; the Standards to be Roses, Juniper, Holly, Bear-berries, (but here and there, because of the smell of their blossom), Red Currans, Gooseberries, Rosemary, Bays, Sweet-Briar, and such like. But these Standards to be kept with Cutting, that they grow not out of course.

For the Side Grounds, you are to fill them with variety of Alleys, private, to give a full shade, some of them, wheresoever the Sun be. You are to frame some of them, likewise for shelter, that when the wind blows sharp, you may walk as in a Gallery. And those Alleys must be likewise hedged at both Ends, to keep out the Wind, and these closer Alleys must be ever finely Gravelled, and no grass, because of going wet. In many of these Alleys likewise, you are to set Fruit Trees of all sorts; as well upon the Walls, as in Ranges. And this would be generally observed, that the Borders wherein you plant your Fruit-Trees be fair and large, and low, and not steep, and set with fine Flowers, but thin and sparingly, lest they deceive the trees. At the end of both the side Grounds, I would have a Mount of some pretty Height, leaving the Wall of the Enclosure breast-high, to look abroad into the Fields.

For the Main Garden, I do not deny, but there should be some fair Alleys ranged on both sides with Fruit-Trees, and some pretty Tufts of Fruit-Trees and Arbors with Seats, set in some decent Order; but these to be by no means set too thick; but to leave the Main Garden, so as it be not close, but the Air open and free; for as for Shade I would have you rest upon the Alleys of the Side Grounds, there to walk, if you be disposed, in the Heat of the Year or Day: but to make account, that the Main Garden is for the more temperate parts of the year, and in the Heat of Summer, for the Morning and the Evening, or Over-cast days.

For Aviaries, I like them not, except they be of that largeness,

# PAUL HENTZNER 73

as they may be turfed, and have Living Plants and Bushes set in them, that the Birds may have more scope, and natural Nestling, and that no foulness appear in the floor of the Aviary. So I have made a Plat-form of a Princely Garden, partly by Precept, partly by Drawing, not a Model, but some general Lines of it, and in this I have spared for no Cost.

But it is nothing for Great Princes, that for the most part taking advice with Work-men, with no less Cost, set their things together, and sometimes add Statua's and such things, for State and Magnificence, but nothing to the true pleasure of a Garden.—*Essays: 'Of Gardens.'*

—◦◦◦—

*Jurisconsult and Traveller: author of 'Itinerarium Germaniæ, Galliæ, Italiæ,' Nuremberg,* 1612.

**PAUL HENTZNER** (1558-1623).

THE first was THEOBALDS, belonging to Lord Burleigh the Treasurer: In the gallery was painted the genealogy of the Kings of England; from this place one goes into the garden, encompassed with a ditch full of water, large enough for one to have the pleasure of going in a boat, and rowing between the shrubs; here are great variety of trees and plants; labyrinths made with a great deal of labour; a jet d'eau, with its bason of white marble; and columns and pyramids of wood and other materials up and down the garden: After seeing these, we were led by the gardiner into the summer-house, in the lower part of which, built semi-circularly, are the twelve Roman emperors in white marble, and a table of touchstone; the upper part of it is set round with cisterns of lead, into which the water is conveyed through pipes, so that fish may be kept in them, and in summer time they are very convenient for bathing; in another room for entertainment very near this, and joined to it by a little bridge, was an oval table of red marble.

WHITEHALL.

In a garden joining to this palace, there is a Jet d'eau, with a sun-dial, which while strangers are looking at, a quantity of water forced by a wheel, which the gardiner turns at a distance, through a number of little pipes, plentifully sprinkles those that are standing round.

OXFORD.

As soon as Grace is said after each meal, every one is at liberty, either to retire to his own chambers, or to walk in the College garden, there being none that has not a delightful one.

HAMPTON COURT.[1]

Afterwards we were led into the gardens, which are most pleasant, here we saw rosemary so planted and nailed to the walls as to cover them entirely, which is a method exceeding common in England.

NONESUCH (a Royal Retreat in a place formerly called
    CUDDINGTON, a very healthful situation chosen by King
    Henry VIII.).

The palace itself is so encompassed with parks full of deer, delicious gardens, groves ornamented with trellis-work, cabinets of verdure, and walks so embrowned by trees, that it seems to be a place pitched upon by *Pleasure* herself, to dwell in along with *Health*.

In the pleasure and artificial gardens are many columns and pyramids of marble, two fountains that spout water one round the other like a pyramid, upon which are perched small birds that stream water out of their bills: In the grove of Diana is a very agreeable fountain, with Actæon turned into a stag, as he was sprinkled by the goddess and her nymphs, with inscriptions.

There is besides another pyramid of marble full of concealed

---

[1] See Illustration in Appendix.

pipes, which spirt upon all who come within their reach.—
*A Journey into England in the year* 1598.[1]

—⁄⁄⁄⁄⁄—

ROSAMOND'S Labyrinth, whose Ruins, together with her Well, being paved with square Stone in the bottom, and also her Tower, from which the Labyrinth did run (are yet remaining) was altogether under ground, being Vaults Arched and Walled with Brick and Stone, almost inextricably wound one within another, by which, if at any time her Lodging were laid about by the Queen, she might easily avoid eminent Peril, and if need be, by secret issues take the Air abroad, many Furlongs round about Woodstock in Oxfordshire, wherein it was situated. Thus much for Rosamond's Labyrinth.—'*England's Heroical Epistles.*' Annotations to '*The Epistle of Rosamond to King Henry II.*'

**MICHAEL DRAYTON** (1563-1631).

—⁄⁄⁄⁄⁄—

*Apothecary to James I.; for his "Theatre of Plants" Charles I. made him "Botanicus Regius Primarius;" he spent nearly 40 years in travelling.*

**JOHN PARKINSON** (1567-1640).

ALTHOUGH many men must be content with any plat of ground, of what form or quantity soever it be, more or less, for their Garden, because a more large or convenient cannot be had to their habitation: Yet I perswade myself, that Gentlemen of the better sort and quality, will provide such a parcel of ground to be laid out for their Garden, and in such convenient manner, as may be fit and answerable to the degree they hold. . . . The orbicular or round form is held in its own

[1] Horace Walpole, who reprinted the text of this work with the translation at his private press at Strawberry Hill in 1757, remarks in his Advertisement: 'We are apt to think that Sir William Temple, and King William, were in a manner the introducers of gardening into England. By the description of Lord Burleigh's gardens at Theobalds, and of those at Nonsuch, we find that the magnificent, though false taste, was known here as early as the reigns of Henry VIII., and his daughter. There is scarce an unnatural and sumptuous impropriety at Versailles which we do not find in Hentzner's description of the gardens above mentioned.'

proper existence to be the most absolute form, containing within it all other forms whatsoever; but few I think will choose such a proportion to be joyned to their habitation, being not accepted any where I think, but for the general Garden to the University at Padua. . . . The four square form is the most usually accepted with all, and doth best agree to any man's dwelling, being (as I said before) behind the house, all the back windows thereof opening into it. Yet if it be longer than the breadth, or broader than the length, the proportion of walks, squares, and knots may be soon brought to the square form and be so cast, as the beauty thereof may be no lesse than the four square proportion, or any other better form, if any be. To form it therefore with walks, cross the middle both wayes, and round about it also with hedges, with squares, knots and trails, or any other work within the four square parts, is according as every man's conceit alloweth of it, and they will be at the charge: For there may be therein walks either open or close, either publick or private, a Maze, or Wildernesse, a Rock, or Mount, with a Fountain in the midst thereof to convey water to every part of the Garden, either in Pipes under the ground or brought by hand, and emptied into large Cisterns, or great Turky Jars, placed in convenient places, to serve as an ease to water the nearest parts thereunto. Arbours also being both graceful and necessary, may be appointed in such convenient places, as the corners or elsewhere, as may be most fit, to serve both for shadow and rest after walking. And because many are desirous to see the forms of trails, knots, and other compartiments, and because the open knots are more proper for these Out-landish flowres; I have here caused some to be drawn, to satisfy their desires; . . . Let every man therefore, if he like of these, take what may please his minde, or out of these or his own conceit frame any other to his fancy, or cause others to be done, as he liketh best, observing this *decorum*, that according to his ground he do cast out his knots, with convenient room for allies and walks; for the fairer and larger your allies and walks be, the more grace your Garden shall have, the lesse harm

# THOMAS HILL

the herbs and flowers shall receive, by passing by them that grow next unto the allies sides, and the better shall your Weeders cleanse both the beds and the allies.—'*Paradisi in Sole Paradisus Terrestris* ( = *The Earthly Paradise of Park-in-Sun.*), *or a garden of all sorts of pleasant flowers,*' *&c.*, *with engraved title-page, a portrait and* 109 *woodcuts* (1629, *folio*).

---

*A hack-writer on Dreams, Physiognomy, Mysteries, Astronomy and Gardening; author of 'A most briefe and pleasaunt Treatyse teachynge howe to Dress, Sowe, and Set a Garden,' London, 8vo,* 1563: *and 'The profitable Arte of Gardening,'* 1567; *and under the Latinized name of 'Dydymus Mountaine' he published 'The Gardener's Labyrinth'* (1571, 4*to*, 𝔅lack 𝔏etter), *and 'The Second Part' in* 1577. *'The Gardener's Labyrinth' was re-edited by H. Dethycke his friend, in* 1586.

**THOMAS HIL** or **'DYDYMUS MOUNTAINE'** (*fl.* 1590).

THE husbandman or Gardener shal enjoy a most commodiouse and delectable garden, whiche bothe knoweth, can, and will orderly dresse the same: yet not sufficient is it to a Gardener, that he knoweth, or would the furtherance of the Garden, without a cost bestowed, which the workes and labours of the same require: nor the will againe of the workeman, in doing and bestowing of charges, shall smally avayle, without he have both arte and skill in the same. For that cause, it is the chiefest poynt in every facultie and busines, to understand and know what to begin and follow: as the learned *Columella* out of *Varronianus Tremellius* aptly uttereth. The person which shall enjoy or have in a readinesse these three, and will purposedly or with diligence frame to him a well dressed Garden, shall after obtayne these two commodities, as utilitie and delight: the utilitie, yeeldeth the plentie of Herbes, floures, and fruytes right delectable: but the pleasure of the same procureth a delight, and (as *Varro* writeth) a jucunditie of minde. For that cause a Garden shal workemanly be handled and dressed unto the necessarie use and commoditie of man's life, next for health, and the recoverie of strength by sicknesse feebled: as the singular *Palladius Rutilius* hath learnedly uttered, and the skilful *Florentinus*, that wrote cunningly of husbandry in the

Greek tunge, certayne yeeres before him: Lastly by sight unto delectation, and jucunditie through the fragrancie of smell: but most of all, that the same may furnishe the owners, and husbande mans table, with sundry seemely and dayntie dishes, to him of small coste. The Garden grounde (if the same may be) ought rather to be placed neere hande, whereby the owner or Gardener may with more ease be partaker of such commodities growing in the garden, and bothe oftner resorte and use his diligence in the same: So that this is the whole care and duetie required of every owner and Gardener in their plot of ground.—*The Gardener's Labyrinth.* A.D. 1577.

—ᴡᴡᴡ—

**LEONARD MASCHAL** (d. 1589). *Clerk of Kitchen in house of Parker, Archbishop of Canterbury: author of 'A Booke of the Arte and maner howe to plant and graffe all sortes of Trees,' 1572; 'On the Government of Cattle' (with portrait), 1596, a later edition (1680) being called "The Countryman's Jewel."*

—ᴡᴡᴡ—

**WILLIAM LAWSON** (c. 1570-1618). *Writer on gardening, whose book 'A new Orchard and Garden,' he says was the result of 48 years' experience. It appeared in 1618, and earned him the name of 'the Isaac Walton of Gardeners.'*

THE very works of, and in an Orchard and Garden, are better than the ease and rest of and from other laboures. When God had made man after his owne Image, in a perfect state, and would have him to represent himselfe in authoritie, tranquilitie, and pleasure upon the Earth, He placed him in *Paradise*. What was *Paradise*? But a Garden and Orchard of trees and hearbs, full of all pleasure? and nothing there but delights. The gods of the Earth, resembling the great God of heaven in authoritie, Majestie, and abundance of all things, wherein is their most delight? And whether doe they withdraw themselves from the troublesome affayres of their estate, being tyred with the hearing and judging of litigious Controversies? choked (as it were), with the close ayres of their sumptuous buildings, their stomacks cloyed with varietie of Banquets, their eares filled and over-burthened with tedious discoursings. Whither? but into

# WILLIAM LAWSON

their Orchards? made and prepared, dressed and destinated for that purpose to renew and refresh their sences, and to call home their over-wearied spirits. Nay, it is (no doubt) a comfort to them, to set open their Cazements into a most delicate Garden and Orchard, whereby they may not only see that, wherein they are so much delighted, but also to give fresh, sweete, and pleasant ayre to their Galleries and Chambers.

What can your eye desire to see, your eares to heare, your mouth to taste, or your nose to smell, that is not to be had in an Orchard? with abundance and variety? What more delightsome than an infinite varietie of sweet smelling flowers? decking with sundry colours the greene mantle of the Earth, the universall Mother of us all, so by them bespotted, so dyed, that all the world cannot sample them, and wherein it is more fit to admire the Dyer, than imitate his workemanship. Colouring not onely the earth, but decking the ayre, and sweetning every breath and spirit.

The Rose red, damaske, velvet, and double double province Rose, the sweet muske Rose double and single, the double and single white Rose. The faire and sweet senting Woodbind, double and single. Purple Cowslips, and double Cowslips, Primrose double and single. The Violet nothing behinde the best, for smelling sweetly. And 1000 more will provoke your content.

And all these, by the skill of your Gardiner, so comely, and orderly placed in your Borders and Squares, and so intermingled, that none looking thereon, cannot but wonder, to see, what Nature corrected by Art can doe.

When you behold in divers corners of your Orchard *Mounts* of stone, or wood curiously wrought within and without, or of earth covered with fruit trees: Kentish Cherry, Damsons, plummes, etc. With stares of precious workmanship And in some corner (or more) a true Dyall or Clock, and some Anticke works, and especially silver s(o)unding Musique, mixt Instruments and voyces, gracing all the rest: How will you be rapt with delight?

Large walks, broad and long, close and open, like the *Tempe*

# 80        THE PRAISE OF GARDENS

groves in *Thessalie*, raysed with gravell and sand, having seats and banks of Camamile, all this delights the minde, and brings health to the body.

View now with delight the works of your owne hands, your fruit trees of all sorts, loaden with sweet blossomes, and fruit of all tasts, operations, and coloures; your trees standing in comely order which way soever you looke.

Your borders on every side hanging and drooping with Feberries, Raspberries, Barberries, Currens, and the roots of your trees powdred with Strawberries, red, white, and greene, what a pleasure is this?

Your Gardiner can frame your lesser wood to the shape of men armed in the field, ready to give battell: or swift running Grey hounds: or of well sented and true running Hounds, to chase the Deere, or hunt the Hare. This kinde of hunting shall not waste your corne, nor much your coyne.

Mazes well framed a man's height, may perhaps make your friend wander in gathering of berries, till he cannot recover himselfe without your helpe.

To have occasion to Exercise within your Orchard: it shall be a pleasure to have a Bowling Alley, or rather (which is more manly, and more healthfull) a payre of Buttes, to stretch your armes.

Rosemary and sweet Eglantine are seemly ornaments about a Doore or Window, so is Woodbine.

Looke *Chap.* 5 and you shall see the forme of a Conduict. It there were two or more it were not amisse.

And in mine opinion, I could highly commend your Orchard, if eyther thorow it, or hard by it there should runne a pleasant River with silver streames : you might sit in your Mount, and angle a peckled Trout, or a sleightie Eele, or some other Fish. Or Moats, whereon you might row with a Boat, and fish with Nets.

Store of Bees in a dry and warme Bee-house, comely made of Firboords, to sing, and sit, and feede upon your flowers and sprouts, make a pleasant noyse and sight. For cleanly and innocent Bees, of all other things, love and become, and thrive in an Orchard. If they thrive (as they must needs if your Gardiner be skilfull, and love them: for they love their friends, and hate none but their Enemies) they will besides the pleasure, yeeld great profit, to pay him his wages. Yea, the increase of twenty Stocks, or Stooles with other fees will keep your Orchard. You need not doubt their stings, for they hurt not, whom they know, and they know their keeper and acquaintance. If you like not to come amongst them, you neede not doubt them : for but neere their store, and in their owne defence, they will not fight, and in that case onely (and who can blame them ?) they are manly and fight desperately. Some (as that Honourable Lady at *Hacknes*, Whose name doth much grace mine Orchard) use to make seats for them in the Stone wall of their Orchard or Garden, which is good, but wood is better. A vine over-shadowing a seat is very comely, though her Grapes with us ripe slowly.

One chiefe grace that adornes an Orchard I cannot let slippe. A broode of Nightingales, who with their several notes and tunes, with a strong delightsome voyce, out of a weake body, will beare you company night and day. She loves (and lives in) hots of wood in her heart. She will help you to cleanse your trees of Caterpillars, and all noysome wormes and flyes. The gentle Robbin-red-brest will helpe her, and in Winter in the coldest stormes will keepe a part.

Neither will the Silly Wren be behind in Summer, with her distinct whistle (like a sweet Recorder) to cheere your spirits.

The Black-bird and Threstle (for I take it the Thrush sings not, but devoures) sing loudly in a May morning, and delights the Eare much (and you neede not want their company, if you have ripe Cherryes or Berries, and would as gladly as the rest doe you pleasure :) But I had rather want their company than my fruit.

What shall I say ? 1000 of delights are in an Orchard : and sooner shall I be weary, then I can reckon the least part of that pleasure, which one, that hath and loves an Orchard may finde therein.

What is there, of all these few that I have reckoned, which

doth not please the eye, the eare, the smell and taste? And by these sences, as Organes, Pipes, and Windowes, these delights are carryed to refresh the gentle, generous, and noble minde.

To conclude, what joy may you have, that you living to such an age, shall see the blessings of God on your labours, while you live, and leave behind you to your heires, or successors (for God will make heires) such a worke, that many ages after your death, shall record your love to your Country. And the rather, when you consider, to what a length of time your worke is like to last.—'*A New Orchard and Garden.*' 1618.[1]

---

**ROBERT LANEHAM** (*fl.* 1575). *Was Clerk of the Council-Chamber Door and Gentleman Usher, under the patronage of the Earl of Leicester. He is the author of a letter describing the 'Entertainment unto the Queen's Majesty at Killingworth Castle in Warwicksheer in this Somers Progress,* 1575,' *which is used by Sir Walter Scott in 'Kenilworth' and characterised by him as 'A very diverting Tract, written by as great a Coxcomb as ever blotted paper.'*

UNTO this, his Honor's (the Earl of Leicester's) exquisite appointment of a beautiful garden, an acre or more in quantity, that lieth on the north there : Whereon hard all along by the Castle wall is reared a pleasant terrace, ten feet high, and twelve feet broad, even under foot, and fresh of fine grass ; as is also the side thereof towards the garden : In which, by sundry equal distances, with obelisks and spheres, and white bears, all of stone upon their curious bases, by goodly shew were set ; To these, two fine arbours redolent by sweet trees and flowers, at each end one, the garden plot under that, with fair alleys, green by grass, even voided from the borders on both sides, and some (for change) with sand, not light, or too soft, or soily by dust, but smooth and firm, pleasant to walk on, as a sea-shore when the water is availed. Then, much gracified by due proportion of four even quarters ; in

---

[1] This work usually forms part of Gervase Markham's 'A way to get Wealth,' which went through many editions.

the midst of each, upon a base of two feet square, and high, seemly bordered of itself, a square pilaster rising pyramidically fifteen feet high. Symmetrically pierced through from a foot beneath to two feet of the top: whereupon, for a Capital, an orb of ten inches thick; every one of these, with its base, from the ground to the top, of one whole piece; hewn out of hard porphyry, and with great art and heed (think me) thither conveyed and there erected. Where, further also, by great cast and cost, the sweetness of savour on all sides, made so respirant from the redolent plants, and fragrant herbs and flowers, in form, colour, and quantity so deliciously variant; and fruit-trees bedecked with apples, pears, and ripe cherries. . . .

A garden then so appointed, as wherein aloft upon sweet shadowed walk of terrace, in heat of summer to feel the pleasant whisking wind above, or delectable coolness of the fountain-spring beneath; to taste of delicious strawberries, cherries, and other fruits, even from their stalks; to smell such fragrancy of sweet odours, breathing from the plants, herbs, and flowers; to hear such natural melodious music and tunes of birds; to have in eye for mirth sometime these underspringing streams; then, the woods, the waters (for both pool and chase were hard at hand in sight), the deer, the people (that out of the East arbour in the base Court, also at hand in view), the fruit-trees, the plants, the herbs, the flowers, the change in colours, the birds flittering, the fountain streaming, the fish swimming, all in such delectable variety, order, and dignity; whereby, at one moment, in one place, at hand, without travel, to have so full fruition of so many God's blessings, by entire delight unto all senses (if all can take) at once; for etymon of the word worthy to be called Paradise: and though not so goodly as Paradise, for want of the fair rivers, yet better a great deal by the lack of so unhappy a tree. Argument most certain of a right noble mind, that in this sort could have thus all contrived.—*Letter describing the Pageants at Kenilworth Castle.* 1575.

SIR HENRY WOTTON (1568-1639). *Was educated at Winchester and Oxford, then travelled for nine years, one year in France, and at Geneva, where he was acquainted with Theodore Beza and Isaac Casaubon; three years in Germany and five in Italy, where (according to Isaac Walton), both in Rome, Venice, and Florence he became acquainted with the most eminent men for learning, and all manner of arts, as picture, sculpture, chemistry, architecture, and other manual arts: on his return became Secretary to the Earl of Essex, upon whose apprehension he returned to Italy. The Grand Duke of Tuscany sent him to James, King of Scotland, to acquaint him with a plot upon his life, which was the beginning of Wotton's fortune. On the King's accession he was sent as Ambassador to Venice—in Augsburg he wrote his famous definition of an Ambassador sent to 'lie abroad for his country'—on his return he was made Provost of Eton.*

*His writings were collected in 'Reliquiæ Wottonianæ' by I. Walton (1651), containing his 'Elements of Architecture.' He is now remembered chiefly by his poems, and his epigram (recorded on his tomb) 'Disputandi pruritus ecclesiarum scabies.'*

FIRST, I must note a certain contrariety between *building* and *gardening*: for as *Fabricks* should be *regular*, so *Gardens* should be *irregular*, or at least cast into a very wild *Regularity*. To exemplifie my conceit, I have seen a *Garden*, for the manner perchance incomparable, into which the first Access was a high walk like a *Tarrace*, from whence might be taken a general view of the whole *Plot* below, but rather in a delightful confusion, then with any plain distinction of the pieces. From this the *Beholder* descending many steps, was afterwards conveyed again by several *mountings* and *valings*, to various entertainments of his *sent* and *sight*: which I shall not need to describe, for that were poetical, let me only note this, that every one of these diversities, was as if he had been *magically* transported into a new *Garden*.

But though other *Countreys* have more benefit of Sun than we, and thereby more properly tyed to contemplate this delight; yet have I seen in our *own*, a delicate and diligent *curiosity*, surely without *parallel* among foreign *Nations*: Namely, in the Garden of Sir *Henry Fanshaw*, at his Seat in *Ware-Park*; where I well remember, he did so precisely examine the *tinctures* and *seasons* of his *flowers*, that in their *settings*, the *inwardest* of which that were to come up at the same time, should be always a little *darker* than the *outmost*, and so serve them for a kind of gentle *shadow*, like a piece not of *Nature*, but of *Art*: which mention (incident to this place) I have willingly made of his *Name*, for the dear *friendship*, that was long between us: though I must confess, with much wrong to his other *vertues*; which deserve a more solid *Memorial*, then among these vacant Observations. So much of *Gardens.—The Elements of Architecture.*

—◦◦◦—

(*Upon the sight of Tulipaes and Marygolds, etc., in his Garden.*) JOSEPH
HALL—
THESE Flowers are true Clients of the Sunne; how observant *Bishop of Exeter and Norwich*
they are of his motion, and influence.
At even, they shut up, as mourning for his departure, without (1574-1656).
whom they neither can nor would flourish in the morning; they welcome his rising with a cheerfull opennesse, and at noone, are fully display'd in a free acknowledgment of his bounty: Thus doth the good hart unto God; When thou turnedst away thy face I was troubled, saith the man after God's owne hart; in thy presence is life; yea the fullnesse of joy: thus doth the carnall hart to the world; when that withdrawes his favour, hee is dejected; and revives with a smile: All is in our choyse; whatsoever is our Sun will thus carry us; O God, be thou to mee, such as thou art in thyselfe; thou shalt bee mercifull in drawing me; I shall be happy in following thee.—*Occasional Meditations.*

—◦◦◦—

TO walk amongst orchards,[1] gardens, bowers, mounts and arbours, ROBERT
BURTON
artificial wildernesses, green thickets, arches, groves, lawns, (1576-1640).
rivulets, fountains, and such like pleasant places, like that Antiochian Daphne, brooks, pools, fishponds, between wood and water, in a fair meadow, by a river side, *ubi variæ avium cantationes florum* park, run up a steep hill sometimes, or sit in a shady seat, must

[1] Ambulationes subdiales, quas hortenses auræ ministrant, sub fornice viridi, pampinis virentibus concameratæ.

*colores, pratorum frutices*,¹ etc.; to disport in some pleasant plain, needs be a delectable recreation. *Hortum principis et domus ad delectationem facta, cum sylvâ, monte et piscinâ, vulgò la Montagna*: the prince's garden at Ferrara Schottus² highly magnifies, with the groves, mountains, ponds, for a delectable prospect, he was much affected with it; a Persian paradise, or pleasant park, could not be more delectable in his sight. St Bernard, in the description of his monastery, is almost ravished with the pleasures of it. *A sick man*³ (saith he) *sits upon a green bank, and when the dog-star parcheth the Plains, and dries up rivers, he lies in a shady bowre!* Fronde sub arborea ferventia temperat astra, *and feeds his eyes with variety of objects, herbs, trees, to comfort his misery, he receives many delightsome smells, and fills his ears with that sweet and various harmony of Birds: good God* (saith he) *what a company of pleasures hast thou made for man!* He that should be admitted on a sudden to the sight of such a Palace as that of *Escurial* in *Spain*, or to that which the *Moors* built at *Granado*, *Fountenblewe* in *France*, the *Turks* gardens in his *seraglio*, wherein all manner of Birds and beasts are kept for pleasure; Wolves, Bears, lynces, Tygers, Lyons, Elephants, *etc.* or upon the banks of that *Thracian Bosphorus*: the Pope's *Belvedere* in *Rome*⁴ as pleasing as those *Horti pensiles* in *Babylon*, or that *Indian* King's delightsome garden in *Ælian*;⁵ or those famous gardens of the Lord *Cantelow* in *France*,⁶ could not choose, though he were never so ill apaid, but be much recreated for the time; or many of our Noblemens gardens at home.—*The Anatomy of Melancholy.*

[1] Theophylact.
[2] Itinerar. Ital.
[3] Sedet ægrotus cespite viridi, et cum inclementia Canicularis terras excoquit, et siccat flumina, ipse securus sedet sub arborea fronde, et ad doloris sui solatium, naribus suis gramineas redolet species, pascit oculos herbarum amœna viriditas, aures suavi modulamine demulcet pictaram concentus avium, etc. Deus bone, quanta pauperibus procuras solatia!
[4] Diod. Siculus, lib. 2.
[5] Lib. 13, De Animal, cap. 13.
[6] Pet. Gillius, Paul Hentznerus, Itinerar. Italiæ, 1617: Iod. Sincerus, Itinerar. Galliæ, 1617; Simp. lib. 1, quest. 4.

Generalife, Granada.
George F. Atwood, Sc. ?

A MONGST the rest, the pains and industry of an ancient gentleman, Mr Adrian Gilbert, must not be forgotten: for there[1] hath he (much to my Lord's cost and his own pains) used such a deal of intricate setting, grafting, planting, inoculating, railing, hedging, plashing, turning, winding, and returning, circular, triangular, quadrangular, orbicular, oval, and every way curiously and chargeably conceited: there hath he made walks, hedges, and arbours, of all manner of most delicate fruit-trees, planting and placing them in such admirable art-like fashions, resembling both divine and moral remembrances, as three arbours standing in a triangle, having each a recourse to a greater arbour in the midst, resembleth three in one and one in three: and he hath there planted certain walks and arbours all with fruit-trees, so pleasing and ravishing to the sense, that he calls it *Paradise*, in which he plays the part of a true *Adamist*, continually toiling and tilling.

Moreover, he hath made his walks most rarely round and spacious, one walk without another (as the rinds of an onion are greatest without, and less towards the centre), and withall, the hedges betwixt each walk are so thickly set that one cannot see through from the one walk, who walks in the other: that, in conclusion, the work seems endless; and I think that in England it is not to be fellowed, or will in haste be followed.—*Of the Gardens at Wilton.*

JOHN TAYLOR ('THE WATER POET') (1580-1654).

—∿∿∿—

*A Moravian Minister: settled in Poland, published 'Janua Linguarum' —was invited to England: travelled in Sweden and finally settled in Amsterdam: author of 'Orbis Sensualium Pictus.'*

JOHN AMOS COMENIUS (1592-1671).

G ARDENING is practised for food's sake in a kitchen garden and orchard, or for pleasure's sake in a green grass-plot and an arbour.

The pleacher (*Topiarius*) prepares a green plot of the more choice flowers and rarer plants, and adorns the garden with pleach-work; that is with pleasant walks and bowers, etc., to conclude with water-works.—'*Janua Trilinguis.*'

[1] At Wilton, the seat of the Earl Pembroke. (See Illustration in Appendix.)

## THE PRAISE OF GARDENS

**WILLIAM HARRISON (1593).**

IF you looke into our gardens annexed to our houses, how woonderfullie is their beauty increased, not onelie with floures, which Col(u)mella calleth *Terrena sydera*, saieng:

*Pingit et in varios terrestria sydera flores,*

and varietie of curious and costlie workmanship, but also with rare and medicinable hearbes sought up in the land within these fortie yeares: so that in comparison of this present, the ancient Gardens were but dunghils and laistowes to such as did possesse them. How art also helpeth nature, in the dailie colouring, dubling and inlarging the proportion of our floures, it is incredible to report, for so curious and cunning are our Gardeners now in these daies, that they presume to doo in maner what they list with nature, and moderate hir course in things as if they were hir superiours. It is a world also to see how manie strange hearbs, plants, and annuall fruits, are dailie brought unto us from the Indies, Americans, Taprobane Canarie Iles, and all parts of the world: the which, albeit that in respect of the constitutions of our bodies they doo not grow for us, because that God hath bestowed sufficient commodities upon everie countrie for hir owne necessitie; yet for delectation sake unto the eie, and their odoriferous savours unto the nose, they are to be cherished, and God to be glorified also in them, because they are his good gifts, and created to doo man help and service. . . .

For mine owne part, good reader, let me boast a little of my garden, which is but small, and the whole *Area* thereof little above 300 foot of ground, and yet, such hath beene my good lucke in purchase of the varietie of simples, that notwithstanding my small abilitie, there are verie neere three hundred of one sort and other conteined therein, no one of them being common or usuallie to bee had. If therefore my little plot, void of all cost in keeping, be so well furnished, what shall we thinke of those of Hampton Court, Nonesuch, Tibaults, Cobham garden, and sundrie other apperteining to diuerse citizens

of London, whom I could particularlie name, if I should not seeme to offend them by such my demeanour and dealing.—
*The Description of England*, 1577 (*in Hollinshed's Chronicles*).

---

YOU may be on land, yet not in a garden.
A noble plant suits not with a stubborn ground.
The charges of building and making of gardens are unknown.
Although it rain, throw not away thy watering-pot.
Fear keeps the garden better than the gardener.
A garden must be looked unto and dressed, as the body.
*Jacula Prudentum, or Outlandish Proverbs.* 1640.

GEORGE
HERBERT
(1593-1632).

In the knowledge of simples, wherein the manifold wisdom of God is wonderfully to be seen, one thing would be carefully observed—which is, to know what herbs may be used instead of drugs of the same nature, and to make the garden the shop; for home-bred medicines are both more easy for the parson's purse, and more familiar for all men's bodies. So, where the apothecary useth either for loosing, rhubarb, or for binding, bolearmena, the parson useth damask or white roses for the one, and plantain, shepherd's-purse, knot-grass for the other, and that with better success. As for spices, he doth not only prefer home-bred things before them, but condemns them for vanities, and so shuts them out of his family, esteeming that there is no spice comparable for herbs to rosemary, thyme, savory, mints; and for seeds to fennel and carraway-seeds. Accordingly, for salves, his wife seeks not the city, but prefers her garden and fields, before all outlandish gums. And surely hyssop, valerian, mercury, adder's tongue, yarrow, melilot, and St John's wort made into a salve, and elder, camomile, mallows, comphrey, and smallage made into a poultice, have done great and rare cures.—*A Priest to the Temple; or the Country Parson, his Character and Rule of Holy Life.* 1652.

# THE PRAISE OF GARDENS

**PIERRE GASSENDI** (1592-1655). *One of the most distinguished naturalists, mathematicians and philosophers of France. 1624, wrote his " Paradoxical Exercises against the Aristotelians," which earned him the influence of Nicolas Peiresc, President of the University of Aix. He then studied Astronomy and Anatomy, and wrote a treatise to show that man was intended to be a Vegetarian. 1628, he visited Holland, and wrote an Examination of Robert Fludd's Mosaic philosophy. 1631, he observed the Transit of Mercury over the Sun's disc, foretold by Kepler. 1641, he was called to Paris, and wrote a metaphysical Disquisition on Doubts upon the " Meditations" of his friend Descartes : they became estranged and reconciled. Gassendi's philosophy of Atoms and a Void was founded upon the Doctrines of Democritus and Epicurus. 1645, appointed Professor of Mathematics in the Collége Royale de Paris by influence of Cardinal du Plessis. 1647, published his chief work on " The Life and Morals of Epicurus," which rehabilitated this philosopher; and in 1653, the Lives of Tycho Brahé, Copernicus, and other Astronomers.*
*Bayle styled him " the greatest philosopher among scholars, and the greatest scholar among philosophers."*

AS concerning Plants, it may be expected that I should in this place reckon up the principal of them; yet I will not stand to speak of such, which though accounted rare are to be seen in other Gardens. I shall only touch at some of those which *Peireskius* was the first, that caused to be brought into, and cherished in Europe. Of which the Indian Gelsemine is one, a wooddy plant, always green, with a clay-coloured yellowish flower, of a most sweet smell.

This was first brought from China, planted at *Beaugensier*, and from thence propagated into the King's and Cardinal *Barlerine* his Gardens. . . . The next is a plant called Lifa, or the Gourd of Meccha . . . also the true Papyrus Ægyptia or Ægyptian paper . . . also the Indian Coco Nuts. . . . In the next place, Ginger, which being brought out of India did wax green in his Garden, from whence it was sent to Paris, to *Vidus Brosseus*, a famous Physician, the chief storer of the King's Garden, and principal shewer thereof. . . .

I say nothing of the broad-leaved Myrtle, with the full flower of the Storax, and Lentise-Tree, which yields Mastick : and other plants mentioned before. Much lesse shall I speak of the great *American Gelsemine*, with the Crimson-coloured flower, not of the

## PIERRE GASSENDI 91

Persian, with a violet-coloured flower, nor the Arabian with a full flower: of the Orenge-Trees, with a red and particoloured flower; of the Medlar and soure Cherry without stones; *Adam's* Fig-Tree, whose fruit *Peireskius* conceived to be one of those which the spies brought back, that went to view the Land of Canaan; the rare Vines which he had from Tunis, Smyrna, Sidon, Damascus, Nova Francia, and other places. Least of all shall I stand to speak of the care he took in ordering his Knots, and planting his trees in such order, as to afford even walks every way between them; in bringing the water every where into his Gardens; in providing that the tenderer sort of Plants might receive no dammage by the Winters cold, in sending for the most skilful Florists, to furnish himself with all variety of Flowers: in a word, omitting nothing that might beautifie and adorn his Grounds.—*The Mirrour of True Nobility and Gentility being the Life of The Renowned Nicolaus Claudius Fabricius Lord of Peiresk, Senator of the Parliament at Aix. Englished by W. Rand, Doctor of Physick. London,* 1657.[1]

[1] *Nicolas de Peiresc, born in Provence in* 1580, *was one of the greatest patrons of letters. The friend of De Thou and Isaac Casaubon, he was called by Bayle* "*Le Procureur Général de la Littérature.*" *In* 1605 *he came to England in the suite of La Boderie, the French Ambassador, and visited Oxford, where he became intimate with Selden, Camden, Sir Robert Cotton and Sir Henry Saville. Scaliger, Holstensius and Saumaise were aided by him with presents of books, and at his instigation Grotius wrote his great work* " *De Jure Belli et Pacis.*"

" *He kept up a noble traffic with all travellers, supplying them with philosophical instruments and recent inventions . . . it was the curiosity of Peiresc which first embellished his own garden, and thence the gardens of Europe with a rich variety of exotic flowers and fruits . . . The correspondence of Peiresc branched out to the farthest bounds of Ethiopia, connected both Americas, and had touched the newly discovered extremities of the Universe.*"—I. Disraeli.

*He died in the arms of his biographer, Pierre Gassendi, on the* 24*th June* 1637.

*Isaac Disraeli thus speaks of this Biography:*—" *A moving picture of the literary life of a man of letters, who was no author, would have been lost to us, had not Peiresc found in Gassendi a twin spirit.*" *When are we to have a reprint of this Life* "*of that incomparable Virtuoso,*" *as Evelyn called Peiresc?*

## THE PRAISE OF GARDENS

**JAMES HOWELL** (1595-1666).  *Educated at Oxford; travelled abroad as agent for first glass manufactory established in England; later M.P. and one of the Clerks of the Privy Council to Charles I.; Secretary to British Ambassador in Denmark; imprisoned in Fleet and released by Cromwell; Historiographer to Charles II.; author of "Dodona's Grove" and "Epistolæ Ho-Elianæ." (Familiar Letters of J. H.)*

THE stables (at Lord Savage's House in Long-Melford) butt upon the Park, which for a cheerful rising Ground, for Groves and Browsings for the Deer, for rivulets of water, may compare with any for its highness in the whole land; it is opposite to the front of the great House, whence from the Gallery one may see much of the Game when they are a-hunting. Now for the gardening and costly choice Flowers, for Ponds, for stately large Walks, green and gravelly, for Orchards and choice Fruits of all sorts, there are few the like in England: here you have your *Bon Christian* Pear, and *Bergamot* in perfection, your *Muscadel grapes* in such plenty, that there are bottles of Wine sent every year to the King; and one Mr *Daniel*, a worthy Gentleman hard by, who, with him long abroad, makes good store in his Vintage. Truly this House of Long-Melford though it be not so great, yet it is so well compacted and contrived with such dainty conveniences every way, that if you saw the Landskip of it, you would be mightily taken with it, and it would serve for a choice pattern to build and contrive a House by.—(*Letter to Dan. Caldwell, Esq., 20th May* 1621).

—∧∧∧—

**SIR WILLIAM WALLER** (1597-1668).  *A Parliamentary General in the Civil Wars, originally of the same family as Edmund Waller the poet.*

HE that *walkes with God* can never want *a good walke*, and good company. There is *no garden well contrived*, but that which hath an *Enoch's walk*[1] in it.

How *cleanly* are these *Allies* kept? and how *orderly* are the *Hedges* cut, and the *Trees* pruned and nailed, and not an irregular

[1] "Enoch walked with God 300 years."—GEN. v. 22.

*Twig* left? there is no such care taken for the *weeds*, and *bushes* and brambles that grow abroad. God is careful to preserve the *Garden of his Church* in all *decency* and *order*; and will not suffer it to be overgrown with *errours* or *prophaness*; but is (like a good Husbandman, if I may say so with all humbleness) ever at work about it; either *weeding* out, what his heavenly hand hath not *planted*; or if need be, lopping, and cutting off luxuriant branches, that bear not *fruit*; or purging those that do bear, that they may bring forth more *fruit.—Divine Meditations (Upon the sight of a pleasant Garden).*

# CHAPTER V

### THE FORMAL GARDEN IN THE SEVENTEENTH CENTURY UNDER FRENCH AND DUTCH INFLUENCE: ORIENTAL TRAVELLERS ON PERSIAN AND JAPANESE GARDENS.

SIR THOMAS BROWNE (1605-1682). FOR though Physick may plead high, from that medical act of God, in casting so deep a sleep upon our first Parent; And Chirurgery find its whole Art, in that one passage concerning the Rib of Adam: yet is there no rivality with Garden-contrivance and Herbery. For if Paradise were planted the third day of the Creation as wiser Divinity concludeth, the Nativity thereof was too early for Horoscopie; Gardens were before Gardiners, and but some hours after the Earth. Of deeper doubt is its topography and local designation; yet being the primitive garden, and without much controversy seated in the East it is more than probable the first curiosity, and cultivation of plants, most flourished in those quarters. . . .

However, the account of the pensile or hanging gardens of Babylon, if made by Semiramis, the third or fourth from Nimrod, is of no slender antiquity; which being not framed upon ordinary level of ground, but raised upon pillars, admitting under-passages, we cannot accept as the first Babylonian gardens,—but a more eminent progress and advancement in that art than any that went before it; somewhat answering or hinting the old opinion concerning Paradise itself, with many conceptions elevated above the plane of the Earth.[1] Nabuchodonosor (whom some will have to

[1] Simon Wilkin, the editor of Browne's Works, quotes a passage from *MS. Sloan*, 1847, which he thinks intended for this work, wherein Browne writes, "We are unwilling to diminish or loose the credit of Paradise, or only pass it over with (the Hebrew word for) *Eden*, though the Greek be of a later name. In this excepted, we know not whether the ancient gardens do equal those of late times, or those at present in Europe. Of the Garden of Hesperies, we know nothing singular but some golden apples."

be the famous Syrian King of Diodorus) beautifully repaired that city, and so magnificently built his hanging gardens,[1] that from succeeding writers he had the honour of the first. From whence, overlooking Babylon, and all the region about it, he found no circumscription to the eye of his ambition; till, over-delighted with the bravery of this Paradise, in his melancholy metamorphosis he found the folly of that delight, and a proper punishment in the contrary habitation—in wild plantations and wanderings of the fields. The Persian gallants, who destroyed this monarchy, maintained their botanical bravery. Unto whom we owe the very name of Paradise, wherewith we meet not in Scripture before the time of Solomon, and conceived originally Persian. The word for that disputed garden, expressing, in the Hebrew, no more than a field enclosed, which from the same root is content to derive a garden and a buckler.—*The Garden of Cyrus, or the Quincuncial*[2] *Lozenge, or Net-work Plantations of the Ancients. Artificially, Naturally, Mystically considered.*[3]

[1] Josephus.
[2] Quid quincunce speciosius, qui in quamcunque partem spectaveris, rectus est.—*Quintilian.*
[3] The *Garden of Cyrus*, though it ends indeed with a passage of wonderful felicity, certainly emphasises (to say the least) the defects of Browne's literary good qualities. His chimeric fancy carries him here into a kind of frivolousness, as if he felt almost too safe with his public, and were himself not quite serious or dealing fairly with it; and in a writer such as Browne, levity must of necessity be a little ponderous. Still, like one of those stiff gardens, halfway between the medieval garden and the true ' English' garden of Temple or Walpole, actually to be seen in the background of some of the conventional portraits of that day, the fantasies of this indescribable exposition of the mysteries of the *quincunx* form part of the complete portrait of Browne himself; and it is in connection with it that once or twice the quaintly delightful pen of Evelyn comes into the correspondence in connexion with the 'hortulane pleasure'—"Norwich" he writes to Browne, "is a place I understand much addicted to the flowery poet." Professing himself a believer in the operation "of the air and genius of gardens upon human spirits, towards virtue and sanctity" he is all for natural gardens as against "those which appear like gardens of paste-board and march-pane, and smell more of paint than of flowers and verdure."—*Walter Pater,* '*Appreciations.*'

## THE PRAISE OF GARDENS

*From the Epistle Dedicatory, to Nicholas Bacon, of Tillingham, Esquire.*—The Turks who past their days in gardens here, will have also gardens hereafter, and delighting in flowers on earth, must have lilies and roses in heaven. In garden delights 'tis not easy to hold a mediocrity; that insinuating pleasure is seldom without some extremity. The ancients venially delighted in flourishing gardens; many were florists that knew not the true use of a flower; and in Pliny's days none had directly treated of that subject. Some commendably affected plantations of venemous vegetables, some confined their delights unto single plants, and Cato seemed to dote upon Cabbage; while the ingenuous delight of tulipists stands saluted with hard language, even by their own professors.[1] That in this garden discourse, we range into extraneous things, and many parts of art and nature, we follow herein the example of old and new plantations, wherein noble spirits contented not themselves with trees, but by the attendance of aviaries, fish-ponds, and all variety of animals, they made their gardens the epitome of the earth, and some resemblance of the secular shows of old. . .

Since the verdant state of things is the symbol of the resurrection, and to flourish in the state of glory, we must first be sown in corruption:—besides the ancient practice of noble persons, to conclude in garden-graves, and urns themselves of old to be wrapt up with flowers and garlands.

—ᴡᴡ—

**JOHN MILTON (1608-1674).**

AND which is the worthiest work of these two, to plant as every minister's office is equally with the bishops, or to tend that which is planted, which the blind and undiscerning prelates call Jurisdiction and would appropriate to themselves as a business of higher dignity?

Have patience therefore and hear a law-case. A certain man of large possessions had a fair garden, and kept therein an honest and laborious servant, whose skill and profession was to set or

[1] "Tulipo-mania;" Narrencruiid, Laurenberg. Pet. Hondius in lib. Belg.

sow all wholesome herbs, and delightful flowers according to every season, and whatever else was to be done in a well-husbanded nursery of plants and fruits. Now, when the time was come that he should cut his hedges, prune his trees, look to his tender slips, and pluck up the weeds that hindered their growth, he gets him up by break of day, and makes account to do what was needful in his garden; and who would think that any other should know better than he how the day's work was to be spent? Yet for all this there comes another strange gardener that never knew the soil, never handled a dibble or spade to set the least pot-herb that grew there, much less had endured an hour's sweat or chilness, and yet challenges as his right the binding or unbinding of every flower, the clipping of every bush, the weeding and worming of every bed, both in that and all other gardens thereabout. The honest gardener, that ever since the day-peep, till now the sun was grown somewhat rank, had wrought painfully about his banks and seed-plots, at his commanding voice turns suddenly about with some wonder; and although he could have well beteemed to have thanked him of the ease he proffered, yet loving his own handywork, modestly refused him, telling him withal, that for his part, if he had thought much of his own pains, he could for once have committed the work to one of his fellow-labourers, for as much as it is well known to be a matter of less skill and less labour to keep a garden handsome, than it is to plant it or contrive it, and that he had already performed himself. No, said the stranger, this is neither for you nor your fellows to meddle with, but for me only that am for this purpose in dignity far above you; and the provision which the Lord of the soil allows me in this office is, and that with good reason, tenfold your wages. The gardener smiled and shook his head; but what was determined, I cannot tell you till the end of this parliament. —*Animadversions upon the Remonstrant's Defence against Smectymnuus.*

## 98    THE PRAISE OF GARDENS

**THOMAS FULLER (1608-1661).** 1631, *Fellow of Sidney Sussex College; Lecturer at the Savoy.* 1639, *published his 'History of the Holy War.'* 1648, *rector of Waltham Abbey, and the same year published his 'Holy State.'* 1653, *joined the King at Oxford and preached before him at St Mary's Church. During his residence at Lincoln College, he was sequestered and lost all his books and MS. He attended the Royal Army from place to place as Chaplain to Lord Hopton, animated the garrison of Basing House, and forced Sir William Waller to raise the siege.* 1655, *published 'Church History of Britain' and 'History of the University of Cambridge.'* 1660, *created D.D. at Cambridge; chaplain extraordinary to the King.* 1662, *his 'History of the Worthies of England,' which had occupied him through his life, was published posthumously.*

WITHIN this circuit of ground, there is still extant, by the rare preservation of the owner, a small Scantlin of some three Acres, which I might call the Tempe of Tempe, and re-epitomiz'd the delicacies of all the rest. It was divided into a *Garden*, in the *upper* Part whereof *Flowers* did grow, in the *lower*, *Hearbs*, and those of all sorts and kinds. And now in the springtime earth did put on her new cloathes, though had some cunning *Herald* beheld the same, he would have condemned her *Coate* to have been of no antient *bearing*, it was so overcharged with variety of *Colours*.

For there was *yellow Marigolds*, Wallflowers, *Auriculusses*, *Gold Knobs*, and abundance of other namelesse *Flowers*, which would pose a *Nomenclator* to call them by their distinct denominations. There was *White, the Dayes Eye, white roses, Lillyes, etc., Blew, Violet, Irisse, Red Roses*, Pionies, etc. The whole field was *vert* or *greene*, and all colours were present save *sable*, as too sad and dolefull for so merry a meeting. All the Children of *Flora* being summoned there, to make their appearance at a great solemnity.

Nor was the lower part of the ground lesse stored with herbs, and those so various, that if *Gerard* himself had bin in the place, upon the beholding thereof he must have been forced to a re-edition of his *Herball*, to adde the recruit of those *Plants*, which formerly were unseen by him, or unknown unto him.

In this solemn Randevouz of *Flowers* and *Herbs*, the *Rose* stood forth, and made an *Oration* to this effect.

It is not unknown to you, how I have the precedency of all Flowers, confirmed unto me under the *Patent* of a double Sence, Sight, smell. What more curious *Colours*? how do all *Diers blush*, when they behold my *blushing* as conscious to themselves that their *Art* cannot imitate that tincture, which *Nature* hath stamped upon me. *Smell*, it is not lusciously *offensive*, nor dangerously *Faint*, but comforteth with a delight, and delighteth with the comfort thereof: Yea, when *Dead*, I am more Soveraigne then *Living*: What Cordials are made of my Syrups? how many corrupted Lungs (those Fans of Nature) sore wasted with consumption that they seem utterly unable any longer to cool the heat of the *Heart*, with their *ventilation*, are with Conserves made of my stamped *Leaves*, restored to their former soundnesse againe: More would I say in mine own cause, but that happily I may be taxed of pride, and selfe-flattery, who speak much in mine own behalf, and therefore I leave the rest to the judgment of such as hear me, and pass from this *discourse* to my just *complaint*.

There is lately a *Flower* (shal I call it so? in courtesie I will tearme it so, though it deserve not the appellation) a *Toolip*, which hath engrafted the love and affections of most people unto it; and what is this Toolip? a well complexion'd stink, an ill favour wrapt up in pleasant colours; as for the use thereof in *Physick*, no *Physitian* hath honoured it yet with the mention, nor with a *Greek*, or Latin name, so inconsiderable hath it hitherto been accompted; and yet this is that which filleth all Gardens, hundred of pounds being given for the root thereof, whilst I the *Rose*, am neglected and contemned, and conceived beneath the honour of noble hands, and fit only to grow in the gardens of Yeomen. I trust the remainder to your apprehensions, to make out that which grief for such undeserved injuries will not suffer me to expresse. —*Antheologia, or The Speech of Flowers: partly Morall, partly Misticall* (1660).

Gardening was first brought into England for profit about seventy years ago, before which we fetched most of our cherries from Flanders, apples from France, and had hardly a mess of rathe-ripe pease but from Holland, which were dainties for ladies, they came so far and cost so dear. Since, gardening hath crept out of Holland to Sandwich, Kent, and thence into this county (Surrey), where though they have given six pounds an aker and upward, they have made their rent, lived comfortably, and set many people on work. Oh, the incredible profit by digging of ground!—for though it be confessed that the plough beats the spade out of distance for speed (almost as much as the press beats the pen), yet what the spade wants in the quantity of the ground it manureth, it recompenseth with the plenty of the fruit it yieldeth, that is *set* multiplying a hundredfold more than that which is *sown*. 'Tis incredible how many poor people in London live therein, so that, in some seasons, the Gardens feed more people than the field.—*History of the Worthies of England* (1662).

---

ABRAHAM COWLEY (1618-1667). THE three first men in the world, were a Gardiner, a Ploughman, and a Grazier; and if any man object, that the second of these was a murtherer, I desire that he would consider that as soon as he was so, he quitted our profession, and turned builder. —*Of Agriculture.*

I never had any other desire so strong, and so like to covetousness, as that one which I have had always, that I might be master at last of a small house and large Garden, with very moderate conveniences joined to them, and there dedicate the remainder of my life only to the culture of them and study of nature,

'And there (with no design beyond my wall) whole and intire to lie,
In no unactive ease, and no unglorious poverty.'

Or as Virgil has said, shorter and better for me, that I might there

'Studiis florere ignobilis otii':

# ABRAHAM COWLEY

(though I could wish that he had rather said, 'Nobilis otii,' when he spoke of his own). But several accidents of my ill fortune have disappointed me hitherto, and do still, of that felicity; for though I have made the first and hardest step to it, by abandoning all ambitions and hopes in this world, and by retiring from the noise of all business and almost company, yet I stick still in the inn of a hired house and garden, among weeds and rubbish; and without that pleasantest work of human industry, the improvement of something which we call (not very properly, but yet we call) our own. I am gone out from Sodom, but I am not yet arrived at my little Zoar. 'O let me escape thither (is it not a little one?) and my soul shall live.' I do not look back yet; but I have been forced to stop, and make too many halts. ... Among many other arts and excellencies, which you enjoy, I am glad to find this favourite of mine the most predominant; that you choose this for your wife, though you have hundreds of other arts for your concubines; though you know them, and beget sons upon them all (to which you are rich enough to allow great legacies), yet the issue of this seems to be designed by you to the main of the estate. You have taken most pleasure in it, and bestowed most charges upon its education: and I doubt not to see that book which you are pleased to promise to the world, and of which you have given us a large earnest in your Calendar,[1] as accomplished as any thing can be expected from an extraordinary wit, and no ordinary expenses, and a long experience. I know nobody that possesses more private happiness than you do in your Garden; and yet no man, who makes his happiness more public, by a free communication of the heart, and knowledge of it to others. All that I myself am able yet to do, is only to recommend to mankind the search of that felicity, which you instruct them how to find and to enjoy.—*The Garden.* (*To J. Evelyn, Esq.*)

[1] Mr Evelyn's 'Calendarium Hortense,' dedicated to Mr Cowley.

## THE PRAISE OF GARDENS

**SAMUEL HARTLIB** (d. 1670).
*Friend of Milton; son of a Polish Merchant. 1628, came to England. 1644, Milton addressed to him his treatise on Education, he having introduced the writings of Comenius. 1646, was pensioned by Parliament for his works on Husbandry. 1655, Evelyn describes a visit to him.*

*He wrote many pamphlets on education and husbandry, (inter alia) 'A Discourse of Husbandry used in Brabant and Flanders'; 'An Essay for Advancement of Husbandry Learning or Propositions for errecting a Colledge of Husbandry'; 'The Reformed Husbandman'; 'His Legacy'; 'Cornu Copia' and 'The Compleat Husband-man.'*

ABOUT 50 years ago, about which time *Ingenuities* first began to flourish in *England*; this *Art* of *Gardening*, began to creep into *England*, into *Sandwich*, and *Surrey*, *Fulham*, and other places.

Some old men in *Surrey*, where it flourisheth very much at present, report, That they knew the first *Gardiners* that came into those parts, to plant *Cabages*, *Colleflowers*, and to sowe *Turneps*, *Carrets*, and *Parsnips*, to sowe *Raith* or (early ripe) *Rape*, *Pease*, all which at that time were great rarities, we having few, or none in *England*, but what came from *Holland* and *Flanders*. These *Gardiners* with much ado procured a plot of good ground, and gave no lesse than 8 pound *per* Acre; yet the *Gentleman* was not content, fearing they would spoil his ground; because they did use to dig it. So ignorant were we of Gardening in those dayes.—*The Compleat Husbandman* (1659).

—ᴡᴡᴡ—

**ANDRÉ LE NÔTRE** (1612-1700).
*The Grand Gardener of the Grand Monarch.*
*Rueil, created by Richelieu (or the Boboli gardens at Florence), said to have suggested the Versailles garden to Le Nôtre; the Parc de Vaux began his reputation; he executed Versailles and Chantilly together for Condé; the terrace at Fontainebleau was his design. He worked at the Château de Meudon for the Duc de Chartres, at St Cloud for Fouquet, and for Colbert at the 'Parc de Sceaux.'*

SAINT SIMON wrote his epitaph:—
"After living 88 years in perfect health, with his intellect untouched, and all his judgment and good taste undiminished, he

[1] See Portrait of Le Nôtre and Illustrations and description of Versailles in Appendix.

# JOHN EVELYN

died, illustrious for having the first designed those beautiful gardens, which decorate France. Le Nôtre possessed a probity, an exactness and uprightness, which made him valued and loved by every one. He worked for private individuals and for the King with the same industry: his only thought was to aid Nature, and to reduce the truly beautiful to the lowest cost. All he did is still far beyond what has been done since, whatever pains have been taken to copy him."—*Memoirs*.

---

WE visited the Haff or Prince's Court at the Hague, with the adjoining gardens, which were full of ornament, close-walks, statues, marbles, grotts, fountains, and artificiall musiq, etc. . . .

JOHN EVELYN (1620-1706).

From hence we walked into the Parke, which for being entirely within the walls of the city is particularly remarkable; nor is it less pleasant than if in the most solitary recesses, so naturally is it furnish'd with whatever may render it agreeable, melancholy, and country-like. Here is a stately heronry, divers springs of water, artificial cascades, rocks, grotts, one whereof is composed of the extravagant rootes of trees cunningly built and hung together. In this Parke are both fallow and red deare.

Bruxelles.
Oct. 8, 1641.

From hence we were lead into the Manege, and out of that into a most sweet and delicious garden, where was another grott, of more neat and costly materials, full of noble statues, and entertaining us with artificial musiq; but the hedge of water, in forme of lattice-worke, which the fontainer caused to ascend out of the earth by degrees exceedingly pleased and supris'd me, for thus with a previous wall, or rather a palisad hedge, of waters, was the whole parterre environ'd.

There is likewise a faire Aviary, and in the Court next it are kept divers sorts of animals, rare and exotic fowle, as eagles, cranes, storks, bustards, pheasants of several kinds, a duck having four wings, etc. In another division of the same close, are rabbits of an almost perfect yellow colour.

**Paris.**
**1644, Feb. 8.**

I took coach and went to see the famous Jardine Royale, which is an enclosure walled in, consisting of all varieties of ground for planting and culture of medical simples. It is well chosen, having in it hills, meadows, wood and upland, naturall and artificial and is richly stor'd with exotic plants. In the middle of the Parterre is a faire fountaine.

In another more privat garden towards the Queene's apartment is a walk or cloister under arches, whose terrace is paved with stones of a great breadth; it looks towards the river, and has a pleasant aviary, fountaine, stately cypresses, etc. . . .

**The Thuilleries.**
**1644, Feb. 27.**

I finished this day with a walk in the great garden of the Thuilleries, which is rarely contrived for privacy, shade, or company, by groves, plantations of tall trees, especially that in the middle, being of elmes, another of mulberys. There is a labyrinth of cypresse, noble hedges of pomegranates, fountains, fishponds, and an aviary. Here is an artificial echo, redoubling the words distinctly, and it is never without some faire nymph singing to it. Standing at one of the focus's, which is under a tree, or little cabinet of hedges, the voice seems to descend from the clouds; at another, as if it were underground. This being at the bottom of the garden, we were let into another which being kept with all imaginable accuratenesse as to the orangery, precious shrubes, and rare fruites seem'd a paradise. From a terrace in this place we saw so many coaches, as one would hardly think could be maintained in the whole City, going, late as it was in the year, towards the course, which is a place adjoyning, of neere an English mile long, planted with four rows of trees, making a large circle in the middle. This course is walled about, neere breast high, with squared freestone, and has a stately arch at the entrance, with sculpture and statues about it, built by Mary di Medices. Here it is that the gallants and ladys of the Court take the ayre and divert themselves, as with us in Hide Park, the circle being capable of containing an hundred coaches to turne commodiously, and the larger of the plantations for five or six coaches a brest.

# JOHN EVELYN

... By the way we alighted at St Cloes, where, on an St Cloud. eminence neere the river, the Archbishop of Paris has a garden, for the house is not very considerable, rarely watered and furnish'd with fountaines, statues, and groves, the walkes are very faire; the fountain of Laocoon is in a large square pool, throwing the water neere 40 feet high, and having about it a multitude of statues and basins, and is a suprising object: but nothing is more esteem'd than the cascade falling from the greate stepps into the lowest and longest walke from the Mount Parnassus, which consists of a grotto, or shell house, on the summit of the hill, wherein are divers water-workes and contrivances, to wet the spectators; this is covered with a fayre cupola, the walls paynted with the Muses, and statues placed thick about it, whereof some are antiq and good. In the upper walkes are two perspectives, seeming to enlarge the allys. In this garden are many other contrivances.

About a league further we went to see Cardinal Richelieu's Rueil. villa at Ruell. The house is small, but fairly built, in form of a castle, moated round. The offices are towards the road, and over against are large vineyards walled in.

Though the house is not of the greatest, the gardens about it are so magnificent that I doubt whether Italy has any exceeding it for all rarities of pleasure. The garden nearest the pavilion is a parterre, having in the middst divers noble brasse statues, perpetually spouting water into an ample bassin, with other figures of the same metal; but what is most admirable is the vast enclosure, and variety of ground, in the large garden, containing vineyards, cornefields, meadows, groves (whereof one is one of perennial greens), and walkes of vast lengthes, so accurately kept and cultivated, that nothing can be more agreeable. On one of these walkes, within a square of tall trees, is a basilisc of copper which managed by the fountainere casts water neere 60 feet high, and will of itself move round so swiftly, that one can hardly escape wetting. This leads to the Citroniere, where is a noble conserve of all those rarities; and at the end of it is the Arch of Constantine, painted on a wall in oyle, as large as the real one at Rome, so well don that even a man skill'd in painting may mistake it for stone and sculpture. The skie and hills which seem to be betweene the arches are so naturall that swallows and other birds, thinking to fly through, have dashed themselves against the wall. At the further parte of this walk is that plentiful though artificial cascade which rolls down a very steepe declivity, and over the marble steps and bassins, with an astonishing noyse and fury; each basin hath a jetto in it, flowing like sheetes of transparent glasse, especialy that which rises over the great shell of lead, from whence it glides silently downe a channell thro' the middle of a spacious gravel walk terminating in a grotto. Here are also fountaines that cast water to a great height, and large ponds, 2 of which have islands for harbour of fowles, of which there is store. One of these islands has a receptacle for them built of vast pieces of rock, neere 50 feet high, growne over with mosse, ivy, etc., shaded at a competent distance with tall trees, in this the fowles lay eggs and breede. We then saw a large and very rare grotto of shell worke, in the shape of satyres and other wild fancys: in the middle stands a marble table, on which a fountaine plays in forms of glasses, cupps, crosses, fanns, crownes, etc. Then the fountaineere represented a showre of raine from the topp, mett by small jetts from below. At going out two extravagant musqueteers shot us with a streme of water from their musket barrells. Before this grotto is a long poole into which ran divers spouts of water from leaden escollop bassins.

1644, *Mch.* 1. I went to see the Count de Liancourt's Palace in the Rue de Seine, which is well built. Towards his study and bedchamber joynes a little garden, which tho' very narrow, by the addition of a well painted perspective is to appearance greatly enlarged; to this there is another part, supported by arches, in which runs a streame of water, rising in the aviary, out of a statue, and seeming to flow for some miles, by being artificially continued in the painting, when it sinkes down at the wall. It is a very agreeable deceipt. At the end of this garden is a little theater, made to change with divers pretty seanes, and the stage so ordered that with figures of men and women paynted on light boards, and cut out, and, by a person who stands underneath, made to act as if they were speaking, by guiding them, and reciting words in diferent tones as the parts require.

Having seen the roomes we went to the Volary, which has a cupola in the middle of it, greate trees and bushes, it being full of birds who drank at two fountaines. There is a faire Tennis Court and noble Stables; but the beauty of all are the Gardens. In the Court of the Fountaines stand divers antiquities and statues, especially a Mercury. In the Queenes Garden is a Diana ejecting a fountaine, with numerous other brasse statues. Fontainebleau.<br>1644, *Mch.* 7.

The Greate Garden, 180 toises long and 154 wide, has in the centre a fountayne of Tyber of a Colossean figure of Brasse, with the Wolfe over Romulus and Rhemus. At each corner of the garden rises a fountaine. In the Garden of the Fish Pond is a Hercules of white marble. Next is the Garden of the Pines, and without that a Canale of an English mile in length, at the end of which rise 3 jettos in the form of a fleur de lys, of a great height; on the margin are excellent walkes planted with trees. The carps come familiarly to hand (to be fed).

Hence they brought us to a spring, which they say being first discover'd by a dog, gave occasion of beautifying this place both with the Palace and Gardens. The rocks at some distance in the Forest yeald one of the most august and stupendous prospects imaginable. The Parke about this place is very large, and the Towne is full of noblemen's houses.

I went to see more exactly the roomes of the fine Palace of Luxemburge, in the Fauxbourg St Germains, built by Mary de Medices, and I think one of the most noble, entire, and finish'd piles, that is to be seen, taking it with the garden and all its accomplishments. Luxemburge.<br>1644, *April* 1.

## THE PRAISE OF GARDENS

The Gardens are neere an English mile in compasse, enclos'd with a stately wall, and in a good ayre. The parterre is indeed of box, but so rarely designed and accurately kept cut, that the embroidery makes a wonderful effect to the lodgings which front it. 'Tis divided into 4 squares, and as many circular knots, having in the center a noble basin of marble neere 30 feet diameter (as I remember), in which a triton of brasse holds a dolphin that casts a girandola of water neere 30 foote high, playing perpetualy, the water being conveyed from Arceuil by an aqueduct of stone, built after the old Roman magnificence. About this ample parterre, the spacious walkes and all included, runs a border of freestone, adorned with pedestalls for potts and statues, and part of it neere the stepps of the terrace, with a raile and baluster of pure white marble.

The walkes are exactly faire, long, and variously descending, and so justly planted with limes, elms, and other trees, that nothing can be more delicious, especially that of the hornebeam hedge, which being high and stately, butts full on the fountaine.

Towards the farther end is an excavation intended for a vast fish-pool, but never finish'd. Neere it is an enclosure for a garden of simples, well kept, and here the Duke keeps tortoises in greate number, who use the poole of water on one side of the garden. Here is also a conservatory for snow. At the upper part towards the palace is a grove of tall elmes, cutt into a starr, every ray being a walk, whose center is a large fountaine.

The rest of the ground is made into severall inclosures (all hedgeworke or rowes of trees) of whole fields, meadowes, boscages, some of them containing divers acres.

Next the streete side, and more contiguous to the house, are knotts in trayle or grasse worke, where likewise runs a fountaine. Towards the grotto and stables, within a wall, is a garden of choyce flowers, in which the Duke spends many thousand pistoles. In sum, nothing is wanted to render this palace and gardens perfectly beautifull and magnificent; nor is it one of the least diversions to see the number of persons of quality, citizens and strangers, who frequent it, and to whom all accesse is freely

# JOHN EVELYN

permitted, so that you shall see some walkes and retirements full of gallants and ladys; in others melancholy fryers; in others studious scholars; in others jolly citizens, some sitting or lying on the grasse, others running, jumping, some playing at bowles and ball, others dancing and singing; and all this without the least disturbance, by reason of the largeness of the place.

What is most admirable is, you see no gardners or men at worke, and yet all is kept in such exquisite order as if they did nothing else but work; it is so early in the morning, that all is despatched and don without the least confusion.

I have been the larger in the description of this Paradise, for the extraordinary delight I have taken in those sweete retirements. The Cabinet and Chapell neerer the garden front have some choyce pictures. All the houses neere this are also noble palaces, especially petite Luxemburge.

The next morning I went to the Garden of Monsieur Morine, who from being an ordinary gardner is become one of the most skilful and curious persons in France for his rare collections of shells, flowers and insects.

His garden is of an exact oval figure, planted with cypresse cutt flat and set as even as a wall; the tulips, anemonies, ranunculus's, crocus's, etc., are held to be of the rarest, and draw all the admirers of such things to his house during the season. He lived in a kind of Hermitage at one side of his garden, where his collection of purselane and coral, whereof one is carved into a large Crucifix, is much esteemed. He has also bookes of prints, by Albert (Durer), Van Leyden, Calot, etc. His collection of all sorts of insects, especially of Butterflys, is most curios; these he spreads and so medicates that no corruption invading them, he keepes them in drawers, so placed as to represent a beautifull piece of tapistre.

I often went to the Palais Cardinal, bequeathed by Richelieu to the King, on condition that it should be called by his name; at this time the King resided in it, because of the building of the Louvre. It is a very noble house, tho' somewhat low; the gallerys, paintings of the most illustrious

## THE PRAISE OF GARDENS

persons of both sexes, the Queenes bathes, presence chamber with its rich carved and gilded roofe, theatre and large garden, in which is an ample fountaine, grove, and maille, are worthy of remark.

Genoa.
1644, *Oct.* 17.

One of the greatest here for circuit is that of the Prince d'Orias, which reaches from the sea to the sum'it of the mountaines. . . . To this Palace belongs three gardens, the first whereof is beautified with a terrace, supported by pillars of marble; there is a fountaine of eagles, and one of Neptune with other Sea-gods, all of the purest white marble; they stand in a most ample basin of the same stone. At the side of this garden is such an aviary as Sir Fra Bacon describes in his Sermones fidelium, or Essays, wherein grow trees of more than two foote diameter, besides cypresse, myrtils, lentises, and other rare shrubs which serve to nestle and pearch all sorts of birds, who have ayre and place enough under their ayrie canopy, supported with huge iron worke, stupendous for its fabrick and the charge. The other two gardens are full of orange trees, citrons and pomegranads, fountaines, grottos, and statues; one of the latter is a Colossal Jupiter, under which is the Sepulchre of a beloved dog, for the care of which one of this family received of the K. of Spaine 500 crownes a yeare during the life of that faithfull animal. The reservoir of water here is a most admirable piece of art; and so is the grotto over against it . . .

Monte Cavallo.
1644, *Nov.* 10.

The garden which is called the Belvedere di Monte Cavallo, in emulation to that of the Vatican, is most excellent for ayre and prospect, its exquisite fountaines, close walkes, grotts, piscinas, or stews for fish, planted about with venerable cypresses, and refresh'd with water musiq, aviaries, and other rarities.

Villa Borghesi.
1644, *Nov.* 17.

I walked to Villa Borghesi, a house and ample garden on Mons Pincius, yet somewhat without the Citty walls, circumscrib'd by another wall full of small turrets and banqueting-houses, which makes it appeare at a distance like a little towne. Within it is an Elysium of delight, having in the centre a noble Palace; but the entrance of the garden presents us with a very glorious fabrick or rather dore case adorn'd with divers excellent marble statues. This garden abounded with all sorts of delicious fruit and exotig simples, fountaines of sundry inventions, groves, and small rivulets. There is also adjoining to it a vivarium for estriges, peacocks, swanns, cranes, etc., and divers strange beasts, deare, and hares. The grotto is very rare, and represents among other devices artificial raine, and sundry shapes of vessells, flowers, etc., which is effected by changing the heades of the fountaines.

Wotton. 1652, *Mch.* 22.
I went with my brother Evelyn to Wotton to give him what directions I was able about his garden, which he was now desirous to put into some forme; but for which he was to remove a mountaine overgrowne with huge trees and thicket, with a moate within 10 yards of the house. This my brother immediately attempted, and that without greate cost, for more than an hundred yards South, by digging downe the mountaine and flinging it into a rapid stream, it not onely carried away the sand, etc., but filled up the moate, and level'd that noble area, where now the garden and fountaine is. The first occasion of my brother making this alteration was my building the little retiring place betweene the greate wood Eastward next the meadow, where some time after my father's death I made a triangular pond, or little stew, with an artificial rock after my coming out of Flanders.

Sayes Court. 1653, *Jan.* 17.
I began to set out the ovall garden at Sayes Court, which was before a rude orchard and all the rest one intire field of 100 acres, without any hedge, except the hither holly hedge joyning to the Bank of the mount walk. This was the beginning of all the succeeding gardens, walks, groves, enclosures, and plantations there.

1653, *Jan.* 19.
I planted the Orchard at Sayes Court, new moone, wind W.

1653, *May* 8.
I went to Hackney to see my Lady Brooke's garden, which was one of the neatest and most celebrated in England, the house well furnish'd, but a despicable building. Returning visited one Mr Lambs's garden; it has large and noble walks, some modern statues, a vineyard, planted in strawberry borders, staked at 10

foote distances; the banqueting house of cedar, where the couch and seates were carv'd à l'antique.

**Wilton.**
1654, *July* 20.
In the afternoon we went to Wilton. . . . The Garden, heretofore esteemed the noblest in England, is a large handsom plaine, with a grotto and water-works, which might be made much more pleasant were the river that passes through cleans'd and rais'd, for all is effected by a meere force. It has a flower garden not inelegant. But after all, that which renders the seate delightful is its being so neere the downes and noble plaines about the country contiguous to it. The stables are well order'd and yield a gracefull front, by reason of the walkes of lime-trees, with the court and fountaine of the stables adorn'd with the Cæsar's heads.

**Audley End.**
The gardens are not in order, tho' well inclos'd. It has also a bowling-alley a noble well wall'd, wooded, and water'd park, full of fine collines and ponds; the river glides before the palace, to which is an avenue of lime trees, but all this is much diminish'd by its being placed in an obscure bottome.

1655, *Aug.* 22.
I went to Box-hill to see those rare natural bowers, cabinets, and shady walkes in the box copses: hence we walk'd to Mickleham, and saw Sir F. Stidolph's seate environ'd with elme trees and walnuts innumerable, and of which last he told us they receiv'd a considerable revenue. Here are such goodly walkes and hills shaded with yew and box as render the place extreamely agreeable, it seeming from these ever-greens to be summer all the winter.

**Hampton Court.**
1662, *June* 9.
The Park formerly a flat naked piece of ground, now planted with sweete rows of lime trees; and the canall for water now neere perfected; also the hare parke. In the garden is a rich and noble fountaine, with syrens, statues, etc., cast in copper by Fanelli, but no plenty of water. The cradle-walk of horne beame in the garden is, for the perplexed twining of the trees, very observable. There is a parterre which they call Paradise, in which is a pretty banquetting-house set over a cave or cellar. All these gardens might be exceedingly improved, as being too narrow for such a palace.

# JOHN EVELYN 113

Next to Wadham, and the Physick Garden, where were two large locust trees, and as many platana, and some rare plants under the culture of old Bobart. *Oxford. 1664, Oct. 24.*

To Alburie to see how that garden proceeded, which I found exactly don to the designe and plot I had made, with the crypta thro' the mountaine in the park 30 perches in length. Such a Pausilippe¹ is no where in England besides. The canall was now digging and the vineyard planted. *Albury. 1670, Sept. 23.*

THERE stand in the garden two handsome stone pyramids, and the avenue planted with rows of fair elms, but the rest of these goodly trees, both of this and of Worcester Park adjoining, were felled by those destructive and avaricious rebels in the late war, which defaced one of the stateliest seats his Majesty had. *Nonesuch.*

For the rest, the fore-court is noble, so are the stables; and above all, the gardens, which are incomparable by reason of the inequality of the ground, and a pretty *piscina*. The holly-hedges on the terrace I advised the planting of. *Berkeley House.*

Above all, are admirable and magnificent the several ample gardens furnished with the choicest fruit, and exquisitely kept. Great plenty of oranges and other curiosities. *Lord Sunderland's Seat at Althorpe.*

After dinner I walked to Ham, to see the house and garden of the Duke of Lauderdale, which is indeed inferior to few of the best villas in Italy itself; the house furnished like a great Prince's; the parterres, flower-gardens, orangeries, groves, avenues, courts, statues, perspectives, fountains, aviaries, and all this at the banks of the sweetest river in the world, must needs be admirable. *Ham.*

The gardens are very rare, and cannot be otherwise, having so skilful an artist to govern them as Mr Cooke, who is, as to the mechanick part, not ignorant in mathematics, and pretends *Earl of Essex's House at Cashiobury, Herts.*

¹ A word adopted by Mr Evelyn for a subterranean passage, from the famous grotto of Pausilippo, at Naples.

H

## THE PRAISE OF GARDENS

to astrology. There is an excellent collection of the choicest fruit.

Next morning I went to see Sir Thomas Browne (with whom I had some time corresponded by letter, tho' I had never seen him before). His whole house and garden being a paradise and cabinet of rarities, and that of the best collection, especially medails, books, plants, and natural things.—*Diary*.

**Wotton.**
**1696,** *Oct.* **28.** Concerning the Gardning and Husbandry of the Antients, which is your inquirie (especialy of the first), that it had certainely nothing approaching the elegancy of the present age, Rapinus (whom I send you) will aboundantly satisfie you. The discourse you will find at the end of Hortorum, lib. 4° capp. 6, 7. What they called their Gardens onely spacious plots of ground planted with platans and other shady trees in walks, and built about with Porticas, Xisti, and noble ranges of pillars, adorn'd with Statues, Fountaines, Piscariæ, Aviaries, etc. But for the flowry parterre, beds of Tulips, Carnations, Auricula, Tuberose, Jonquills, Ranunculas, and other of our rare Coronaries, we heare nothing of, nor that they had such a store and variety of Exotics, Orangeries, Myrtils, and other curious Greenes; nor do I believe they had their Orchards in such perfection, nor by far our furnitrue for the Kitchen. Pliny indeed enumerates a world of vulgar plants and olitories, but they fall infinitely short of our Physic gardens, books and herbals, every day augmented by our sedulous Botanists and brought to us from all the quarters of the world. And as for their Husbandry and more rural skill, of which the same author has written so many books in his Nat. History, especial lib. 17, 18, etc., you'l soone be judge what it was. They tooke great care indeede of their Vines and Olives, stercorations, ingraftings, and were diligent in observing seasons, the course of the stars, etc., and doubtlesse were very industrious, but when you shall have read over Cato, Varro, Columella, Palladio, with the Greek Geoponics, I do not think you will have cause to prefer them before the modern agriculture, so exceedingly of late improv'd, for which you may consult and compare our old

Tusser, Markham, the Maison Rustic, Hartlib, Walter Blith, the Philosophical Transactions, and other books, which you know better than my selfe.

—⁂—

BEHOLD the Disposition and Order of these finer sorts of Apartments, Gardens, *Villas*! The kind of Harmony to the Eye, from the various Shapes and Colours agreeably mixt, and rang'd in Lines, intercrossing without confusion, and fortunately co-incident.—A *Parterre*, Cypresses, Groves, Wildernesses.—Statues, here and there, of *Virtue*, *Fortitude*, *Temperance*—*Heroes*-Busts, *Philosophers*-Heads; with sutable Mottos and Inscriptions—Solemn Representations of things deeply natural—*Caves*, *Grottos*, *Rocks*—*Urns* and *Obelisks* in retir'd places, and dispos'd at proper distances and points of Sight: with all those Symmetrys which silently express a reigning *Order*, *Peace*, *Harmony*, and *Beauty*!—But what is there answerable to this, in the MINDS of the *Possessors*? What *Possession* or *Propriety* is theirs? What *Constancy* or *Security* of Enjoyment? What *Peace*, what *Harmony* WITHIN?"—*Miscellaneous Reflections*.

ANTHONY ASHLEY COOPER, EARL OF SHAFTESBURY (1621-1683).

—⁂—

*The greatest fruit and kitchen gardener who ever lived was born at Poictiers 1626; he gave up study of law to accompany son of M. Tambonneau (whose garden he planned and directed) to Italy, to study plants; made experiments and discoveries on sap of plants. His "Traité des Jardins Fruitiers et Potagers" (Amsterd. 1690), translated by Evelyn as "Compleat Gardiner," and abridged by London and Wise. Friend of Louis XIV. and Condé. Charles II. offered him pension. He visited England twice. Perrault says his letters were published in London. He stayed with Evelyn, who had his portrait engraved for him, and Quintinye imparted to him his mode of cultivating melons. He was Director-General of the King's Fruit and Kitchen Garden at Versailles, which he laid out, covering thirty acres, of which he gives the plan. Here the Confrères de Saint Fiacre, the Tutelar Saint of Horticulturists, still hold their Gardeners' Lodge. He died 1700, and Louis XIV. said to his widow, 'I am as great a sufferer by his death as you, and I despair of ever supplying his loss.' His system of pruning and training wall and espalier trees surpassed that of all previous writers.*

JEAN DE LA QUINTINYE (1626-1700).

I KNOW well enough that all Books of Gardening have usually begun with a Preface full of the praises given to it, and that consequently it may be thought this ought to begin so too.

## THE PRAISE OF GARDENS

But since I am far from presuming myself able to say anything new, that may at all enhance the Esteem which is due to *Gardens*, or to the *Art* that teaches their Construction, and therefore cannot but think it very impertinent to go about to persuade any one to study it; when I observe the most part of Men possess'd with a natural passion for so sweet and profitable an Occupation, I shall wave those Complements, and fall down right upon the pursuit of my Design, which is to instruct, in case I can show myself really master enough of the *Art*, worthily to perform it.

And further, the affectation of Men to gratifie the Pleasures of their Eyes, inciting them to push on things to more and more Perfection; there came first into the minds of Noble Persons, some conceits of ranging those *Flowers* with a little more agreeableness and *Symmetry* than was practised by the first *Curiosi's*, which gave the first beginnings to *Parterres*, or *Flower-Pots* among *Florist's*, the first of which, in all probability, were but cut pieces (découpéz) shaped after but a plain and gross manner. But afterwards there were some made of another fashion, called *Embroidery Fashion* which were better contrived and more delightful than the other, with which two sorts the World contented themselves for several *Ages*, so that Gardens were not accompanied with any other Beauties than those, till in these last times *Curiosity*, *Good Judgment*, and *Fancy*, and *Magnificence* itself being grown by little and little, to an extraordinary heighth, our Age, which excells in all that Humane industry is able to invent, has given in particular by the ingenious skill of the famous Mr *Le Nostre* the best perfection to this part of *Gardening*, which appears by so many *Canals*, *Water-Works*, *Cascades*, *Spouting-Fountains*, *Labyrinths*, *Bowling Greens*, *Terraces*, *etc.*, ornaments indeed that are new, but such as in earnest do wonderfully set off the natural Beauty of a Garden.—*Preface to the Compleat Gard'ner, translated by John Evelyn (or his son).*

MY little trees are of a surprising beauty. Pilois raises them up to the clouds with a wonderful adroitness: all the same, nothing is so beautiful as those alleys whose birth you have seen. You know I gave you a kind of device which pleased you: here is a motto I have written on a tree for my son who has returned from Candia, *Vago di fama*: is it not pretty although so brief? Only yesterday I had written in honour of the idle, *Bella cosa far niente*. *Aux Rochers*. 31 *May*, 1671.

MADAME DE SÉVIGNÉ (1626-1696).

As to my labyrinth, it is neat, it has green plots, and the palissades are breast-high; it is a lovable spot; but, alas! my dear child, there is scarcely a sign of my ever seeing you in it.

*Di memoria nudrirsi, piu che di speme.*

It is indeed my true device.—*Aux Rochers*, 26 *July*, 1671.

I do not know what you have done this morning; for my part, I have been in the dew up to my knees laying lines; I am making winding alleys all round my park, which will be of great beauty; if my son loves woods and walks, he will be sure to bless my memory.—28 *October*, 1671.

There is the Palace of the Luxemburg belonging to Mademoiselle,[1] and we shall enter it soon. Madame had ordered all the trees in the garden on her side to be cut down, out of pure contradiction: this beautiful garden had become ridiculous; Providence has provided for it. Mademoiselle will be able to have it cleared on both sides, and put Le Nôtre in it, to make it like the Tuileries.—*Paris*. 6 *April*, 1672.

We were at Clagny . . . the building is growing visibly, the Gardens are made. You know the manner of Le Nôtre; he has left a little dark wood, which does very well. There is a grove of orange-trees in great tubs; you walk there; and they form alleys in the shade; and to hide the tubs there are two rows of pallisades high enough to lean on, all aflower with tube-roses,

[1] Marguerite de Lorraine, second wife of Gaston, Duke of Orleans.

118     THE PRAISE OF GARDENS

roses, jasmines, carnations. It is assuredly the most beautiful, the most surprising, and the most enchanted novelty imaginable. 7 *Aug.*, 1675.—*Letters to Madame Grignan.*

—⁓⁓—

JOHN
BUNYAN
(1628-1688).

AFTER this, he (the Interpreter) led them into his Garden, where was great Variety of Flowers: And he said, Do you see all these? So Christian said, Yes. Then said he again, Behold the Flowers are divers in Stature, in Quality, and Colour, and Smell, and Virtue; and some are better than some: Also where the Gardener hath set them, there they stand, and quarrel not one with another. . . . When the Interpreter had done, he takes them out into his Garden again, and had them to a Tree, whose inside was all rotten and gone, and yet it grew and had leaves. Then said *Mercy*, What means this? This Tree, said he, whose Outside is fair and whose Inside is rotten, it is, to which may be compared, that are in the Garden of God: Who with their Mouths speak high in Behalf of God, but in deed will do nothing for him; whose Leaves are fair, but their Hearts good for nothing but to be Tinder for the Devil's Tinder-Box.—*The Pilgrim's Progress.*

—⁓⁓—

JOHN RAY,     *One of the founders of modern Zoology and Botany: originally Greek Lecturer*
(1627-1705).   *at Cambridge, where he was Fellow of Trinity with Sir Isaac Newton. He published in 1660 A Catalogue of Plants around that town, and in 1673 'Observations made in a Journey through the Low Countries, Germany, Italy and France,' giving information of animals and plants seen during three years.   1667, elected Fellow of Royal Society.   1682, "Methodus Plantarum nova," as altered by himself, formed the basis of the System of Jussieu received at present day.   1670, his 'Catalogus Plantarum Angliæ,' the basis of all subsequent Floras of this Country.   1686, his Historia Plantarum (Vol. I. appeared); made many researches in Vegetable Physiology.*
*Cuvier states, he was the model of the Systematists during the whole of the 18th Century (Whewell).   Ray meditated a work to be entitled " Horti Angliæ." See his Letters.   (Daines Barrington).*

BUT whether there be such a constant circulation of the Sap in Plants as there is of the blood in Animals, as they would from hence infer, there is some reason to doubt.

# LEONARD MEAGER

I might add hereto the pleasant and delectable, cooling and refreshing Shade they afford in the Summer-time; which was very much esteem'd by the Inhabitants of hot Countries, who always took great delight and pleasure to sit in the open Air, under shady Trees; Hence that Expression so often repeated in Scripture, of every Man's *sitting under his own Vine, and under his own Fig-tree*, where also they us'd to eat; as appears by *Abraham's* entertaining the Angels under a Tree, and standing by them whem they did eat, *Gen.* 18, 8. Moreover the Leaves of Plants are very beautiful and ornamental. That there is great pulchritude and comeliness of Proportion in the Leaves, Flowers and Fruits of Plants, is attested by the general Verdict of Mankind, as *Dr. More* and others well observe. The adorning and beautifying of Temples and Buildings in all Ages, is an evident and undeniable Testimony of this: For what is more ordinary with *Architects* than the taking in Leaves and Flowers and Fruitage for the garnishing of their Work; as the *Roman* the Leaves of *Acanthus*, and the *Jewish* of *Palm-Trees* and *Pomegranets*: and these more frequently than any of the five regular Solids, as being more comely and pleasant to behold.—*The Wisdom of God in the Creation.*

—〰〰—

*Gardener in service of P. Holmlan of Warkworth: author of 'The English Gardener,' with engravings,* 4*to,* 1670; *'The New Art of Gardening, with The Gardener's Almanack,'* 1697, 12*mo; and The Mystery of Husbandry,'* 1697.

LEONARD MEAGER (1624?-1704?)

—〰〰—

IN every Garden Four Things are necessary to be provided for, Flowers, Fruit, Shade, and Water, and whoever lays out a Garden without all these, must not pretend it in any Perfection. It ought to lie to the best Parts of the House, or to those of the Master's commonest Use, so as to be but like one of the Rooms out of which you step into another. The Part of your Garden next your House (besides the Walks that go round it) should be a Parterre for flowers, or Grass-Plots bordered with

SIR WILLIAM TEMPLE (1628-1700).

Flowers; or if, according to the Newest Mode, it be cast all into Grass-Plots and Gravel-Walks, the Driness of these should be relieved with Fountains, and the Plainness of those with Statues; otherwise, if large, they have an ill effect upon the Eye. However, the Part next the House should be open, and no other Fruit but upon the Walls. If this take up one Half of the Garden, the other should be Fruit-Trees, unless some Grove for Shade lie in the Middle. If it take up a Third Part only, then the next Third may be Dwarf-Trees, and the Last Standard-Fruit; or else the Second Part Fruit-Trees, and the Third all Sorts of Winter-Greens, which provide for all Seasons of the Year. . . .

The perfectest Figure of a Garden I ever saw, either at Home or Abroad, was that of *Moor-Park*, in *Hertfordshire*, when I knew it about thirty years ago. It was made by the Countess of *Bedford*, esteemed among the greatest Wits of her Time, and celebrated by Doctor *Donne*; and with very great Care, excellent Contrivance, and much Cost; but greater sums may be thrown away without Effect or Honour if there want Sense in Proportion to Money, or if Nature be not followed; which I take to be the great Rule in this, and perhaps in every thing else, as far as the Conduct not only of our Lives, but our Governments. And whether the Greatest of Mortal Men should attempt the forcing of Nature may best be judged by observing how seldom God Almighty does it Himself, by so few, true, and undisputed Miracles, as we see or hear of in the World. For my own Part, I know not three wiser Precepts for the Conduct either of Princes or Private Men, than

—— Servare Modum, Finemque tueri,
Naturamque sequi.

Because I take the Garden I have named to have been in all Kinds the most beautiful and perfect, at least in the Figure and Disposition, that I have ever seen, I will describe it for a model to those that meet with such a Situation, and are above the Regards of common Expence. It lies on the Side of a Hill, (upon which the House stands) but not very steep. The Length

## SIR WILLIAM TEMPLE

of the House, where the best Rooms and of most Use or Pleasure are, lies upon the Breadth of the Garden, the Great Parlour opens into the Middle of a Terras Gravel-Walk that lies even with it, and which may be, as I remember, about three hundred Paces long, and broad in Proportion, the Border set with Standard Laurels, and at large Distances, which have the Beauty of Orange-Trees, out of Flower and Fruit: From this Walk are Three Descents by many Stone Steps, in the Middle and at each End, into a very large Parterre. This is divided into Quarters by Gravel-Walks, and adorned with Two Fountains and Eight Statues in the several Quarters; at the End of the Terras-Walk are Two Summer-Houses, and the Sides of the Parterre are ranged with two large Cloisters, open to the Garden, upon Arches of Stone, and ending with two other Summer-Houses even with the Cloisters, which are paved with Stone, and designed for Walks of Shade, there being none other in the whole Parterre. Over these two Cloisters are two Terrasses covered with Lead, and fenced with Balusters; and the Passage into these Airy Walks, is out of the two Summer-Houses, at the End of the first Terras-Walk. The Cloister facing the *South* is covered with Vines, and would have been proper for an Orange-House, and the other for Myrtles, or other more common Greens; and had, I doubt not, been cast for that Purpose, if this Piece of Gardening had been then in as much Vogue as it is now.

From the Middle of this Parterre is a Descent by many Steps flying on each side of a Grotto, that lies between them (covered with Lead, and flat) into the lower Garden, which is all Fruit-Trees ranged about the several Quarters of a Wilderness which is very Shady; the Walks here are all Green, the Grotto embellish'd with Figures of Shell-Rock-work, Fountains and Waterworks. If the Hill had not ended with the lower Garden, and the Wall were not bounded by a common Way that goes through the Park, they might have added a Third Quarter of all Greens; but this Want is supplied by a Garden on the other Side of the House, which is all of that Sort, very Wild, Shady, and adorned with rough Rock-work and Fountains.—*Upon the Gardens of Epicurus, or of Gardening.*

## THE PRAISE OF GARDENS

**PIERRE DANIEL HUET (1630-1721).** 1670, *appointed Tutor to the Dauphin, and for twenty years published the Edition of the Classics "in usum Delphini."* 1674, *Member of the French Academy.* 1685, *Bishop of Avranches.*

ALTHOUGH natural beauties are preferable to artistic ones, that is not the taste of this century. Nothing pleases, if not costly. A fountain issuing in great cascades from the foot of a rock, tumbling over a golden sand the clearest and freshest water in the world, will not please the people at court as much as a jet of fœtid and muddy water drawn up at enormous cost from a frog-marsh. A factitious parterre, composed of earth brought together according to a plan of Monsieur Le Nôtre, having for its whole decoration but a few rows of box, which never distinguish the seasons by change of colour; surrounded by vast sanded alleys, very compact and very bare; such a parterre forms the delight of polite society.

It leaves to small cits and peasants these rustic lawns, this rural turf. It requires palissades erected with the line, and at the point of the shears. The green shades of these tufted birches, and of those great oaks which were found at the birth of time, are in bad taste and worthy of the grossness of our fathers. Is not to think thus to prefer a painted face to the natural colour of a beautiful countenance? But the depravity of this judgment is discovered in our pictures and in our tapestries. Paint on the one side a fashionable garden, and on the other one of those beautiful landscapes, in which Nature spreads her riches undisguised; one will present a very tedious object, the other will charm you by its delight. You will be tired of the one at first glance, you will never weary of looking at the other, such is the force of nature to make itself beloved, in spite of the pilferings and deceits of art.—*Huetiana*, '*Natural Beauties preferable to Artistic ones*' (1722).[1]

I have no more approval for the gardens in fashion than for iron-screens (clairvoyées). I mean those gardens, composed

---

[1] Böttiger contends that the Bishop of Avranches has in these remarks foreshadowed the modern landscape garden before the *Spectator*.

of large broad sand-strewn allies, of trellises, parterres, adorned only with a few delicate beds, defined by strips of box and edged with a few flowers, and a few stunted trees, and in which you can scarce distinguish summer from winter.

M. le Nostre, who is quoted as the author of this sort of garden, which it is asserted he brought back from Italy, did, it is true, adapt it to the King's Gardens, but he did not adapt it alone, for he added covered alleys, shaped woods, trees of lofty trunk, pallisades, and green shades. The majority of private persons, possessing neither sufficient ground, nor sufficient means to give their gardens all these ornaments, and keep them up, have only adopted its parterres, which require little time and expense, but in which walking is out of the question throughout the day, and in which ladies, regardful of their complexion, would only venture to appear after sun-set.

Père Rapin was not of this way of thinking, and has left very different lessons in his agreeable Poem on gardening; and if Virgil had been able to satisfy the desire he had to handle that subject, he would not have been content to give precepts for cultivating fruit- and kitchen-gardens; but in imitation of the good old man of Cilicia, whom he had seen at Tarentum, and whose care and industry he describes so agreeably, he would have painted in his verse the pleasures created by tall trees, unfruitful though they may be, by their foliage, their shadows, and their decoration.—*Ibid: Of the gardens in fashion.*

(Lord Paulet's garden at Hinton St George is) very different **XVIIth Century.** from the common style of English gardens; these are usually walks of sand, made perfectly level, by rolling them with a stone cylinder, through the axis of which a lever of iron is passed whose ends being brought forward and united together in form of a triangle, serve to move it backwards or forwards, and between the walks are smooth grass-plats, covered with the greenest tuft, without any other ornament. This of my Lord Paulet is a Meadow divided into several compartments of brick-work, which are filled with flowers.—*Harleian Miscellanies*, vol. vii. p. 141.

**SAMUEL PEPYS**
(1632-1703).

THEN to Mr Evelyn's, to discourse of our confounded business of prisoners, and sick and wounded seamen, wherein he and we are so much put out of order. And here he showed me his Gardens, which are, for variety of evergreens, and hedge of holly, the finest things I ever saw in my life. Thence in his coach to Greenwich, and there to my office, all the way having fine discourse of trees and the nature of vegetables.—'*Diary*.' 5*th October*, 1665.

By water to Deptford, and there made a visit to Mr Evelyn. . . . He read to me very much also of his discourse, he hath been many years and now is about, about Gardenage; which will be a most noble and pleasant piece.—5 *Novr.*, 1665.

22nd (Lord's Day). Walked to White Hall, where saw nobody almost, but walked up and down with Hugh May, who is a very ingenious man.

Among other things, discoursing of our present fashion of gardens to make them plain, that we have the best walks of gravell in the world, France having none nor Italy; and our green of our bowling allies is better than any they have. So our business here being ayre, this is the best way, only with a little mixture of statues or pots, which may be handsome, and so filled with another pot of such or such a flower or greene, as the season of the year will bear. And then for flowers, they are best seen in a little plat by themselves: besides, their borders spoil the walks of another garden: and then for fruit, the best way is to have walls built circularly one within another, to the South, on purpose for fruit, and leave the walking Garden only for that use. Thence walked through the House, where most people mighty hush, and methinks, melancholy.—22*nd July*, 1666.

# GEORGE LONDON

*London was a pupil of Rose, Gardener to Charles II., and founder of the* **GEORGE**
*Brompton Park Nursery. He and Wise were authors of 'The Compleat* **LONDON**
*Gardener' (abridged from de la Quintinye), and of 'The Retir'd Gard'ner' in* (d. 1717), and
*two volumes. Vol. I., a Translation of 'Le Jardinier Solitaire, or Dialogues* **HENRY**
*between a Gentleman and a Gard'ner' (Fruit and Kitchen Garden). Vol. II.,* **WISE.**
*containing the manner of planting and cultivating all sorts of Flowers* ....
*being a translation from 'Le Jardinier Fleuriste et Historiographe' written
by the Sieur Liger of Auxerre.*

Evelyn devotes the "Advertisement" of his translation of La Quintinye's 'Compleat Gard'ner' to an eulogy of London and Wise, in which he commends their industry, knowledge of Nature and genius of Soils, their powers of Design, and their ample Collection at Brompton Park, near Kensington.

When Wise was appointed to the care of the Royal Gardens by Queen Anne, London used to make riding Circuits of the principal Gardens of England.

*Gard'ner.*

THE Distribution of Four acres for a fruit and kitchin garden, according to the figure I here present you, is the most approv'd of, both in regard to fruit-trees and legumes.

*Gentleman.*

Wherein does the beauty of it consist?

*Gard'ner.*

You may observe it in the figure before you: you see 'tis more deep than broad; the Alleys are of a good size, adorn'd with Borders Three Foot deep on each side, edged with several sorts of Aromatick Herbs. . . . In my Opinion there's nothing more ingenious belonging to a Garden, than the different Ways of marking our different Figures in a Parterre, especially when the design happens to be well contrived, and the Execution of it perform'd by a skilful Hand.

Formerly Gardens did not require so great Exactness as now, and Art suffer'd Nature to bring forth her Productions as confus'd as she pleas'd; a Flower that should have been the chief Ornament of the Garden lay hid, and languish'd among others of less Value, which tarnish'd all its Beauty. It was not then known what was meant by knots parted by Box, which had it been form'd in all the figures Fancy could suggest, would have afforded a pleasure to the Eye not easie to be express'd.

In former Times, the use of Box was not known, and the Manner of using it, if we believe the Fable, was introduc'd by the Goddess *Flora*, who believing it to be an Ornament prepared for Gardens, order'd it to be made use of accordingly.

. . . Some Parterres are said to be imbroider'd, others partly imbroider'd, and partly Cut-work with Borders ; a Third Sort compos'd of Grass-work only ; a Fourth made up of Imbroidery and Grass-work ; a Fifth only Cut-work ; a Sixth nothing but Cut-work and Turfs of Grass ; a Seventh of Cut-work of Grass and Imbroidery ; an Eighth whose middle is all Cut-work, and the Borders Imbroidery ; a Ninth, on the contrary, whose Borders are all Cut-work, and the Middle Imbroidery ; and lastly another Sort, whose Middle is partly Imbroidery, partly Cut-work and Green Turf, with Borders of Turf and Cut-work.

NOTE.—*Imbroidery* = those Draughts which represent in Effect those we have on our Cloaths, and look like Foliage ; in Gard'ners' language call'd *Branch-work*. Below the Foliage certain Flowers called *Flourishings.*—*The Retir'd Gard'ner*, chap. iii.

---

**MANDELSLO**
(1640.)

*A traveller who visited England in 1640 thus describes the Garden at Theobalds, the Palace of James I :—*

IT is large and square, having all its walls covered with sillery and a beautiful jet d'eau in the centre. The parterre hath many pleasant walks, many of which are planted on the sides with espaliers, and others arched over. Some of the trees are limes and elms, and at the end is a small mount called the *Mount of Venus*, which is placed in the midst of a labyrinth and is upon the whole, one of the most beautiful spots in the world.—'*Voyages de Mandelslo*' (*quoted by Daines Barrington*).

---

**SIR JOHN CHARDIN**
(1643-1713).

AFTER what I have said of the number and beauty of the flowers in Persia, one might easily imagine that the most beautiful gardens in the world are to be found there ; but this

The Garden of Sir Kenelm Digby

## CHARLES DUFRESNY

is not at all the case. On the contrary, by a rule I find very general where nature is fertile and aisée, art is coarser and more unknown, as in this matter of gardens. This happens from the fact that when Nature is so excellent a gardener, if I may so express it, there is nothing for art to do. The Gardens of the Persians consist commonly of a grand alley or straight avenue in the centre, planted with plane (the zinzar, or Chenar of the East), which divides the garden into two parts. There is a basin of water in the middle, proportionate to the garden, and two other lesser ones on the two sides. The space between them is sown with a mixture of flowers in natural confusion, and planted with fruit trees and roses; and this is the whole of the plan and execution. They know nothing of parterres and cabinets of verdure, labyrinths, terraces and such other ornaments of our gardens. The reason of which is, that the Persians do not walk in their gardens, as we do; but content themselves with having the view of them, and breathing the fresh air. For this purpose they seat themselves in some part of the garden as soon as they come into it, and remain there till they go out.—*Travels into Persia* (1686).

"Of the older travellers (in Persia) the palm will be conceded, *nemine contradicente*, to the French Huguenot, and English Knight, Chardin. He is apt to exaggerate, and he cannot invariably be relied upon, but he is always painstaking, frequently ingenious, and not seldom profound."—*Hon. George N. Curzon.* "*Persia*" (1892).

—⁂—

*Said to be descended from a natural son of Henry IV. and the wife of a gardener; a very* irregular *man in every way; improviser alike of gardens and comedies; the soi-disant rival of Lenôtre ; laid out the Gardens of Mignaux, near Poissy, and of the Abbé Pajot, near Vincennes; was valet de Chambre to Louis XIV. ; a "man of ideas" one of which Montesquieu adopted in his "Letters Persanes"; collaborated with Regnard, and had something in him of Marivaux—* (*Brunetière*).

*The first indications by the Jesuits of Chinese gardens* (1690) *had struck his ardent and paradoxical imagination. He loved to work upon an unequal and*

**CHARLES DUFRESNY** (1648-1724).

128    THE PRAISE OF GARDENS

*irregular ground (Alphana). He wanted obstacles to overcome, if there were none, he raised a mountain on a plain.*

*His style had something of the modern English manner, but his projects were rarely carried into execution. Gabriel Thouin asserts (" Plans Raisonnés,") that the first example of modern Landscape gardening was given by Dufresny in the Faubourg St Antoine.*

—ᴡᴡ—

ENGELBERT KAEMPFER (1651-1716). *Doctor and Traveller. Born at Lemgow in Westphalia; travelled while youth in North Germany, Holland and Poland; at 32 joined Swedish Diplomatic service and travelled through Russia and Tartary to Ispahan. Entered Dutch East India Company as surgeon and sailed to Batavia (1688) and Japan (1690), with which countries the Dutch were then the only traders. 1694, returned to Europe, first to Leyden then Lemgow where he wrote "History of Japan" (1727-8) and "Amœnitates Exoticæ" and practised as Physician. Kämpfer is called by Mr B. H. Chamberlain "the scientific discoverer of Japan."*

THE Garden is the only place we Dutchmen, being treated in all respects little better than prisoners, have liberty to walk into. It takes in all the room behind the house, it is commonly square, with a back door, and wall'd in very neatly like a cistern or pond, for which reason it is called *Tsubo*, which in the Japanese language signifies a large water-trough or cistern. If there be not room enough for a garden, they have at least an old ingrotted plane, cherry or apricock tree. The older, the more crooked and monstrous this tree is, the greater value they put upon it. Sometimes they let the branches grow into the rooms. . .

If the *Tsubo* or Garden be a good one, it must have at least 30 foot square and consist of the following essential parts. 1. The ground is partly cover'd with roundish stones, of different colours, gather'd in rivers or upon the sea-shore, well-wash'd and clean'd, and those of the same kind laid together in form of beds, partly with gravel, which is swept every day, and kept clean and neat to admiration, the large stones being laid in the middle, as a path to walk upon, without injuring the gravel, the whole in a seeming but ingenious confusion. 2. Some few flower-bearing plants planted confusedly, tho' not without some certain rules.

Amidst the plants stands sometimes a Saguer, as they call it, or scarce outlandish tree, sometimes a dwarf-tree or two. 3. A small rock or hill in a corner of the garden, made in imitation of nature, curiously adorn'd with birds and insects, cast in brass, and placed between the stones, sometimes the model of a temple stands upon it, built, as for the sake of the prospect they generally are, on a remarkable eminence, or the borders of a precipice Often a small rivulet rushes down the stones with an agreeable noise, the whole in due proportions and as near as possible resembling nature. 4. A small bush, or wood, on the side of the hill, for which the gardiners chuse such trees, as will grow close to one another, and plant and cut them according to their largeness, nature, and the colour of their flowers and leaves, so as to make the whole very accurately imitate a natural wood, or forest. 5. A cistern or pond, as mention'd above, with alive fish kept in it, and surrounded with proper plants, that is such, as love a watry soil, and would lose their beauty and greeness if planted in a dry ground. It is a particular profession to lay out these gardens, and to keep them so curiously and nicely as they ought to be, as I shall have an opportunity to shew more at large in the sequel of this history. Nor doth it require less skill and ingenuity to contrive and fit out the rocks and hills above mention'd according to the rules of art. What I have hitherto observed will be sufficient to give the reader a general idea of the Inns of Japan.—*History of Japan.*

—WW—

*Author of* '*Systema Agriculturæ*,' 1669, *and* '*Systema Horticulturæ*,' 1677. **JOHN WORLIDGE (17th cent.).**

THE excellency of a *Garden* is better manifested by experience, which is the best Mistress, than indicated by an imperfect Pen, which can never sufficiently convince the Reader of those transcendent pleasures, that the Owner of a Complete *Garden* with its Magnificent *Ornaments*, its Stately *Groves*, and infinite variety of never dying *Objects of Delight* every day enjoys; Nor how all his Senses are satiated with the great variety of

I

Objects it yields to every of them: Nor what an influence they have upon the passions of the mind, reducing a discomposed fancy to a more sedate temper by contemplating on those miracles of Nature *Gardens* afford; deemed Miracles because their admired and strange forms and effects proceed from occult causes. . . .

The Italians, in the time of their Ancient Glory, thought no Palace nor Habitation Complete without its Garden, on which they spared for no cost as well in their forming.

Neither is there a noble or pleasant seat in England, but hath its gardens for pleasure and delight. So that we may, without vanity, conclude, that a garden of pleasant avenues, walks, fruits, flowers, grots, and other branches springing from it, well composed, is the only complete and permanent inanimate object of delight the world affords.—*Systema Horticulturæ.*

# CHAPTER VI

DECLINE OF THE FORMAL, AND EARLY INDICATIONS OF THE NATURAL OR LANDSCAPE GARDEN IN THE FIRST HALF OF THE EIGHTEENTH CENTURY

WANSTEAD, the noble seat of Sir Richard Child, with the finest gardens in the world. You descend from the Salon into the parterre, which hath a Canal in the middle; on the right a wilderness, and on the left a fine green walk, which ends in a banqueting house. On one side of this green walk stands the green-house, finely adorned with statues, and uncommonly furnished with greens: while behind this green-house are variety of high-hedged walks, affording delicious vistas. At the bottom of the canal is a bowling-green encircled with grottos and seats, with antique statues between each seat; this bowling-green is separated by a balustrade of iron from another long green walk, which leads you to another long canal.

DANIEL DEFOE (1663-1731).

On Richmond Green is a fine house and gardens, made by Sir Charles Hedges, but now belonging to Sir Matthew Decker, which are very curios. The longest, largest, and highest hedge of holly I ever saw is in this garden, with several other hedges of evergreens, vistas cut through woods, grottos with fountains, and a fine canal running up from the river. His duckery, which is an oval pond bricked round, and his pretty summer-house by it, in which to drink a bottle, his stove houses, which are always kept of an equal heat for his citrons and other Indian plants, with gardeners brought from foreign countries to manage them, are very curious and entertaining.

Sutton Court is *une bijoux*; it hath three parterres from the three fronts of the house, each finely adorned with statues. The

Sutton Court.

gardens are irregular, but that, I think, adds to their beauty, for every walk affords variety; the hedges, grottos, statues, mounts, and canals, are so many surprising beauties.

**Durdans.** There are several very good seats in and about Epsom. That of Lord Guildford, called Durdans, at the extremity of the village, was built by the Earl of Barclay out of the materials of Nonsuch, a royal palace in this neighbourhood, built by Henry VIII., and given by King Charles II. to the Duchess of Cleveland, who pulled it down and sold the materials. This house of Durdans is built *a-la-moderne* of free-stone; the front to the garden, and that to the Downs, are very noble; the apartments within are also very regular, and in the garden is the most charming grove imaginable; famous for that scene of love between Lord Grey and his lady's sister, which you have read of.

**Cannons.** The parterre fronting the west is separated from the great avenue, and the great court leading to the great staircase by balustrades of iron, as it is also from the gardens on the other side. There is a large terrace walk, from whence you descend to the parterre; this parterre hath a row of gilded vases on pedestals on each side down to the great canal, and in the middle fronting the canal, is a gladiator, gilded also; through the whole parterre, abundance of statues as big as the life, are regularly disposed. The canal runs a great way, and indeed one would wonder to see such a vast quantity of water in a country where are neither rivers or springs; but they tell me that the Duke hath his water in pipes from the mountains of Stanmore, about two miles off. The gardens are very large and well disposed; but the greatest pleasure of all is that the divisions of the whole, being only made by balustrades of iron and not by walls, you see the whole at once, be you in what part of the garden or parterre you will.—*A Journey through England and Scotland in* 1714.

*Professional gardener and seedsman in the reign of Anne and George I.,* **STEPHEN**
*and for several years a pupil of London and Wise, under the former of whom* **SWITZER**
*he was employed in 1706 in laying out the grounds at Blenheim. His own* (1665-1745).
*garden was at Milbank. (See G. W. Johnson's 'History of English Gardening,'*
*for a long analysis of his chief work ' Ichnographia Rustica.')*

IF a little Regularity is allow'd near the main Building and as soon as the Designer has stroke out by Art some of the roughest and boldest of his strokes, he ought to pursue Nature afterwards, and by as many Twinings and Windings as his *Villa* will allow, will endeavour to diversify his Views, always striving that they may be so intermixt, as not to be all discover'd at once; but that there should be as much as possible, something appearing new and diverting, while the whole should correspond together by the magic Error of its natural Avenues and Meanders. . . . And to the End that he may know the better, how to make the best use of natural Advantage, he ought to make himself Master of all Rural Scenes: And the Writings of the Poets on this Subject, will give him considerable Hints, for in Design the *Designer* as well as the *Poet should take as much Pains in forming his Imagination, as a Philosopher in cultivating his Understanding.*—*Ichnographia Rustica,* 1742 *(first edition* 1718).

—⁂—

I WISH I were just now in my little garden at Laracor. I **JONATHAN**
would set out for Dublin early on Monday and bring you **SWIFT**[1]
an account of my young trees, which you are better acquainted (1667-1745).
with than the ministry, and so am I.

It is now high cherry time with us; take notice is it so soon with you? And we have early apricots; and gooseberries are ripe.—(*Kensington, July* 1, 1712.)

[1] Swift had an odd humour of making extempore proverbs. Observing that a gentleman, in whose garden he walked with some friends, seemed to have no intention to request them to eat any of the fruit, Swift observed, 'It was a saying of his dear grandmother,

Always pull a peach
When it is within your reach';

and helping himself accordingly, his example was followed by the whole company.—*Sir W. Scott: Memoirs of Jonathan Swift.*

# THE PRAISE OF GARDENS

Pray why don't MD go to 'Trim, and see Laracor, and give me an account of the garden, and the river, and the holly and the cherry-trees on the river-walk.—*Journal to Stella.*

---

**JOSEPH ADDISON**
(1672-1719).

SIR,—Having lately read your essay on The Pleasures of the Imagination, I was so taken with your thoughts upon some of our English gardens, that I cannot forbear troubling you with a letter upon that subject. I am one, you must know, who am looked upon as a humourist in gardening. I have several acres about my house, which I call my garden, and which a skilful gardener would not know what to call. It is a confusion of kitchen and parterre, orchard and flower-garden, which lie so mixt and interwoven with one another, that if a foreigner, who had seen nothing of our country, should be conveyed into my garden at his first landing, he would look upon it as a natural wilderness, and one of the uncultivated parts of our country. My flowers grow up in several parts of the garden in the greatest luxuriancy and profusion. I am so far from being fond of any particular one, by reason of its rarity, that if I meet with any one in a field which pleases me, I give it a place in my garden. By this means, when a stranger walks with me, he is surprised to see several large spots of ground covered with ten thousand different colours, and has often singled out flowers he might have met with under a common hedge, in a field, or in a meadow, as some of the greatest beauties of the place. The only method I observe in this particular, is to range in the same quarter the products of the same season, that they may make their appearance together, and compose a picture of the greatest variety. There is the same irregularity in my plantations, which run into as great a wilderness as their natures will permit. I take in none that do not naturally rejoice in the soil; and am pleased, when I am walking in a labyrinth of my own raising, not to know whether the next tree I shall meet with is an apple or an oak; an elm or a pear tree. My kitchen has likewise its particular quarters assigned it; for besides the wholesome luxury which that place abounds with, I have always thought a kitchen garden a more pleasant sight than the finest orangery, or artificial greenhouse. I love to see everything in its perfection: and am more pleased to survey my rows of coleworts and cabbages, with a thousand nameless pot-herbs, springing up in their full fragrancy and verdure, than to see the tender plants of foreign countries kept alive by artificial heats, or withering in an air and soil that are not adapted to them. I must not omit, that there is a fountain rising in the upper part of my garden, which forms a little wandering rill, and administers to the pleasure as well as the plenty of the place. I have so conducted it that it visits most of my plantations; and have taken particular care to let it run in the same manner as it would do in an open field, so that it generally passes through banks of violets and primroses, plats of willow or other plants, that seem to be of its own producing. There is another circumstance in which I am very particular, or, as my neighbours call me, very whimsical; as my garden invites into it all the birds of the country, by offering them the conveniency of springs and shades, solitude and shelter, I do not suffer any one to destroy their nests in the Spring, or drive them from their usual haunts in fruit-time; I value my garden more for being full of blackbirds than cherries, and very frankly give them fruit for their songs. By this means I have always the music of the season in its perfection, and am highly delighted to see the jay or the thrush hopping about my walks, and shooting before my eye across the several little glades and alleys that I pass through. I think there are as many kinds of gardening as of poetry: your makers of parterres and flower-gardens are epigrammatists and sonneteers in this art; contrivers of bowers and grottos, treillages and cascades, are romance writers. Wise and London are our heroic poets; and if, as a critic, I may single out any passage of their works to commend, I shall take notice of that part in the upper garden at Kensington, which was at first nothing but a gravel pit. It must have been a fine genius for gardening, that could have thought of forming such an unsightly hollow into so beautiful an area, and to have hit the eye with so uncommon

## THE PRAISE OF GARDENS

and agreeable a scene as that which it is now wrought into. To give this particular spot of ground the greater effect, they have made a very pleasing contrast; for as on one side of the walk you see this hollow basin, with its several little plantations, lying so conveniently under the eye of the beholder, on the other side of it there appears a seeming mount, made up of trees, rising one higher than another, in proportion as they approach the centre. A spectator, who has not heard this account of it, would think this circular mount was not only a real one, but that it actually had been scooped out of that hollow space which I have before mentioned. I never yet met anyone who has walked in this garden, who was not struck with that part of it which I have here mentioned. As for myself, you will find, by the account which I have already given you, that my compositions in gardening are altogether after the Pindaric manner, and run into the beautiful wildness of nature, without affecting the nicer elegancies of art. What I am now going to mention, will, perhaps, deserve your attention more than anything I have yet said. I find, that in the discourse which I spoke of in the beginning of my letter, you are against filling an English garden with evergreens; and indeed I am so far of your opinion, that I can by no means think the verdure of an evergreen comparable to that which shoots out annually, and clothes our trees in the summer season. But I have often wondered that those who are like myself, and love to live in gardens, have never thought of contriving a winter garden, which should consist of such trees only as never cast their leaves. We have very often little snatches of sunshine and fair weather in the most uncomfortable parts of the year, and have frequently several days in November and January that are as agreeable as any in the finest months. At such times, therefore, I think there could not be a greater pleasure than to walk in such a winter garden as I have proposed. In the summer season, the whole country blooms, and is a kind of garden; for which reason we are not so sensible of those beauties that at this time may be everywhere met with; but when Nature is in her desolation, and presents us with nothing but bleak and barren prospects, there is something unspeakably cheerful in a spot of ground which is covered with trees that smile amidst all the rigours of winter, and give us a view of the most gay season, in the midst of that which is most dead and melancholy. I have so far indulged myself in this thought, that I have set apart a whole acre of ground for the executing of it. The walls are covered with ivy instead of vines. The laurel, the hornbeam, and the holly, with many other trees and plants of the same nature, grow so thick in it that you cannot imagine a more lively scene. The glowing redness of the berries with which they are hung at this time, vies with the verdure of their leaves, and is apt to inspire the heart of the beholder with that vernal delight which you have somewhere taken notice of in your former papers. It is very pleasant, at the same time to see the several kinds of birds retiring into this little green spot, and enjoying themselves amongst the branches and foliage, when my great garden, which I have before mentioned to you, does not afford a single leaf for their shelter.

You must know, Sir, that I look upon the pleasure which we take in a Garden, as one of the most innocent delights in human life. A Garden was the habitation of our first parents before the fall. It is naturally apt to fill the mind with calmness and tranquillity, and to lay all its turbulent passions at rest. It gives us a great insight into the contrivance and wisdom of providence, and suggests innumerable subjects for meditation. I cannot but think the very complacency and satisfaction which a man takes in these works of Nature to be a laudable if not a virtuous habit of mind. For all which reasons I hope you will pardon the length of my present letter.

I am, Sir, etc.

—*The Spectator*, No. 477 (*Saturday, Sept.* 6, 1712).

Writers who have given us an account of China, tell us the inhabitants of that country laugh at the plantations of our Europeans, which are laid out by the rule and line; because they say, any one may place trees in equal rows and uniform figures.

They choose rather to shew a genius in works of this nature, and therefore always conceal the art by which they direct themselves. They have a word, it seems, in their language, by which they express the particular beauty of a plantation, that thus strikes the imagination at first sight, without discovering what it is, that has so agreeable an effect.

Our British gardeners, on the contrary, instead of humouring nature, love to deviate from it as much as possible. Our trees rise in cones, globes, and pyramids. We see the marks of the scissors upon every plant and bush. I do not know whether I am singular in my opinion, but for my own part, I would rather look upon a tree in all its luxuriancy and diffusion of boughs and branches, than when it is thus cut and trimmed into a mathematical figure: and cannot but fancy that an orchard in flower looks infinitely more delightful, than all the little labyrinths of the most finished parterre. But as our great modellers of gardens have their magazines of plants to dispose of, it is very natural for them to tear up all the beautiful plantations of fruit-trees, and contrive a plan that may most turn to their own profit, in taking off their evergreens, and the like movable plants, with which their shops are plentifully stocked.—*The Spectator, No.* 414. *Wednesday, June* 25, 1712.

I have often looked upon it as a piece of happiness that I have never fallen into any of these fantastical tastes, nor esteemed anything the more for its being uncommon and hard to be met with. For this reason I look upon the whole country in Springtime as a spacious garden, and make as many visits to a spot of daisies, or a bank of violets, as a florist does to his borders or parterres.

There is not a bush in blossom within a mile of me, which I am not acquainted with, nor scarce a daffodil or cowslip that withers away in my neighbourhood without my missing it. I walked home in this temper of mind through several fields and meadows with an unspeakable pleasure, not without reflecting on the bounty of providence, which has made the most pleasing and most beautiful objects the most ordinary and most common.—*The Tatler, No.* 218.

*Soldier, Diplomatist, Historian.*

L'HERMITAGE (de Marly) fut fait : ce n'était que pour y coucher trois nuits du Mercredi au Samedi, deux ou trois fois l'année, avec une douzaine de courtisans en charge, les plus indispensables ; peu à peu l'hermitage fut augmenté. D'accroissement en accroissement les collines furent taillées pour faire place et y bâtir, et celles du bout légèrement emportées pour donner au moins une échappée de vue fort imparfaite. Enfin en bâtiments, en jardins, en eaux, en aqueducs, en ce qui est si curieux sous le nom de *Machine de Marly*, en parcs, en forêts ornées et enfermées, en statues, en meubles précieux, en grands arbres qu'on y a apportés sans cesse de Compiègne et de bien plus loin, dont les trois quarts mouraient, et qu'on remplacait aussitôt, en allées obscures subitement changées en d'immenses pièces d'eau où l'on se promenait en gondoles, en remises, en forêts à n'y pas voir le jour dès le moment qu'on les plantait, en bassins changés cent fois, en casçades de même, en figures successives et toutes différentes, en sejours de carpes ornés de dorures, et de peintures les plus exquises, à peine achevés, rechangés et rétablis par les mêmes maîtres une infinité de fois ; que si on ajoute les dépenses de ces continuels voyages qui devinrent enfin égaux aux séjours de Versailles, souvent presque aussi nombreux, et tout à la fin de la vie du roi, le séjour le plus ordinaire, on ne dira pas trop sur Marly en comptant par milliards.—*Memoirs.*

SAINT-SIMON, (1675-1755).

I AM in my farm, and here I shoot strong and tenacious roots. I have caught hold of the earth, to use a gardener's phrase, and neither my friends nor my enemies will find it an easy matter to transplant me again.—*Letter to Swift.*

HENRY ST JOHN, LORD BOLINGBROKE (1678-1751).

**WILLIAM KENT (1684-1748).** *Coach-painter, portrait and historical painter, sculptor, architect, furniture and dress designer, and landscape gardener; patronised by the Earl of Burlington, the great amateur-architect, with whom he lived and died. He sculptured Shakespeare's monument in Westminster Abbey, and painted an altar-piece for St Clement Dane's Church, of St Cecilia, afterwards removed to the Vestry Hall. Hogarth's Caricature 'The Man of Taste' places Kent on the summit of Burlington Gate, with Pope his patron lower down; and his opinion of Kent as a painter was that 'neither England nor Italy ever produced a more contemptible dauber.'*

WHEN Kent had returned to England, about 1730, he first distinguished himself as an architect and ornamental gardener at his great patron's, Lord Burlington's villa at Chiswick; and his additions to the plans of Bridgman and Vanbrugh, at Stowe, firmly established his fame. Esher[1] and Claremont[2] are cited as his best works; yet the garden laid out for General Dormer at Rousham, in Oxfordshire, was more agreeable to our noble author.

Of the beautiful scenes which have been created upon Kent's system, and since his death, some account is necessary with a view to the date and progress of the art.

A new application of it, comprehending the grounds destined to agriculture, by including them in the whole scheme, and imperceptibly connecting them with the more embellished portion, was first successfully practised by Mr Philip Southcote, at Woburn farm, in Surrey. Hence the origin of that description of pleasure-ground which has since received the French designation of *ferme ornée*. Pain's hill, in the same country, soon followed the new attempt, and exceeded it in point of taste, variety, and extent. Its author, the Hon. C. Hamilton, was a man of genius, who dedicated all his powers to this pursuit, and sad to say, expended his private fortune in the completion of improvements which continually presented themselves.

[1] See Illustration in Appendix.
[2] Whateley, when speaking of Kent's work at Claremont, confers a very elegant eulogy, and communicates an idea of a perfect garden. 'The whole is a place wherein to tarry with secure delight, or to saunter with perpetual amusement.'

# ALEXANDER POPE

Dr Burgh in his notes on the English Garden calls 'Bacon, the prophet; Milton, the herald; and Addison, Pope and Kent, the champions of this true taste in gardening, because they absolutely brought it into execution.'

Mr Price, in his Essay on the Picturesque, objects to Kent, that his ideas of painting were uncommonly mean, contracted and perverse; and that as he painted trees without form, so he planted them without life. 'Kent, it is true, was by profession a painter, as well as an improver; but we may learn from his example how little a certain degree of mechanical practice can qualify its possessor to direct the taste of the nation in either of these arts.'—*Rev. James Dallaway, 'Supplementary Anecdotes of Gardening in England.'*

—⁓⌇⌇⁓—

HOW contrary to this simplicity (of Homer) is the modern practice of gardening! We seem to make it our study to recede from nature, not only in the various tonsure of greens into the most regular and formal shape, but even in monstrous attempts beyond the reach of the art itself: we run into sculpture, and are yet better pleased to have our trees in the most aukward figures of men and animals, than in the most regular of their own. . . .

A citizen is no sooner proprietor of a couple of yews, but he entertains thoughts of erecting them into giants, like those of

ALEXANDER POPE[1]
(1688-1744).

[1] Mr Pope undoubtedly contributed to form his (Kent's) taste. The design of the Prince of Wales's garden at Carlton House was evidently borrowed from the poet's at Twickenham. There was a little of affected modesty in the latter, when he said, of all his works he was most proud of his garden. And yet it was a singular effort of art and taste to impress so much variety and scenery on a spot of five acres. The passing through the gloom from the grotto to the opening day, the retiring and again assembling shades, the dusky groves, the larger lawn, and the solemnity of the termination at the cypresses that lead up to his mother's tomb, are managed with exquisite judgment; and though Lord Peterborough assisted him

To form his quincunx and to rank his vines,

those were not the most pleasing ingredients of his little perspective.—*Horace Walpole. On Modern Gardening.*

Guildhall. I know an eminent cook, who beautified his country-seat with a coronation-dinner in greens, where you see the champion flourishing on horseback at one end of the table, and the Queen in perpetual youth at the other.

For the benefit of all my loving countrymen of this curious taste, I shall here publish a catalogue of greens to be disposed of by an eminent town-gardener, who has lately applied to me upon this head. He represents that for the advancement of a politer sort of ornament in the villas and gardens adjacent to this great city, and in order to distinguish those places from the mere barbarous countries of gross nature, the world stands much in need of a virtuoso gardener, who has a turn to sculpture, and is thereby capable of improving upon the ancients in the imagery of evergreens. I proceed to this catalogue:

Adam and Eve in yew; Adam a little shattered by the fall of the tree of Knowledge in the great storm; Eve and the serpent very flourishing.

Noah's Ark in holly, the ribs a little damaged for want of water.

The tower of Babel not yet finished.

St. George in Box; his arm scarce long enough, but will be in a condition to stick the dragon by next April.

A green dragon of the same, with a tail of ground-ivy for the present.

*N.B.*—Those two are not to be sold separately.

Edward the Black Prince in Cypress. . . .

A Queen Elizabeth in Phyllirea, a little inclining to the Green sickness, but of full growth. . . .

An old Maid of honour in wormwood.

A topping Ben Johnson in Laurel.

Divers eminent modern poets in bays, somewhat blighted, to be disposed of a penny worth. . . .—*The Guardian, No.* 173.

I can afford room for your self and two servants; I have indeed room enough, nothing but myself at home; the kind and hearty house-wife is dead! the agreeable and instructive neighbour is gone! yet my house is inlarg'd, and the gardens extend and flourish, as knowing nothing of the guests they have lost. I have more fruit-trees and kitchen garden than you have any thought of; nay I have good Melons and Pine-apples of my own growth. I am as much a better Gardiner, as I am a worse Poet, than when you saw me: but gardening is near a-kin to Philosophy, for Tully says "Agricultura proxima sapientiæ." For God's sake why should not you (that are a step higher than a Philosopher, a Divine, yet have too much grace and wit than to be a Bishop) e'en give all you have to the poor of Ireland (for whom you have already done every thing else) so quit the place, and live and die with me? And let "Tales Animæ Concordes" be our Motto and our Epitaph.—*Letter to Dean Swift, March 25, 1736.*

Let the young ladies be assured I make nothing new in my gardens, without wishing to see the print of their fairy steps in every part of them. I have put the last hand to my works of this kind, in happily finishing the subterraneous way and grotto. I there found a spring of the clearest water, which falls in a perpetual rill, that echoes through the Cavern day and night. From the river Thames, you see through my arch up a walk of the wilderness, to a kind of open temple, wholly composed of shells in the rustic manner; and from that distance under the temple, you look down through a sloping arcade of trees, and see the sails on the river passing suddenly and vanishing as through a perspective glass. When you shut the doors of this grotto it becomes on the instant, from a luminous room, a *Camera obscura*, on the walls of which all the objects of the river, hills, woods and boats are forming a moving picture in their visible radiations; and when you have a mind to light it up, it affords you a very different scene. It is finished with shells interspersed with pieces of looking-glass in angular forms; and in the ceiling is a star of the same material, at which when a lamp, of an orbicular figure of thin alabaster, is hung in the middle, a thousand pointed rays glitter, and are reflected over the place. There are connected to this grotto by a narrower passage two porches with niches and seats,—one towards the river, of smooth stones, full of light, and open; the other towards the arch of trees, rough with shells, flints and iron-ore. The bottom is paved with simple pebble, as the adjoining walk up the wilderness to the temple is to be cockle-shells, in the natural taste, agreeing not ill with the little dripping murmur, and the aquatic idea of the whole place. It wants nothing to complete it but a good Statue with an inscription, like that beautiful antique one which you know I am so fond of:—

> " Hujus Nympha loci, sacri custodia fontis,
> Dormio, dum blandae sentio murmur aquæ;
> Parce meum, quisquis tangis cava murmura, somnum
> Rumpere; sive bibas, sive lavare, tace.

> " Nymph of the Grot, those sacred springs steep,
> And to the murmur of these waters sleep;
> Ah, spare my slumbers, gently tread the cave!
> And drink in silence, or in silence lave."

*Letter to Edward Blount, Twickenham, June* 3, 1725.

My Lord Chesterfield tells me your Lordship has got ahead of all the gardening lords; that you have distanced Lord Burlington and Lord Cobham in the true scientific past; but he is studying after you, and has here lying before him those Thesauruses from which he affirms you draw all your knowledge—Miller's Dictionaries; but I informed him better, and told him your chief lights were from Johannes Serlius,[1] whose books he is now enquiring for of Leake, the bookseller, who has wrote for them to his correspondents.—*Letter to Lord Marchmont*, 1743.

—᭸᭸—

**MONTESQUIEU** IT is, then, the pleasure which an object gives us, which carries
(1689-1755). us on to another; it is for this reason that the soul is always seeking new things, and is never at rest.

[1] This looks like a joke of Pope's—John Serle being his gardener and factotum at Twickenham, who has left a "Plan of Mr Pope's Garden and Grotto," and an account of the materials composing the latter, published by Dodsley, 1745. (See Plan in Appendix.)

# PHILIP MILLER

Thus, you will be always certain to please the soul, whenever you show it many things or more than it had hoped to see.

In this way may be explained the reason why we take pleasure in seeing a perfectly regular garden, and yet are pleased to see a wild and rural spot; the same cause produces these effects.

As we like to see a large number of objects, we would wish to extend our view, to be in several places, traverse greater space: in short, our soul escapes from bounds, and wishes, so to speak, to widen the sphere of its presence; and derives great pleasure from a distant view. But how to effect this? In towns, our view is confined by houses; in the country, by a thousand obstacles; we can scarcely see three or four trees. Art comes to our assistance, and discovers to us nature which hides itself; we love art, and we love it better than nature, that is to say, nature concealed from our eyes: but when we find beautiful situations, when our unfettered view can see in the distance meadows, streams, hills, and these dispositions are, so to speak, expressly created, it is enchanted otherwise than when it sees the gardens of Le Nôtre; because nature does not copy itself, whereas art always bears its own likeness. That is why, in painting, we prefer a landscape to the plan of the most beautiful garden in the world; it is because painting only chooses nature where it is beautiful, where the sight can extend to a distance and to its full scope, where it is varied, where it can be viewed with pleasure.—*Essay on Taste.*

---

**PHILIP MILLER, F.R.S. (1691-1771).**

"*Hortulanorum Princeps:*" *for nearly fifty years gardener to the Botanic Garden at Chelsea belonging to the company of Apothecaries.* "*In him the perfect Botanist and Horticulturist were combined*" (*G. W. Johnson*). *In* 1792 *appeared the* 9*th edition of his* '*Gardener's Dictionary*' *edited by Professor Martyn of Cambridge, it having been already translated into Dutch, German and French. Linnæus said of it,* "*Non est Lexicon Hortulanorum sed Botanicorum.*"

THE Area of a handsom *Garden* may take up thirty or forty Acres, not more.

And as for the Disposition and Distribution of this Garden, the following Directions may be observed.

1st. There ought always to be a Descent from the house to the garden not fewer than three steps. This elevation of the Building will make it more dry and wholesome: Also, from the Head of these steps there will be a prospect or view of a great part of the Garden.

In a fine Garden, the first thing that should present itself to the sight, is a parterre, which should be next to the House, whether in the front or on the sides, as well upon account of the Opening it affords to the House, as for the Beauty with which it constantly entertains the sight from all the windows on that side of the House.

As for the Parterres, they must be furnished with such works as will improve and set them off; and they being low and flat, do necessarily require something that is raised, as Groves and Pallisades. . . .

Groves make the chief of a garden, being great Ornaments to all the rest of its Parts; so that there cannot be too many of them planted, if the Places designed for them don't take up those of the Kitchen and Fruit-Garden, which are very necessary for a House, and should always be placed near the Stabling.

To accompany Parterres, it is useful to make choice of those designs of Wood-work that are the finest; as Groves opened in Compartiments, Quincunces, Verdant Halls, with Bowling-greens, Arbour-work, and Fountains in the Middle.

These small Groves, being placed near the House, are so much the more agreeable, in that you have no need to go far to find shades; and besides this, they communicate a coolness to the Apartments, which is very agreeable in hot weather.

It would also be very proper to plant some Groves of Evergreens, that may afford the pleasure of seeing a Wood always verdant in Winter, when the other trees and plants are deprived of their Ornaments; and also to plant some squares of them to be a diversity from the other Woods.

It is also usual to adorn the Head of a Parterre with Basons, Water-works: and beyond it, with a circular line of Pallisades or Wood-work cut into a Goosefoot, leading into the great Walks,

# PHILIP MILLER 147

and to fill the space between the Bason and the Pallisade with small pieces of Embroidery or Grass-work, set off with Yews, Vases and flower-pots.

In Gardens, which have Terrasses, either in the side or front of the house, where there is a delightful prospect, so that you cannot shut up the Parterre by a circular Pallisade; in order to continue the new view, you should lay several compartiments of a parterre together, such as plain green pots after the modern fashion, or cut-work; which ought to be divided at convenient distances by Cross-walks: But the parterre or plain Green plot must always be next to the House, because it is very agreeable to the eye. . . .

When the great lines and chief walks are laid out, and the Parterres and Works about the sides and head of them are disposed so as is most suitable to the Ground, then the rest of the Garden is to be furnished with many different designs, as tall groves, Close walks, Quincunces, Galleries and Halls of Verdure, Green Arbours, Labyrinths, Bowling greens, and Amphitheatres, adorned with Fountains, Canals, Figures, etc. Which sort of Works distinguish a Garden well, and do also greatly contribute to the rendring of it magnificent. . . .

Before the design of a Garden be put into execution, it ought to be considered what it will be in twenty or thirty years time, when the Pallisades are grown up, and the trees are spread: For it often happens that a design which looks handsome when it is first planted, and in good proportion, becomes so small and ridiculous in process of time, that there is a necessity either to alter it, or destroy it entirely, and so plant it anew.

The corners and angles of every part of a Garden ought to be sloped, or cut hollow: This will make the cross-paths more agreeable to the eye, and more convenient for walking, than to find points and corners advancing, which look very ill upon the ground, and are very inconvenient.

There is a peculiar Excellency in Gardens that have terrasses; because from the height of one Terrass, all the lower parts of the Garden may be discovered; and from others the Compartiments are seen, which form so many several Gardens one under another, and present us with very agreeable Views, and different Scenes of Things, if the Terrasses are not too frequent, and there be good lengths of Level between them.—*The Gardener's Dictionary* (1st edition 1724).

—ww—

**VOLTAIRE,**
(1694-1778).

AFTER having thus passed in review all the books, they descended into the garden. Candide praised all its beauties. I know nothing in such bad taste, said the master; here are only gee-gaws : but I shall begin to-morrow to have one planted of a nobler design.—*Candide ou l'Optimisme*, chap. xxv.

—ww—

**EARL OF CHESTER-FIELD**
(1694-1773).

I HAVE been a Country Gentleman a great while, for me, that is; for I have now been a fortnight together at Blackheath, and stay three or four days longer. The *furor hortensis* has seized me, and my acre of ground here affords me more pleasure than Kingdoms do to Kings; for my object is not to extend but to enrich it.

My Gardener calls me, and I must obey.—*Letter to the Bishop of Waterford.* (*Blackheath*, 1751.)

—ww—

**BATTY LANGLEY**
(1696-1751),
*Architect and Garden Designer.*

OF THE DISPOSITION OF GARDENS IN GENERAL.

NOW as the Beauty of Gardens in general depends upon an elegant Disposition of all their Parts, which cannot be determined without a perfect Knowledge of its several Ascendings, Descendings, Views, etc., how is it possible that any Person can make a good Design for any Garden, whose Situation they never saw?

To draw a beautiful regular Draught, is not to the Purpose; for altho' it makes a handsome Figure on the paper, yet it has quite a different Effect when executed on the ground : Nor is there any Thing more ridiculous, and forbidding, than a Garden which is regular; which, instead of entertaining the Eye with fresh

# BATTY LANGLEY 149

Objects, after you have seen a quarter Part, you only see the very same part repeated again, without any variety.

And what still adds to this wretched Method, is, that to execute these still regular Designs, they destroy many a noble Oak, and in its place plant, perhaps, a clumsy-bred Yew, Holley, etc., which, with me, is a Crime of so high a Nature, as not to be pardon'd.

There is nothing adds so much to the pleasure of a Garden, as these great Beauties of Nature, Hills and Valleys, which, by our regular Coxcombs, have ever been destroyed, and at a very great Expence also in Levelling.

For, to their great Misfortune, they always deviate from Nature, instead of imitating it.

There are many other absurdities I could mention, which those wretched Creatures have, and are daily guilty of: But as the preceding are sufficient to arm worthy Gentlemen against such Mortals, I shall at present forbear, and instead thereof, proceed to General Directions for laying out Gardens in a more grand and delightful Manner than has been done before. But first observe,

That the several Parts of a beautiful Rural Garden, are Walks, Slopes, Borders, Open Plains, Plain Parterres, Avenues, Groves, Wildernesses, Labyrinths, Fruit-Gardens, Flower-Gardens, Vineyards, Hop-Gardens, Nurseries, Coppiced Quarters, Green Openings, like Meadows: Small Inclosures of Corn, Cones of Ever-Greens, of Flowering-Shrubs, of Fruit Trees, of Forest-Trees, and mix'd together: Mounts, Terraces, Winding Valleys, Dales, Purling Streams, Basons, Canals, Fountains, Cascades, Grottos, Rocks, Ruins, Serpentine Meanders, Rude Coppies, Hay-Stacks, Wood-Piles, Rabbit and Hare-Warrens, Cold Baths, Aviaries, Cabinets, Statues, Obelisks, Manazeries, Pheasant and Partridge-Grounds, Orangeries, Melon-Grounds, Kitchen-Gardens, Physick or Herb-Garden, Orchard, Bowling Green, Dials, Precipices, Ampthitheatres, etc.

GENERAL DIRECTIONS, ETC.

I. That the Grand Front of a Building lie open upon an

elegant Lawn or Plain of Grass, adorn'd with beautiful Statues, (of which hereafter in their Place,) terminated on its sides with open Groves.

II. That Grand Avenues be planted from such large open plains, with a Breadth proportionable to the Building, as well as to its Length of view.

III. That Views in Gardens be as extensive as possible.

IV. That such Walks, whose Views cannot be extended, terminate in Woods, Forests, mishapen Rocks, strange Precipices, Mountains, old Ruins, grand Buildings, etc.

V. That no regular Ever-Greens etc., be planted in any part of an open Plain or Parterre.

VI. That no Borders be made, or Scroll-Work cut, in any such Lawn or plain Parterre; for the Grandeur of those beautiful Carpets consists in their native Plainness.

VII. That all Gardens be grand, beautiful and natural.

VIII. That shady Walks be planted from the End-Views of a House, and terminate in those open Groves that enclose the Sides of the plain Parterre, that thereby you may enter into immediate shade, as soon as out of the House, without being heated by the scorching Rays of the Sun.

> " Without a Shade no Beauty Gardens know:
> And all the Country's but a naked Show."

IX. That all the Trees of your shady Walks and Groves be planted with Sweet-Brier, White Jessamine, and Honey-Suckles, environ'd at Bottom with a small Circle of Dwarf-Stock, Candy Turf and Pinks.

X. That all those Parts which are out of view from the House, be form'd into Wildernesses, Labyrinths, etc.

XI. That Hills and Dales, of easy Ascents, be made by Art, where Nature has not perform'd that work before.

XII. That Earths cast out of Foundations, etc., be carried to such Places for raising of Mounts, from which, fine Views may be seen.

XIII. That the Slopes of Mounts, etc., be laid with a moderate

Reclination, and planted with all sorts of Ever-Greens in a promiscuous Manner, so as to grow all in a Thicket; which has a prodigious fine Effect.

In this very Manner are planted two beautiful Mounts in the Gardens of the Honourable Sir Fisher Tench at Low Laxton in Essex.

XIV. That the Walks leading up the Slope of a Mount, have their Breadth contracted at the Top, full one half part; and if that contracted Part be enclosed on the sides with a Hedge whose Leaves are of a Light Green, 'twill seemingly add a great Addition to the Length of the Walk, when view'd from the other End.

XV. That all Walks whose Lengths are short, and lead away from any point of View, be made narrower at their further Ends than at the hither part; for by the Inclination of their Sides, they appear to be of a much greater Length than they really are; and the further end of every long Walk, Avenue, etc., appears to be much narrower than that End where you stand.

And the Reason is, that notwithstanding the Sides of such Walks are parallel to each other, yet as the Breadth of the further End is seen under a lesser Angle, than the Breadth of that Part where you stand, it will therefore appear as if contracted, although the Sides are actually parallel; for equal Objects always appear under equal Angles, Q.E.D.

XVI. That the Walks of a Wilderness be never narrower than 10 feet, or wider than 25 feet.

XVII. That the Walks of a Wilderness be so plac'd as to respect the best Views of the Country.

XVIII. That the Intersections of Walks be adorn'd with Statues, large open Plains, Groves, Cones of Fruit, of Ever-Greens, of Flowering Shrubs, of Forest Trees, Basons, Fountains, Sun-Dials, and Obelisks.

" When in the Garden's Entrance you provide,
The Waters, there united, to divide:
First, in the Center a large Fountain make;
Which from a narrow Pipe its Rise may take,

## THE PRAISE OF GARDENS

<blockquote>
And to the Air those Waves, by which 'tis fed,<br>
Remit agen ; About it raise a Bed<br>
Of Moss, or Grass ; but if you think this base,<br>
With well-wrought Marble circle in the Place."
</blockquote>

XIX. That in those Serpentine Meanders, be placed at proper Distances, large Openings, which you surprisingly come to; and in the first are entertain'd with a pretty Fruit-Garden, or Paradice-Stocks, with a curious Fountain, from which you are insensibly led through the pleasant Meanders of a shady delightful plantation; first into an even Plain environ'd with lofty Pines, in whose Center is a pleasant Fountain adorn'd with Neptune and his Tritons, etc., secondly into a Flower Garden, enrich'd with the most fragrant Flowers and beautiful Statues; and from thence through small Inclosures of Corn, open Plains, or small Meadows, Hop-Gardens, Orangeries, Melon-Grounds, Vineyards, Orchards, Nurseries, Physick Gardens, Warrens, Paddocks of Deer, Sheep, Cows, etc., with the rural Enrichments of Hay Stacks, Wood-Piles, etc.

<blockquote>
" Which endless are, with no fixed Limits bound,<br>
But fill in various forms the spacious Round,<br>
And endless Walks the pleas'd Spectator views,<br>
As ev'ry Turn the verdant scene renews."
</blockquote>

These agreeable surprising Entertainments in the pleasant Passage through a Wilderness, must without doubt, create new Pleasures at every Turn: And more especially when the Whole is so happily situated, as to be blessed with small Rivulets and purling Streams of clear Water, which generally admit of fine Canals, Fountains, Cascades, etc., which are the very Life of a delightful rural Garden.

<blockquote>
" Of pleasant Floods, and Streams, my Muse now sings,<br>
Of chrystal Lakes, Grotts, and transparent Springs;<br>
By these a Garden is more charming made,<br>
They chiefly beautify the rural Shade."
</blockquote>

And to add to the Pleasure of these delightful Meanders, I advise that the Hedge-Rows of the Walks be intermix'd with Cherries, Plumbs, Apples, Pears, Bruxel Apricots, Figs, Goose-

# BATTY LANGLEY 153

berries, Currants, Rasberries, etc., and the Borders planted with Strawberries, Violets, etc.

The most beautiful Forest-Trees for Hedges, are the English Elm, the Dutch Elm, the Lime-Tree, and Hornbeam: And although I have advis'd the Mixing of these Hedges of Forest-Trees with the aforesaid Fruits, yet you must not forget a Place for those pleasant and delightful Flowering-Shrubs, the White Jessemine, Honey Suckle, and Sweet-Brier.

*New Principles of Gardening, or The Laying out and Planting Parterres, Groves, Wildernesses, Labyrinths, Avenues, Parks, etc., after a more Grand and Rural Manner than has been done before. 1728.*

## CHAPTER VII.

THE SENTIMENTAL, LANDSCAPE, AND PARK SCHOOLS OF GARDENING, FOUNDED UPON PAINTING; AND THE CHINESE AND ENGLISH 'NATURAL' STYLES IN THE SECOND HALF OF THE EIGHTEENTH CENTURY.

**HENRY HOME, LORD KAMES (1696-1782).** THE emotions raised by the fine arts, are generally too nearly related to make a figure by resemblance; and for that reason their succession ought to be regulated as much as possible by contrast. . . . In gardening there is an additional reason for the rule: the emotions raised by that art are at best so faint, that every artifice should be used to give them their utmost strength: a field may be laid out in grand, sweet, gay, neat, wild, melancholy scenes; and when these are viewed in succession, grandeur ought to be contrasted with neatness, regularity with wildness, and gaiety with melancholy, so as that each emotion may succeed its opposite: nay it is an improvement to intermix in the succession, rude, uncultivated spots as well as unbounded views, which in themselves are disagreeable, but in succession heighten the feeling of the agreeable objects; and we have nature for our guide, who in her most beautiful landscapes often intermixes rugged rocks, dirty marshes, and barren stony heaths.—*Elements of Criticism*. (*Resemblance and Contrast*.)

Gardening, besides the emotions of beauty by means of regularity, order, proportion, colour, and utility, can raise emotions of grandeur, of sweetness, of gaiety, melancholy, wildness, and even of surprise or wonder. . . . In gardening as well as in architecture simplicity ought to be the governing taste. Profuse ornament hath no better effect than to confound the eye, and to prevent the object from making an impression as one entire whole. . . .

# LORD KAMES

The simplest idea of a garden, is that of a spot embellished with a number of natural objects, trees, walks, polished parterres, flowers, streams, etc. One more complex comprehends statues and buildings, that nature and art may be mutually ornamental. A third, approaching nearer perfection, is of objects assembled together, in order to produce, not only an emotion of beauty, essential to gardens of every kind, but also some other particular emotion, grandeur, for example, gaiety, or any other of those above mentioned.

The most perfect idea of a garden is an improvement upon the third, requiring the several parts to be arranged in such a manner, as to inspire all the different emotions that can be raised by gardening. In this idea of a garden, the arrangement is an important circumstance; for it has been shown that some emotions figure best in conjunction, and that others ought always to appear in succession and never in conjunction.

. . . Kent's method of embellishing a field is admirable; which is, to paint a field with beautiful objects, natural and artificial, disposed like colours upon a canvas. It requires indeed more genius to paint in the gardening way: in forming a landscape upon a canvas, no more is required but to adjust the figures to each other: an artist who lays out ground in Kent's manner, has an additional task; he ought to adjust his figures to the several varieties of the field. . . .

It seems to me far from an exaggeration that good professors are not more essential to a college, than a spacious garden, which ought to be formed with the nicest elegance, tempered with simplicity, rejecting sumptuous and glaring ornaments. In this respect so grand and important, the university of Oxford may justly be deemed a perfect model.—*Ibid.* (*Gardening and Architecture.*)

*Millin,* (*Dictionnaire des Beaux Arts*) thus comments on the above :—

"On peut dire que ce chapitre fut le prélude d'un bavardage esthétique et vague qui a été à la mode pendant quelque temps sur l'art des jardins, mais par lequel certainement personne n'aura appris l'art d'établir un beau jardin."

—vvv—

JOSEPH
SPENCE,
D.D.
(1698-1768). *Friend of Pope and Horace Walpole; in 1747 published 'Polymetis,' and later, 'Remarks on Virgil': in 1757, under the pseudonym of Sir Harry Beaumont, he translated the Jesuit Père Attiret's 'Account of the Emperor of China's Gardens, near Pekin,' which largely contributed to the revolution in European Garden-taste.*

. . . . . . .

AS for the Pleasure Houses, they are really charming. They stand in vast Compass of Ground. They have raised Hills from Twenty to Sixty foot high; which form a great Number of Little Valleys between them. The Bottoms of these Valleys are watered with clear streams; which run on till they join together, and form Larger pieces of Water and Lakes: They pass these Streams, Lakes, and Rivers, in beautiful and magnificent Boats: I have seen one, in particular, Seventy eight feet long, and Twenty four feet broad, with a very handsome House raised upon it. In each of these Valleys, there are Houses about the Banks of the Water, very well disposed; with their different Courts, open and close Porticos, Parterres, Gardens and Cascades; which, when viewed all together, have an admirable effect upon the eye.

They go from one of the Valleys to another, not by formal strait Walks as in Europe; but by various Turnings and Windings, adorned on the sides with little Pavilions and Charming Grottos; and each of these Valleys is diversified from all the rest, both by their manner of laying out the Ground, and in the Structure and Disposition of its Buildings.

All the Risings and Hills are sprinkled with Trees; and particularly with Flowering Trees, which are here very common. The sides of the Canals, or lesser Streams, are not faced (as they are with us) with smooth Stone, and in a straight Line; but look rude and rustic, with different Pieces of Rock, some of which jut out, and others recede inwards; and are pleased with so much Art, that you would take it to be the work of Nature.

# EARL OF CHATHAM

In some Parts the Water is wide, in others narrow; here it serpentises, and there spreads away, as if it was really pushed off by the Hills and Rocks. The Banks are sprinkled with Flowers, which rise up even through the Hollows in the Rock work, as if they had been produced there naturally. They have a great variety of them, for every season of the year.

Beyond these streams there are always Walks, or rather Paths, paved with small Stones; which lead from one Valley to another. These Paths too are irregular; and sometimes wind along the Banks of the Water, and at others run out wide from them.

. . . I have already told you that these little Streams, or Rivers, are carried on to supply several larger Pieces of Water, and Lakes. One of these Lakes is very near Five Miles round; and they call it a Meer or Sea. This is one of the most beautiful Parts in the whole Pleasure Grounds.

On the Banks are several Pieces of Buildings, separated from each other by the Rivulets and artificial Hills above mentioned.

But what is the most charming Thing of all is, an Island, or Rock, in the Middle of this Sea; raised, in a natural and rustic Manner about Six Feet above the Surface of the Water. On this rock there is a little Palace, which, however, contains an hundred different Apartments.—*A particular account of the Emperor of China's Gardens near Pekin, in a letter from F. Attiret,* 1757.[1]

―⋁⋁⋁―

LORD CHATHAM'S taste in laying out his grounds was exquisite. In the pleasing gardens of South Lodge, Enfield Chase, he designed a Temple of Pan, and its accompaniments, which are highly commended by Mr Whately, in his "Observations on Modern Gardening." Mr Hayley likewise mentions Mr Pitt's admirable taste in selecting points of picturesque scenery.

About 1754, Hayes Place, Kent, was purchased by Pitt. He rebuilt the house, and considerably added to the Grounds. Here

EARL OF CHATHAM
(1708-1778).

[1] See Illustration in Appendix.

## THE PRAISE OF GARDENS

General Wolfe dined the evening before he left England for Quebec, Chatham died, and William Pitt was born.

Lord Mahon, in his History of England, says that at Hayes in former years Chatham "had made improvements, which his memory fondly recalled: plantations for example, pursued with so much ardour and eagerness, that they were not even interrupted at nightfall, but were continued by torchlight, and with relays of labourers." The belts thus planted are pointed out to this day at Hayes (Timbs's "Anecdote Biography," which has a vignette of Hayes Place on the title-page).

—⁂—

**SAMUEL JOHNSON**
(1709-1784).

NOW was excited his (Shenstone's) delight in rural pleasures, and his ambition of rural elegance: he began from this time to point his prospects, to diversify his surface, to entangle his walks, and to wind his waters; which he did with such judgment and such fancy as made his little domain the envy of the great and the admiration of the skilful—a place to be visited by travellers and copied by designers. Whether to plant a walk in undulating curves, and to place a bench at every turn where there is an object to catch the view—to make water run where it will be heard, and to stagnate where it will be seen—to leave intervals where the eye will be pleased, and to thicken the plantation where there is something to be hidden—demand any great powers of the mind, I will not enquire: perhaps a surly and sullen spectator may think such performances rather the sport than the business of human reason. But it must at least be confessed that to embellish the form of nature is an innocent amusement, and some praise must be allowed by the most scrupulous observer to him who does best what multitudes are contending to do well.—*Lives of the Poets.* (*Shenstone.*)

The truth is, he (Dr Johnson) hated to hear about prospects and views, and laying out ground, and taste in gardening: "That was the best garden," he said, "which produced most roots and fruits; and that water was most to be prized which contained

## CHARLES DE BROSSES 159

most fish." He used to laugh at Shenstone most unmercifully for not caring whether there was anything good to *eat* in the streams he was so fond of; "as if," says Johnson, "one could fill one's belly with hearing soft murmurs, or looking at rough cascades!" He loved the sight of fine forest trees, however, and detested Brighthelmstone Downs, "because it was a country so truly desolate," he said, "that if one had a mind to hang one's self for desperation at being obliged to live there, it would be difficult to find a tree on which to fasten the rope." Walking in a wood, when it rained, was, I think, the only rural image he pleased his fancy with; "for," says he, "after one has gathered the apples in the orchard, one wishes them well-baked, and removed to a London eating-house for enjoyment."[1] With such notions who can wonder he passed his time uncomfortably enough with us, whom he often complained of for living so much in the country; "feeding the chickens," as he said I did, "till I starved my own understanding. Get, however," said he, "a book about gardening, and study it hard, since you will pass your life with birds and flowers, and learn to raise the *largest* turnips, and to breed the *biggest* fowls." It was vain to assure him that the goodness of such dishes did not depend upon their size; he laughed at the people who covered their canals with foreign fowls, "when," says he, "our own geese and ganders are twice as large: if we fetched better animals from distant nations, there might be some sense in the preference; but to get cows from Alderney, or water-fowl from China, only to see Nature degenerating round one, is a poor ambition indeed.—*Mrs Piozzi.* ("*Johnsoniana.*")

—◊◊◊—

**CHARLES DE BROSSES (1709-1777).**
*Comte de Tournai et de Montfalcon, first President of the Parliament of Dijon (the Burgundian Parliament.) Translator and editor of Sallust. The first edition of his Letters from Italy, written at the age of thirty, appeared in 1839.*

WHEN we reached them we forgot all our troubles, so singular is the appearance of that called the Beautiful Island (Isola Bella). Imagine a quantity of arcades, formed in

[1] This reminds one of Caraccioli's remark that "the only fruit in England that ripened in the open air were apples, for they were roasted."—*Founereau.*

the centre of the Lake, supporting a conical-shaped hill, cut on four sides, covered with thirty-six terraces, one over the other, nine on each side, and one of these sides covered with buildings. Each of these terraces is hung with palisades of jessamine, orange trees, or pomegranates, with pots of flowers placed on the ledge.

At the top of the hill is an equestrian figure, which forms a fountain, although we saw no water come from it, and there are also four statues on the angles. We have in France artificial and natural beauties better than this, but I have seen none more singular and curious than this isle, which resembles a palace in a fairy tale.

I would advise you, my dear Quinton, if you intend having a pleasant time in Rome, to take this house; you will have also the advantage of living within a stone's throw of Ludovisi Gardens. We go there every evening; they were Sallust's gardens in the olden times. They are worth describing, and I shall make honourable mention of them in the life of my old friend which I am now engaged in writing. One has not to go outside of Rome to enter these Gardens; they are the largest in the town, the best kept, and, being near to the most populous part of the City are much frequented. They contain numerous alleys, orange groves, and cypress copses, fountains, statues, vases and obelisk found *in situ quo* (which obelisk was formerly in Sallust's garden), and two little villas, not much in themselves, but full of treasures. These gardens although they might be better kept, have a delightful rural look about them. You must not expect to find gardens here like those of the Tuileries, nor arranged like those of the Palais Royal—little as the latter are to compare to the former. We have greatly surpassed the Italians in our gardens, although we owe ours to them. To compare gardens to buildings, those of the Tuileries are as superior to others as is St Peter's to other churches—that is to say, that none can be compared with them on the same scale. After all, the Italians follow their own taste, and adapt their gardens to their climate. They wish to have green trees all the year round, grass in their walks instead of

sand, long and palisaded walks, which always afford shade in their sunny land, and they require many fountains, great and small, a crowd of statues, obelisks and bas-reliefs, of which they possess a far greater store than we can show. They do not care a morsel for the keeping up of their gardens, nor for their cleanliness, and they cannot spend much on them. None of their gardens outside the town, not excepting the finest of all, that of Pamphili, which is the most rural and park-like, can compare to St Cloud in charm of rusticity or to Marly in picturesqueness. The best statues in the Ludovisi gardens are those of Silenus and Priapus.

. . . . The Belvedere and the park of the Ludovisi villas are mountains cut into terraces, covered with verdure, containing grottoes and superb cascades. The great fountain in the Belvedere is nearly equal to that of St Cloud; it is one of the finest things of its kind that can be seen. It descends, with a terrific sound of air and water, through pipes arranged expressly to make a perpetual cannonade. Besides this great fountain, there are numerous smaller ones; many in very good taste. The hill of the Belvedere is scooped out into three terraces, ornamented with grottoes and with façades, in rustic architecture, all ornamented with cascades in full play. The great cascade is crowned with columns with twisted flutings, through which the water circulates in spiral lines. The Ludovisi cascade has above it a platform containing a huge fountain basin. The long façades of grottoes, with porticoes, fountains, and statues are beautiful, both here and in the Aldobrandini gardens. In the latter, at the foot of the hill, is a very fine building designed by Porta. The Avenues below are fringed with oranges and palisades of laurel, with balustrades, on which are placed vases full of myrtle and pomegranates.—*Letters of Charles de Brosses, translated by Lord Ronald Gower.*

I BEGAN to traverse in ecstacy the orchard thus transformed; **ROUSSEAU**
and if I did not find exotics, and plants of Indian growth, (1712-1778).
I found those of the country arranged and blended so as to

produce a more smiling and pleasing effect. The turf verdant, yet close and crisp, was strewn with wild thyme, balsam, marjoram, and other sweet-scented herbs: A thousand lustrous wild-flowers were in sight, among which the eye distinguished with surprise some from the garden, which seemed to grow up naturally with the others. I encountered from time to time dark thickets, as impenetrable to the sun's rays as the depths of the forest: these thickets were formed of trees of the most flexible wood, whose branches had been made to bend back, hang on the ground, and take root, by an art akin to the natural habit of the mango in America.

In the more open places, I saw here and there, unordered and unsymmetrical, bushes of roses, raspberries, and gooseberries; patches of lilac, hazel, alders, seringas, broom, and clover, which clothed the earth whilst giving it an appearance of being uncultivated. I followed the serpentine and irregular alleys edged with these flowering thickets, and roofed with a thousand garlands of Judæa-vines, virgin-vines, hops, rose-weed, snake-weed, clematis, and other plants of this kind, with which honeysuckle and jasmine deigned to mingle. These garlands appeared to be thrown carelessly from one tree to another, as I had sometimes observed in forests, and formed above us, as it were, draperies, which sheltered us from the sun, whilst under foot we had soft, pleasant, and dry walking upon fine moss, without sand, grass, or rough shoots. Only then I discovered, not without surprise, that these green and bushy shades, which in the distance had looked so imposing, were only formed of these creeping parasite plants, which, trained along the trees, wrapped their heads in the thickest foliage, and their feet in shadow and coolness. I observed too, that by means of a very simple industry, several of these plants had been induced to take root on the trunks of trees and so to spread more, being nearer the top, while requiring less room. You will easily understand that the fruitage is none the better for all these additions; but only in this spot has the useful been sacrificed to the agreeable, and in the rest of the grounds such care has been bestowed upon the plants and trees, that with this orchard the less, the fruit crop is larger than before.

If you think how charming it is, sometimes deep in the wood, to see wild fruit and even to refresh yourself with it, you will understand the pleasure it gives to find in this artificial desert excellent and ripe fruit, although thinly sown and of bad complexion, but which, for all that, affords the pleasure of search and choice.

All these little paths were confined and crossed by a limpid and clear stream, sometimes circling amid the grass and flowers in almost imperceptible threads, now in larger streams flowing over a pure mosaic of gravel, which made the water more transparent.

I can imagine, said I to them, a rich man from Paris or London, master of this house, bringing with him an expensive architect to spoil Nature. With what disdain would he enter this simple and mean place! With what contempt would he have all these weeds up-rooted! What fine avenues he would open out! what beautiful alleys he would have pierced! what fine goose-feet, what fine trees like parasols and fans! what finely fretted trellises! what beautifully drawn yew-hedges, finely squared and rounded! what fine bowling-greens of fine English turf, rounded, squared, sloped, ovaled: what fine yews carved into dragons, pagodas, marmosets, every kind of monster! With what fine bronze vases, what fine stone-fruits he would adorn his garden![1]

When all that is carried out, said M. de Wolmar, he will have made a very fine place, which one will scarcely enter, and will always be anxious to leave to seek the country: a dismal spot, where no one will walk, but through which one will pass to go for a walk; whereas in my country strolls I am often eager to return, that I may come and walk here.

[1] I am convinced the time is at hand, when we shall no longer have in gardens anything that is found in the country; we shall tolerate neither plants nor shrubs; we shall only like porcelain flowers, baboons, arbour-work, sand of all colours, and fine vases full of nothing.

## THE PRAISE OF GARDENS

I only see in these vast and richly ornamented estates the vanity of the proprietor and of the artist, who, always eager to display, the one his wealth and the other his talent, prepare, at a great expense, ennui for any one desirous of enjoying their work. A false taste for grandeur, which is not made for man, poisons his pleasures.

The "grand air" is always melancholy: it makes us think of the miseries of the man who affects it. Amid his parterres and grand alleys, his littleness does not increase: a tree twenty feet high shelters him as well as one of sixty feet: he never occupies more than his three feet of space, and is lost like a worm in his immense possessions.

There is another taste directly opposed to that, and still more ridiculous, in so far as it does not even permit the enjoyment of the walk, for which gardens are made.

I understand, I replied: it is that of those pretty virtuosi, those small florists, who swoon at the sight of a ranunculus, and prostrate themselves before a tulip. Whereupon I related to them what had formerly happened to me in London, in that flower-garden into which we were ushered with so much formality, and where we saw displayed so pompously all the treasures of Holland on four beds of dung. I did not forget the ceremony of the parasol, and of the little wand, with which they honoured me, all unworthy as I was, as well as the other spectators.

I humbly confessed to them, how, being desirous to exert myself when my turn came, and to venture to go into ecstacies at the sight of a tulip, of which the colour appeared to me striking, and the form elegant, I was mocked, hooted, hissed by all the connoisseurs; and how the garden-professor, passing from his contempt for the flower to that for the panegyrist, did not condescend to look at me during the whole interview. I think, I added, that he greatly regretted having profaned his wand and parasol. . . .

What then will the man of taste do, who lives for the sake of living, who can enjoy by himself, who seeks real and simple pleasures, and who wishes to make for himself a walk within

reach of his house. He will make it so commodious and so
agreeable, that he can please himself there at all hours of the
day, and moreover so simple and so natural, that he seems to
have done nothing. He will combine water, verdure, shade and
coolness; for Nature too combines all these things. He will
give symmetry to nothing; it is the enemy to nature and variety;
and all the alleys of an ordinary garden have so strong a
resemblance, that you think you are always in the same one:
he will level the soil to walk on it comfortably: but the two
sides of his alleys will not be always exactly parallel; its direction will not be always in a straight line, it will have a certain
vagueness, like the gait of a leisurely man who sways as he
walks. He will not be anxious to open up fine prospects in
the distance: the taste for points of view and distances comes
from the tendency which most men have to be pleased only
where they do not happen to be: they are always longing for
what is far from them, and the artist, who does not know how
to make them sufficiently satisfied with what surrounds them,
allows himself this resource to amuse them: but the man of
whom I speak, has not this anxiety: and when he is well where
he is, he does not desire to be elsewhere.—*Julie, or the New
Héloise.*

—〰〰—

**STERNE**
(1713-1768).

M ETHINKS I see my contemplative girl now in the gardens,
watching the gradual approaches of Spring. Dost not thou
mark with delight the first vernal buds? the snow-drop, and
primrose, these early and welcome visitors, spring beneath thy
feet. Flora and Pomena already consider thee as their handmaid; and in a little time will load thee with their sweetest
blessing. The feathered race are all thy own, and with them,
untaught harmony will soon begin to cheer thy morning and
evening walks. Sweet as this may be, return—return, the birds
of Yorkshire will tune their pipes, and sing as melodiously as
those of Staffordshire.

I think I see you looking twenty times a day at the house,

almost counting every brick and pane of glass, and telling them at the same time, with a sigh, you are going to leave them. Oh! happy modification of matter! they will remain insensible of thy loss. But how wilt thou be able to part with thy garden? The recollection of so many pleasing walks must have endeared it to you. The trees, the shrubs, the flowers, which thou rearedst with thy own hands, will they not droop and fade away sooner upon thy departure? Who will be thy successor to nurse them in thy absence? Thou wilt leave thy name upon the myrtle-tree. If trees and shrubs and flowers could compose an elegy, I should expect a very plaintive one upon this subject.—*Letters to Miss L. (afterwards Sterne's wife and Editress of his Letters dedicated to David Garrick, June 1775, by Lydia Sterne de Medalle).*

—ᴡᴡᴡ—

**DIDEROT'S "ENCYCLOPÆDIA" (1751-1765).** THE French, plunged so long in barbarism, had no ideas of the decoration of gardens or of gardening, before the age of Louis XIV. It is in the reign of that prince that this art was on the one hand created, perfected by la Quintinie for utility, and by le Nôtre for pleasure. . . .

Let us, without partiality, cast our eye over this century. How do we at present decorate the most beautiful situations of our choice, with which, le Nôtre would have been able to achieve wonders? We bring to bear upon them a ridiculous and paltry taste. The long straight alleys appear to us insipid; the palissades cold and formless; we delight in devising twisted alleys, scroll-work parterres and shrubs pruned into tufts; the largest portions are divided-up into little lots always decorated without grace, without nobility, without simplicity. Baskets of flowers, faded after a few days, have taken the place of lasting flower-beds; we see everywhere vases of terra-cotta, Chinese grotesques, caricatures, and other such works in sculpture of mean workmanship, which plainly enough prove to us that mediocrity has extended its empire over all our productions of this kind.

It is not so with a neighbouring nation, amongst whom gardens in good taste are as common as magnificent palaces are rare. In England, these kinds of walks, practicable in all weathers, seem made to be the sanctuary of a sweet and placid pleasure; the body is there relaxed, the mind diverted, the eyes are enchanted by the verdure of the turf, and bowling-greens; the variety of flowers offers pleasant flattery to the smell and sight. There is no pretence of lavishing on these places, I do not say small, but even the most beautiful works of art.

Nature alone, modestly arrayed, and never made up, there spreads out her ornaments and benefits. How the fountains beget the shrubs and beautify them! How the shadows of the woods put the streams to sleep in beds of herbage! Let us call the birds in these places of delight; their concerts will draw man hither, and will form a hundred times better eulogy of a taste for sentiment, than marble and bronze whose display but produces a stupid wonderment.—*Encyclopædia.* (*Jardin.*)

---

*Poet and author. Seems to have been the inventor of the term "landscape-gardening," as well as of the actual "Sentimental Farm," the "Leasowes."* **WILLIAM SHENSTONE** (1714-1763).

GARDENING may be divided into three species—kitchen-gardening—parterre gardening—and landscape or picturesque-gardening: which latter is the subject intended in the following pages. It consists in pleasing the imagination by scenes of grandeur, beauty or variety. Convenience merely has no share here any further than it pleases the imagination. . . .

Objects should indeed be less calculated to strike the immediate eyes than the judgment or well-informed imagination, as in painting. . . .

I believe, however, the sublime has generally a deeper effect than the merely beautiful.

I use the words landscape and prospect, the former so expressive of home scenes, the latter of distant images. Prospects should take in the blue distant hills; but never so remotely, that they be not distinguishable from clouds. Yet this mere effect is what the vulgar value.

Landscape should contain variety enough to form a picture upon canvass; and this is no bad test, as I think the landscape-painter is the gardener's best designer. The eye requires a sort of balance here; but not so as to encroach upon probable nature. A wood or hill may balance a house or obelisk; for exactness would be displeasing. . . . The eye should look rather down upon water: customary nature makes this requisite. . . . It is not easy to account for the fondness of former times for straight-lined avenues to their houses; straight-lined walks through their woods; and in short every kind of a straight-line; where the foot is to travel over what the eye has done before. . . .

By the way I wonder that lead statues are not more in vogue in our gardens. Though they may not express the finer lines of a human body, yet they seem perfectly well calculated, on account of their duration, to embellish landscapes, were they some degrees inferior to what we generally behold.[1] . .

It is always to be remembered in gardening, that sublimity or magnificence, and beauty or variety, are very different things. Every scene we see in nature is either tame and insipid, or compounded of those. . . .

Gardeners may be divided into three sorts, the landscape-gardener, the parterre-gardener, and the kitchen-gardener, agreeably to our first division of gardens.

I have used the word landscape-gardeners, because, in pursuance of our present taste in gardening, every good painter of landscape appears to me the most proper designer. The misfortune of it is that these painters are apt to regard the execution of their work, much more than the choice of subject. . . .

Hedges, appearing as such, are universally bad. They discover art in nature's province.

[1] The taste for lead statues and vases in gardens is now being stimulated by Mr W. R. Lethaby, Mr Inigo Thomas, and other Architects. See the former's admirable monograph on "Leadwork." (Macmillan, 1893.)

Water should ever appear, as an irregular lake, or winding stream. . . .
In gardening, it is no small point to enforce either grandeur or beauty by surprize; for instance, by abrupt transition from their contraries—but to lay a stress upon surprize only; for example, on the surprize occasioned by an aha! (Ha! Ha!) without including any nobler purpose; is a symptom of bad taste, and a violent fondness for mere concetto.—*Unconnected Thoughts on Gardening.*

—⋘—

*As a boy, entered service of Lord Cobham at Stowe and became his head gardener. On his recommendation was appointed Royal Gardener at Hampton Court in 1750 by George II. Brown, asked by the King to "improve" the gardens at Hampton Court, declined, "out of respect to himself and his profession." He probably planted the famous vine in 1769, from a slip of one at Valentines, Ilford, Essex ; he resided many years at Hampton Court. Chatham, who corresponded with Brown, writes of him in a letter to Lady Stanhope: " The writer, Lancelot Brown, Esquire, en titre d'office: please to consider he shares the private hours of the King, dines familiarly with his neighbour of Sion (Duke of Northumberland) and sits down at the tables of all the House of Lords."*

**LANCELOT BROWN ("CAPABILITY")**
**(1715-1783).**

LANCELOT BROWN had the supreme control over the art of modern gardening for nearly half a century. He had been bred as a kitchen gardener at Stowe. Having been recommended by Lord Cobham to the Duke of Grafton at Wakefield Lodge, Northamptonshire, he directed the formation of a large lake, and afterwards at Blenheim, where he covered a narrow valley with an artificial river, and gave a character to a lofty bridge. He exultingly said, that "the Thames would never forgive him!" . . . Croome in Worcestershire and Fisherwick in Staffordshire are his only works entirely new, as taken from fields. But it would be barely possible to enumerate all the villas and their environs which he remodelled, according to the system upon which he acted, with persevering uniformity, for he was a consummate mannerist. His reputation and consequent wealth gave him almost exclusive pretensions. Clumps and belts were multiplied to a disgusting monotony, and abounded in every part of the kingdom. The ancient avenues disappeared, as if before the wand of a magician; every vestige of the formal or the reformed taste was forcibly removed. Whatever approached to a right line was held in abhorrence. Brown's influence upon public opinion produced, in time, two memorable controversies, which may be styled the "Chinese," and the "Picturesque."

Yet during his high career, he found some of the most approved theorists to gratify him with no measured praise. Walpole is courtly and discreet, as far as not becoming his partizan. Whately treats him with bare allusion; but Mason gives an unequivocal encomium, whilst he afterwards combats his principles.[1]

By his partizans, Brown has been complimented as 'the living leader of the powers of nature, and the realiser of Kent's Elysian scenes'; an immoderate praise which has excited the most severe contempt. But, in candour, he should not have been charged with all the faults of his numerous followers. He was not likely to form himself upon the pictures of Salvator, Claude, or Poussin, who was himself ignorant of mechanical drawing. His principles were known, and his plans manufactured by others. His management of water was more worthy of admiration than of grounds or plantations, in which his mind appears to have been occupied by a single object, not consulting, in some instances, the genius of the place. The uniformity of 'clumps and belts' (as he called them) by such constant repetition has lost its claim to our surprise or approbation; and that claim originated as much in the novelty as the beauty of the objects. Unlike the instance of the prophet of old, his mantle has been appropriated to themselves by numerous successors; unless indeed, the precedence claimed by

[1] 'Bards yet unborn
Shall pay to Brown, that tribute fitliest paid
In strains the beauty of his scenes inspire.'
—*English Garden, Book I.*

Repton be allowed by the public.¹—*Dallaway's* '*Anecdotes of Gardening.*'²

—⁓⁓⁓—

H E (Count Algarotti) is highly civil to our nation, but there is one little point, in which he does not do us justice. I am the more solicitous about it, because it relates to the only taste which we can call our own, the only proof of our original talent in matter of pleasure; I mean, our skill in gardening, and laying out grounds. That the Chinese have this beautiful art in high perfection, seems very probable from the *Jesuit's Letters*, and more from Chamber's little discourse published some few years ago. But it is very certain, we copied nothing from them, nor had anything but nature for our model. It is not forty years since the art was born among us; and it is sure, that there was nothing in Europe like it, and as sure, we then had no information on this head from China at all.—*Letter to William Taylor Howe, dated Cambridge, September* 10, 1763.

THOMAS GRAY (1716-1771).

And so you have a garden of your own, and you plant and transplant, and are dirty and amused; are not you ashamed of yourself? Why, I have no such thing, you monster; nor ever shall be either dirty or amused as long as I live! My gardens

¹ Repton, in his enquiry into the changes of taste in Landscape Gardening, offers the following defence of Brown :—' After his death he was immediately succceded by a numerous herd of his foremen and working gardeners, who from having executed his designs, became consulted as well as employed in the several works which he had entrusted them to superintend. And this introduced all the bad taste attributed to Brown, by enlarging his plans. Hence came the mistaken notion, that greatness of dimensions would produce greatness of character: hence proceeded the immeasurable length of naked lawn : the tedious length of belts and drives : the useless breadth of meandering roads: the tiresome monotony of shrubberies and pleasure-grounds : the naked expanse of water accompanied by trees, and all the unpicturesque features which disgrace modern gardening, and which brought on Brown's system the opprobrious epithets of " bare and bald." '

² What may be called the literary history of gardening shall be succinctly and impartially attempted.—*Dallaway.*

are in a window like those of a lodger up three pair of stairs in Petticoat Lane or Camomile Street, and they go to bed regularly under the same roof that I do: dear, how charming it must be to walk out in one's own garden, and sit on a bench in the open air with a fountain and a leaden statue and a rolling stone and an arbour! have a care of sore throat though, and the *agoe.—Letter to the Rev. Norton Nicholls.* (*Pembroke College, June* 24, 1769.)

---

**HORACE WALPOLE**
(1717-1797).

WHEN I had drank tea I strolled into the garden. They told me it was now called the '*pleasure-ground*.' What a dissonant idea of pleasure! Those groves, those *alleys*, where I have passed so many charming moments, are now stripped up, or overgrown; many fond paths I could not unravel, though with a very exact clue in my memory. I met two gamekeepers and a thousand hares! In the days when all my soul was tuned to pleasure and vivacity, I hated Houghton and its solitude; yet I loved this garden; as now, with many regrets, I love Houghton; —Houghton, I know not what to call it: a monument of grandeur or ruin!—*Letters.*

A cottage and a slip of ground for a cabbage and a gooseberry-bush such as we see by the side of a common, were in all probability the earliest seats and gardens: a well and bucket succeeded to the Pison and Euphrates.[1]

As settlements increased, the orchard and the vine-yard followed; and the earliest princes of tribes possessed just the necessaries of a modern farmer.

Matters, we may well believe, remained long in this situation; and though the generality of mankind form their ideas from the import of words in their own age, we have no reason to think that for many centuries the term *garden* implied more than a kitchen-garden or orchard. When a Frenchman reads of the

[1] Two of the four rivers enclosing Paradise, the others being Gihon and Hiddekel.

# HORACE WALPOLE 173

Garden of Eden, I do not doubt but he concludes it was something approaching to that of Versailles, with clipt hedges, berceaus, and trellis-work. If his devotion humbles him so far as to allow that, considering who designed it, there might be a labyrinth full of Æsop's fables, yet he does not conceive that four of the largest rivers in the world were half so magnificent as an hundred fountains full of statues by Girardon. It is thus that the word *garden* has at all times passed for whatever was understood by that term in different countries. But that it meant no more than a kitchen-garden or orchard for several centuries, is evident from those few descriptions that are preserved of the most famous gardens of antiquity.

(Walpole then describes Alcinous's garden in Homer; the hanging gardens of Babylon; Pliny's gardens, at his Laurentine and Tusculan villas; the gardens of Herculaneum, of which latter he says:)

In the paintings found at Herculaneum are a few traces of gardens, as may be seen in the second volume of the prints. They are small square inclosures formed by trellis-work, and espaliers,[1] and regularly ornamented with vases, fountains and Caryatides, elegantly symmetrical, and proper for the narrow spaces allotted to the garden of a house in a capital city. From such I would not banish those playful waters that refresh a sultry mansion in town, nor the neat trellis, which preserves its wooden verdure better than natural greens exposed to dust. Those treillages in the gardens at Paris, particularly on the Boulevard, have a gay and delightful effect. They form light corridores, and transpicuous arbours through which the sunbeams play and chequer the shade, set off the statues, vases, and flowers, that marry with their gaudy hotels, and suit the galant and idle society who paint the walks between their parterres, and realize the fantastic scenes of Watteau and Durfé.

From what I have said, it appears how naturally and insensibly the idea of a kitchen-garden slid into that which has for so many ages been peculiarly termed a garden, and by our

[1] At Warwick castle is an ancient suit of arras, in which there is a garden exactly resembling these pictures of Herculaneum.—*Walpole's Note.*

ancestors in this country, distinguished by the name of a pleasure-garden.

A square piece of ground was originally parted off in early ages for the use of the family—to exclude cattle and ascertain the property, it was separated from the fields by a hedge. As pride and desire of privacy increased, the inclosure was dignified by walls; and in climes where fruits were not lavished by the ripening glow of nature and soil, fruit-trees were assisted and sheltered from surrounding winds by the like expedient; for the inundation of luxuries which have swelled into general necessities, have almost all taken their source from the simple fountain of reason.

When the custom of making square gardens enclosed with walls was thus established, to the exclusion of nature and prospect, pomp and solitude combined to call for something that might enrich and enliven the insipid and unanimated partition. Fountains, first invented for use, which grandeur loves to disguise and throw out of the question, received embellishments from costly marbles, and at last, to contradict utility, tossed their waste of waters into air in spouting columns. Art, in the hands of rude man, had at first been made a succedaneum to nature; in the hands of ostentatious wealth it became the means of opposing nature; and the more it traversed the march of the latter, the more nobility thought its power was demonstrated.

Canals measured by the line were introduced instead of meandering streams, and terrasses were hoisted aloft in opposition to the facile slopes that imperceptibly unite the valley to the hill. Balustrades defended these precipitate and dangerous elevations, and flights of steps rejoined them to the subjacent flat from which the terrass had been dug. Vases and sculpture were added to these unnecessary balconies, and statues furnished the lifeless spot with mimic representations of the excluded sons of men. Thus difficulty and expense were the constituent parts of those sumptuous and selfish solitudes; and every improvement that was made, was but a step farther from nature. The tricks of water-works to wet the unwary, not to refresh the panting spectator, and parterres embroidered in patterns like a petticoat, were but the childish endeavours of fashion and novelty to reconcile greatness to what it had surfeited on.

To crown these impotent displays of false taste, the sheers were applied to the lovely wildness of form with which nature has distinguished each various species of tree and shrub.

The venerable oak, the romantic beech, the useful elm, even the aspiring circuit of the lime, the regular round of the chesnut, and the almost moulded orange-tree, were corrected by such fantastic admirers of symmetry. The compass and square were of more use in plantations than the nursery-man. The measured walk, the quincunx, and the etoile imposed their unsatisfying sameness on every royal and noble garden. Trees were headed, and their sides pared away; many French groves seem green chests set upon poles. Seats of marble, arbours and summer-houses terminated every visto; and symmetry, even where the space was too large to permit its being remarked at one view, was so essential, that, as Pope observed:

> '... Each alley has a brother,
> And half the garden just reflects the other.'

Knots of flowers were more defensibly subjected to the same regularity. Leisure, as Milton expressed it,

> 'In trim gardens took his pleasure.'

In the garden of Marshal de Biron at Paris, consisting of fourteen acres, every walk is buttoned on each side by lines of flower-pots which succeed in their seasons. When I saw it, there were nine thousand pots of Asters, or la Reine Marguerite.

We do not precisely know what our ancestors meant by a bower, it was probably an arbour; sometimes it meant the whole frittered enclosure, and in one instance it certainly included a labyrinth. Rosamund's bower was indisputably of that kind, though whether composed of walls or hedges we cannot determine. A square and a round labyrinth were so capital ingredients of a garden formerly, that in Du Cerceau's architecture, who lived in the time of Charles IX. and Henry III., there is scarce a ground plot without one of each. The enchantment of antique appellations have consecrated a pleasing idea of a royal residence, of which we now regret the extinction. Havering in the Bower, the jointure of many dowager queens, conveys to us the notion of a romantic scene.

In Kip's views of the seats of our nobility and gentry, we see the same tiresome and returning uniformity. Every house is approached by two or three gardens, consisting perhaps of a gravel-walk and two grass-plats, or borders of flowers. Each rises above the other by two or three steps, and as many walks and terrasses; and so many iron gates, that we recollect those ancient romances, in which every entrance was guarded by nymphs or dragons. At Lady Oxford's at Piddletown in Dorsetshire, there was, when my brother married, a double enclosure of thirteen gardens each I suppose not a hundred yards square, with an enfilade of correspondent gates; and before you arrived at these, you passed a narrow gut between two stone terrasses, that rose above your head, and which were crowned by a line of pyramidal yews. A bowling-green was all the lawn admitted in those times, a circular lake the extent of magnificence.

(Then follows reference to Hentzner, and the origin of parks, 'the principle of modern gardening':—

Eulogy of Milton's idea of Paradise, about which he says: 'He seems with the prophetic eye of taste to have conceived, to have foreseen modern gardening. . . . The description of Eden is a warmer and more just picture of the present style than Claud Lorraine could have painted from Hagley or Stourhead.'—

Analysis of Milton's description: 'And recollect that the conceits in Italian gardens, and Theobalds and Nonsuch, were the brightest originals that his memory could furnish.'—

. Censure of Sir William Temple's idea of a garden: quotation from his essay, describing Moor Park in Hertfordshire.

Spence's account of Chinese Emperor's garden.—)

But the capital stroke, the leading step to all that has followed, was (I believe the first thought was Bridgman's) the destruction of walls for boundaries, and the invention of fossès—an attempt then deemed so astonishing that the common people called them Ha! Ha's! to express their surprise at finding a sudden and unperceived check to their walk.

... I call a sunk fence the leading step, for these reasons No sooner was this simple enchantment made, than levelling, mowing and rolling, followed. The contiguous ground of the park without the sunk fence was to be harmonized with the lawn within; and the garden in its turn was to be set free from its prim regularity, that it might assort with the wilder country without. The sunk fence ascertained the specific garden, but that it might not draw too obvious a line of distinction between the neat and the rude, the contiguous out-lying parts came to be included in a kind of general design: and when nature was taken into the plan, under improvements, every step that was made, pointed out new beauties and inspired new ideas.

At that moment appeared Kent; painter enough to taste the charms of landscape, bold and opinionative enough to dare and dictate, and born with a genius to strike out a great system from the twilight of imperfect essays. He leaped the fence, and saw that all nature was a garden. He felt the delicious contrast of hill and valley changing imperceptibly into each other, tasted the beauty of the gentle swell, or concave scoop, and remarked how loose groves crowned an easy eminence with happy ornament, and while they called in the distant view between their graceful stems, removed and extended the perspective by delusive comparison.

Thus the pencil of his imagination bestowed all the arts of landscape on the scenes he handled. The great principles on which he worked were perspective, and light and shade. Groups of trees broke too uniform or too extensive a lawn; evergreens and woods were opposed to the glare of the champain, and where the view was less fortunate, or so much exposed as to be beheld at once, he blotted out some parts by thick shades, to divide it into variety, or to make the richest scene more enchanting by reserving it to a farther advance of the spectator's step. Thus selecting favourite objects, and veiling deformities by screens of plantation; sometimes allowing the rudest waste to add its foil to the richest theatre, he realized the compositions of the greatest masters in painting. Where objects were wanting to animate his

## THE PRAISE OF GARDENS

horizon, his taste as an architect could bestow immediate termination. His buildings, his seats, his temples, were more the works of his pencil than of his compasses. We owe the restoration of Greece and the diffusion of architecture to his skill in landscape.

But of all the beauties he added to the face of this beautiful country, none surpassed his management of water. Adieu to canals, circular basons, and cascades tumbling down marble steps, that last absurd magnificence of Italian and French villas. The forced elevation of cataracts was no more. The gentle stream was taught to serpentize seemingly at its pleasure, and where discontinued by different levels, its course appeared to be concealed by thickets properly interspersed, and glittered again at a distance where it might be supposed naturally to arrive. Its borders were smoothed, but preserved their waving irregularity. A few trees scattered here and there on its edges sprinkled the tame bank that accompanied its mæanders; and when it disappeared among the hills, shades descending from the heights leaned towards its progress, and framed the distant point of light under which it was lost, as it turned aside to either hand of the blue horizon.—*On Modern Gardening.*

—∿∿∿—

CLAUDE HENRI WATELET, (1718-1786). *Receiver-General of Finances, Member of the French Academy and of the Royal Academy of Painting and Sculpture, author of poem on 'The Art of Painting' and 'Essay on Gardens'; a critic of the type of the Comte de Caylus. He created the Moulin-Joli (near Paris) of which the Prince de Ligne wrote:—*

'*Voici un lieu peut-être encore plus selon mon cœur (qu'Ermenonville), et plus près de Paris. C'est en quittant un jour son vain tourbillon, qu'errant à l'aventure, le long de la Seine, je le perdis de vue au Moulin-Joli, et que je me trouvai moi-même, car ce n'est qu'aux champs qu'on peut se trouver. Qui que vous soyez, si vous n'êtes pas des cœurs endurcis, asseyez-vous entre les bras d'un saule, au Moulin-Joli, sur le bord de la rivière. Lisez, voyez et pleurez, ce ne sera pas de tristesse, mais d'une sensibilité délicieuse. Le tableau de votre âme viendra s'offrir à vous. . . . Allez-y, incrédules. . . . Méditez sur les inscriptions que le goût y a dictées. Méditez avec le sage, soupirez avec l'amant, et bénissez Watelet.*'

# WATELET

*Watelet divides his 'Essay on Gardens' into 'useful establishments and places of pleasure'; the first is represented by the 'Ferme ornée,' which he depicts in detail. He next treats of ancient Parks, which owed their origin to feudal pride; Modern Parks, the three characters of which he classes under the heads Picturesque, Poetic and Romantic (Romanesque). In the 'Places of Pleasure' he finds the power of fashion and imitation too strong, good taste yielding to artifice 'impotently busy' ('péniblment industrieux') and the 'mechanical' overwhelming the 'liberal.'*

ON verra donc, dans les Jardins, les ornemens factices préférés aux agrémens naturels. Les arbres seront soumis à des formes et à des usages qui les défigurent. . . . Les branches et les feuillages mutilés et transformés en plafond, ou en murs, n'oseront végéter que sous les loix du fer, des distributions semblables à celle des appartemens reproduiront, en plein air, des salles, des cabinets, des boudoirs, où se trouvera le même ennui qui remplit ceux que couvrent les lambris dorés. L'eau stagnera dans des bassins ronds ou quarrés; elle sera emprisonnée dans des tuyaux, pour attendre quelques instants de liberté de la volonté du fontainier. Le marbre qui prétendra ennoblir par la richesse ce qui dans la Nature est bien au-dessus de la somptuosité, s'y montrera souvent dans un état de dépérissement, qui contraste avec ses prétentions à la magnificence. Le triste bronze ternira l'émail riant des fleurs. . . .

Cependant, dans quelques coins oubliés, la Nature encore hasardera d'user de ses droits à la liberté; et s'il arrive que ces arbres, tourmentés par le fer et le niveau, vieillissent, ils acquerront, en dépit de leurs tirans, des proportions grandes, nobles et robustes. Alors, parvenus à élever leurs cimes au-dessus de la portée des échelles et des croissans, ils reprendront les traits de cette beauté majestueuse et pittoresque qui appelle et fixe les regards. C'est alors que de larges allées, devenues de superbes galeries, formeront leur voûte au sommet des airs. Les branchages étendus sans gêne, s'approcheront à leur gré, s'entrelasseront sans contrainte, et se feront justement admirer par des effets que l'art ne peut imiter. . . .

Dans les parcs l'utile doit prêter des secours à l'agrément, et l'Art doit être subordonné généralement à la Nature.

Dans les lieux de plaisance l'Art peut s'arroger le droit de se montrer avec moins de réserve.

Enfin, dans les jardins destinés à des sensations plus délicates et plus recherchées, l'artifice et la richesse employés à des effets surnaturels et à des prodiges, s'effacent de l'emporter sur la Nature.

Mais pour revenir encore un instant à des notions primitives et simples ; dans quelques dispositions de promenades et de jardins que ce soit, le premier principe est d'entremêler sans cesse les motifs de curiosité qui engagent à changer de place aux objets qui attachent et qui invitent à s'arrêter.

. . . Aussi, des Arts connus, celui qui a plus de relations d'idée avec l'Art des Jardins, c'est celui de la Peinture.

L'Architecture s'en est cependant presque toujours occupé jusqu'ici, et il était assez naturel que ne regardant pas les jardins comme susceptibles d'une certaine perfection *liberale* qu'on y désiré aujourd'hui, l'Artiste à qui l'on confiait le soin des édifices, fût chargé de ce qui ne semblait en être que les accessoires. D'ailleurs on appercevait une relation, en apparence assez fondée, entre les formes adoptées pour les jardins, et celles qu'employait l'Architecture ; mais on ne faisait pas attention à la différence qu'apporte dans les deux Arts la seule nature des plans sur lesquels ils s'exercent.

L'Architecte, dans la partie libérale de son Art, a pour objet de rendre agréable toutes les parties d'un plan vertical.

Le décorateur de jardin exerce ses talens pour embellir un plan horizontal.

Le premier doit satisfaire le plutôt et avec le moins d'effort possible, le spectateur qui ne destine à son plaisir que des regards et quelques momens.

Le second ne doit découvrir que l'une après l'autre les beautés de son ouvrage à ceux qui consacrent à cette jouissance des heures entières.

D'après des intentions si différentes ; les plans simples, les formes symmétriques, les proportions faciles à saisir, les masses régulières seront préférées par l'Architecte ; tandis que les plans

mistérieux, les formes dissemblables, les effets plus appérçus que leurs principes, les accidents qui combattent la régularité offriront les moyens les plus favorables au décorateur. La précision du trait, la propreté des détails seront les recherches de l'Architecture ; une certaine indécision pleine d'agrémens, cette négligence qui sied si bien à la Nature seront les finesses de l'Art des Jardins.—
*Essai sur les Jardins*, 1774.

—ww—

AS to the produce of a Garden, every middle-aged person of observation may perceive, within his own memory, both in town and country, how vastly the consumption of vegetables is increased. Green stalls in cities now support multitudes in a comfortable state, while gardeners get fortunes. Every decent labourer also has his garden, which is half his support as well as his delight; and common farmers provide plenty of beans, peas, and greens, for their hinds to eat with their bacon; and those few that do not are despised for their sordid parsimony, and looked upon as regardless of the welfare of their dependants. Potatoes have prevailed in this little district by means of premiums, within these twenty years only, and are much esteemed here now by the poor, who would scarce have ventured to taste them in the last reign.

GILBERT WHITE, of SELBORNE (1720-1793).

Our Saxon ancestors certainly had some sort of cabbage, because they call the month of February Sprout-cale; but long after their days, the cultivation of gardens was little attended to. The religious being men of leisure, and keeping up a constant correspondence with Italy, were the first people among us that had gardens and fruit-trees in any perfection, within the walls of their abbies, priories, and monasteries, where the lamp of knowledge continued to burn, however dimly. In them men of business were formed for the state: the art of writing was cultivated by the monks; they were the only proficients in mechanics, gardening, and architecture. The barons neglected every pursuit that did not lead to war, or tend to the pleasure of the chase.

It was not till gentlemen took up the study of horticulture

themselves, that the knowledge of gardening made such hasty advances. Lord Cobham, Lord Ila, and Mr Waller of Beaconsfield, were some of the first people of rank that promoted the elegant science of ornamenting without despising the superintendence of the kitchen quarters and fruit walls.—*The Natural History of Selborne.* (*Letter LXXIX.*)

ADAM SMITH (1723-1790).

THE circumstances of gardeners, generally mean, and always moderate, may satisfy us that their great ingenuity is not commonly over-recompenced. Their delightful art is practised by so many rich people for amusement, that little advantage is to be made by those who practise it for profit; because the persons who should naturally be their best customers, supply themselves with all their most precious productions. — *The Nature and Causes of the Wealth of Nations.*

WILLIAM GILPIN (1724-1804).

*Owner of a school at Cheam; Rector of Boldre, near New Forest; author of Lives of Bernard Gilpin, Cranmer, Wycliffe, and others; also of 'Forest Scenery,' 'Essay on Prints,' and many volumes on Picturesque Beauty and Travels in the British Isles, from the year 1776, with his own illustrations; his name is generally joined with those of Uvedale Price and Payne Knight on the 'Picturesque' side of the Controversy with the 'Improvers' and Landscape Gardeners, 'Capability' Brown and 'Amenity' Repton.*

FROM clumps we naturally proceed to Park scenery, which is generally composed of combinations of clumps, interspersed with lawns. . . . As the park is an appendage of the house, it follows that it should participate of its neatness and elegance. Nature, in all her great walks of landscape, observes this accommodating rule. She seldom passes abruptly from one mode of scenery to another, but generally connects different species of landscape by some third species, which participates of both. Thus, as the house is connected with the country through the medium of the park, the park should partake of the neatness of the one, and of the wildness of the other. As the park is a scene either planted by art, or if naturally woody, artificially improved, we expect a beauty and contrast in its clumps, which we do not look for in the wild scenes of Nature. We expect to see its lawns and their appendages contrasted with each other, in shape, size and disposition, from which a variety of artificial scenes will arise. We expect, that when trees are left standing as individuals, they should be the most beautiful of their kind, elegant and well balanced. . . . If there be a natural river or a real ruin in the scene, it may be a happy circumstance: let the best use be made of it; but I should be cautious in advising the creation of either. At least I have rarely seen either ruins or rivers well manufactured. Mr Brown, I think, has failed more in river making than in any of his attempts. An artificial lake has sometimes a good effect; but neither propriety nor beauty can arise from it, unless the heads and extremities of it are perfectly well managed and concealed; and after all the success is hazardous. . . .

As the garden, or pleasure ground, as it is commonly called, approaches nearer to the house than the park, it takes of course a higher polish. Here the lawns are shorn instead of being grazed; the roughness of the road is changed into an elegant, gravel walk; and knots of flowers and flowering shrubs are introduced, yet blended with clumps of forest trees, which connect it with the park. Single trees also take their station here with great propriety. Here too, if the situation suits it, the elegant temple may find a place. But it is an expensive, a hazardous and often a useless decoration. . . . In the most polished landscape, unless nature and simplicity lead the way, the whole will be deformed.— '*Remarks on Forest Scenery*,' *edited by Sir T. Dick Lauder*, 1834 (*who has also edited Humphry Repton's complete works*).

—∿∿∿—

*Mason was Author of two tragedies and of the poem* '*The English Garden*,' 1772.
Dallaway says these Notes and Commentaries to "The English Garden" are by W. Burgh. Loudon quotes them as by Mason.—See '*Encyclopædia of Gardening.*'

WILLIAM MASON (1725-1797) and WILLIAM BURGH, LL.D.

THE first book (of 'The English Garden') contains the general principles of the art, which are shown to be no other than those which constitute beauty in the sister art of landscape-painting; beauty which results from a well-chosen variety of curves, in contradistinction to that of architecture, which arises from a judicious symmetry of right lines, and which is thus shown to have afforded the principle on which that formal disposition of garden ground, which our ancestors borrowed from the French and Dutch, proceeded: a principle never adopted by nature herself, and therefore constantly to be avoided by those whose business it is to embellish nature. . . .

The picturesque principle being thus established, the second book proceeds to a more practical discussion of the subject, but confines itself to one point only, the disposition of the ground plan, and that very material business immediately united with it, the proper disposition and formation of the paths and fences. The necessity of attending constantly to the curvilinear principle is first shown, not only in the formation of the ground plan, with respect to its external boundary, but in its internal swellings and sinkings where all abruptness or angular appearances are as much to be avoided, as in the form of the outline that surrounds the whole.

The pathways or walks are next considered, and that peculiar curve recommended for their imitation, which is so frequently found in common roads, footpaths, etc., and which being casually produced appears to be the general curve of nature.

The rest of the book is employed in minutely describing the method of making sunk fences, and other necessary divisions of the pleasure-ground or lawn from the adjacent field or park. . . .

The third book proceeds to add natural ornament to that ground-plan, which the second book has ascertained, in its two capital branches, wood and water. . . . Factitious or artificial ornaments (apparently including flowers) in contradistinction to natural ones last treated, form the general subject of the fourth book, and conclude the plan.

I had before called Bacon the prophet, and Milton the herald, of true taste in Gardening (on account of their introducing 'natural wildness'). I here call Addison, Pope, Kent, etc., the champions of this free taste, because they absolutely brought it into execution.
—*General Postscript to the 'English Garden.'*

# SIR WILLIAM CHAMBERS

*Born at Stockholm; employed by George III. to plan the gardens at Kew, of* **SIR**
*which he published the 'Plans, Elevations and Views' in folio, 1763, having in* **WILLIAM**
*1757 issued 'Designs of Chinese Buildings,' etc., drawn by him as a youth* **CHAMBERS**
*in China. 1772, appeared his 'Dissertation on Oriental Gardening' and a* (1726-1796).
*'Treatise on Civil Architecture'; he built Somerset House.*

THE Gardens of Italy, France, Germany and Spain, and of all the other countries where the antient style still prevails, are in general mere cities of verdure; the walks are like streets conducted in strait lines, regularly diverging from different large open spaces, resembling public squares; and the hedges with which they are bordered, are raised, in imitation of walls, adorned with pilasters, niches, windows and doors, or cut into colonades, arcades and porticos; all the detached trees are shaped into obelisks, pyramids and vases; and all the recesses in the thickets bear the names and forms of theatres, amphitheatres, temples, banqueting halls, ball rooms, cabinets and saloons. The streets and squares are well manned with statues of marble or lead, ranged in regular lines, like soldiers at a procession; which, to make them more natural, are sometimes painted in proper colours, and finely gilt. The lakes and rivers are confined by quais of hewn stone, and taught to flow in geometrick order; and the cascades glide from the heights by many a succession of marble steps: not a twig is suffered to grow as nature directs, nor is a form admitted but what is scientific, and determinable by the line or compass.

In England, where this antient style is held in detestation, and where, in opposition to the rest of Europe, a new manner is universally adopted, in which no appearance of art is tolerated, our gardens differ very little from common fields, so closely is common nature copied in most of them; there is generally so little variety in the objects, such a poverty of imagination in the contrivance, and of art in the arrangement that these compositions rather appear the offspring of chance than design; and a stranger is often at a loss to know whether he be walking in a meadow, or in a pleasure-ground, made and kept at a very considerable expence: he sees nothing to amuse him, nothing to excite his curiosity, nor anything to keep up his attention.

## THE PRAISE OF GARDENS

At his first entrance, he is treated with the sight of a large green field, scattered over with a few straggling trees, and verged with a confused border of little shrubs and flowers; upon farther inspection, he finds a little serpentine path, twining in regular S's amongst the shrubs of the border, upon which he is to go round, to look on one side at what he has already seen, the large green field; and on the other side at the boundary, which is never more than a few yards from him, and always obtruding upon his sight: from time to time he perceives a little seat or temple stuck up against the wall; he rejoices at the discovery, sits down, rests his weary limbs, and then reels on again, cursing the line of beauty, till spent with fatigue, half roasted by the sun, for there is never any shade, and tired for want of entertainment, he resolves to see no more: vain resolution! there is but one path; he must either drag on to the end, or return back by the tedious way he came.

Such is the favourite plan of all our smaller gardens: and our larger works are only a repetition of the small ones; more green fields, more shrubberies, more serpentine walks and more seats; like the honest bachelor's feast, which consisted in nothing but a multiplication of his own dinner; three legs of mutton and turneps, three roasted geese, and three buttered apple-pies.

It is, I think, obvious that neither the artful, nor the simple style of Gardening here mentioned, is right: the one being too extravagant a deviation from nature; the other too scrupulous an adherence to her. One manner is absurd; the other insipid and vulgar: a judicious mixture of both would certainly be more perfect than either.

But how this union can be effected is difficult to say. The men of art and the friends of nature, are equally violent in defence of their favourite system; and, like all other partizans, loth to give up anything, however unreasonable. . . .

Whether the Chinese manner of Gardening be better or worse than those now in use amongst the Europeans, I will not determine: comparison is the surest as well as the easiest test of truth; it is in every man's power to compare and to judge for himself. . . .

Though the Chinese artists have nature for their general model, yet they are not so attached to her as to exclude all appearance of art; on the contrary they think it on many occasions necessary to make an ostentatious shew of their labour. Nature, say they, affords us but few materials to work with. . . .

The Chinese are therefore no enemies to strait lines; because they are, generally speaking, productive of grandeur, which often cannot be attained without them: nor have they any aversion to regular geometrical figures, which they say are beautiful in themselves, and well suited to small compositions, where the luxuriant irregularities of nature would fill up and embarrass the parts they should adorn. . . .

The usual method of distributing Gardens in China, is to contrive a great variety of scenes to be seen from certain points of view; at which are placed seats or buildings adapted to the different purposes of mental or sensual enjoyments.

The perfection of their Gardens consists in the number and diversity of these scenes, and in the artful combination of their parts; which they endeavour to dispose in such a manner, as not only separately to appear to the best advantage, but also to unite in forming an elegant and striking whole. . . . In their large Gardens they contrive different scenes for the different times of the day; disposing at the points of view buildings, which from their use point out the proper hour for enjoying the view in its perfections. . . . They have beside, scenes for every season of the year: some for the winter, generally exposed to the southern sun, and composed of pines, firs, cedars, evergreen oaks, phillyreas, hollies, yews, and many other evergreens.—'*A Dissertation on Oriental Gardening,*' *by Sir William Chambers, Knt., Comptroller General of his Majesty's Works,* 1772.

—ᜠᜠ—

I CUT off all the rosebuds of the trees in our little garden (which is a secret) to make them blow at the end of the season, when I hope to enjoy your company there after our trees.
—*Letter to his Daughter.*

JOHN WILKES
(1727-1797).

**OLIVER GOLDSMITH (1728-1774).**

THE English have not yet brought the art of gardening to the same perfection with the Chinese, but have lately begun to imitate them; Nature is now followed with greater assiduity than formerly; the trees are suffered to shoot out into the utmost luxuriance; the streams no longer forced from their native beds, are permitted to wind along the vallies: spontaneous flowers take the place of the finished parterre, and the enamelled meadow of the shaven green.

Yet still the English are far behind us in this charming art: their designers have not yet attained a power of uniting instruction with beauty. An European will scarcely conceive my meaning, when I say, that there is scarce a garden in China which does not contain some fine moral, couch'd under the general design, where one is not taught wisdom as he walks, and feels the force of some noble truth or delicate precept resulting from the disposition of the groves, streams or grotto's.

Permit me to illustrate what I mean by a description of my gardens at Quamsi. My heart still hovers round those scenes of former happiness with pleasure; and I find satisfaction in enjoying them at this distance, though but in imagination.

You descended from the house between two groves of trees, planted in such a manner that they were impenetrable to the eye; while on each hand the way was adorned with all that was beautiful in porcelaine, statuary and painting.

This passage from the house opened into an area surrounded with rocks, flowers, trees and shrubs, but all so disposed as if each was the spontaneous production of nature. As you proceeded forward on this lawn, to your right and left hand were two gates, opposite each other, of very different architecture and design; and before you lay a temple built rather with minute elegance than ostentation.

The right-hand gate was planned with the utmost simplicity or rather rudeness; ivy clasp'd round the pillars, the baleful cyprus hung over it; time seemed to have destroyed all the smoothness and regularity of the stone: two champions with lifted clubs appeared in the act of guarding its access; dragons and serpents were seen in the most hideous attitudes, to deter the spectator from approaching; and the perspective view that lay behind seemed dark and gloomy to the last degree; the stranger was tempted to enter only from the motto: PERVIA VIRTUTI. The opposite gate was formed in a very different manner; the architecture was light, elegant and inviting; flowers hung in wreaths round the pillars; all was finished in the most exact and masterly manner; the very stone of which it was built still preserved its polish; nymphs wrought by the hand of a master, in the most alluring attitudes, beckoned the stranger to approach, while all that lay behind as far as the eye could reach, seemed gay, luxuriant, and capable of affording endless pleasure. The motto itself contributed to invite him; for over the gate was written these words, FACILIS DESCENSUS.—*The Citizen of the World.*

I was led into this train of thinking upon lately visiting the beautiful gardens of the late Mr Shenstone,[1] who was himself a poet, and possessed of that warm imagination, which made him ever foremost in the pursuit of flying happiness. Could he but have foreseen the end of all his schemes, for whom he was improving, and what changes his designs were to undergo, he would have scarcely amused his innocent life with what, for several years, employed him in a most harmless manner, and abridged his scanty fortune. As the progress of this improvement is a true picture of sublunary vicissitude, I could not help calling up my imagination, which, while I walked pensively along, suggested the following reverie.

As I was turning my back upon a beautiful piece of water, enlivened with cascades, and rock-work, and entering a dark walk, by which ran a prattling brook, the Genius of the place appeared before me, but more resembling the God of Time, than him more peculiarly appointed to the care of gardens. Instead of shears, he bore a scythe; and he appeared rather with the implements of husbandry, than those of a modern gardener.

[1] At the Leasowes.

## THE PRAISE OF GARDENS

Having remembered this place in its pristine beauty, I could not help condoling with him on its present ruinous situation. I spoke to him of the many alterations which had been made, and all for the worse; of the many shades which had been taken away, of the bowers that were destroyed by neglect, and the hedge-rows that were spoiled by clipping. The Genius, with a sigh, received my condolement and assured me that he was equally a martyr to ignorance and taste, to refinement and rusticity.

Seeing me desirous of knowing farther, he went on:

'You see in the place before you the paternal inheritance of a poet; and, to a man content with little, fully sufficient for his subsistence: but a strong imagination, and a long acquaintance with the rich, are dangerous foes to contentment.

'Our poet, instead of sitting down to enjoy life, resolved to prepare for its future enjoyment, and set about converting a place of profit into a scene of pleasure. This he at first supposed could be accomplished at a small expense; and he was willing for a while to stint his income, to have an opportunity of displaying his taste. The improvement in this manner went forward; one beauty attained led him to wish for some other; but still he hoped that every emendation would be the last. It was now, therefore, found that the improvement exceeded the subsidy— that the place was grown too large and too fine for the inhabitant. But that pride which was once exhibited, could not retire; the garden was made for the owner, and though it was become unfit for him, he could not willingly resign it to another. Thus the first idea of its beauties contributing to the happiness of his life, was found unfaithful; so that, instead of looking within for satisfaction, he began to think of having recourse to the praises of those who came to visit his Improvement.

'In consequence of this hope, which now took possession of his mind, the gardens were open to the visits of every stranger; and the country flocked round to walk, to criticise, to admire, and to do mischief. He soon found that the admirers of his taste left by no means such strong marks of their applause, as the envious did of their malignity. All the windows of his temples,

# IMMANUEL KANT

and the walls of his retreats, were impressed with the characters of profaneness, ignorance and obscenity; his hedges were broken, his statues and urns defaced, and his lawns worn bare. It was now, therefore, necessary to shut up the gardens once more, and to deprive the public of that happiness which had before ceased to be his own.—*Essays: 'On the Tenants of the Leasowes.'*

---

I WOULD divide the Art of Painting, as one of the second kind of Formative Arts, representing sense-appearance (*Sinnen-schein*) artistically united with ideas, into that of beautiful presentation of Nature, and beautiful combination of her products. The first would be pure Painting, the second Pleasure-gardening. For the first gives only the appearance of physical extent, whereas the second represents this according to truth, but only the appearance of its application and use for other ends, as merely for the play of the imagination in the contemplation of its forms. The latter is nothing else but decoration of the ground with the same variety (grasses, flowers, bushes and trees, even waters, hills and valleys) as Nature presents to the sight, only in different combinations and according to certain ideas. But the beautiful juxtaposition of material things is also only presented to the eye, as in painting. —*Criticism of the Aesthetic Judgment.*

IMMANUEL KANT (1724-1804).

---

*Professor of Botany at Cambridge, a post he obtained by fraud. 'One of the first writers on Horticulture, who concentrated in any considerable degree, the light of other Sciences for its improvement. His works abound in information collected from books and men of learning.'*—G. W. Johnson. *He was the author of twenty-nine different works on Botany, Husbandry and Gardening. His 'General Treatise of Husbandry and Gardening' is a summary of what he had previously written on the subject.*

RICHARD BRADLEY, F.R.S. (d. 1732).

WHEN I consider these things, I cannot enough lament the want of learning among the gardeners of this nation; who in their spare hours, were they Men of Letters, might very greatly improve themselves by reading the works of the Ancients, and bringing their several propositions to practice; and also might bring to light many of the most hidden branches of the art of Gardening, and have the pleasure of producing several effects, as good and useful, perhaps, as most of those that are called modern discoveries. For upon a deliberate perusal of Columella, Varro, and the other gentlemen I am to descant upon in the following work, I find many excellent pieces, which have not hitherto been made common with us; many more that have not yet been try'd in our fields and gardens.—*A Survey of the Ancient Husbandry and Gardening.*

—⁂—

**ERASMUS DARWIN, F.R.S., (1731-1802).** *M.D., Edin., and practised as Physician at Derby; grandfather of Charles Darwin; author of 'Botanic Garden or Loves of the Plants,' and 'Zoonomia.'*

THE beautiful colours of the petals of flowers with their polished surfaces are scarcely rivalled by those of shells, of feathers, or of precious stones. Many of these transient beauties, which give such brilliancy to our gardens, delight at the same time the sense of smell with their odours: yet have they not been extensively used as articles, either of diet, medicine, or the arts.—*Phytologia, or The Philosophy of Agriculture and Gardening,* 1800.

—⁂—

**WILLIAM COWPER (1731-1780).** MY green-house is never so pleasant as when we are just upon the point of being turned out of it. The gentleness of the autumnal suns, and the calmness of this latter season, make it a much more agreeable retreat than we ever find it in the summer; when the winds being generally brisk, we cannot cool it by admitting a sufficient quantity of air, without being at the same time incommoded by it. But now I sit with all the windows and the door wide open, and am regaled with the scent of every flower, in a garden as full of flowers as I have known how to make it. We keep no bees, but if I lived in a hive, I should hardly hear more of their music. All the bees in the neighbourhood resort to a bed of mignonette opposite to the window, and pay me for the honey they get out of it by a hum, which, though rather monotonous, is as agreeable to my ear as the whistling of my linnets. All the sounds that Nature utters are delightful, at least in this country.—*Letter to Rev. John Newton.* (*Sept.* 18, 1784.)

My dear, I will not let you come till the end of May, or beginning of June, because before that time my green-house will not be ready to receive us, and it is the only pleasant room belonging to us. When the plants go out, we go in. I line it with mats, and spread the floor with mats; and there you shall sit with a bed of mignonette at your side, and a hedge of honeysuckles, roses, and jasmine; and I will make you a bouquet of myrtle every day. Sooner than the time I mention, the country will not be in complete beauty.—*Letter to Lady Hesketh.* (*Olney, February* 9, 1786.)

I write in a nook that I call my boudoir; it is a summer-house not bigger than a sedan-chair; the door of it opens into the garden that is now crowded with pinks, roses, and honeysuckles, and the window into my neighbour's orchard. It formerly served an apothecary as a smoking-room; at present, however, it is dedicated to sublimer uses.—*Letter to Hill.*

## CHAPTER VIII

GARDEN DESIGN AS A LIBERAL OR FINE ART: THE 'COMPOSITION' OF NATURE OR LANDSCAPE — REACTION OF THE 'PICTURESQUE' WRITERS — COSMOPOLITANISM AND ECLECTICISM IN THE GARDEN.

**THOMAS WHATELY** (d. 1772). *Loudon in the 'Encyclopædia of Gardening' says of him:—' His " Observations on Modern Gardening," published in 1770, is the grand fundamental and standard work on English gardening. It is entirely analytical; treating first of the materials, then of the scenes, and lastly, of the subjects of gardening. Its style has been pronounced by the learned Eason, inimitable; and the descriptions with which his investigations are accompanied have been largely copied and amply praised by Alison in his work on "Taste." The book was soon translated into the continental languages, and is judiciously praised in the* Mercure de France, Journal Encyclopédique *and* Wieland's Journal. *G. Mason alone dissents from the general opinion, enlarging on the very few faults or peculiarities which are to be found in the book.' Whately was the brother of the then proprietor of Nonsuch Park, near Epsom in Surrey, which place he mainly assisted in 'laying out.' He was for a short time secretary to the Earl of Suffolk; then M.P. and secretary to the Treasury; besides this work, he published two anonymous English pamphlets, and died in 1772. After his death his* Remarks on Shakespeare *were published in 1785 by his brother, the Rev. Dr J. Whately, and a second edition in 1808 by his nephew Dr R. Whately, Archbishop of Dublin, 1831.*

GARDENING, in the perfection to which it has been lately brought in England, is entitled to a place of considerable rank among the liberal arts. It is as superior to landskip-painting as a reality to a representation: it is an exertion of fancy, a subject for taste; and being released now from the restraints of regularity and enlarged beyond the purposes of domestic convenience, the most beautiful, the most simple, the most noble scenes of nature are all within its province: for it is no longer confined to the spots from which it borrows its name, but regulates also the disposition and embellishments of a park, a farm, or a riding; and the business of a gardener is to select and to apply whatever is great, elegant, or characteristic in any of them; to discover and to shew all the advantages of the place upon which he is employed; to supply its defects, to correct its faults, and to improve its beauties. For all these operations, the objects of nature are still his only materials. . . . Nature, always simple, employs but four materials in the composition of her scenes, *ground*, *wood*, *water*, and *rocks*. The cultivation of nature has introduced a fifth species, the *buildings* requisite for the accommodation of men.

But the art of gardening aspires to more than imitation: it can create *original* characters and give expressions to the several scenes superior to any they can receive from illusions. Certain properties and certain dispositions of the objects of nature are adapted to excite particular ideas and sensations.

*Elegance* is the peculiar excellence of a garden; *greatness* of a park; *simplicity* of a farm; and *pleasantness* of a riding.

Whatever contributes to render the scenes of nature delightful is amongst the subjects of gardening; and animate as well as inanimate objects are circumstances of beauty or character. Nothing is unworthy of the attention of a gardener which can tend to improve his compositions, whether by immediate effects or by suggesting a train of pleasing ideas. The whole range of nature is open to him, from the parterre to the forest; and whatever is agreeable to the senses or the imagination he may appropriate to the spot he is to improve; it is a part of his business to collect into one place the delights which are generally dispersed through different species of country.

But in this application, the genius of the place must always be particularly considered; to force it is hazardous; and an attempt to contradict it is always unsuccessful.

The art of laying out gardens has, within a little more than a hundred years in Europe, and within a much less time in Great

Britain started up from being one of the mechanical arts, in which mere utility is intended, to be one of the fine arts, which join utility to pleasure. In all ages men have known the use of fruits, flowers and herbs for the pleasure of the senses: it is almost only in our age that they have introduced into gardens one half of the pleasing objects of art and nature for the entertainment of the imagination. . . .

There seem in nature to be four different dispositions of grounds distinct from each other, and which create distinct and separate sentiments.

The first situation is that of a high-land country, consisting of great and steep mountains, rocks, lakes, impetuous rivers, etc. Such a place is Inverary.

The sentiment which a situation like this creates in the breast of a beholder is obviously, and every one feels it, that of Grandeur.

The next is what one may call a romantic disposition of grounds, consisting of small valleys, woods hanging over them, smooth rivers, the banks steep but accessible, etc. Places like this we have on the banks of many of our small rivers in the low countries of Scotland.

The sentiment which such a situation seems to flatter, is that of composure of mind, and perhaps even of melancholy.

A third situation is that of grounds running by gentle falls and risings easily into each other. In situations of this kind are placed many of the English modern gardens; and particularly those which Kent delighted in laying out. Such a situation, as it is generally attended with great verdure, cultivation and populousness, naturally creates in the mind that sentiment of cheerfulness which society and action are apt to create.

The last situation is that of a dead flat. A situation of this kind may, from its verdure, or from its extent, or from its contrast with other grounds that surround it, create some particular sentiment, but merely considered in itself, it appears to create little or none. . . .

The English in such a situation attempt to humour nature; the French in such a situation attempt to hide her. . . . In a small flat the serpentine river, the open planting, the lake and island, the moulding the flat into the gentle unevennesses of Kent, have a rural and cheerful aspect; of this last particularly there is a fine instance in Kent's plantation at the back of the house at Chiswick, compared with the phlegmatic plantation of Bridgeman on the same side of the garden. But these contrivances though proper for a small plain, are too few and simple for a great one. . . . We must frankly call in the assistance of art to make the chief parts of the garden. For this reason bosquets, statues, vases, trees cut into great arches, jets-d'eau, cascades forced up and made to tumble down an hundred steps, regular basins, peristiles, temples, long vistas, the star plantation, etc., are in taste here. All the magnificence of Versailles, without its conceits or its too often repeated symmetry, should be admitted. To supply the defects of natural prospect the walks should terminate in artificial vistas; and in the light, perhaps even painted cascades and buildings, as practised by some of our English gardeners, if pardonable anywhere, are pardonable here. To get too, as far as can be, the advantage of natural prospects, the artificial mounts of the flat Dutch gardens should here be introduced. . . . As there is but little pleasure to the imagination arising from this situation itself, so it should be contrived to give as much pleasure to the senses as possible; for this reason, the flowers should be sown in beds and parterres, to be the more obviously seen, and to throw out their sweets stronger into the air; fruits of the finest kinds should be spread through the compartments; the flowering shrubs should be planted in clumps, and assorted in their colours and flowers with all the nicety of a well made-up flower-pot; to strike with the stronger surprize, the trees should be all exotics, and of the rarest kinds; and to create a greater variety, though the Chinese form from its fantastical appearance and the Corinthian order from its magnificence, be, in general, the prospect for such an adorned garden, yet buildings of all species under the sun that have dignity in them should here find place. In short, every agreeable object that creates surprize and that exhibits a view of magnificent art should enter into the composition of such a garden. It is more proper when in the neighbourhood of a great city and thrown open to all the world than when in a remote province, and for that reason some of the French gardens have an excuse which those at Stow have not.

A garden like this is a kind of fairy land. It is in comparison of other gardens what an opera is in comparison of a tragedy: neither of them should be judged by the ordinary rules of experience or taste, but by the capricious ones of variety and Fancy.— *Observations on Modern Gardening, and laying out Pleasure-Grounds, Parks, Ridings, &c.* (*A new edition* 1801, *with notes by Horace Walpole, late Earl of Orford; and ornamented with coloured plates, chiefly designed by Mr Woollet, of Hall Barn, Esher, Carlton House, Wooburn, Pain's Hill and Hagley.*)

—⁂—

CHARLES JOSEPH, PRINCE DE LIGNE (1735-1814).

*One of the most cosmopolitan and accomplished men of arms and letters who ever lived: ' Le seul étranger,' said Mme. de Staël, ' qui dans le genre Français, soit devenu modèle, au lieu d'être imitateur.' ' I have six or seven countries,' he declared. Born in Brussels, he entered the Austrian army at the age of* 17, *fought with distinction in the Seven Years War, and was then invited to the French Court by the Comte d'Artois. Sent on a mission to Russia, he was made a Field-Marshal by Catherine the Great, with an estate in the Crimea. A Citizen of the World with the freedom of all the Courts of Europe, a dandy of the first water and a brilliant wit and ' causeur,' he had also a most delicate instinct for letters, a vein of serious reflection worked in epigram, and a fine taste in designing gardens.*

SAINTE-BEUVE writes thus of the Prince's Essay on Gardens:—
Parmi les ouvrages décousus échappés au prince de Ligne dans la première moitié de sa vie, et qui le peignent le mieux à cette date, je distingue ce qu'il a écrit sur les jardins à l'occasion de ceux de Belœil. *Coup d'œil sur Belœil*, avait-il intitulé son Essai (1781) par un de ces jeux de mots et de ces sortes de calembours qui sont un de ses petits travers. C'était le temps où l'abbé Delille publiait son poëme des *Jardins*, et disait de ce

beau lieu de Belœil près d'Ath en Belgique, qui était la propriété et en partie la création du Prince de Ligne.[1]

'Belœil, tout à la fois magnifique et champêtre.' On était alors en France dans une veine de création et de renouvellement pour les jardins : le genre anglais s'y introduisait et y rompait l'harmonie de le Nôtre. C'était à qui s'étudierait à diversifier la nature et à en profiter pour l'embellir. M. de Girardin créait Ermenonville, M. de Laborde Méréville ; M. Boutin avait Tivoli, et M. Watelet Moulin-Joli. Belœil était, et j'aime à le croire, est encore un assemblage et un composé charmant de jardins anglais et français, quelque chose de naturel et de regulier, d'élégant et de majestueux. Tout ce qui, à Belœil, était grand, regulier, dans le genre de Le Nôtre, venait du Père du prince : lui, il s'occupa d'y jeter le varié et l'imprévu ; il ne lui manque que plus de temps pour achever son œuvre, son poëme. Il n'est pas exclusif ; il serait bien fâché de bannir la ligne droite ; il ne veut pas substituer la monotonie anglaise à la monotonie française, ce qui de son temps arrivait déjà ; mais en jardins comme en amour, il est d'avis qu'il ne faut pas tout montrer d'abord, sans quoi, le premier moment passé, l'on baille et l'on s'ennuie. Il traite des bâtiments dans leurs rapports avec la campagne : autre doit être une *résidence* et un *palais*, autre un *château*, autre une maison de *plaisance*, une maison de *campagne*, une maison des *vignes*, etc. ; mais quels que soient les bâtiments, 'j'exclus,' dit-il, 'tous ceux qui ont une façade bourgeoise, sans mouvement dans le toit ou la bâtisse, sans milieu, sans saillant sur les ailes, ou en plâtre avec un air vulgaire ; et je recommande encore le beau ou le simple, le magnifique ou le joli, et *toujours le propre*, le piquant et le distingué.'—*Causeries du Lundi.* Vol. viii.

---

[1] 'His patrimonial house, the Castle of Belœil, still stands in quaint supremacy over the modest village of Ligne, about six miles from Ath, in Belgium. It has endured seven centuries of change ; and its gothic peculiarities, with its old-world garden, and its ancient horn-beam, yet answer to the prolix description thereof given in the Prince's published letters.'—*Dr Doran's* '*Habits and Men.*'

## THE PRAISE OF GARDENS

I should like to inflame the whole world with my taste for gardens. It seems to me impossible for an evil-doer to share it. He is not capable of any taste at all. But if, for this reason, I rate highly the wild-herborist, the deft and agile butterfly-hunter, the minute scrutinizer of shells, the stern lover of minerals, the icy geometrician, the three frenetics of poetry, music and painting, the abstract thinker and the subtle chemist, there is no virtue which I do not attribute to the man who loves to project and execute gardening.

Engrossed in this passion, the only one which keeps pace with advancing years, a man day by day casts off such as disturb peace of mind or social order. When he has passed the draw-bridge at the gate of the city, that refuge of moral and physical corruption, to work in or enjoy the country, his heart laughs with Nature, and experiences the same feeling as his lungs in absorbing the fresh air, which regenerates them.

Fathers, instil into your children the garden-mania. They will grow up the better for it. Let other arts be only studied to heighten the beauty of the one I advocate. Engaged in planning how to shade a glen, or in contriving how to divert the course of a stream, one is too busy ever to become a dangerous citizen, an intriguing general, or a caballing courtier. If such a man had designs to write against the laws, to lay his grievances before the ministry of war, to overthrow a superior, or hatch plots at court, he would arrive too late, for his head would be full of his Judæa trees, or his flower-borders, or with the ordering of his grove of plane-trees. . . .

Let not the mason's art come in awkwardly to overload the Earth, under pretence of supporting it: let not their lime burn up the enamel of the meadows—let not their cement make the daisy, the violet and the pansy lie low, let not their feet soil the bed of the Nymphs. I love to see them sport with young Sylvan boys, for whom they begin to have a budding passion, as yet unconscious. Steps are alarming. Gentle slopes are required for their sports.

Let all trades be banished from gardens. Above all no

PRINCE DE LIGNE 201

scaffolding, no trellises, paintings, hoops: let the branches at their own will try to find one another.

I see no other rule for bridges, than not to make two alike. We can give ourselves up to all the extravagances of our imagination. Happily architecture did not take possession of these at the time it usurped gardens; if however, a highly decorated garden scene neighbour to some august temple, required an elaborate bridge, without copying that of Czarskozelo[1] or Wilton, a colonnade may be permitted. With that exception, the more fantastic they are, the more pleasure they will give: let them be high enough not to impede navigation, but not arched enough to cause one to slip when crossing. Taste, or rather the situation, will decide if they should be partially concealed, or entirely exposed.

I detest sketches of great things. There must be no failure when one takes them in hand. No Ruins of Palmyra in the taste of General Conway. Their whiteness, their low columns, are a bad example: their vaults, too well kept, are ridiculous. Ruins ought to offer an idea of things deserving respect, which have passed, and of celebrated people who inhabited them; but when we see the Greek of many Englishmen and the Gothic of Mr Walpole, one is tempted to think the delirium of a nightmare has presided over their work. I like his 'Castle of Otranto,' as much as that on the Thames, which is as mad, and not more lively.

Temples ought to inspire pleasure, or recall that secret terror,

[1] The Garden of Zarskojeselo or Tzarsco-Celo (Imperial Spot) mentioned by de Ligne was laid out by Catherine II. of Russia about 1768. She acquired the English taste in gardening from reading the 'Hausvater' by Count Munchhausen. Her own architect and gardener being unable to satisfy her orders 'to follow Nature' she sent to England for a landscape gardener in the person of John Busch of Hackney. In 1772 he commenced his work at Pulkova, about five miles from Tzarsco-Celo, which, visited by Catherine in 1774 completely satisfied her, with its winding, shady, gravel walks and fine lawn. 'This is what I have long wished to have,' she exclaimed. From 1775 till 1789 Busch worked in the Tzarsco-Celo gardens, and was succeeded by his son Joseph Busch. The Emperor Paul, her successor, preferred straight walks and clipped trees, and Alexander patronised both styles.—(*Loudon.*)

which one felt of old on entering them. But what is the sensation when one sees one above the other, spoiling by a *templo-mania*, those which like the temple of friendship, would deserve our commendation? My Lord Temple has been too much led astray by his name.[1] I should prize the house of Lord Batita (*sic*) near Bristol, but it has only the water which falls from the sky. In vain are Chinese bridges often thrown across hollows, to make believe there is something beneath. We are not long duped, and what I saw at Lord Mansfield's, from the windows of his house, only shews the sorry privations of several Gardens in England.

This would be lessened, if they had not the rage for separating themselves from the Thames. They do not know how to profit by it. The Duke of Marlborough makes up for it by the river which he brought into his park, which increases in breadth and swiftness and falls with much noise. I do not forgive Lord Pembroke for making his flow like a canal.—*Coup d'œil sur les Jardins.*

—⋘—

**MARQUIS DE GIRARDIN** (1735-1808).  *Was largely instrumental in introducing the ' English' Style of Gardening into France at his Park of Ermenonville, where he was assisted by J. M. Morel (' the Kent of France' and author o, the ' Théorie des Jardins') and the Landscape-painter, G. F. Meyer. Rousseau, his guest, died here and was first buried on the ' Ile des Peupliers,' before he was removed to the Pantheon (see the description by Arthur Young). Author of ' De la Composition des Paysages, ou des Moyens d'embellir la Nature près des habitations, en y joignant l'utile à l'agréable. —Paris 1777, 4to, translated by Daniel Malthus.*

MUCH has of late been said upon the subject of Gardens; but in the more common sense of the word, by which we understand a piece of ground enclosed and laid out in straight lines, or in some form or other, this by no means defines the species of garden which I have undertaken to describe; the first express condition of which is that neither garden nor enclosure should

[1] Alluding to Lord Temple's Gardens at Stowe, which swarmed with Temples to every conceivable Deity and Virtue.

appear; for stiff forms can only produce the effect of a mathematical plan, cut paper or an ornament for a dessert, and can never produce the picturesque effect of a landscape. . . .

Symmetry certainly owed its origin to vanity and indolence ; to vanity, in attempting to force the situation to accord with the building, instead of making the building suit the situation ; to idleness, because it was more easy to work upon paper, which will allow of any form, than to examine and combine the real objects, which can only take the forms that suit them.—*The Composition of Landscape.*

---

**GEORGE MASON (1735-1806).**

MILTON, as well as SIDNEY, lived at a time when rural graces were but little understood ; yet *his* model of EDEN remains unimpeachable. CLAREMONT could not be freed from the fetters of regularity, when celebrated by GARTH ; nevertheless regularity is concealed without violating truth in the description.

> ' 'Tis he can paint in verse those rising hills,
> Those gentle vallies, and their silver rills ;
> Close groves and opening glades with verdure spread ;
> Flowers sighing sweets, and shrubs that balsam bleed.'
> GARTH'S *Claremont.*

The elegance and propriety of rural designs seems greatly to depend on a nice distinction between *contrast* and *incongruity.* . . . At PAINE'S HILL the banks of the lake are admirably *contrasted* by the wild rusticity on the other side of the arch : but I could wish the *separation* more perfect. The *species* of design should generally conform to the nature of the place, but even this rule may sometimes be neglected without any *visible incongruity.* . . .

There is an art in the management of grounds little understood, and possibly the most difficult to be accomplished ; 'tis analogous to what is called *keeping under* in painting : by some parts being seemingly neglected, the succeeding are more strikingly beautiful. The effect of this management is very apparent at the LEASOWES. . . .

From a general view of our present gardens in populous

## 204   THE PRAISE OF GARDENS

districts, a stranger might imagine they were calculated for a race of LILLIPUTIANS. Are their *shade*, their *ponds*, or their *islands* proportionable to common mortals? Their winding walks—such as no human foot-step (except a reeling drunkard's) could have traced.[1] Yet these, in the eyes of the proprietors, are perfect models of CHINESE. . . .

OATLANDS, WINDSOR-PARK, and WENTWORTH CASTLE will show you how rivers can be imitated: PERESFIELD (*sic*) may bring to your imagination some romantic paradise of Semiramis. PAINE'S-HILL has every mark of *creative genius*, and HAGLEY of *correctest fancy*; but the most intimate *alliance* with *nature* was formed by SHENSTONE. . . . NATURE'S favourite haunts are the *school* of gardening—she appears in sublimest *rudeness* on the forest of MACCLESFIELD, and the *Welch* mountains—her milder *train of graces* disperse themselves along the banks of THAMES—her *majestic retirements* are situated on the streams of DOVE and DERWENT, in the vale of HACKNESS, and the groves of EASTWELL —she assumes on RICHMOND-BROW a *gayer* and a *softer* dignity, making every sprightly work of art serve for her embellishment.— *An Essay on Design in Gardening*, 1768 (*greatly enlarged*, 1795— *two Appendices*, 1798).

—∿∿∿—

**GIBBON**
(1737-1794).

WE now enjoy the genial influence of the Climate and the Season; and no station was ever more calculated to enjoy them than Deyverdun's house and garden, which are now become my own. You will not expect that the pen should describe, what the pencil would imperfectly delineate. A few circumstances may, however, be mentioned. My library is about the same size with that in Bentinck Street, with this difference, however, that instead of looking on a paved court

[1] This looks like the *fons et origo* of the *mot* usually attributed to a Frenchman, of intoxicating your gardener and following his steps, to design a modern garden. France was 'translating' our garden-ideas pretty freely just then—many into verse, more into prose, most into execution—but often without acknowledgment.

twelve feet square, I command a boundless prospect of vale, mountain, and water from my three windows. . . . A Terrace, one hundred yards long, extends beyond the front of the House, and leads to a close impenetrable shrubbery; and from thence the circuit of a long and various walk carries me round a meadow and vineyard. The intervals afford abundant supply of fruit, and every sort of vegetables; and if you add, that this villa (which has been much ornamented by my friend) touches the best and most sociable part of the town, you will agree with me, that few persons, either princes or philosophers, enjoy a more desirable residence.

Deyverdun, who is proud of his own works, often walks me round, pointing out with knowledge and enthusiasm, the beauties that change with every step and with every variation of light. I share, or at least I sympathise, with his pleasure — he appears content with my progress, and has already told several people, that he does not despair of making me a Gardener." . . . (*To his step-mother*—*Lausanne*, 1784).

. . . The glories of the landskip I have always enjoyed; but Deyverdun has almost given me a taste for minute observation, and I can dwell with pleasure on the shape and colour of the leaves, the various hues of the blossoms, and successive progress of vegetation. These pleasures are not without cares; and there is a white Acacia just under the windows of my library, which in my opinion was too closely pruned last Autumn, and whose recovery is the daily subject of anxiety and conversation! My romantic wishes led sometimes to an idea which was impracticable in England, the possession of an house and garden, which should unite the society of town with the beauties and freedom of the country. That idea is now realised in a degree of perfection to which I never aspired, and if I could convey in words a just picture of my library, apartments, terrace, wilderness, vineyard, with the prospect of land and water, terminated by the mountains; and this position at the gate of a populous and lively town where I have some friends and many acquaintance, you would envy or rather applaud the singular propriety of my choice.—(*To his step-mother, May 3rd*, 1786.) *Private Letters of Edward Gibbon*, 1753-1794 (*edited by Rowland E. Prothero*).

—⁂—

L'ABBÉ DELILLE (1738-1813). *Called 'L'Abbé Virgile' by Rivarol, from his rendering of the Georgics in 1769; translated 'Paradise Lost,' in London, and like Milton lost his sight. Author of 'L'homme des Champs' and 'La Conversation.'*

RAPIN has sung Gardens of the regular style, and the monotony attached to the great regularity has passed from the subject into the poem. The imagination, naturally a friend to liberty, here walks painfully in the involved design of a parterre, anon expires at the end of a long straight alley. Everywhere it regrets the slightly disordered beauty and the piquant irregularity of nature. Finally he has only treated the mechanical part of the art of gardening; he has entirely forgotten the most essential part, which seeks in our sensations, in our feeling, the source of the pleasures, which country scenes and the beauties of nature perfected by art occasion us. In a word, his gardens are those of the architect; the others are those of the philosopher, the painter, the poet.

This style has gained much in the last few years; and if this is but the effect of fashion, we ought to be grateful to it. The art of gardens, which might be called the luxury of agriculture, appears to me one of the most suitable, I might almost say, one of the most virtuous amusements of rich people. . . .

When Rapin wrote a Latin poem on regular gardens, it was easy for him to present in the four Cantos which compose it—(1) the flowers, (2) orchards, (3) waters, (4) forests. But in picturesque and free gardens, in which all these objects are often mixed together, where it has been necessary to go back to the philosophic causes of the pleasure, which the sight of Nature, embellished and not tortured by art, gives us; from which it has been necessary to exclude straight lines, symmetrical distributions, and formal beauties, another plan was necessary. The author has thus shown in the first Canto the art of borrowing from nature

## L'ABBÉ DELILLE

and of happily employing the rich materials of the picturesque decoration of irregular gardens, of changing landscapes into pictures; with what care we must choose the locality and the site, profit by its advantages, correct its inconveniences; what in nature lends itself to, or resists imitation; finally the distinction between different kinds of gardens and landscapes, free gardens and regular gardens. . . .

The second Canto concerns itself entirely with plantations, the most important part of the landscape, and the beauty of prospective and distant views, which depend upon the artifice of plantations. The third contains objects, each of which would not suffice to fill a canto, without falling into sterility or monotonousness; such are lawns, flowers, rocks and waters.

The fourth Canto contains the distribution of different scenes, majestic or touching, voluptuous or severe, melancholy or smiling, the artifice with which the paths leading to them ought to be traced, finally what the other arts, and particularly agriculture and sculpture can add to the art of landscape.—*Preface to 'Les Jardins,' 20th edition*, 1801.

>   Moins pompeux qu'élégant, moins décoré que beau,
>   Un jardin à mes yeux est un vaste tableau.
>
>   Les arbres, les rochers, et les eaux et les fleurs
>   Ce sont là vos pinceaux, vos toiles, vos couleurs.
>
>   C'est peu de charmer l'œil, il faut parler au cœur
>
>   Partout entremêlés d'arbres pyramidaux,
>   Marbres, bronzes, palais, urnes, temples, tombeaux,
>   Parlent de Rome antique ; et la vue abusée
>   Croit, au lieu d'un jardin, parcourir un musée.
>
>   Loin donc ces froids jardins, colifichet champêtre,
>   Insipides réduits, dont l'insipide maître
>   Vous vante, en s'admirant, ses arbres bien peignés,
>   Ses petits salons verds bien tondus, bien soignés,

208    THE PRAISE OF GARDENS

Son plan bien symmétrique, où, jamais solitaire,
Chaque allée à sa sœur, chaque berceau son frère ;
Ses sentiers ennuyés d'obéir au cordeau,
Son parterre brodé, son maigre filet d'eau,
Ses buis tournés en globe, en pyramide, en vase,
Et ses petits bergers bien guindés sur leur base.
Laissez-le s'applaudir de son luxe mesquin ;
Je préfere un champ brut à son triste jardin.—
                                            *Les Jardins.*

—⁓⁓—

ARTHUR     '*The Columella of the North,*' 1768, *published* '*A Six weeks' Tour through*
YOUNG      *the Southern Counties of England and Wales*'; 1771, '*A Six months' Tour*
(1741-1820). *through the North of England*'; '*The Farmer's Tour through the East of*
           *England*'; 1780, '*Tour in Ireland*'; 1792-4, '*Travels in France during*
           *1787-1790*'; '*The Farmer's Letters to the People of England*'; '*The*
           *Farmer's Guide,*' '*Rural Economy,*' *and* '*A Course of Experimental Agri-*
           *culture*'; *Agricultural Surveys, and many other works.*
              *His name is a 'household word' in France, while in England confined to*
           *agricultural and literary circles.*

Chantilly.  I HAD been so accustomed to the imitation in water of the
waving and irregular lines of nature that I came to Chantilly
prepossessed against the idea of a canal, but the view of one
here is striking and had the effect which magnificent scenes
impress. It arises from extent and from the right lines of the
water uniting with the regularity of the objects in view. It is
Lord Kames, I think, who says the part of the garden contiguous
to the house should partake of the regularity of the building ;
with much magnificence about a place this is unavoidable. The
effect here, however, is lessened by the parterre before the Castle,
in which the division and the diminutive jets d'eau are not of a
size to correspond with the magnificence of the canal. The
*hameau* contains an imitation of an English garden ; the taste is
but just introduced into France, so that it will not stand a critical
examination. The most English idea I saw is the lawn in front
of the stables ; it is large, of a good verdure and well kept ; proving clearly that they may have as fine lawns in the North of

France as in England. The labyrinth is the only complete one I have seen, and I have no inclination to see another: it is in gardening what a rebus is in poetry. In the Sylvae are many very fine and scarce plants.—*May 25th,* 1787.

As to the garden, it is beneath all contempt, except as an St Martino. object to make a man stare at the efforts to which folly can arrive: in the space of an acre, there are hills of genuine earth, mountains of pasteboard, rocks of canvas: abbés, cows, sheep and shepherdesses in lead; monkeys and peasants, asses and altars, in stone. Fine ladies and blacksmiths, parrots and lovers, in wood. Windmills and cottages, shops and villages, nothing excluded except nature. . . .

Give a man the secure possession of a bleak rock, and he will turn it into a garden; give him a nine years' lease of a garden, and he will convert it into a desert.

We passed by Chantilly to Morefountain, the country seat of Morefontaine. Mons. de Morefountain, Prevost des Marchands of Paris; the place has been mentioned as decorated in the English style. It consists of two scenes; one a garden of winding walks, and ornamented with a profusion of temples, benches, grottos, columns, ruins, and I know not what: I hope the French who have not been in England do not consider this as the English taste. It is in fact as remote from it as the most regular style of the last age. The water view is fine. There is a gaiety and cheerfulness in it that contrast well with the brown and unpleasing hills that surround it, and which partake of the waste character of the worst part of the surrounding country. Much has been done here; and it wants but few additions to be as perfect as the ground admits.

Reach Ermenonville, through another part of the Prince of Ermenonville. Condé's forest, which join the ornamented grounds of the Marquis Girardon.[1] This place, after the residence and death of the

[1] Marquis de Girardin, friend of Rousseau, died 1808.

persecuted, but immortal Rousseau, whose tomb every one knows is here, became so famous as to be resorted to very generally. It has been described, and plates published of the chief views; to enter into a particular description would therefore be tiresome, I shall only make one or two observations, which I do not recollect having been touched on by others. It consists of three distinct water scenes; or of two lakes and a river. We were first shown that which is so famous for the small Isle of Poplars, in which reposes all that was mortal of that extraordinary and inimitable writer. This scene is as well imagined, and as well executed as could be wished. The water is between forty and fifty acres; hills rise from it on both sides, and it is sufficiently closed in by tall wood at both ends, to render it sequestered. The remains of departed genius stamp a melancholy idea, from which decoration would depart too much, and accordingly there is little. We viewed the scene in a still evening. The declining sun threw a lengthened shade on the lake, and silence seemed to repose on its unruffled bosom; as some poet says, I forget who. The worthies to whom the temple of philosophers is dedicated, and whose names are marked on the columns, are Newton, *Lucem.*—Descartes, *Nil in rebus inane.*—Voltaire, *Ridiculum.*—Rousseau, *Naturam.*—And on another unfinished column, *Quis hoc perficiet?* The other lake is larger; it nearly fills the bottom of the vale, around which are some rough, rocky, wild and barren sand hills; either broken or spread with heath; in some places wooded, and in others scattered thinly with junipers. The character of the scene is that of wild and undecorated nature, in which the hand of art was meant to be concealed as much as was consistent with ease of access. The last scene is that of a river, which is made to wind through a lawn, receding from the house, and broken by wood: the ground is not fortunate; it is too dead a flat, and no where viewed to much advantage.

**Trianon.** To Trianon, to view the Queen's Jardin Anglais. I had a letter to Mons. Richard, which procured admittance. It contains about 100 acres, disposed in the taste of what we read of in books

# ARTHUR YOUNG

of Chinese gardening, whence it is supposed the English style was taken. There is more of Sir William Chambers here than of Mr Brown, more effort than nature—and more expence than taste. It is not easy to conceive anything that art can introduce in a garden that is not here; woods, rocks, lawns, lakes, rivers, islands, cascades, grottos, walks, temples, and even villages. There are parts of the design very pretty, and well executed. The only fault is too much crouding; which has led to another, that of cutting the lawn by too many gravel walks, an error to be seen in almost every garden I have met with in France. But the glory of La Petite Trianon is the exotic trees and shrubs. The world has been successfully rifled to decorate it. Here are curious and beautiful ones to please the eye of ignorance; and to exercise the memory of science. Of the buildings the temple of Love is truly elegant.

Pass Rosoy to Maupertuis, through a country chearfully **Maupertuis.** diversified by woods, and scattered with villages; and single farms spread every where as about Nangis. Maupertuis seems to have been the creation of the marquis de Montesquiou, who has here a very fine chateau of his own building; an extensive English garden, made by the Count d'Artois' gardener,[1] with the town, has all been of his own forming. I viewed the garden with pleasure; a proper advantage has been taken of a good command of a stream, and many fine springs which rise in the grounds; they are well conducted, and the whole executed with taste. In the kitchen garden, which is on the slope of a hill, one of these springs has been applied to excellent use, it is made to wind in many doubles through the whole on a paved bed, forming numerous basons for watering the garden, and might with little trouble, be conducted alternately to every bed as in Spain. This is a bit of real utility to all those who form gardens on the sides of hills; for watering with pots and pails is a miserable, as well as expensive succedaneum to this infinitely more

[1] Thomas Blaikie, a Scotsman, who laid out many of the best gardens in France before and after the Revolution (see Loudon, p. 88).

effective method. There is but one fault in this garden, which is its being placed near the house, where there should be nothing but lawn and scattered trees when viewed from the Chateau.—*Travels in France*, 1787-9.

—◦◦◦—

**SIR UVEDALE PRICE**
**1747-1829).**

1780, *Translated Pausanias: his various works on the Picturesque, Beauty and Landscape were collected in one volume by Sir T. D. Lauder in* 1842.

I MAY perhaps have spoken more feelingly on this subject, from having done myself what I so condemn in others—destroyed an old-fashioned garden. . . .

I remember, that even this garden (so infinitely inferior to those of Italy) had an air of decoration, and of gaiety, arising from that decoration—*un air paré*—a distinction from mere unimbellished nature, which, whatever the advocates for extreme simplicity may allege, is surely essential to an ornamented garden : all the beauties of undulating ground, of shrubs, and of verdure are to be found in places where no art has ever been employed, and consequently cannot bestow a distinction which they do not possess. . . .

Among other circumstances, I have a strong recollection of a raised terrace, seen sideways from that in front of the house, in the middle of which was a flight of steps with its iron rails, and an arched recess below it backed by a wood : these steps conducted you from the terrace to a lower compartment, where there was a mixture of fruit-trees, shrubs, and statues, disposed, indeed, with some formality, yet which formed a dressed foreground to the woods ; and with a little alteration would have richly and happily blended with the general landscape. . . .

I regret extremely, not only the compartment I have just mentioned, but another garden immediately beyond it : and I cannot forget the sort of curiosity and surprise that was excited after a short absence, even in me to whom it was familiar, by the simple and common circumstance of a door that led from the first compartment to the second, and the pleasure I always experienced on entering that inner and more secluded garden. There was nothing, however, in the garden itself to excite any

extraordinary sensations; the middle part was merely planted with the lesser fruits, and dwarf trees, but on the opening of the door, the lofty trees of a fine grove appeared immediately over the opposite wall; the trees are still there, they are more distinctly and openly seen, but the striking impression is gone.—*Essay on the Picturesque*, 1794.

IN the public garden at Palermo, adjoining the road, I peacefully **GOETHE** passed the most pleasurable hours. It is the most marvellous (1749-1832). spot in the world. Though laid out in regular order, it is like fairy-land; planted no great time since, it sets us down amidst antiquity. Green parterres embrace foreign shrubs, lemon-espaliers arch themselves into comely leaf-shaded walks, lofty walls of oleander, gemmed with a thousand red clove-like blossoms, arrest the eye. Foreign trees entirely unknown to me, still leafless, probably from warmer climes, spread forth curious branches. A bench raised behind the level ground brings into view vegetation so wonderfully interwoven, and guides the gaze at last to great basins, wherein gold and silver fish dart fascinatingly about, now hiding under mossy reeds, now assembling again in shoals, lured by a bit of bread. Everywhere upon the plants appears a green that we are not used to see, now yellower, now bluer than with us. But that which threw over the whole the rarest grace was a hazy vapour, pervading everything uniformly with so striking effect, that objects but a few steps' distance behind one another, stood forth by a distinct shade of light blue from each other, so that their own colour was finally lost, or at least presented itself to the eye through a blue medium.—*Italian Journey*, (*Sicily* 1787).[1]

ADVANTAGES OF DILETTANTISM IN THE GARDEN-ART.

Ideal in the Real.
Striving after form in formless masses.

[1] See Lewes's 'Life of Goethe,' for a charming description of his Garden-House at Weimar.

Selection.
Beautiful composition.
To make a picture out of reality, in short, first entrance into art.
A pure and completely beautiful surrounding always has a beneficial effect upon the company.

HARM OF DILETTANTISM IN THE GARDEN-ART.
The real is treated as a work of Fancy.
Garden amateurism is pursuing something infinite :—
1. Because it is not definite and limited in idea.
2. Because the material, always accidental, is ever changing and ever resisting the idea.
Garden-dilettantism often allows the nobler arts to serve it in an unworthy manner, and makes a plaything of their solid tendency.

Furthers sentimental and fantastic Nullity.
It dwarfs the sublime in Nature and neutralises it by imitation.
It perpetuates the reigning degeneracy of the age by its desire to be unconditioned and lawless in Æsthetics, to give way to arbitrary fancy, by not correcting itself like other arts and holding itself in check.
The blending of Art and Nature.
Its preference for appearances.—*Ferneres über Kunst.*

—www—

**RICHARD PAYNE KNIGHT (1750-1824).** *Greek scholar :* 1784-1806, *M.P. for Ludlow ;* 1814, *Trustee of the British Museum, to which he bequeathed his collection of coins and ancient bronzes, and where his bust is placed ;* 1794, *published '* The Landscape,*' a didactic poem ; united with Sir Uvedale Price in reacting against the extremes and exaggerations of the '* Landscape*' School of Brown and Repton.*

*June 26th,* 1839.—Delbury. I rode to Dowton Castle on Monday—a gimcrack Castle and bad-house, built by Payne Knight, an epicurean Philosopher, who, after building the Castle went and lived in a lodge or cottage in the park : there he died, not without suspicion of having put an end to himself, which would have been fully conformable to his notions. He was a sensualist in all ways, but a quiet and self-educated scholar. His property is now in Chancery, because he chose to make his own will. The prospect from the windows is beautiful, and the walk through the wood overhanging the river Teme, surpasses any thing I have ever seen of the kind.—*The Greville Memoirs.*

FOR this reason we require, immediately adjoining the dwellings of opulence and luxury, that every thing should assume its character; and not only be, but appear to be dressed and cultivated. In such situations, neat gravel walks, mown turf, and flowering plants and shrubs, trained and distributed by art, are perfectly in character; although, if the same buildings were abandoned, and in ruins, we should, on the same principle of consistency and propriety, require neglected paths, ragged lanes and wild uncultivated thickets; which are, in themselves, more pleasing, both to the eye and the imagination, but unfit accompaniments for objects, not only originally produced by art, but in which art is constantly employed and exhibited. . . .

On this account, I think the avowed character of art of the Italian Gardens preferable, in garden scenery, to the concealed one now in fashion; which is, in reality, rather counterfeited than concealed; for it appears in every thing; but appears in a dress that does not belong to it: at every step we perceive its exertions; but at the same time perceive that it has laboured much to effect little; and that while it seeks to hide its character, it only discovers it the more. In the decorations, however, of ground adjoining a house, much should depend upon the character of the house itself: if it be neat and regular, neatness and regularity should accompany it; but if it be rugged and picturesque, and situated amidst scenery of the same character, art should approach it with more caution: for though it be in itself an avowed work of art, yet the influence of time, with the accompaniments of trees and creepers may have given it a character of nature, which ought to be as little disturbed as is consistent with comfort: for, after all, the character of nature, is more pleasing than any that can be given by art. At all events, the character of dress and artificial neatness ought never to be suffered to encroach upon the park or the forest; where it is as contrary to propriety as it is to beauty; and where its introduction by our modern landscape gardeners affords one of the most memorable instances of any recorded in the history of fashions, of the extravagant absurdity, with which an insatiate passion for novelty may infect a whole nation.

. . . . . .

By the old system of laying out ground, indeed, this incongruity was in a great degree obviated: for the house being surrounded by gardens, as uniform as itself, and only seen through vistas at right angles, every visible accompaniment was in union with it; and the systematic regularity of the whole discernible from every point of sight: but when, according to the modern fashion, all around is levelled and thrown open; and the poor square edifice exposed alone, or with the accompaniment only of its regular wings and portico, amidst spacious lawns interspersed with irregular clumps or masses of wood, and sheets of water, I do not know a more melancholy object; it neither associates nor harmonizes with anything; and as the beauties of symmetry, which might appear in its regularity, are only perceived when that regularity is seen; that is, when the building is shown from a point of sight at right angles with one of the fronts, the man of taste takes care that it never shall be so shown; but that every view of it shall be oblique, from the tangent of a curve in a serpentine walk; from whence it appears neither quite regular, nor quite irregular, but with that sort of lame and defective uniformity which we see in an animal that has lost a limb.

The view from one of these solitary mansions is still more dismal than that towards it: for, at the hall door, a boundless extent of open lawn presents itself in every direction, which the despairing visitant must traverse before he can get into any change of scenery: and to complete the congruity of the whole, the clumps with which this monotonous tract is dotted, and the winding stream or canal, by which it is intersected, are made as neat and determinate as ever the ancient gardens were; which having been professedly a work of art, and an appendage to the house, the neatness and even formality of architecture were its proper characteristics; and when its terraces and borders were

# WILLIAM WINDHAM

intermixed with vines and flowers (as I have seen them in Italian villas and in some old English gardens in the same style) the mixture of splendor, richness and neatness was beautiful and pleasing in the highest degree. But the modern art of landscape gardening, as it is called, takes away all natural enrichment, and adds none of its own; unless, indeed, meagre and formal clumps of trees, and still more formal patches of shrubs may be called enrichment. Why this art has been called landscape gardening, perhaps he, who gave it the title, may explain. I can see no reason unless it be the efficacy which it has shown in destroying landscapes, in which, indeed, it seems to be infallible; not one complete painter's composition being, I believe, to be found in any of the numerous, and many of them beautiful and picturesque spots, which it has visited in different parts of this island.—*An Analytical Enquiry into the Principles of Taste*, 1805.

RT. HON. WILLIAM WINDHAM (1750-1810).

I HOPE therefore that you will publish the system which I conceive you to have adopted, and vindicate to the art of laying out ground its true principles, which are wholly different from those which these wild improvers (Payne Knight and Uvedale Price) would wish to introduce. Places are not to be laid out with a view to their appearance in a picture, but to their uses, and the enjoyment of them in real life; and their conformity to those purposes is that which constitutes their beauty: with this view, gravel walks and neat mown lawns, and in some situations, straight alleys, fountains, terraces, and for aught I know, parterres and cut hedges are in perfect good taste, and infinitely more conformable to the principles which form the basis of our pleasure in these instances, than the docks, and thistles, and litter and disorder, that may make a much better figure in a picture.—*Letter to Humphry Repton, on his controversy with Uvedale Price*, 1794.

# THE PRAISE OF GARDENS

**HUMPHRY REPTON (1752-1818).** *Was the first to assume professionally the title of 'Landscape Gardener.' Having failed as a merchant, he settled in Norfolk, and tried Agricultural Experiments and gardening—was Confidential Secretary to Mr Windham, Lord Lieutenant of Ireland in 1783—then resided in Harestreet, Essex, till his death. He lost more money in Palmer's mail-coach system, and then announced himself as 'Landscape Gardener.' 'Capability' Brown, by his death in 1784, having left the field open, Repton began a period of uninterrupted prosperity. He published, 1795, 'Sketches and Hints on Landscape Gardening'; 1803, 'Observations on the Theory and Practice of Landscape Gardening'; 1806, 'Inquiry into the Changes of Taste in Landscape Gardening'; 1808, 'Designs for the Pavillon at Brighton' (not accepted); 1816, 'Fragments on the Theory of Landscape Gardening,' assisted by his son; all reprinted by J. C. Loudon, in 1840, in one volume, with a Memoir of the author.—(Knight's Biography.)*

Humphry Repton next occupied the attention of many, who confirmed their opinion of his skill and taste by greatly encouraging his professional labours. Considered as an élève of Brown's school, and, at first, the zealous defender both of his system and practice, it is clear, that when he became more firmly established, he invented for himself, and trusted to his own talents. He declared himself a professor of an art, to which he gave the designation of 'Landscape Gardening,' about the year 1788, and continued his practice of 'producing beautiful effects,' till his death in 1818. If the character of this artist's talents be fairly examined and defined, it was more for elegant ornament and prettiness, than for any decided effort of original genius. He studied, in most instances, rather to gratify his employers by acceding to their previous intentions, than to attempt grandeur in any scene. Amenity was his leading object—colonnades of wicker work covered with flowering shrubs, or large conservatories, in fanciful forms, were made the appendage of mansions, no longer as Brown had left them, bald and exposed. He continued to be admired and popular, as long as the ardour for improving places and the fashion itself lasted. Nor can it now be said that it has passed away.—*Dallaway's 'Anecdotes of Modern Gardening.'*

TO improve the scenery of a country, and to display its native beauties with advantage, is an Art which originated in England, and has therefore been called *English Gardening*; yet as this expression is not sufficiently appropriate, especially since gardening, in its more confined sense of *Horticulture*, has been likewise brought to the greatest perfection in this country, I have adopted the term *Landscape Gardening*, as most proper, because the art can only be advanced and perfected by the united powers of the *landscape painter* and the *practical gardener*. The former must conceive a plan, which the latter may be able to execute; for though a painter may represent a beautiful landscape on his canvas, and even surpass Nature by the combination of her choicest materials, yet the luxuriant imagination of the *painter* must be subjected to the *gardener's* practical knowledge in planting, digging and moving earth; that the simplest and readiest means of accomplishing each design may be suggested.

The perfection of Landscape Gardening consists in the four following requisites: First, it must display the Natural beauties, and hide the natural defects of every situation. Secondly, it should give the appearance of extent and freedom, by carefully disguising or hiding the boundary. Thirdly, it must studiously conceal every interference of art, however expensive, by which the Scenery is improved; making the whole appear the production of Nature only; and fourthly, all objects of mere convenience or comfort, if incapable of being made ornamental, or of becoming proper parts of the general scenery, must be removed or concealed.[1]

Each of the four objects here enumerated are directly opposite to the principles of ancient gardening, which may be thus stated. First, the natural beauties or defects of a situation had an influence, when it was the fashion to exclude by lofty walls every surrounding object. Secondly, these walls were never considered as defects, but were ornamented with vases, expensive iron gates, and palisades to render them more conspicuous. Thirdly, so far from making gardens appear natural, every expedient was used to display the expensive efforts of Art, by which Nature had been subdued:—the ground was levelled by a line; the water was squared or scalloped into regular basins; the trees, if not clipped into artificial shape, were at least so planted by line and measurement, that the formal hand of art could not here be

[1] This last article, I confess, has occasionally misled modern improvers into the absurdity of not only banishing the appearance but the reality of all comfort and convenience to a distance; as I have frequently found in the bad choice of a spot for the kitchen garden.

mistaken. And lastly, with respect to objects of convenience, they were placed as near the house as possible :—the stables, the barns, and the kitchen garden, were among the ornaments of a place; while the village, the alms house, the parish school, and churchyard were not attempted to be concealed by the walls or palisades that divided them from the Embellished pleasure ground.
—*Sketches and Hints on Landscape Gardening*, 1794.

*Sources of pleasure in Landscape Gardening* :—1, Conformity; 2, Utility; 3, Order; 4, Symmetry; 5, Picturesque Effect; 6, Intricacy; 7, Simplicity; 8, Variety; 9, Novelty; 10, Contrast; 11, Continuity; 12, Association; 13, Grandeur; 14, Appropriation; 15, Animation.—*Ibid.*

JOSEPH JOUBERT (1754-1824).

SCENTS are the souls of flowers: they may be even perceptible in the land of shadows.

The tulip is a flower without a soul; but the rose and lily seem to have one.

We ought to gather nothing which grows in our cemeteries, and to let even the grass in them enjoy a pious uselessness.

We enjoy in gardening the pure delicacies of agriculture.

Our gardens in Paris smell musty. I do not like these evergreen trees. There is something of blackness in their greenery, of coldness in their shade, something sharp, dry, and thorny in their leafage. Besides, since they neither lose anything, nor have anything to fear, they seem to me unfeeling, and hence have little interest for me.[1]

When a regular building commands the garden which surrounds it, it ought, so to speak, to radiate regularity, by throwing it round itself to all distances, whence it can be easily seen.

It is a centre, and the centre ought to be in harmony with all points of the circumference, which is itself nothing but the

---

[1] 'I hate those trees that never lose their foliage:
They seem to have no sympathy with Nature:
Winter and Summer are alike to them.'
*W. S. Landor.*

development of a central point. Those irregular gardens, which we call English gardens, require a labyrinth for a dwelling.—*Thoughts*.

---

**ARCHIBALD ALISON (1757-1839).**

THE Art of Gardening seems to have been governed, and long governed, by the same principle. When men first began to consider a garden as a subject capable of Beauty, or of bestowing any distinction upon its possession, it was natural that they should endeavour to render its Form as different as possible from that of the country around it; and to mark to the Spectator, as strongly as they could, both the design and the labour which they had bestowed upon it. Irregular Forms, however convenient or agreeable, might still be the production of Nature; but forms perfectly regular, and Divisions completely uniform,—immediately excited the belief of Design, and with this belief all the admiration which follows the employment of Skill, or even of Expense. That this Principle would naturally lead the first Artists in Gardening to the production of Uniformity, may easily be conceived, as even at present, when so different a System of Gardening prevails, the common People universally follow the first System; and even the Men of the best Taste, in the cultivation of waste or neglected lands, still enclose them by uniform Lines and in regular Divisions, as more immediately signifying what they wish should be signified, their Industry or Spirit in their improvement.

As gardens, however, are both a costly and permanent subject, and are of consequence less liable to the influence of Fashion, this Taste would not easily be altered; and the principal improvements which they would receive, would consist rather in the greater employment of uniformity and expense, than in the introduction of any new Design. The whole History of Antiquity, accordingly, contains not, I believe, a single instance where this character was deviated from, in a spot considered solely as a garden; and till within the last century, and in this country, it seems not any where to have been imagined, that a garden was capable of any other Beauty than what might arise from Utility, and from the display of Art and Design. It deserves also further to be remarked, that the additional ornaments of gardening have in every country partaken of the same character, and have been directed to the purpose of increasing the appearance and the Beauty of Art and of Design. Hence Jets d'Eau, artificial Fountains, regular Cascades, Trees in the form of animals, etc., have in all countries been the principal ornaments of gardening. The violation of the usual appearances of Nature in such objects, strongly exhibited the employment of Art. They accorded perfectly, therefore, with the character which the scene was intended to have; and they increased its Beauty as they increased the effect of that quality upon which this Beauty was founded, and intended to be founded.—*Essays on the Nature and Principles of Taste*, 1790.

—⁓⁓⁓—

**SCHILLER**
(1759-1805).

THERE will be found in all probability a very good middle course between the formality of the French gardening-taste and the lawless freedom of the so-called English style; it will become manifest that this art may not indeed soar into such lofty spheres as they would persuade us, who, in their designs, overlook nothing but the means of putting them into execution; and that it is certainly tasteless and inconsistent to desire to encompass the world with a garden-wall, but very practicable and reasonable to make a garden, satisfying all the demands of a good husbandman, into a characteristic whole to the eye, heart, and understanding alike.

The road from Stuttgart to Hohenheim is, in some measure, an embodied history of the art of gardening, which offers to the attentive observer an interesting commentary. In the orchards, vineyards, and kitchen-gardens, past which the high road stretches, the first natural beginning of the garden-art is revealed to him, stripped of all æsthetic ornament. But now the French style of gardening greets him with dignified formality beneath the gaunt and abrupt walls of poplar, which unite the open landscape with Hohenheim and arouse expectation by their well-balanced form. This solemn impression rises to an almost painful intensity, as you roam through the chambers of the ducal palace, which for splendour and elegance has few peers, and in a certain rare manner combines taste with profusion. By the brilliance which here strikes the eye from every side, and by the exquisite architecture of the rooms and furniture, the craving for simplicity is wrought to the highest pitch, and the most conspicuous triumph is in waiting for rural Nature, which all at once welcomes the traveller into the so-called English Park.

Meantime the monuments of sunken splendour, against whose decaying walls the gardener leans his peaceful hut, make a quite peculiar impression upon the heart, and it is with a secret joy that in these mouldering ruins we see ourselves revenged upon the art, which in the gorgeous building hard by had wielded its power over us to excess. But the Nature we meet in this English Park is no more the same as that we have issued from. It is a Nature quickened with soul and exalted by art, which satisfies not only the man of simple taste, but also the spoiled child of culture, charming the one into reflection, and leading back the other to emotion.—*Miscellaneous Writings: On the Garden-Calendar for the Year* 1795.

—ᴡᴡ—

*Son of a Lord Mayor, he began life with unusual material, physical and* **WILLIAM**
*intellectual advantages. He did many extraordinary things, writing ' Vathek'* **BECKFORD**
*in a few hours, building the fabulous Fonthill, and shutting himself up in it* (1760-1844).
*alone with dogs and a magnificent library; but perhaps the most extraordinary thing was his declaration, at the close of a long luxurious life, that he had never known an hour's ennui.*

I RETURNED towards the Hague, and looked into a country-house of the late Count Bentinck, with parterres and bosquets by no means resembling, one should conjecture, the gardens of the Hesperides. But, considering that the whole group of trees, terraces, and verdure were in a manner created out of hills of sand, the place may claim some portion of merit. The walks and alleys have all the stiffness and formality which our ancestors admired, but the intermediate spaces, being dotted with clumps and sprinkled with flowers, are imagined in Holland to be in the English style. An Englishman ought certainly to behold it with partial eyes, since every possible attempt has been made to twist it into the taste of his country.

I need not say how liberally I bestowed my encomiums on Count Bentinck's tasteful inventions; nor how happy I was, when I had duly serpentized over his garden, to find myself once more in the grand avenue.

All the way home, I reflected upon the unyielding perseverance of the Dutch, who raise gardens from heaps of sand, and cities out of the bosom of the waters.—*Italy, Spain, and Portugal.* (*Letter II. Ostend, June* 21, 1780.)

Having remained some time in this pious hue, I returned home and feasted upon grapes and ortolans with great edification; then walked to one of the bridges across the Arno, and from thence to the garden of Boboli, which lies behind the Grand Duke's palace, stretched out on the side of a mountain. I ascended terrace after terrace, robed by a thick underwood of bay and myrtle, above which rise several nodding towers, and a long sweep of venerable wall, almost entirely concealed by ivy. You would have been enraptured with the broad masses of shade and dusky alleys that opened as I advanced, with white statues of fauns and sylvans glimmering amongst them: some of which pour water into sarcophagi of the purest marble, covered with antique rilievos. The capitals of columns and ancient friezes are scattered about as seats.

On these I reposed myself, and looked up to the cypress groves which spring above the thickets; then, plunging into their retirements, I followed a winding path, which led me by a series of steep ascents to a green platform overlooking the whole extent of wood, with Florence deep beneath, and the tops of the hills which encircle it jagged with pines; here and there a convent, or villa, whitening in the sun. This scene extends as far as the eye can reach.

Still ascending I attained the brow of the eminence, and had nothing but the fortress of Belvedere and two or three open porticoes above me. On this elevated situation, I found several walks of trellis-work, clothed with luxuriant vines. A colossal statue of Ceres, her hands extended in the act of scattering fertility over the country, crowns the summit.

Descending alley after alley, and bank after bank, I came to the orangery in front of the palace, disposed in a grand amphitheatre, with marble niches relieved by dark foliage, out of which spring cedars and tall aërial cypresses. This spot brought the scenery of an antique Roman garden so vividly into my mind, that, lost in the train of recollections this idea excited, I expected every instant to be called to the table of Lucullus hard by, in one of the porticoes, and to stretch myself on his purple triclinias; but waiting in vain for a summons till the approach of night, I returned delighted with a ramble that had led my imagination so far into antiquity.—*Ibid.* (*Florence, Sept.* 14, 1780.)

I dined in peace and solitude, and repaired, as evening drew on, to the thickets of Boboli.

What a serene sky! what mellowness in the tints of the mountains! a purple haze concealed the bases, whilst their summits were invested with saffron light, discovering every white cot and every copse that clothed their declivities. The prospect widened as I ascended the terraces of the garden.

After traversing many long dusky alleys, I reached the opening on the brow of the hill, and, seating myself under the statue of Ceres, took a sketch of the huge mountainous cupola of the Duomo, the adjoining lovely tower and one more massive in its neighbourhood, built not improbably in the style of ancient Etruria. Beyond this historic group of buildings a plain stretches itself far and wide, most richly studded with villas and gardens, and groves of pine and olive, quite to the feet of the mountains.

Having marked the sun's going down and all the soothing

effects cast by his declining rays on every object, I went through a plat of vines to a favourite haunt of mine:—a little garden of the most fragrant roses, with a spring under a rustic arch of grotto-work fringed with ivy. Thousands of fish inhabit here, of that beautiful glittering species which comes from China. This golden nation were leaping after insects as I stood gazing upon the deep clear water, listening to the drops that trickle from the cove. Opposite to which, at the end of a green alley, you discover an oval basin, and in the midst of it an antique statue full of that graceful languor so peculiarly Grecian.

Whilst I was musing on the margin of the spring (for I returned to it after casting a look upon the sculpture), the moon rose above the tufted foliage of the terraces, which I descended by several flights of steps, with marble balustrades crowned by vases of aloes.
—*Florence, Oct.* 5, 1780.

As soon as the sun declined I strolled into the Villa Medici; but finding it haunted by pompous people, nay, even by the Spanish Ambassador, and several red-legged Cardinals, I moved off to the Negroni garden. There I found what my soul desired, thickets of jasmine, and wild spots overgrown with bay; long alleys of cypress totally neglected, and almost impassable through the luxuriance of the vegetation; on every side antique fragments, vases, sarcophagi, and altars sacred to the Manes, in deep, shady recesses, which I am certain the Manes must love. The air was filled with the murmurs of water trickling down basins of porphyry, and losing itself amongst overgrown weeds and grasses.

Above the wood and between its boughs appeared several domes, and a strange lofty tower. I will not say they belonged to St. Maria Maggiore; no, they are fanes and porticoes dedicated to Cybele, who delights in sylvan situations. The forlorn air of this garden, with its high and reverend shades, make me imagine it as old as the baths of Dioclesian, which peep over one of its walls.—*Rome, June* 30, 1782.

Horne persuaded me much against my will to accompany him in his Portuguese chaise to Pagliavam, the residence of John the

Fifth's bastards, instead of following my usual track along the sea-shore. . . . A great flat space before the garden-front of the villa is laid out in dismal labyrinths of clipped myrtle, with lofty pyramids rising from them, in the style of that vile Dutch maze planted by King William at Kensington, and rooted up some years ago by King George the Third.

Beyond this puzzling ground are several long alleys of stiff dark verdure, called *ruas*, *i.e.* literally streets, with great propriety, being more close, more formal, and not less dusty than High Holborn. I deviated from them into plats of well-watered vegetables and aromatic herbs, inclosed by neat fences of cane, covered with an embroidery of the freshest and most perfect roses, quite free from insects and cankers, worthy to have strewn the couches and graced the bosom of Lais, Aspasia, or Lady ———, You know how warmly every mortal of taste delights in these lovely flowers; how frequently, and in what harmonious numbers, Ariosto has celebrated them. Has not Lady ——— a whole apartment painted over with roses? Does she not fill her bath with their leaves, and deck her idols with garlands of no other flowers? and is she not quite in the right of it?—*May* 30, 1787.

At length, after a tedious drive through vast tracts of desolate country, scarce a house, scarce a shrub, scarce a human being to meet with, we descended a rapid declivity, and I once more found myself in the valley of Aranjuez.

. . . Charles the Fifth's elms in the island-garden close to the palace are decaying apace. I visited the nine venerable stumps close to a hideous brick ruin; the largest measures forty or fifty feet in girth; the roots are picturesquely fantastic. The fountains, like the shades in which they are embowered, are rapidly going to decay: the bronze Venus, at the fountain which takes its name from Don John of Austria, has lost her arm.

Notwithstanding the dreariness of the season, with all its accompaniment of dry leaves and faded herbage, this historic garden had still charms; the air was mild and the sunbeams played on the Tagus, and many a bird flitted from spray to spray.

Several long alleys of the loftiest elms, their huge rough trunks mantled with ivy, and their grotesque roots advancing and receding like grotto-work into the walk, struck me as singularly pleasing.—*December* 1, 1795.

—∿∿—

**WILLIAM COBBETT (1762-1835).** *As a boy of sixteen was engaged in the Gardens of Farnham Castle: fired by a description of Kew gardens, he started off to see them himself: enlisted in 54th Foot and served at Halifax, N. S. 1792, visited France for six months: settled near Philadelphia, teaching English, and is said to have refused to give Talleyrand lessons; edited a French grammar. 1796, wrote 'Life and Adventures of Peter Porcupine,' (an autobiography). 1802, started 'Cobbett's Political Register,' continued till his death. 1806, he began farming at Botley in Hampshire; wrote 'The Woodlands,' 'English Gardener,' 'American Gardener.' 1810, was prosecuted by government for libel, and sentenced to two years' imprisonment and £1000 fine. 1820, he became insolvent with debts of £34,000. 1821, commenced his 'Rural Rides.' 1832, after Reform Bill was returned M.P. for Oldham.*

THEY say that these Gardens (of Mr Drummond, at Shere, Surrey) were laid out for one of the Howards, in the reign of Charles the Second, by Mr Evelyn, who wrote the *Sylva*. The mansion house, which is by no means magnificent, stands on a little flat by the side of a parish church, having a steep, but not lofty hill, rising up on the south side. It looks right across the gardens, which lie on the slope of a hill which runs along at about a quarter of a mile distant from the front of the house. The gardens, of course, lie facing the south. At the back of them under the hill, is a high wall; and there is also a wall at each end, running from north to south. Between the house and the gardens there is a very beautiful run of water, with a sort of little wild narrow sedgy meadow. The gardens are separated from this by a hedge, running along from east to west. From this hedge there go up the hill, at right angles, several other hedges, which divide the land here into distinct gardens, or orchards. Along at the top of these there goes a yew hedge, or, rather, a row of small yew trees, the trunks of which are bare for about eight or ten feet high, and the tops of which form one

# WILLIAM COBBETT

solid head of about ten feet high, while the bottom branches come out on each side of the row about eight feet horizontally. This hedge, or row, is a quarter of a mile long. There is a nice hard sand-road under this species of umbrella; and, summer and winter, here is a most delightful walk! Behind this row of yews, there is a space, or garden (a quarter of a mile long you will observe) about thirty or forty feet wide, as nearly as I can recollect. At the back of this garden, and facing the yew tree row, is a wall probably ten feet high, which forms the breastwork of a terrace; and it is this terrace which is the most beautiful thing that I ever saw in the gardening way. It is a quarter of a mile long, and, I believe, between thirty and forty feet wide; of the finest green sward, and as level as a die.

We came hither by the way of Waverley Abbey and Moor(e) Park. . . . We got leave to go and see the grounds at Waverley, where all the old monks' garden walls are totally gone, and where the spot is become a sort of lawn.[1] I showed him the spot where the strawberry garden was, and where I, when sent to gather *hautboys*, used to eat every remarkably fine one, instead of letting it go to be eaten by Sir Robert Rich. . . .

From Waverley we went to Moore Park once the seat of Sir William Temple, and, when I was a very little boy, the seat of a Lady, or a Mrs Temple. Here I showed Richard Mother Ludlam's Hole; but alas, it is not the enchanting place that I knew it, nor that which Grose describes in his Antiquities! . . . Near the mansion, I showed Richard the hill, upon which Dean Swift tells us, he used to run for exercise, while he was pursuing his studies

---

[1] Cobbett was born at Farnham, in a house still existing, and the ancient kitchen garden of the Monks at Waverley Abbey was where he first worked. 'It was the spot where I first began to learn to work, or rather where I first began to eat fine fruit in a garden ; and though I have now seen and observed upon as many fine gardens as any man in England, I have never seen a garden equal to that of Waverley.'—(*The English Gardener.*)

The Abbey gave the title to the Waverley Novels, Scott having explored its monastic chronicles in early life—the *Annales Waverlienses* of the Cistercian Monks from 1066 to 1291, were published by Gale in vol ii. of his *Hist. Anglican. Scriptores.*

here; and I would have showed him the garden-seat, under which Sir William Temple's heart was buried, agreeably to his will;[1] but the seat was gone, also the wall at the back of it; and the exquisitely beautiful little lawn in which the seat stood was turned into a parcel of divers-shaped Cockney clumps, planted according to the strictest rules of artificial and refined vulgarity.[2]—*Rural Rides.*

---

**MADAME DE STAËL (1766-1817).**

GARDENS are almost as beautiful in some parts of Germany as in England; the luxury of gardens always implies a love of the Country. In England simple mansions are often built in the middle of the most magnificent parks; the proprietor neglects his dwelling to attend to the ornament of nature. This magnificence and simplicity united do not, it is true, exist in the same degree in Germany; yet, in spite of the want of wealth, and the pride of feudal dignity, there is everywhere to be remarked a certain love of the beautiful, which sooner or later must be followed by taste and elegance, of which it is the only real source. Often, in the midst of the superb gardens of the German princes, are placed Æolian harps close by grottoes, encircled with flowers, that the wind may waft the sound and the perfume together. The imagination of the northern people thus endeavours to create for itself a sort of Italy; and during the brilliant days of a short-lived summer, it sometimes attains the deception it seeks.—*Germany, Chap. I.*

---

**MAINE DE BIRAN (1766-1824).** *One of the few true Psychologists France has produced, who anticipated Schopenhauer in making the Will the main-spring of his Philosophy.*

I HAVE experienced, this evening, in a solitary walk taken during the finest weather, some instantaneous flashes of that ineffable enjoyment, which I have tasted at other times, and at

[1] Is Cobbett accurate here? It has always been supposed that it was a sundial (near the east end of the house) under which Temple's heart was buried in a silver box in 1698.

[2] About 1858 Moor Park was a Hydropathic Establishment. In 1896 it was again for sale.

such a season; of that pure pleasure, which seems to snatch us away from all that is of the earth, to give us a foretaste of heaven. The verdure had a new freshness, and took beauty from the last rays of the sinking sun; all things were instinct with a soft splendour; the trees waved tenderly their majestic crests; the air was full of balm, and the nightingales interchanged sighs of love, which yielded to accents of pleasure and joy.

I walked gently in an alley of young plane-trees, which I planted a few years since. Above all the vague incomplete impressions and images, which were born of the presence of the objects and my moods, hovered this feeling of the infinite which bears us onward sometimes towards a world superior to phenomena, towards this world of realities, which links itself to God, as the first and only reality. It seems in this condition, when all sensations without and within are calm and happy, as if there were a peculiar sense appropriate to heavenly things, which, wrapped up in the actual fashion of our existence, is destined perhaps to develop itself one day, when the soul shall have quitted its mortal husk.—*His Life and Thoughts* (*May* 17, 1815).

THERE has been a class of men, whose patriotic affection, or whose general benevolence, have been usually defrauded of the gratitude their country owes them : these have been the introducers of new flowers, new plants, and new roots into Europe; the greater part which we now enjoy was drawn from the luxuriant climates of Asia, and the profusion which now covers our land originated in the most anxious nursing, and were the gifts of individuals. Monuments are reared, and medals struck to commemorate events and names which are less deserving our regard than those, who have transplanted into the colder regions of the North, the rich fruits, the beautiful flowers, and the succulent pulse and roots of more favoured spots; and carrying into their own country, as it were, another Nature, they have, as old Gerard well expresses

ISAAC DISRAELI (1767-1848).

it, 'laboured with the soil to make it fit for the plants, and with the plants to make them delight in the soil.'

There is no part of the characters of Peiresc and Evelyn, accomplished as they are in so many, which seems more delightful to me, than their enthusiasm for the garden, the orchard, and the forest.—*Curiosities of Literature.*

—⋙—

**ALEXANDER VON HUMBOLDT** (1769-1859).

LANDSCAPE-PAINTING, notwithstanding the multiplication of its productions by engravings, and by the recent improvements in lithography, is still productive of a less powerful effect than that excited in minds susceptible of natural beauty, by the immediate aspect of groups of exotic plants in hot-houses or in gardens. I have already alluded to the subject of my own youthful experience, and mentioned that the sight of a colossal dragon-tree and of a fan-palm in an old tower of the botanical garden at Berlin, implanted in my mind the seeds of an irresistible desire to undertake distant travels.

He who is able to trace through the whole course of his impressions that which gave the first leading direction to his whole career, will not deny the influence of such a power.—*Cosmos,* Part I., § ii.

## CHAPTER IX

THE GARDEN IN THE NINETEENTH CENTURY

LAYING out grounds, as it is called, may be considered as a **WILLIAM WORDSWORTH** liberal art, in some sort like poetry and painting; and its ob- (1770-1850). ject, like that of all the liberal arts is, or ought to be, to move the affections under the control of good sense; that is, those of the best and wisest: but speaking with more precision, it is to assist Nature in moving the affections, and surely, as I have said, the affections of those who have the deepest perception of the beauty of Nature ; who have the most valuable feelings, that is, the most permanent, and most independent, the most ennobling, connected with Nature and human life. No liberal art aims merely at the gratification of an individual or a class: the painter or poet is degraded in proportion as he does so; the true servants of the arts pay homage to the human kind as impersonated in unwarped enlightened minds. If this be so when we are merely putting together words or colours, how much more ought the feeling to prevail when we are in the midst of the realities of things ; of the beauty and harmony, of the joy and happiness of living creatures ; of men and children, of birds and beasts, of hills and streams, and trees and flowers; with the changes of night and day, evening and morning, summer and winter; and all their unwearied actions and energies, as benign in the spirit that animates them, as they are beautiful and grand in that form and clothing which is given to them for the delights of our senses.—*Letter to Sir G. Beaumont*, 1805.

—ᴡᴡ—

YET now that these ridiculous anomalies have fallen into **SIR** general disuse, it must be acknowledged that there exist **WALTER SCOTT** gardens, the work of Loudon, Wise, and such persons as laid out (1771-1832). ground in the Dutch taste, which would be much better subjects

233

for modification than for absolute destruction. Their rarity now entitles them to some care as a species of antiques, and unquestionably they give character to some snug, quiet, and sequestered situations which would otherwise have no marked feature of any kind. We ourselves retain an early and pleasing recollection of the seclusion of such a scene. A small cottage, adjacent to a beautiful village, the habitation of an ancient maiden lady, was for some time our abode. It was situated in a garden of seven or eight acres, planted about the beginning of the eighteenth century, by one of the Millars, related to the author of the Gardener's Dictionary, or, for aught we know, by himself. It was full of long straight walks between hedges of yew and hornbeam, which rose tall and close on every side. There were thickets of flowering shrubs, a bower, and an arbour, to which access was obtained through a little maze of contorted walks, calling itself a labyrinth. In the centre of the bower was a splendid Platanus, or oriental plane—a huge hill of leaves—one of the noblest specimens of that regularly beautiful tree which we remember to have seen.[1] In different parts of the garden were fine ornamental trees which had attained great size, and the orchard was filled with fruit-trees of the best description. There were seats and trellis-walks and a banqueting house. Even in our time this little scene, intended to present a formal exhibition of vegetable beauty, was going fast to decay. The parterres of flowers were no longer watched by the quiet and simple *friends* under whose auspices they had been planted, and much of the ornament of the domain had been neglected or destroyed to increase its productive value. We visited it lately, after an absence of many years. Its air of retreat, the seclusion which its alleys afforded, was entirely gone; the huge Platanus had died, like most of its kind, in the beginning of this century; the hedges were cut down, the trees stubbed up and the whole character of the place so much destroyed, that I

[1] It was under this *Platanus* that Scott first devoured Percy's Reliques. I remember well being with him, in 1820, or 1821, when he revisited the favourite scene, and the sadness of his looks, when he discovered that 'the huge hill of leaves was no more.'—*J. G. Lockhart: Life of Sir Walter Scott.*

was glad when I could leave it.[1]—*Essay on Landscape Gardening.*
(*Quarterly Review*, 1828.)

—ww—

BUT out of doors as much regard was shown to beauty as to **ROBERT**
utility. Miss Allison and Betsey claimed the little garden **SOUTHEY**
in front of the house for themselves. It was in so neglected a (1774-1843).
state when they took possession that, between children and
poultry and stray pigs, not a garden flower was left there to grow
wild: and the gravel walk from the gate to the porch was overgrown with weeds and grass, except a path in the middle which
had been kept bare by use. On each side of the gate were three
yew-trees, at equal distances. In the old days of the Grange they
had been squared in three lessening stages, the uppermost tapering pyramidally to a point. While the house had been shorn of
its honours, the yews remained unshorn; but when it was once
more occupied by a wealthy habitant, and a new gate had been
set up and the pillars and their stone balls cleaned from moss
and lichen and short ferns, the unfortunate evergreens were again
reduced to the formal shape in which Mr Allison and his sister
remembered them in their childhood.

This was with them a matter of feeling, which is a better thing
than taste. And indeed the yews must either have been trimmed,
or cut down, because they intercepted sunshine from the garden,
and the prospect from the upper windows. The garden would
have been better without them, for they were bad neighbours:
but they belonged to old times, aud it would have seemed a sort
of sacrilege to destroy them.

Flower-beds used, like beds in the kitchen-garden, to be raised
a little above the path, with nothing to divide them from it, till
about the beginning of the seventeenth century; the fashion of
bordering them was introduced either by the Italians or the
French. Daisies, periwinkles, feverfew, hyssop, lavender, rosemary, rue, sage, wormwood, camomile, thyme, and box were used
for this purpose: a German horticulturist observes that hyssop

[1] See Note on page 234.

was preferred as the most convenient; box, however, gradually obtained the preference. The Jesuit Rapin claims for the French the merit of bringing this plant into use, and embellishes his account of it by one of those school-boy fictions which passed for poetry in his day, and may still pass for it in his country. He describes a feast of the rural Gods. . . .

Adfuit et Cybele, Phrygias celebrata per urbes, *etc*.

The fashion which this buxom Flora introduced had at one time the effect of banishing flowers from what should have been the flower garden; the ground was set with box in their stead, disposed in patterns more or less formal, some intricate as a labyrinth and not little resembling those of Turkey carpets, where Mahommedan laws interdict the likeness of any living thing, and the taste of Turkish weavers excludes any combination of graceful forms. One sense at least was gratified when fragrant herbs were used in these 'rare figures of composures,' or knots as they were called, hyssop being mixed in them with thyme, as aiders the one to the other, the one being dry, the other moist. Box had the disadvantage of a disagreeable odour; but it was greener in winter and more compact in all seasons. To lay out these knots and tread them required the skill of a master-gardener: much labour was thus expended without producing any beauty. The walks between them were sometimes of different colours; some would be of lighter or darker gravel, red or yellow sand ; and when such materials were at hand, pulverised coal, and pulverised shells.

Such a garden Mr Cradock saw at Bordeaux no longer ago than the year 1785; it belonged to Monsieur Rabi, a very rich Jew merchant, and was surrounded by a bank of earth, on which there stood about two hundred blue and white flower-pots; the garden itself was a scroll-work cut very narrow, and the interstices filled with sand of different colours to imitate embroidery; it required repairing after every shower, and if the wind rose, the eyes were sure to suffer. Yet the French admired this and exclaimed, *Superbe! magnifique!*

Neither Miss Allison nor her niece would have taken any

pleasure in gardens of this kind, which had nothing of a garden but the name. They both delighted in flowers; the aunt because flowers to her were 'redolent of youth,' and never failed to awaken tender recollections; Betsey for an opposite reason: having been born and bred in London, a nosegay there had seemed always to bring her a foretaste of those enjoyments for which she was looking forward with eager hope. They had stocked their front-garden therefore with the gayest and the sweetest flowers that were cultivated in those days; larkspurs, both of the giant and dwarf species, and of all colours; sweet-williams of the richest hues; monk's-hood for its stately growth; Betsey called it the dumbledore's delight, and was not aware that the plant, in whose helmet, rather than cowl-shaped flowers that busy and best-natured of all insects appears to revel more than in any other, is the deadly aconite of which she read in poetry: the white lily, and the fleur-de-lis; pœonies, which are still the glory of the English garden: stocks and gillyflowers which make the air sweet as the gales of Arabia; wall-flowers, which for a while are little less fragrant, and not less beautiful; pinks and carnations added their spicy odours; roses, red and white, peeped at the lower casements, and the jessamine climbed to those of the chambers above. You must nurse your own flowers, if you would have them flourish, unless you happen to have a gardener, who is as fond of them as yourself.

Eve was not busier with hers in Paradise, her 'pleasant task injoined,' than Betsey Allison and her aunt, from the time that early spring invited them to their cheerful employment, till late and monitory autumn closed it for the year.

'Solomon in all his glory was not arrayed like one of these'; and Solomon in all his wisdom never taught more wholesome lessons than these silent monitors convey to a thoughtful mind and an understanding heart. 'There are two books,' says Sir Thomas Browne, 'from whence I collect my Divinity; besides that written one of God, another of his servant Nature—that universal and public manuscript that lies expansed unto the eyes of all. Those that never saw him in the one have discovered him in the other. This was the scripture and theology of the heathens: the natural motion of the sun made them more admire him than its supernatural station did the children of Israel; the ordinary effects of nature wrought more admiration in them, than in the other all his miracles. Surely the heathens knew better how to join and read these mystical letters, than we Christians, who cast a more careless eye on those common hieroglyphics, and disdain to suck divinity from the flowers of Nature.'—*The Doctor.*

**SYDNEY SMITH (1774-1847).** *Canon of St Paul's, first Editor of* Edinburgh Review, *author of 'Peter Plymley's Letters,' 'Sketches of Moral Philosophy,' and countless witticisms.*

I WENT for the first time in my life, some years ago, to stay at a very grand and beautiful place in the country, where the grounds are said to be laid out with consummate taste. For the first three or four days I was perfectly enchanted; it seemed something so much better than nature, that I really began to wish the earth had been laid out according to the latest principles of improvement, and that the whole face of nature were a little more the appearance of a park. In three days' time I was tired to death; a thistle, a nettle, a heap of dead bushes, anything that wore the appearance of accident and want of intention, was quite a relief. I used to escape from the made grounds, and walk upon an adjacent goose-common, where the cart-ruts, gravel-pits, bumps, irregularities, coarse ungentlemanlike grass, and all the varieties produced by neglect, were a thousand times more gratifying than the monotony of beauties the result of design, and crowded into narrow confines with a luxuriance and abundance utterly unknown to nature.

**CHARLES LAMB (1775-1834).**

MINE too,—whose else?—thy costly fruit-garden, with its sun-baked southern wall; the ampler pleasure-garden, rising backwards from the house in triple terraces, with flower-pots now of palest lead, save that a speck here and there, saved from the elements, bespake their pristine state to have been gilt and glittering; the verdant quarters backwarder still; and stretching still beyond, in old formality, thy firry wilderness, the haunt of the squirrel, and the day-long murmuring wood-pigeon, with that antique image in the centre, god or goddess I wist not; but child of Athens or old Rome paid never a sincerer worship to Pan or to Sylvanus in their native groves, than I to that fragmental mystery.—*Essays of Elia (Blakesmoor in H——shire)*.

What a transition for a countryman visiting London for the first time—the passing from the crowded Strand or Fleet Street, by unexpected avenues, into its (the Temple's) magnificent ample squares, its classic green recesses! What a cheerful, liberal look hath that portion of it, which, from three sides, overlooks the greater garden; that goodly pile

'Of building strong, albeit of Paper hight,'

confronting with massy contrast, the lighter, older, more fantastically shrouded one, named of Harcourt, with the cheerful Crown Office-row (place of my kindly engendure), right opposite the stately stream, which washes the garden-foot with her yet scarcely trade-polluted waters, and seems but just weaned from her Twickenham Naïades! a man would give something to have been born in such places.

What a collegiate aspect has that fine Elizabethan hall, where the fountain plays, which I have made to rise and fall, how many times! to the astonishment of the young urchins, my contemporaries, who, not being able to guess at its recondite machinery, were almost tempted to hail the wondrous work as magic! What an antique air had the now almost effaced sun-dials, with their moral inscriptions, seeming coevals with that Time which they measured, and to take their revelations of its flight immediately from heaven, holding correspondence with the fountain of light! How would the dark line steal imperceptibly on, watched by the eye of childhood, eager to detect its movement, never catched, nice as an evanescent cloud, or the first arrests of sleep!

> Ah ! yet doth beauty, like a dial-hand,
> Steal from his figure, and no pace perceived !

What a dead thing is a clock, with its ponderous embowelments of lead or brass, its pert or solemn dulness of communication, compared with the simple altar-like structure and silent heart-language of the old dial ! It stood as the garden god of Christian gardens. Why is it almost everywhere banished? If its business-use be superseded by more elaborate inventions, its moral uses, its beauty, might have pleaded for its continuance. It spoke of moderate labours, of pleasures not protracted after sunset, of temperance, and good hours. It was the primitive clock, the horologe of the first world. Adam could scarce have missed it in Paradise. It was the measure appropriate for sweet plants and flowers to spring by, for the birds to apportion their silver warblings by, for flocks to pasture and be led to fold by. The 'shepherd carved it out quaintly in the sun'; and turning philosopher by the very occupation, provided it with mottoes more touching than tombstones. It was a pretty device of the gardener, recorded by Marvell, who, in the days of artificial gardening, made a dial out of herbs and flowers.

I must quote his verses a little higher up, for they are full, as all his serious poetry was, of a witty delicacy. They will not come in awkwardly, I hope, in a talk of fountains and sun-dials.

He is speaking of sweet garden scenes :—

> What wondrous life is this I lead !
> Rich apples drop about my head.
> The luscious clusters of the vine
> Upon my mouth do crush their wine.
> The nectarine and curious peach
> Into my hands themselves do reach.
> Stumbling on melons, as I pass,
> Insnared with flowers, I fall on grass.
> Meanwhile the mind from pleasure less
> Withdraws into its happiness.
> The mind, that ocean, where each kind
> Does straight its own resemblance find ;
> Yet it creates, transcending these,
> Far other worlds, and other seas,

> Annihilating all that's made
> To a green thought in a green shade.
> Here at the fountain's sliding foot,
> Or at some fruit-tree's mossy root,
> Casting the body's vest aside,
> My soul into the boughs does glide;
> There, like a bird, it sits and sings,
> Then whets and claps its silver wings,
> And till prepared for longer flight
> Waves in its plumes the various light.
> How well the skilful gardener drew
> Of flowers and herbs this dial new,
> Where from above the milder sun
> Does through a fragrant zodiac run;
> And as it works, the industrious bee
> Computes its time as well as we.
> How could such sweet and wholesome hours
> Be reckoned but with herbs and flowers?[1]

—*The Old Benchers of the Inner Temple.*

I am ill at dates, but I think it is now better than five-and-twenty years ago, that walking in the gardens of Gray's Inn—they were then far finer than they are now—the accursed Verulam Buildings had not encroached upon all the east side of them, cutting out the delicate green crankles, and shouldering away one or two of the stately alcoves of the terrace—the survivor stands gaping and relationless as if it remembered its brother—they are still the best gardens of any of the Inns of Court, my beloved Temple not forgotten—have the gravest character; their aspect being altogether reverend and law-breathing—Bacon has left the impress of his foot upon their gravel walks—taking my afternoon solace on a summer day upon the aforesaid terrace, a comely sad personage came towards me, whom from his grave air and deportment, I judged to be one of the old Benchers of the Inn. . . .—
*On some of the old Actors.*

When you come Londonward, you will find me no longer in Covent Garden; I have a cottage in Colebrook Row, Islington;

[1] From a copy of verses entitled 'The Garden.'

—a cottage, for it is detached; a white house with six good rooms in it; the New River (rather elderly by this time) runs (if a moderate walking pace can be so termed) close to the foot of the house; and behind is a spacious garden, with vines (I assure you); pears, strawberries, parsnips, leeks, carrots, cabbages, to delight the heart of old Alcinous. . . . I heard of you from Mr P. this morning, and that gave a fillip to my laziness, which has been intolerable; but I am so taken up with pruning and gardening, quite a new sort of occupation to me. I have gathered my jargonels, but my winter pears are backward. The former were of exquisite raciness. I do now sit under my own vine, and contemplate the growth of vegetable nature. I can now understand in what sense they speak of *Father Adam*. I recognise the paternity, while I watch my tulips. I almost feel with him too; for the first day I turned a drunken gardener (as he let in the serpent) into my Eden, and he laid about him, lopping off some choice boughs, etc., which hung over from a neighbour's garden, and in his blind zeal laid waste a shade, which had sheltered their window from the gaze of passers-by. The old gentlewoman (fury made her not handsome) could scarcely be reconciled by all my fine words. There was no buttering her parsnips. She talked of the law. What a lapse to commit on the first day of my happy 'garden state!'—*Letter to Bernard Barton.* (*Sept.* 2, 1823.)

—⋘⋙—

**WALTER SAVAGE LANDOR**
(1775-1865).

*TERNISSA.* I promise you I never will hate a tree again.
*Epicurus.* I told you so.
*Leontion.* Nevertheless I suspect, my Ternissa, you will often be surprised into it. I was very near saying, 'I hate these rude square stones!' Why did you leave them here, Epicurus?
*Epicurus.* It is true, they are the greater part square, and seem to have been cut out in ancient times for plinths and columns: they are also rude. Removing the smaller, that I might plant violets and cyclamens and convolvuluses and strawberries, and

such other herbs as grow willingly in dry places, I left a few of these for seats, a few for tables and for couches.

*Leontion.* Delectable couches!

*Epicurus.* Laugh as you may, they will become so when they are covered with moss and ivy, and those other two sweet plants, whose names I do not remember to have found in any ancient treatise, but which I fancy I have heard Theophrastus call 'Leontion' and 'Ternissa.' . . .

*Leontion.* Why have you torn up by the root all these little mountain ash-trees? This is the season of their beauty: come, Ternissa, let us make ourselves necklaces and armlets, such as may captivate old Sylvanus and Pan: you shall have your choice. But why have you torn them up?

*Epicurus.* On the contrary, they were brought hither this morning. Sosimenes is spending large sums of money on an olive-ground, and has uprooted some hundreds of them, of all ages and sizes. I shall cover the rougher part of the hill with them, setting the clematis and vine and honey-suckle against them, to unite them.

*Ternissa.* O what a pleasant thing it is to walk in the green light of the vine-leaves, and to breathe the sweet odour of their invisible flowers!

*Epicurus.* The scent of them is so delicate that it requires a sigh to inhale it; and, this, being accompanied and followed by enjoyment, renders the fragrance so exquisite. Ternissa, it is this, my sweet friend, that made you remember the green light of the foliage, and think of the invisible flowers as you would of some blessing from heaven.—*Imaginary Conversations.* (*Epicurus, Leontion, and Ternissa.*)

*Fillipo.* It is delightful to see their (the Moors') gardens, when one has not the weeding and irrigation of them. What fruit! what foliage! what trellises! what alcoves! what a contest of rose and jessamine for supremacy in odor! of lute and nightingale for victory in song! And how the little bright ripples of the docile brooks, the fresher for their races, leap up against one another to look on! And how they chirrup and applaud, as if they too had a voice of some importance in these parties of pleasure they are loath to separate.

*Eugenius.* Parties of pleasure! birds, fruits, shallow running waters, lute-players and wantons! Parties of pleasure! and composed of these! Tell me now, Filippo, tell me truly, what complexion in general have the discreeter females of that hapless country.

*Filippo.* The colour of an orange-flower, on which an overladen bee has left a suffusion of her purest honey.—*Ibid.* (*Fra Filippo Lippi and Pope Eugenius IV.*)

*Landor.* Enter the gardens and approach the vases: do you perceive the rarity, the beauty, the fragrance of the flowers? In one is a bush of box, in another a knot of tansy. Neptune is recumbent on a bed of cabbages, and from the shell of a Triton sprout three turnips ... to be sold.

*Pallavicini.* Our first object in the garden is profit. The vicinity of Genoa produces a large quantity of lemons, and many families are supported by renting, at about thirty crowns, half an acre or less of lemon ground. ...

*Landor.* We Englishmen talk of *planting* a garden; the modern Italians and ancient Romans talk of *building* one. Ours, the most beautiful in the universe, are not exempt from absurdities; but in the shadiness of the English garden it is the love of retirement that triumphs over taste, and over a sense of the inconveniences.

Inhabiting a moist and chilly climate, we draw our woods almost into our dining-rooms; you, inhabiting a sultry one, condemn your innocent children to the ordeal of a red-hot gravel. The shallow well called *pescina*, in the middle of every garden, contains just enough water to drown them—which happens frequently—and to supply a generation of gnats for the *villegianti*. We again may be ridiculed in our turn: our serpentine ditches are fog-beds.

You should cover your reservoirs (an old hat or wig would do it), and we should invite our Naiads to dance along the green a good half-mile from our windows.

The English are more zealous of introducing new fruits, shrubs and plants, than other nations; you Italians are less so than any civilised one. Better fruit is eaten in Scotland than in the most fertile and most cultivated parts of your peninsula. As for flowers, there is a greater variety in the worst of your fields than in the best of your gardens. As for shrubs, I have rarely seen a lilac, a laburnum, a mezereon, in any of them: and yet they flourish before almost every cottage in our poorest villages. I now come among the ordinary fruits. The currant, the gooseberry, and the raspberry—the most wholesome and not the least delicious—were domesticated among you by the French in some few places: they begin to degenerate already. I have eaten good apples in this country, and pears and cherries much better than ours; the other kinds of fruitage appeared to me unfit for the table, not to say uneatable; and as your gentlemen send the best to market, whether the produce of their own gardens or presents, I have probably tasted the most highly-flavored. Although the sister of Bonaparte introduced peaches, nectarines, and apricots from France, and planted them at Marlia, near Lucca, no person cares about taking grafts from them.

We wonder in England, when we hear it related by travellers, that peaches in Italy are left under the trees for swine; but, when we ourselves come into the country, our wonder is rather that the swine do not leave them for animals less nice.

I have now, Signor Marchese, performed the conditions you imposed on me, to the extent of my observation; hastily I confess it, and pre-occupied by the interest you excited.—*Ibid.* (*Marchese Pallavicini and Walter Landor.*)

—∿∿∿—

A FAR superior performance is the poem on Gardens by the Jesuit René Rapin. For skill in varying and adorning his subject, for a truly Virgilian spirit in expression, for the exclusion of feeble, prosaic, or awkward lines, he may perhaps be equal to

**HENRY HALLAM** (1777-1859).

any poet, to Sammarthanus or to Sannazarius himself. His cadences are generally very gratifying to the ear, and in this respect he is much above Vida. But his subject or his genius, has prevented him from rising very high; he is the poet of Gardens, and what Gardens are to nature, that is he to mightier poets. There is also too monotonous a repetition of nearly the same images, as in his long enumeration of flowers in the first book; the descriptions are separately good, and great artifice is shown in varying them; but the variety could not be sufficient to vary the general sameness that belongs to an horticultural catalogue. Rapin was a great admirer of box and all topiary works, or trees cut into artificial forms.

The first book of the Gardens of Rapin is on flowers, the second on trees, the third on waters, and the fourth on fruits. The poem is of about 3000 lines, sustained with equable dignity. All kinds of graceful associations are mingled with the description of his flowers, in the fanciful style of Ovid and Darwin; the violet is Ianthis, who lurked in valleys to shun the love of Apollo, and stained her face with purple to preserve her chastity: the rose is Rhodanthe, proud of her beauty, and worshipped by the people in the place of Diana, but changed by the indignant Apollo to a tree, while the populace, who had adored her, are converted into her thorns, and her chief lovers into snails and butterflies. A tendency to conceit is perceived in Rapin, as in the two poets to whom we have just compared him. Thus, in some pretty lines, he supposes Nature to have 'tried her prentice hand' in making a convolvulus, before she ventured upon a lily.

In Rapin there will generally be remarked a certain redundancy, which fastidious critics might call tautology of expression. But this is not uncommon in Virgil. The Georgics have rarely been more happily imitated, especially in their didactic parts, than by Rapin in the Gardens; but he has not the high flights of his prototype: his digressions are short and belong closely to the subject; we have no plague, no civil war, no Eurydice. If he praises Louis XIV., it is more as the Founder of the Garden of Versailles, than as the conqueror of Flanders, though his con-

# LORD CAMPBELL

cluding lines emulate with no unworthy spirit, those of the last Georgic. It may be added, that some French critics have thought the famous poem of Delille on the same subject inferior to that of Rapin.—*Introduction to the Literature of Europe.*

—ᴡᴡ—

*While reading for the Bar, acted as dramatic critic to the* Morning **LORD**
Chronicle; *later Lord Chief Justice and Lord Chancellor of England, and* **CAMPBELL**
*biographer of his predecessors in those offices. He declared himself on the* (1779-1861).
*hustings to be 'Plain Jock Campbell,' introduced and carried the 'Divorce Act' of* 1857, *defended Lord Melbourne and Mrs Norton, and is most often quoted in the Law Courts as the godfather of the Act for the protection of the British Workman.*

THE house, garden and pleasure-grounds (at Hartrigge, in Roxburghshire) were in a sad state of neglect, the former laird having been in embarrassed circumstances. I began with some zeal to repair and improve. I am a decided lover of London life, admiring the saying of the old Duke of Queensberry, who still sticking to his house in Piccadilly in the month of September, and being asked whether the town was not now rather empty, replied, 'Yes, but the country is much emptier.' Nevertheless, I am by no means insensible to the beauties of nature, and although I could not write a treatise *De Utilitate Stercorandi*, and most of the rural occupations enumerated by Cicero in his *De Senectute* are much above me, I have great delight in gardening. I have even a little farm in my own hands, and my heart swells within me when my turnips are praised as the most luxuriant, and my *stooks* are declared to be the most crowded to be seen in Teviotdale.—*Life of Lord Campbell, by his daughter, the Hon. Mrs Hardcastle.*

—ᴡᴡ—

IT is in society as in nature—not the useful, but the ornamental, **SIR**
that strikes the imagination. **HUMPHRY**
The monstrous flower, which produces nothing, arrests the eye; **DAVY**
the modest and humble germ of the grain, the staff of human (1778-1829).

## THE PRAISE OF GARDENS

life, is passed by with neglect: but the one is the fancy of the florist, and fades, and dies, and disappears for ever; the other is propagated from generation to generation, eternal in its use.

To raise a chestnut on the mountain, or a palm in the plain, which may afford shade, shelter, and fruit for generations yet unborn, and which, if they have once fixed their roots, require no culture, is better than to raise annual flowers in a garden, which must be watered daily, and in which a cold wind may chill or too ardent a sunshine may dry.—*Extracts from his Note-Books.*

---

**WASHINGTON IRVING**
(1783-1859).

THE taste of the English in the cultivation of land, and in what is called landscape-gardening, is unrivalled. They have studied nature intently, and discover an exquisite sense of her beautiful forms and harmonious combinations.

Those charms, which in other countries she lavishes in wild solitudes, are here assembled round the haunts of domestic life. They seem to have caught her coy and furtive graces, and spread them, like witchery, about their rural abodes.

Nothing can be more imposing than the magnificence of English park scenery. Vast lawns that extend like sheets of vivid green, with here and there clumps of gigantic trees, heaping up rich piles of foliage; the solemn pomp of groves and woodland glades, with the deer trooping in silent herds across them; the hare, bounding away to the covert; or the pheasant, suddenly bursting upon the wing: the brook, taught to wind in natural meanderings, or expand into a glassy lake: the sequestered pool, reflecting the quivering trees, with the yellow leaf sleeping on its bosom, and the trout roaming fearlessly about its limpid waters, while some rustic temple or sylvan statue, grown green and dark with age, gives an air of classic sanctity to the seclusion.

These are but a few of the features of park scenery; but what most delights me is the creative talent with which the English decorate the unostentatious abodes of middle life. The rudest habitation, the most unpromising and scanty portion of land, in the hands of an Englishman of taste, becomes a little paradise.

With a nicely discriminating eye, he seizes at once upon its capabilities, and pictures in his mind the future landscape. The sterile spot grows into loveliness under his hand; and yet the operations of art which produce the effect are scarcely to be perceived. The cherishing and training of some trees; the cautious pruning of others; the nice distribution of flowers and plants of tender and graceful foliage; the introduction of a green slope of velvet turf; the partial opening to a peep of blue distance, or silver gleam of water: all these are managed with a delicate tact, a pervading yet quiet assiduity, like the magic touchings with which a painter finishes up a favourite picture.— *The Sketch Book* ('*Rural Life in England.*')

---

*Describing his two years' imprisonment in the King's Bench for 'libelling' the Prince Regent as an ' Adonis of Fifty,' writes :—*

**LEIGH HUNT**
(1784-1859).

BUT I had another surprise, which was a garden. There was a little yard outside, railed off from another belonging to the neighbouring ward. This yard I shut in with green palings, adorned it with a trellis, bordered it with a thick bed of earth from a nursery, and even contrived to have a grass-plot. The earth I filled with flowers and young trees. There was an apple-tree from which we managed to get a pudding the second year. As to my flowers they were allowed to be perfect. A poet from Derbyshire (Mr Moore) told me he had seen no such heartsease. I bought the *Parnaso Italiano* while in prison, and used often to think of a passage in it, while looking at this miniature piece of horticulture :—

    Mio picciol orto,
  A me sei vigna, e campo, e silva, e prato.
          —*Baldi.*
    My little garden,
  To me thou'rt vineyard, field, and wood, and meadow.

Here I wrote and read in fine weather, sometimes under an awning. In autumn my trellises were hung with scarlet-runners, which added to the flowery investment. I used to shut my eyes in my arm-chair, and affect to think myself hundreds of miles off. But my triumph was in issuing forth of a morning. A wicket out of the garden led into the large one belonging to the prison. The latter was only for vegetables, but it contained a cherry-tree, which I twice saw in blossom.—*Lord Byron, and some of his Contemporaries.*

Variations of flowers are like variations in music, often beautiful as such, but almost always inferior to the theme on which they are founded—the original air. And the rule holds good in beds of flowers, if they be not very large, or in any other small assemblage of them. Nay, the largest bed will look well, if of one beautiful colour; while the most beautiful varieties may be inharmoniously mixed up. Contrast is a good thing, but we should first get a good sense of the thing to be contrasted, and we shall find this preferable to the contrast, if we are not rich enough to have both in due measure. We do not in general love and honour any one single colour enough, and we are instinctively struck with a conviction to this effect when we see it abundantly set forth. The other day we saw a little garden-wall completely covered with nasturtiums, and felt how much more beautiful it was than if anything had been mixed with it. For the leaves, and the light and shade, offer variety enough. The rest is all richness and simplicity united—which is the triumph of an intense perception. Embower a cottage thickly and completely with nothing but roses, and nobody would desire the interference of another plant.—*The Seer* ('*A Flower for your Window*').

—∿∿∿—

JOHN WILSON
(*Christopher North*)
(1785-1854).

AND thus it is, that to us all gardens are beautiful—and all gardeners Adam's favourite sons. An orchard! Families of fruit-trees 'high planted by a river,' and that river the Clyde. Till we gazed on you, we knew not how dazzling may be the

# JOHN WILSON 251

delicate spring, even more than the gorgeous autumn with all her purple and gold. No frost can wither, no blast can scatter such a power of blossoming as there brightens the day with promise that the gladdened heart may not for a moment doubt will be fulfilled ! And now we walk arm in arm with a venerable lady along a terrace hung high above a river—but between us and the brink of the precipice a leafless lawn—not of grass, but of moss, whereon centuries seem softly embedded—and lo ! we are looking—to the right down down the glen, and to the left up up the glen—though to the left it takes a majestic bend, so that yonder castle, seemingly almost in front of us, stands on one of its cliffs—now we are looking over the top of holly-hedges twenty feet high, and over the stately yew-pawns and peacocks—but hark ! the flesh-and-blood peacock shrieking from the pine ! An old English garden—such as Bacon, or Evelyn or Cowley would have loved—felicitously placed, with all its solemn calm, above the reach of the roar of a Scottish Flood !

But we shall not permit the visions of gardens thus to steady themselves before our imagination; and, since come they will, away must they pass like magic shadows on a sheet. There you keep gliding in hundreds along with your old English halls, or rectories, or parsonages—some, alas ! looking dilapidated and forlorn, but few in ruins, and thank heaven ! many of you in the decay of time renewed by love, and many more still fresh and strong, though breathing of antiquity, as when there was not one leaf of all that mass of ivy in which the highest chimneys are swathed and buried all the gables.—Oh ! stay but for one moment longer, thou garden of the cliffs ! Gone by ! with all thine imagery, half-garden and half-forest—reflected in thine own tarn—and with thee a glimmer of green mountains and of dusky woods ! Sweet visionary shadow of the poor man's cot and garden ! A blessing be upon thee, almost on the edge of the bleak moor !—But villages, and towns, and cities travel by mistily, carrying before our ken many a green series of little rural or suburban gardens, all cultivated by owners' or tenants' hands, and beneath the blossomed fruit-trees, the ground variegated with many a flush of flowers.—What pinks! Aye, we know them well—the beautiful garden plats on the banks and braes all round about our native town, pretty Paisley—and in among the very houses in nooks and corners which the sunshine does not scorn to visit—and as the glamour goes by, sweet to our soul is the thought of the Kilbarchan, the loveliest flower in heaven or on earth—for 'tis the prize pink of our childhood, given us by our Father's hand, and we see now the spot where the fine-grained glory grew.—*Loudon on the Education of Gardeners.* (*Blackwood's Magazine*, 1834.)

—ww—

**THOMAS LOVE PEACOCK (1785-1866).** *Friend of Shelley; for thirty-seven years clerk to the East India Company; married the 'Beauty of Carnarvonshire,' and wrote the poem 'Rhododaphne,' and the satyrical novels 'Headlong Hall,' 'Nightmare Abbey,' and 'Crotchet Castle.'*

*MR MILESTONE.*[1]—This, you perceive, is the natural state of one part of the grounds. Here is a wood, never yet touched by the finger of taste; thick, intricate, gloomy. Here is a little stream, dashing from stone to stone, and overshadowed with these untrimmed boughs.

*Miss Tenorina.*—The sweet romantic spot! How beautifully the birds must sing there on a summer evening!

*Miss Graziosa.*—Dear sister! How can you endure the horrid thicket?

*Mr Milestone.*—You are right, Miss Graziosa; your taste is correct, perfectly *en règle*. Now, here is the same place corrected —trimmed—polished—decorated—adorned. Here sweeps a plantation, in that beautiful regular curve; there winds a gravel walk; here are parts of the old wood, left in these majestic circular clumps, disposed at equal distances with wonderful symmetry; there are some singular shrubs scattered in elegant profusion; here a Portugal laurel, there a juniper; here a laurustinus, there a spruce fir; here a larch, there a lilac; here a

[1] Possibly a caricature of 'Capability' Brown or of Humphry Repton.

rhododendron, there an arbutus. The stream, you see, is become a canal: the banks are perfectly smooth and green, sloping to the water's edge: and there is Lord Littlebrain, rowing in an elegant boat.
*Squire Headlong.*—Magical, faith!
*Mr Milestone.*—Here is another part of the ground in its natural state. Here is a large rock, with the mountain-ash rooted in its fissures, over-grown, as you see, with ivy and moss, and from this part of it bursts a little fountain, that runs bubbling down its rugged sides.
*Miss Tenorina.*—O how beautiful! How I should love the melody of that miniature cascade!
*Mr Milestone.*—Beautiful, Miss Tenorina! Hideous. Base, common, and popular. Such a thing as you may see anywhere, in wild and mountainous districts. Now, observe the metamorphosis. Here is the same rock, cut into the shape of a giant. In one hand he holds a horn, through which the little fountain is thrown to a prodigious elevation. In the other is a ponderous stone, so exactly balanced as to be apparently ready to fall on the head of any person who may happen to be beneath, and there is Lord Littlebrain walking under it.
*Squire Headlong.*—Miraculous, by Mahomet!—*Headlong Hall.*

—∿∿∿—

I HAVE sent for my daughter from Venice, and I ride daily and walk in a garden, under a purple canopy of grapes, and sit by a fountain, and talk with the gardener of his tools, which seem greater than Adam's, and with his wife, and with his son's wife, who is the youngest of the party, and, I think, talks best of the three.—*Letter to Mr Murray. Bologna, Aug.* 24, 1819.

**LORD BYRON (1788-1824).**

It is worthy of remark that after all this outcry about '*indoor* nature,' and 'artificial images,' Pope was the principal inventor of that boast of the English, *Modern Gardening*. He divides this honour with Milton. . . . His various excellence is really wonderful: architecture, painting, *gardening*, are all alike subject to his genius. Be it remembered, that English *gardening* is the purposed perfectioning of niggard *Nature*, and that without it England is but a hedge-and-ditch, double-post-and-rail, Hounslow-heath and Clapham-common sort of a country, since the principal forests have been felled. It is in general far from a picturesque country. —Moore's ' *Notices of the Life of Lord Byron*,' 1821.

—∿∿∿—

ARTHUR SCHOPEN-HAUER (1788-1860).

YET how æsthetic is nature! Every spot that is entirely uncultivated and wild, *i.e.*, left free to himself, however small it may be, if only the hand of man remains absent, it decorates at once in the most tasteful manner, clothes it with plants, flowers and shrubs, whose unforced nature, natural grace, and tasteful grouping, bear witness that they have not grown up under the rod of correction of the great egoist, but that nature has here moved freely. Every neglected plant at once becomes beautiful. Upon this rests the principle of the English garden, which is as much as possible to conceal art, so that it may appear as if nature had here moved freely; for only then is it perfectly beautiful, *i.e.*, shows in the greatest distinctness the objectivication of the still unconscious will to live, which here unfolds itself with the greatest naïveté, because the forms are not, as in the animal world, determined by external ends, but only immediately by the soil, climate, and a mysterious third influence, on account of which so many plants which have originally sprung up in the same soil and climate yet show such different forms and characters.

The great difference between the English, or more correctly the Chinese, garden and the old French, which is now always becoming more rare, yet still exists in a few magnificent examples, ultimately rests upon the fact that the former is planned in an objective spirit, the latter in a subjective. In the former the will of nature, as it objectifies itself in tree and shrub, mountain and waterfall, is brought to the purest possible expression of these its Ideas, thus of its own inner being. In the French garden, on the other hand, only the will of the possessor of it is mirrored, which has subdued nature, so that instead of its Ideas it bears as tokens of its slavery the forms which correspond to that will, and which are forcibly imposed upon it—clipped hedges, trees cut into all kinds of forms, straight alleys, aud arched avenues.—*Arthur Schopenhauer*, '*The World as Will and Idea*' (*Isolated Remarks on Natural Beauty*).

—⁓⁓⁓—

*ET in Arcadia Ego!* 'I, too, have been a gardener'! Yes, I, too, have had as my first cradle a little rustic garden, hemmed in by a wall of unmortared stones, upon one of those parched and sombre hills which you see from here to the limits of your horizon ; there were to be found (for the more than modest mediocrity of my father's fortune did not allow it) neither vast tracts, nor majestic shade, nor gushing waters, nor rare flowers, nor precious fruits, nor costly plants ; a few narrow alleys strewn with red sand, edged with wild carnations, violets and primroses, and bordering plots of vegetables for the nurture of the family. Well, there, and not in the gardens of Italy or of the great proprietors of the parks of France, Germany, or England, I have experienced the first and most poignant delights that it is given to Nature to inspire in a soul, in a child's or youth's imagination. I dwell now in gardens vaster and more artistically planted but I have kept my predilection for that one. I keep it as a precious possession, in its ancient poverty of shade, water, flowers, and fruits; and when I have a few rare hours of liberty and solitude snatched from public affairs or labours of the mind to give to vague self-communings, it is to this garden I go to spend them. Yes, in this poor enclosure, long since deserted, emptied by death ; in these alleys overrun by weeds, by moss, and the pinks from the beds under those old trunks drained of sap, but not of souvenirs—on this unraked sand, my eye still seeks the footprints of my mother, of my sisters, old friends, old servants of the family, and I go and sit under the fence opposite the house, which is buried year by year deeper under the ivy, beneath the

ALPHONSE DE LAMARTINE (1790-1869).

rays of the setting sun to the hum of insects, the sound of the lizards of the old wall, whom I seem to recognise as old garden guests, and to whom it seems I might gossip about old times.—*An Address to Gardeners.*

---

PERCY BYSSHE SHELLEY (1792-1822).

WE saw the palace and gardens of Versailles and le Grand et Petit Trianon. They surpass Fontainebleau. The gardens are full of statues, vases, fountains, and colonnades. In all that essentially belongs to a garden they are extraordinarily deficient. The orangery is a stupid piece of expense. There was one orange-tree not apparently so old, sown in 1442. We saw also the gardens and the theatre at the Petit Trianon. The gardens are in the English taste and extremely pretty.—*Journal* (*Sept.* 3, 1816).

This shore of the Lake (Como) is one continued village, and the Milanese nobility have their villas here. The union of culture and the untameable profusion and loveliness of nature is here so close, that the line where they are divided can hardly be discovered. But the finest scenery is that of the Villa Pliniana; so called from a fountain which ebbs and flows every three hours, described by the younger Pliny, which is in the court-yard.

This house, which was once a magnificent palace and is now half in ruins, we are endeavouring to procure. It is built upon terraces *raised from* the bottom of the lake, together with its garden at the foot of a semi-circular precipice, overshadowed by profound forests of chestnut.

The scene from the colonnade is the most extraordinary, at once, and the most lovely that eye ever beheld. On one side is the mountain, and immediately over you are clusters of cypress-trees of an astonishing height, which seem to pierce the sky. Above you, from among the clouds, as it were, descends a waterfall of immense size, broken by the woody rocks into a thousand channels to the lake. On the other side is seen the blue extent of the lake and the mountains, speckled with sails and spires. The apartments of the Pliniana are immensely large, but ill-furnished and antique. The terraces which overlook the lake, and conduct under the shade of such immense laurel-trees as deserve the epithet of Pythian, are most delightful.—*Letters from Italy. To T. L. Peacock.* (*Milan, April* 20, 1818.)

In Rome, at least in the first enthusiasm of your recognition of ancient time, you see nothing of the Italians. The nature of the city assists the delusion, for its vast and antique walls describe a circumference of sixteen miles, and thus the population is thinly scattered over this place, nearly as great as London. Wide, wild fields are enclosed within it, and there are grassy lanes and copses winding among the ruins, and a great green hill, lonely and bare, which overhangs the Tiber. The gardens of the modern palaces are like wild woods of cedar, and cypress, and pine, and the neglected walks are overgrown with weeds. The English burying-place is a green slope near the walls, under the pyramidal tomb of Cestius, and is, I think, the most beautiful and solemn cemetery I ever beheld. To see the sun shining on its bright grass, fresh, when we first visited it, with the autumnal dews, and hear the whispering of the wind among the leaves of the trees which have overgrown the tomb of Cestius, and the soil which is stirring in the sun-warm earth, and to mark the tombs, mostly of women and young people who were buried there, one might, if one were to die, desire the sleep they seem to sleep. Such is the human mind, and so it peoples with its wishes vacancy and oblivion.— *Ibid.* (*Naples, Dec.* 22, 1818.)

—⋙—

AS it is, my garden claims a good portion of my spare time in the middle of the day, when I am not engaged at home or taking a walk; there is always something to interest me even in

**THOMAS ARNOLD**
(1795-1842).

the very sight of the weeds and litter, for then I think how much improved the place will be when they are removed; and it is very delightful to watch the progress of any work of this sort, and observe the gradual change from disorder and neglect to neatness and finish. In the course of the autumn I have done much in planting and altering, but these labours are now over, and I have now only to hope for a mild winter as far as the shrubs are concerned, that they may not all be dead when the Spring comes.—*Letter to J. T. Coleridge, Esq., Laleham. Nov.* 29, 1819.

—⁂—

**WILLIAM WHEWELL (1795-1866).**

THE reader need hardly be reminded that in the early periods of man's mental culture, he acquires those opinions on which he loves to dwell, not by the exercise of observation subordinate to reason; but, far more, by his fancy and his emotions, his love of the marvellous, his hopes and fears. It cannot surprise us, therefore, that the earliest lore concerning plants, which we discovered in the records of the past, consists of mythological legends, marvellous relations, and extraordinary medicinal qualities. To the lively fancy of the Greeks, the Narcissus, which bends its head over the stream, was originally a youth who in such an attitude, became enamoured of his own beauty; the hyacinth,[1] on whose petals the notes of grief were traced (AI, AI,),[2] recorded the sorrow of Apollo for the death of his favourite Hyacinthus; the beautiful Lotus of India,[3] which floats with its splendid flower on the surface of the water, is the chosen seat of the goddess Lackshmi, the daughter of Ocean.[4] In Egypt, too,[5] Osiris swam on a lotus-leaf, and Harpocrates was cradled in one. The lotus-

[1] Lilium Martagon.
[2] αἴ, αἴ: the Greek expression of woe.
   Ipse suos gemitus foliis inscribit et AI, AI,
   Flor habet inscriptum funestaque litera ducta est.—*Ovid.*
[3] Nelumbium Speciosum.
[4] Sprengel, *Geschichte der Botanik*, i. 27.   [5] *Ibid.* i. 28.

eaters of Homer lost immediately their love of home.—*History of the Inductive Sciences.*

AND from my heart poured out the feeling of love; it poured forth with wild longing into the broad night. The flowers in the garden beneath my window breathed a stronger perfume. Perfumes are the feelings of flowers, and as the human heart feels most powerful emotions in the night, when it believes itself to be alone and unperceived, so also do the flowers, soft-minded, yet ashamed, appear to await for concealing darkness, that they may give themselves wholly up to their feelings, and breathe them out in sweet odours.[1] Pour forth, ye perfumes of my heart, and seek beyond yon blue mountain for the loved one of my dreams.— *Pictures of Travel: The Hartz Journey.* (*Translated by Charles Godfrey Leland.*)

HENRI HEINE (1799-1856).

When I think of the great Emperor, all in my memory again becomes summer-green and golden. A long avenue of lindens rises blooming around, on the leafy twigs sit singing nightingales, the water-fall rustles, flowers are growing from full round beds, dreamily nodding their fair heads—I stood amidst them once in wondrous intimacy, the rouged tulips proud as beggars, condescendingly greeted me, the nervous sick lilies nodded with woeful tenderness, the tipsy red roses nodded at me at first sight from a distance, the night-violets sighed—with the myrtle and laurel I was not then acquainted, for they did not entice me with a shining bloom, but the *reseda*, with whom I am now on such bad terms, was my very particular friend.—I am speaking of the Court garden of Dusseldorf, where I often lay upon the bank and piously listened there when Monsieur Le Grand told of the warlike feats of the great Emperor, beating meanwhile the marches which were drummed during the deeds, so that I saw and heard all to the life.—*Ideas. Book Le Grand.* (*C. G. Leland.*)

[1] 'Les odeurs sont comme les âmes des fleurs : elles peuvent être sensibles dans le pays même des ombres.'—*J. Joubert.*

**AMOS BRONSON ALCOTT**
(b. 1799).

THUS we associate gardens and orchards with the perfect condition of mankind. Gardeners ourselves by birthright, we also mythologize and plant our Edens in the East of us, like our ancestors; the sacredness of earth and heaven still clinging to the tiller of the ground. Him we esteem the pattern man, the most favoured of any. His labours have a charming innocency. They yield the gains of a self-respect denied to other callings. His is an occupation friendly to every virtue; the freest of any from covetousness and debasing cares. It is full of honest profits, manly labours, and brings and administers all necessaries; gives the largest leisure for study and recreation, while it answers most tenderly the hospitalities of friendship, and the claims of home. The delight of children, the pastime of woman, the privilege of the poor man, as it is the ornament of the gentleman, the praise of the scholar, the security of the citizen, it places man in his truest relations to the world in which he lives. And he who is insensible to these pleasures, must lack some chord in the harp of humanity, worshipping, if he worship, at some strange shrine.

> Who loves a garden still his Eden keeps;
> Perennial pleasures plants, and wholesome harvests reaps.

—*Tablets.* (*The Garden, I. Antiquity.*)

Orchards are even more personal in their charms than gardens, as they are more nearly human creations. Ornaments of the homestead, they subordinate other features of it; and such is their sway over the landscape that house and owner appear accidents without them. So men delight to build in an ancient orchard, when so fortunate as to possess one, that they may live in the beauty of its surroundings. Orchards are among the most coveted possessions; trees' of ancient standing, and vines, being firm friends and royal neighbors for ever. The profits, too, are as wonderful as their longevity. And if antiquity can add any worth to a thing, what possession has a man more noble than these? So unlike most others, which are best at first, and grow worse till worth nothing; while fruit-trees and vines increase in worth and goodness for ages.—(*The Orchard.*)

'Thick-growing thyme, and roses wet with dew,
Are sacred to the sisterhood divine.'

As orchards to man, so are flowers and herbs to women. Indeed the garden appears celibate, as does the house, without womanly hands to plant and care for it. Here she is in place—suggests lovely images of her personal accomplishments, as if civility were first conceived in such cares, and retired unwillingly, even to houses and chambers; something being taken from their elegancy and her nobleness by an undue absorption of her thoughts in household affairs.

But there is a fitness in her association with flowers and sweet herbs, as with social hospitalities, showing her affinities with the magical and medical, as if she were the plant All-Heal, and mother of comforts and spices. Once the herb-garden was a necessary part of every homestead; every country house had one well stocked, and there was a matron inside skilled in their secret virtues, having the knowledge of how her

'Herbs gladly cure our flesh, because that they
Have their acquaintance there,'

her memory running back to the old country from whence they first came, and of which they retained the fragrance. Are not their names refreshing? with the superstitions concerning the sign under which they were to be gathered, the quaint spellings; mint, roses, fennel, coriander, sweet-cicely, celandine, summer savory, smellage, rosemary, dill, caraway, lavender, tanzy, thyme, balm, myrrh; these and many more, and all good for many an ail; sage, too, sovereign sage, best of all—excellent for longevity—of which to-day's stock seems running low—for

'Why should man die? So doth the sentence say,
When sage grows in his garden day by day?'
—(*Sweet Herbs.*)

EVERYTHING has its own perfection, be it higher or lower in the scale of things; and the perfection of one is not the perfection of another. Things animate, inanimate, visible, invisible, all are good in their kind, and have a best of themselves,

JOHN HENRY, CARDINAL NEWMAN (1801-1890).

which is an object of pursuit. Why do you take such pains with your garden or your park? You see to your walks, and turf, and shrubberies; to your trees and drives; not as if you meant to make an orchard of the one, or corn or pasture land of the other, but because there is a special beauty in all that is goodly in wood, water, plain, and slope, brought all together by art into one shape, and grouped into one whole.—*The Idea of a University.* (*Knowledge its own End.*)

---

**VICTOR HUGO (1802-1885).** THOUGHT is a virgin and fruitful soil, whose products insist on growing in freedom, and, so to speak, by chance, without arrangement, without being drilled into borders like the knots in one of Le Nôtre's classical gardens, or the flowers of language in a treatise on rhetoric.

Let it not, however, be supposed that this freedom must beget disorder; quite the reverse. Let us expand our idea.

Compare for an instant a royal garden of Versailles, well levelled, well clipped, well swept, well raked, well gravelled, quite full of little cascades, little basins, little groves, bronze tritons in ceremonious dalliance with oceans pumped up at great cost from the Seine, marble fauns wooing dryads allegorically imprisoned in a multitude of conical yews, cylindrical laurels, spherical orange-trees, elliptical myrtles, and other trees, whose natural form, too trivial, no doubt, has been gracefully corrected by the gardener's shears; compare this garden, so extolled, with a primitive forest of the New World, with its giant trees, its tall grasses, its deep vegetation, its thousand birds of a thousand hues, its broad avenues, where light and shadow play only upon the verdure, its wild harmonies, its great rivers which drift along islands of flowers, its stupendous waterfalls, over which hover rainbows! We will not say where is the magnificence? Where is the grandeur? Where is the beauty? But simply: where is the order? where is the disorder?

In the one, fountains, imprisoned or diverted from their course, gush from petrified gods, only to stagnate; trees transplanted from their native soil, torn away from their climate and forced to submit to the grotesque caprices of the shears and line; in a word natural order everywhere contradicted, inverted, upset, destroyed. In the other, on the contrary, all obeys an unchangeable law; in all a God seems to dwell. Drops of water follow their course and form rivers, which will form seas: seeds choose their soil and produce a forest. The very bramble is beautiful there. Again we ask, where is the order?

Choose, then, between the masterpiece of gardening and the work of nature; between what is conventionally beautiful, and what is beautiful without rule; between an artificial literature, and an original poesy!—*Preface to ' Odes and Ballads'* (1826).

—∿∿∿—

NOTHING more stamps the true Cockney than his hate for the sound of Bow bells. It is in vain that we squirearchs affect to sneer at the rural tastes of the cit in his rood of ground by the high-road to Hampstead; the aquarium stored with minnows and tittle-bats; the rock work of vitrified clinkers, rich with ferns borne from Wales and the Highlands. His taste is not without knowledge. He may tell us secrets in horticulture that would startle our Scotch gardener; and if ever he be rich and bold enough to have a farm, the chances are that he will teach more than he learns from the knowing ones who bet five to one on his ruin. And when these fameless students of Nature ramble forth from the suburb, and get for a while to the real heart of the country—when, on rare summer holidays they recline, in *remoto gramine*,—they need no choice Falernian, no unguents and brief-

EDWARD BULWER, LORD LYTTON[1] (1803-1873).

[1] 'This place of Lord Lytton's (Knebworth) stands well on a hill in the pretty part of Hertfordshire. It is a house originally of Henry VII.'s reign, and has been elaborately restored. The grounds, too, are very elaborate, and full of statues, kiosks, and knick-knacks of every kind. . . . But, like Lord Lytton himself, the place is a strange mixture of what is really romantic and interesting with what is tawdry, and gimcracky; and one is constantly coming upon stucco for stone, and bits in the taste of a second-rate Vauxhall stuck down in a beautiful recess of garden.'—*Matthew Arnold: Letter to his Mother, May* 12, 1869.

lived roses for that interval of full beatitude which the poet invites his friend to snatch from reprieving fates. Their delight proves the truth of my favourite aphorism—'that our happiest moments are those of which the memories are the most innocent.'—*Caxtoniana.*

—⁂—

**DOUGLAS JERROLD**
(1803-1857).

A SMALL quiet nook of a place nestled among trees, and carpeted with green around. And there a brook should murmur with a voice of out-door happiness; and a little garden brimming over with flowers should mark the days and weeks and months, with bud and blossom; and the worst injuries of time be fallen leaves. And then, health in balm should come about my path and my mind be as a part of every fragrant thing that shone and grew around me.

A garden is a beautiful book, writ by the finger of God; every flower and every leaf is a letter. You have only to learn them —and he is a poor dunce that cannot, if he will, do that—to learn them and join them, and then to go on reading and reading, and you will find yourself carried away from the earth to the skies by the beautiful story you are going through. You do not know what beautiful thoughts—for they are nothing short —grow out of the ground, and seem to talk to a man. And then there are some flowers, they always seem to me like over-dutiful children: tend them ever so little, and they come up and flourish, and show, as I may say, their bright and happy faces to you.

—⁂—

**GEORGE SAND**
(1804-1876).

LE nouveau jardin vallonné et semé de corbeilles de fleurs exotiques, c'est toujours, en somme, le petit Trianon de la décadence classique et le jardin anglais du commencement de ce siècle, perfectionnés en ce sens qu'on en a multiplié les mouvements et les accidents afin de réussir à réaliser l'aspect du paysage naturel dans un espace limité. Rien de moins justifié, selon nous, que ce titre de *jardin paysager* dont s'empare aujourd'hui tout bourgeois dans sa ville de province. Même, dans les espaces plus vastes que Paris consacre à cette fiction, n'espérez pas trouver le charme de la nature. Le plus petit recoin des roches de Fontainebleau ou des collines boisées de l'Auvergne, la plus mince cascatelle de Gargilesse, le plus ignoré des méandres de l'Indre ont une autre tournure, une autre saveur, une autre puissance de pénétration que les plus somptueuses compositions de nos *paysagistes* de Paris! si vous voulez voir le jardin, de la création, n'allez pas au bout du monde. Il y en a dix mille en France dans des endroits où personne n'a affaire ou dont personne ne s'avise. Cherchez, vous trouverez!

Mais si vous voulez voir le jardin *décoratif* par excellence, vous l'aurez à Paris, et disons bien vite que l'invention en est ravissante. C'est du décor, pas autre chose, prenez-en votre parti, mais du décor adorable et merveilleux. La science et le goût s'y sont donné la main; inclinez-vous, c'est un jeune ménage.—*La Rêverie à Paris* (*Paris Guide*. 1867.)[1]

—∿∿∿—

ARMINE PLACE, before Sir Ferdinand, unfortunately for his descendants, determined in the eighteenth century on building a feudal castle, had been situate in famous pleasure-grounds, which extended at the back of the mansion over a space of some hundred acres. The grounds in the immediate vicinity of the buildings had of course suffered severely, but the far greater portion had only been neglected; and there were some indeed who deemed, as they wandered through the arbour-walks of this enchanting wilderness, that its beauty had been enhanced even by this very neglect. It seemed like a forest in a beautiful romance; a green and bowery wilderness where Boccacio would have loved to woo, and Watteau to paint. So artfully had the walks been planned that they seemed interminable; nor was

BENJAMIN DISRAELI (1804-1881).

[1] Never before or since has such a constellation of the genius of a whole nation gathered together to produce such a Guide-book, as Paris out-did herself by publishing in 1867. It is perhaps the highest achievement of the Third Empire.

there a single point in the whole pleasaunce, where the keenest eye could have detected a limit. Sometimes you wandered in those arched and winding walks dear to pensive spirits: sometimes you emerged on a plot of turf blazing in the sunshine, a small and bright savannah, and gazed with wonder on the group of black and mighty cedars that rose from its centre, with their sharp and spreading foliage. The beautiful and the vast blended together; and the moment after you had beheld with delight a bed of geraniums or of myrtles, you found yourself in an amphitheatre of Italian pines. A strange exotic perfume filled the air; you trod on the flowers of other lands; and shrubs and plants, that usually are only trusted from their conservatories, like Sultanas from their jalousies, to sniff the air and recall their bloom, here learning from hardship the philosophy of endurance, had struggled successfully even against northern winters, and wantoned now in native and unpruned luxuriance. Sir Ferdinand, when he resided at Armine, was accustomed to fill these pleasure-grounds with macaws, and other birds of gorgeous plumage; but these had fled away with their master, all but some swans, which still floated on the surface of a lake which marked the centre of this paradise.—*Henrietta Temple.*

—ww—

**NATHANIEL HAWTHORNE** (1807-1864).

THESE gardens of New College are indescribably beautiful,—not gardens in our American sense, but lawns of the richest green and softest velvet grass, shadowed over by ancient trees, that have lived a quiet life here for centuries, and have been nursed and tended with such care, and so sheltered from rude winds, that certainly they must have been the happiest of all trees. Such a sweet, quiet, sacred, stately seclusion—so age-long as this has been, and, I hope, will continue to be—cannot exist anywhere else.

We concluded the rambles of the day by visiting the gardens of St John's College; and I desire, if possible, to say even more in admiration of them than of those of New College,—such beautiful lawns with tall ancient trees, and heavy clouds of foliage, and sunny glimpses through archways of leafy branches, where, to-day, we could see parties of girls, making cheerful contrast with the sombre walls and solemn shade. The world, surely, has not another place like Oxford; it is a despair to see such a place, and ever to leave it, for it would take a lifetime, and more than one, to comprehend and enjoy it satisfactorily.—*English Note-Books.* (*Oxford.*)

Positively the garden of Eden cannot have been more beautiful than this private garden of Blenheim. It contains three hundred acres, and by the artful circumlocution of the paths, and the undulations, and the skilfully interposed clumps of trees, is made to appear limitless. The sylvan delights of a whole country are compressed into this space, as whole fields of Persian roses go to the concoction of an ounce of precious attar. The world within that garden fence is not the same weary and dusty world with which we outside mortals are conversant; it is a finer, lovelier, more harmonious Nature; and the Great Mother lends herself kindly to the gardener's will, knowing that he will make evident the half-obliterated traits of her pristine and ideal beauty, and allow her to take all the credit and praise to herself. I doubt whether there is ever any winter within that precinct,—any clouds, except the fleecy ones of summer. The sunshine that I saw there rests upon my recollection of it as if it were eternal. The lawns and glades are like the memory of places where one has wandered when first in love.—*Our Old Home.* (*Near Oxford.*)

My garden, that skirted the avenue of the Manse, was of precisely the right extent. An hour or two of morning labour was all that it required. But I used to visit and revisit it a dozen times a day, and stand in deep contemplation over my vegetable progeny with a love that nobody could share or conceive of, who had never taken part in the process of creation.

It was one of the most bewitching sights in the world to

observe a hill of beans thrusting aside the soil, or a row of early peas just peeping forth sufficiently to trace a line of delicate green. Later in the season the humming-birds were attracted by the blossoms of a peculiar variety of bean; and they were a joy to me, those little spiritual visitants, for deigning to sip airy food out of my nectar-cups. Multitudes of bees used to bury themselves in the yellow blossoms of the summer-squashes. This, too, was a deep satisfaction; although, when they had laden themselves with sweets, they flew away to some unknown hive, which would give back nothing in requital of what my garden had contributed. But I was glad thus to fling a benefaction upon the passing breeze with the certainty that somebody must profit by it, and that there would be a little more honey in the world to allay the sourness and bitterness which mankind is always complaining of. Yes, indeed; my life was the sweeter for that honey.—*The Old Manse*.[1]

—vvv—

**ALPHONSE KARR (1808-1890).**

ONE of the chief charms I find in a garden, is to say to myself: 'I am shut up, I and my imagination, my body and spirit, in a place filled with flowers, that is to say, with rich colours, dulcet perfumes, and songs of birds (enchanting harmony, which nothing can interrupt), where no one will come, except a friend; but neither mar-joys, the evil-minded, nor enemies can find entrance, any more than my spirit can issue forth to visit them. I keep them imprisoned outside as I keep myself imprisoned within; I create for myself a part of the earth, of the sky, of the grass, and of the flowers, but that part is my own.' To do this, a garden must not be too large; you must feel yourself enclosed in it.

It may be possible not to see the walls, but you must not forget them. It seems as though Nature and Providence have intended man to surround himself with walls, by creating so many beautiful plants, which hide and decorate them wondrously, and which are

[1] The Old Manse was Emerson's residence on the Concord, when he wrote 'Nature.'

nowhere so luxuriant, so beautiful, and so happy, as when beaming upon and spreading over a wall.—*Letters written from my Garden.*

At the bottom of my garden, the vine stretches in long piazzas, through whose arcades are seen trees of every kind, and foliage of every hue.

On this side is an *azerolier*, which in the Fall is hung with little scarlet berries of the richest lustre. I have given several cuttings from it: far from obtaining pleasure from the privation of others, I strive to scatter and make common and vulgar the trees and plants which I prefer; it is to me, as to those who really love flowers for their brilliance, their grace, and their perfume, a multiplication of pleasure, and of the chance of seeing them. They who, on the contrary, are misers of their plants, and who only value them in so far as they are satisfied no one else possesses them, do not love flowers; and rest assured that either accident or poverty has driven them to collect flowers, instead of collecting pictures, gems, or medals, or in a word any other thing which might serve as a pretext for all the joys of possession, heightened by their being owned by no one else.

I have carried the vulgarization of beautiful flowers a step further.

I go for walks round about the place where I live into the wildest and most deserted nooks.

There, after having properly prepared a few inches of ground, I scatter the seeds of my richest plants, which re-sow themselves, are perpetuated, and multiply. Already, whilst the fields round about have only the scarlet wild poppy, it must surprise passers-by to see in certain wild ingles of our little country the finest double poppies, white, rose, red, edged with white, etc; and the most splendid garden poppies, violet, white, lilac, scarlet, and white tipped with scarlet, etc.; at the foot of a lonely tree, instead of the bindweed with its white field-flowers, are to be found here and there patches of convolvulus major, blue, violet, pink, white streaked with red and violet, etc.

Then I enjoy all alone and in advance the pleasures of surprise, which the solitary dreamer will feel, who chances in his walks upon these beautiful flowers or luscious fruits.

That will one day afford some learned botanist, who will go and herborize thereabouts a hundred years hence, long after my death, opportunity to publish a ridiculous system. All these beautiful flowers will have grown common in the country, and will give it a quite unique look, and maybe chance and wind will cast some of their seeds amid the grass which hides my lonely grave. Vale.—*A Voyage round my Garden.*

—ww—

OLIVER
WENDELL
HOLMES
(1809-1894).

I KNOW this, that the way Mother Earth treats a boy shapes out a kind of natural theology for him. I fell into Manichean ways of thinking from the teaching of my garden experiences. Like other boys in the country, I had my patch of ground, to which, in the spring-time, I intrusted the seeds furnished me, with a confident trust in their resurrection and glorification in the better world of summer.

But I soon found that my lines had fallen in a place where a vegetable growth had to run the gauntlet of as many foes and trials as a Christian pilgrim. Flowers would not blow; daffodils perished like criminals in their condemned cups, without their petals ever seeing daylight; roses were disfigured with monstrous protrusions through their very centres,—something that looked like a second bud pushing through the middle of the corolla; lettuces and cabbages would not head; radishes knotted themselves until they looked like centenarian's fingers; and on every stem, on every leaf, and both sides of it, and at the root of everything that grew, was a professional specialist in the shape of a gnat, caterpillar, aphis, or other expert, whose business it was to devour that particular part, and help murder the whole attempt at vegetation. Such experiences must influence a child born to them. A sandy soil, where nothing flourishes but weeds and evil beasts of small dimensions, must breed different qualities in its human offspring from one of those fat and fertile spots which the wit whom I have once before quoted described so happily, that, if I quoted the passage, its brilliancy would spoil one of my pages, as a diamond breastpin sometimes kills the social effect of the wearer, who might have passed for a gentleman without it.—*The Poet at the Breakfast Table.*

---

NO definition has spoken of the landscape-gardener as of the poet; yet it seemed to my friend that the creation of the landscape-garden offered to the proper Muse the most magnificent of opportunities.

EDGAR ALLAN POE (1811-1849).

Here, indeed, was the fairest field for the display of imagination in the endless combining of forms of novel beauty; the elements to enter into combination being, by a vast superiority, the most glorious which the earth could afford. In the multiform and multicolour of the flowers and the trees, he recognised the most direct and energetic efforts of Nature at physical loveliness. And in the direction or concentration of this effort—or, more properly, in its adaptation to the eyes, which were to behold it on earth—he perceived that he should be employing the best means—labouring to the greatest advantage—in the fulfilment, not only of his own destiny as poet, but of the august purposes for which the Deity had implanted the poetic sentiment in man.—*The Domain of Arnheim.*

---

LA Chénaie is a sort of oasis in the midst of the steppes of Brittany. In front of the château stretches a very large garden cut in two by a terrace with a lime avenue, at the end of which is a tiny chapel. I am extremely fond of this little oratory, where one breathes a two-fold peace,—the peace of solitude and the peace of the Lord. When Spring comes we shall walk to prayers between two borders of flowers. On the east side, and only a few yards from the château, sleeps a small mere between

MAURICE DE GUÉRIN (1811-1839).

two woods, where the birds in warm weather sing all day long; and then,—right, left, on all sides,—woods, woods, everywhere woods.—*Letter to M. de Bayne, Christmas Day*, 1832.

One can actually *see* the progress of the green; it has made a start from the garden to the shrubberies, it is getting the upper hand all along the mere; it leaps, one may say, from tree to tree, from thicket to thicket, in the fields and on the hill-sides; and I can see it already arrived at the forest hedge and beginning to spread itself over the broad back of the forest.—*Letters (translated by Matthew Arnold.)*

**THÉOPHILE GAUTIER (1811-1872).** SOME time ago we dreamed to plan a garden wherein Nature should have full liberty. Never should the bill-hook cut one branch in it, nor shears trim a hedge or a border. The twigs would have been quite free to interlace themselves according to their own fancy: the plants, to creep and climb; the mosses, to cover with their patches the trunks of trees; the lichens, to make the statues white with their grey bands; the brambles, to bar the walks and arrest you with their thorns; the wild poppy, to raise its red spark near the untrained rose; the ivy, to shoot its roving wreaths, and hang over the balustrades of terraces. Full license would have been granted to the nettle, the thistle, the celandine, the cleavers, which cling to you like a burr; to the burdock, the nightshade, the quitch—to all the gipsy horde of undisciplined plants—to grow, multiply, invade, obliterate every trace of cultivation, and to turn the flower-garden into a miniature forest.

This forsaken paradise, we should, besides, have liked to see surrounded with walls green with moss, clothed with mural plants, and crowned with stocks, iris, gilliflowers, and seagreens, in place of the broken glass, wherewith it is usual to deter the intruding urchins; and over the rain-washed gate, bare of paint, and having no trace of that green colour beloved by Rousseau, we would have written this inscription in black letters, stone-like in shape, and threatening of aspect: 'Gardeners are prohibited from entering here.'—*Nature at Home.*

Gardens were then (under Louis XIV.) built as much as planted, and the trees had to approximate to architectural forms. The hedges were folded back at right angles like the leaves of a screen of verdure. The yews were sharpened to a pyramid, or rounded to a ball; deft shears outlined arches in clumps of foliage, and what we now know as the 'picturesque,' was sedulously avoided. This taste, improperly called the French taste, reached us from Italy, where the villas and vines of the popes and Roman princes set the example of this mixture of terraces, fabrics, statues, vases, green trees and spouting waters.

We ourselves, in the day of Romanticism, had more or less paraphrased the ingenious antithesis, which Victor Hugo,[1] in the preface of *Cromwell*, made between a virgin forest of America and the gardens of Versailles, and we have jested, like others, about 'the little yews in onion-rows.'[2]

We were wrong; this garden was quite the garden of this château, and there was a marvellous harmony in this collection of regular forms, in which the life of the period could develop at ease its majestic and rather sluggish evolutions. The result is an impression of grandeur, symmetry and beauty, which no one can resist. Versailles ever remains unrivalled in the world: it is the supreme formula of a complete art, and the expression, at its highest power, of a civilisation arrived at its complete expansion.

When, under Louis XVI., the garden was replanted, taste had changed. The Citizen Rousseau of Geneva had discovered Nature; English ideas invaded the Continent, fashion was with 'the landscape gardeners,' that is to say, with hilly sites, clumps

---

[1] See p. 262.
[2] O dieux ! O bergers ! O rocailles !
Vieux Satyres, Termes grognons,
   Vieux petits ifs en rang d'oignons,
O bassins, quinconces, charmilles,
   Boulingrins pleins de majesté,
Où, les dimanches, tout l'été
   Bâillent tant d'honnêtes familles.

*Alfred de Musset.*

of untrimmed trees, sinuous alleys, green lawns, sheets of water crossed by rustic bridges, sham grottoes, artificial ruins, cottages containing automata performing country labours. By admiring such things, one showed that one had a soul of *sensibility*, a great pretension of the period, and the thought arose of remodelling the garden in the modern style . . . this transformation was effected by the plans of Hubert Robert, the designer in fashion, the painter of ruins, the 'Romantique' of the day, an artist endowed with a decorative and picturesque feeling still appreciated in our day, whose pictures and sketches full of intelligence are still collected by amateurs.—*Tableaux de Siège* (*Le Versailles de Louis XIV.*).[1]

---

**ALEXANDER WILLIAM KINGLAKE (1811-1891).**

WILD as the nighest woodland of a deserted home in England, but without its sweet sadness, is the sumptuous Garden of Damascus. Forest trees tall and stately enough, if you could see their lofty crests, yet lead a bustling life of it below, with their branches struggling against strong numbers of bushes and wilful shrubs. The shade upon the earth is black as night. High, high above your head, and on every side all down to the ground, the thicket is hemmed in and choked up by the interlacing boughs that droop with the weight of roses, and load the slow air with their damask breath. The rose-trees which I saw were all of the kind we call *damask*—they grow to an immense height and size. There are no other flowers. Here and there are patches of ground made clear from the cover, and these are either carelessly planted with some common and useful vegetable, or else are left free to the wayward ways of nature, and bear rank weeds, moist-looking and cool to your eyes, and freshening the sense with their earthy and bitter fragrance. There is a lane opened through the thicket, so broad in some places that you can pass along side by side—in some so narrow (the shrubs are for ever encroaching) that you ought, if you can,

[1] See Account of Versailles in Appendix.

to go on the first and hold back the bough of the rose-tree. And
through this wilderness there tumbles a loud rushing stream, which
is halted at last in the lowest corner of the garden, and then tossed
up in the fountain by the side of the simple alcove. This is all.
Never for an instant will the people of Damascus attempt to
separate the idea of bliss from these wild gardens and rushing
waters.—*Eöthen*.

—ᗯᗯ—

MEANWHILE my beans, the length of whose rows, added HENRY
together, was seven miles already planted, were impatient DAVID
to be hoed, for the earliest had grown considerably before the (1817-1862).
latest were in the ground; indeed, they were not easily to be put
off. What was the meaning of this so steady and self-respecting,
this small Herculean labour, I knew not. I came to love my
rows, my beans, though so many more than I wanted. They
attached me to the Earth, and so I got strength like Antœus.
But why should I raise them? Only Heaven knows. This was
my curious labour all summer,—to make this portion of the
Earth's surface, which had yielded only cinquefoil, blackberries,
johnswort, and the like, before, sweet wild fruits and pleasant
flowers, produce instead this pulse? What shall I learn of beans
or beans of me? I cherish them, I owe them, early and late I
have an eye to them, and this is my day's work. It is a fine
broad leaf to look on. My auxiliaries are the dews and rains,
which water this dry soil, and what fertility is in the soil itself,
which for the most part is lean and effete. My enemies are
worms, cool days, and most of all woodchucks. The last have
nibbled for me a quarter of an acre clean. But what right had I
to oust johnswort and the rest, and break up their ancient herb-
garden.—*Walden*.

—ᗯᗯ—

JE me suis toujours plu à chercher dans la nature extérieure et CHARLES
visible des exemples et des métaphores qui me servissent à BAUDELAIRE
caractériser les jouissances et les impressions d'un ordre spirituel. (1821-1867).
Je rêve à ce que me faisait éprouver la poésie de Madame Valmore

quand je la parcourus avec ces yeux de l'adolescence qui sont, chez les hommes nerveux, à la fois si ardents et si clairvoyants. Cette poésie m'apparait comme un jardin : mais ce n'est pas la solennité grandiose de Versailles ; ce n'est pas non plus le pittoresque vaste et théâtral de la savante Italie qui connaît si bien l'art *d'édifier des jardins* (*œdificat hortos*) ; pas même, non pas même *la Vallée des Flutes* ou le *Tenare* de notre vieux Jean Paul. C'est un simple jardin anglais, romantique et romanesque. Des massifs de fleurs y représentent les abondants expressions du sentiment. Des étangs, limpides et immobiles, qui réfléchissent toutes choses s'appuyant à l'envers sur la voûte renversée des cieux, figurent la profonde résignation toute parsemée de souvenirs. Rien ne manque à ce charmant jardin d'un autre âge : ni quelques ruines gothiques se cachant dans un lieu agreste, ni le mausolée inconnu qui, au détour d'une allée, surprend notre âme et lui commande de penser à l'éternité. Des allées sinueuses et ombragées aboutissent à des horizons subits. Ainsi la pensée du poëte, après avoir suivi de capricieux méandres, débouche sur les vastes perspectives du passé ou de l'avenir ; mais ces ciels sont trop vastes pour être généralement purs, et la température du climat trop chaude pour n'y pas amasser des orages. Le promeneur, en contemplant ces étendues voilées de deuil, sent monter à ses yeux les pleurs de l'hystérie, *hysterical tears*. Les fleurs se penchent vaincues, et les oiseaux ne parlent qu' à voix basse. Après un éclair précurseur, un coup de tonnerre a retenti : c'est l'explosion lyrique ; enfin un déluge inévitable de larmes rend à toutes ces choses, prostrées, souffrantes et découragées la fraîcheur et la solidité d'une nouvelle jeunesse !—*Literary Notice of Madame Desbordes-Valmore* (*Les Poëtes Français*).

—〰〰—

HENRI
FREDERIC
AMIEL
(1821-1881).

THIS morning the air was calm, the sky slightly veiled. I went out into the garden to see what progress the spring was making. I strolled from the irises to the lilacs, round the flower-beds and in the shrubberies. Delightful surprise !

at the corner of the walk, half hidden under a thick clump of shrubs, a small-leaved *chorchorus* had flowered during the night. Gay and fresh as a bunch of bridal flowers, the little shrub glittered before me in all the attraction of its opening beauty. What spring-like innocence, what soft and modest loveliness there was in these white corollas, opening gently to the sun, like thoughts which smile upon us at waking, and perched upon their young leaves of virginal green like bees upon the wing! Mother of marvels, mysterious and tender Nature, why do we not live more in thee? . . . A modest garden and a country rectory, the narrow horizon of a garret, contain for those who know how to look and to wait, more instruction than a library.—*29th April* 1852 (*Lancy*).

*31st October* 1852 (*Lancy*). Walked for half an hour in the garden. A fine rain was falling, and the landscape was that of autumn. The sky was hung with various shades of gray, and mists hovered about the distant mountains,—a melancholy nature. The leaves were falling on all sides like the last illusions of youth under the tears of irremediable grief. A brood of chattering birds were chasing each other through the shrubberies, and playing games among the branches, like a knot of hiding schoolboys. Every landscape is, as it were, a state of the soul, and whoever penetrates into both is astonished to find how much likeness there is in each detail.—*Journal Intime* (*translated by Mrs Humphry Ward*).

THE garden, which I had bought with my house, although planted with common, vulgar, philistine shrubs, still possessed one beauty. At the bottom of it stood a superb group of huge trees of the ancient Montmorency Park, all draped in ivy and unfolding over the head of a low rock one of those great fans of verdure, with which Watteau shades the repose and siesta of his courtly groups. This I had to preserve, while uprooting all the rest, and to set this bouquet of great trees in a centre of hardy evergreen shrubs, which under winter sunlight simulate a summer garden; and these shrubs I had to choose from rare sources, for the rare in everything, whatever may be said, is almost always the beautiful. . . . There was something further to do in the state of research and actual progress of horticulture, and in the rehandling and *artist* recolouring of natural verdure; it was the duty of a *colourist* man-of-letters to make a painter's garden, and to set before his eyes on a large scale a palette of greens shading from the deep greens to the tender ones, through the range of the blue-greens of the Juniper tree, the golden-brown greens of the Cryptomerias, and all the varied blendings of hue of Hollies, Spindle trees and Aucubas, which, by the pallor of their leaves, give an illusion of flowers in their absence. Let us confess that in this style of gardening, which has a touch of bric-à-brac about it, the bush elegantly branched, charmingly trained, coquettishly variegated, becomes a kind of art-object, which we see again with closed eyes, dream of in bed, and imagine ourselves seeking in the private garden of a great horticulturist, just as we might pursue a rarity hidden upon the shelf of the private collection of a great curio-hunter. . . .

Here is June with the flowering of the rhododendrons, and the crumpling of their pink and mauve tulle, which calls up visions of ball dresses; and with their lovely tawny and black spots like drones cradled in the core of the flower; and here with the flowering of the rhododendrons come the blossoms of the climbing roses which mount into the great trees and are lost in the ivy. Trails, wreaths, cascades, arranged as deftly as those of the old Venetian masters around the curves of their ewers; cascades of white, yellow, and pink roses, which, with the sun enclosed in their translucent petals, illumine the dark verdure. And, at dusk, days which fade to the scent of pepper blent with the savours of Eastern spices, to the slowly modulated songs of the weary birds, and where, upon a sunless day, a lingering ray of the vanished sun gilds even at eight o'clock the green of the lawn. It is the moment beneath the twilight for the sport of young and imprudent blackbirds still unfledged, watched over by an old, grave, and very ebon blackbird. And amid the sinking into sleep of Colour, when the white of a great-headed viburnum, the yellow of a bunch of iris, the cerise of a broughton rhododendron, are no more than phantoms of white, yellow, and cerise, the zigzags of little blurred bats no longer seem like flights, but the shades of flights. At last, in the mist of things in the darkened garden, nothing but the almost spectral pallor of a streaked negundo, silvery pink in foliage beneath the rising moon, calls to mind an enchanted midnight tree, whither, in a shroud of white satin, a slender wraith of old Italian Comedy comes to cut ghostly capers.—*La Maison d'un Artiste*.[1]

AND how preferable for such historical work would be the peaceful conditions presented by provincial life, to the narrow, troubled, instable, precarious conditions of life in Paris. One of the necessities of erudition is a spacious and pleasant installation, where there is no fear of being either unsettled or disturbed. . . . The love of truth, moreover, makes us solitary: the provinces possess solitude, repose, liberty.

I will add to this the pleasure and the smile of Nature. These austere labours require calm and joy of mind, leisure, complete self-possession. A pretty house in the suburb of a large town; a long work-room furnished with books, the exterior tapestried with Bengal roses; a garden with straight alleys, where we can distract ourselves a moment with our flowers from the conversation of our books: nothing of all this is useless for that health of the soul necessary to the works of the mind.—*Feuilles Détachées* ('*Peut on travailler en Province?*')

**ERNEST RENAN** (1823-1892).

WE venture to think that artistic and scientific gardening might become an admirable profession for gentlemen not ambitious of making great fortunes. No occupation is healthier; none is fuller of variety and interest. Every day in

**MORTIMER COLLINS** (1827-1876).

[1] No. 53 Boulevard Montmorency, Auteil. For a translation of the whole article, see 'The Garden,' May 28, 1898.

garden and greenhouse brings a new surprise—a new delight; and the man who becomes a thorough gardener will often recall Cowley's famous line:

'God the first garden made, and the first city, Cain.'

The leaves of autumn are flying before rain and wind. They drive athwart my lawn, a versi-coloured shower. The copper-beech is burning its deepest russet, the Canadian oak is a tangled web of shivering saffron; soon the turf will be clear swept, to the weary gardener's high delight, and the eye's chief solace will be the glossy green of laurel and holly.—*Thoughts in my Garden.*

---

**T. JAMES** *in* 'The Carthusian' (1839). OF all the vain assumptions of these coxcombical times, that which arrogates the pre-eminence in the true science of gardening is the vainest. True, our conservatories are full of the choicest plants from every clime; we ripen the grape and the pine-apple with an art unknown before, and even the mango, the mangosteen, and the guava are made to yield their matured fruits; but the real beauty and poetry of a garden are lost in our efforts after rarity, and strangeness, and variety. To be the possessor of a unique pansy, the introducer of a new specimen of the Orchidaceæ, or the cultivator of 500 choice varieties of the dahlia, is now the only claim to gardening celebrity and Horticultural medals.

And then our lot has fallen in the evil days of system. We are proud of our natural or English style; and scores of unmeaning flower-beds, disfiguring the lawn in the shapes of kidneys, and tadpoles and sausages, and leeches, and commas, are the result. Landscape-gardening has encroached too much upon gardening proper; and this has had the same effect upon our gardens that horticultural societies have had on our fruits,—to make us entertain the vulgar notion that size is virtue. . . . If we review the various styles that have prevailed in England, from the knotted gardens of Elizabeth, the pleach-work and intricate flower-borders of James I., the painted Dutch statues and canals of William and Mary, the winding gravel walks, and lake-making of Brown, to poor Shenstone's sentimental farm and the landscape fashion of the present day,—we shall have little reason to pride ourselves on the advance which national taste has made upon the earliest efforts in this department.

If I am to have a system at all, give me the good old system of terraces and angled walks, and clipt yew-hedges, against whose dark and rich verdure the bright old-fashioned flowers glittered in the sun.

I love the topiary art, with its trimness and primness, and its open avowal of its artificial character. It repudiates at the first glance the skulking and cowardly '*celare artem*' principle, and, in its vegetable sculpture, is the properest transition from the architecture of the house to the natural beauties of the grove and paddock.

Who, to whom the elegance, and gentlemanliness, and poetry—the Boccaccio-spirit—of a scene of Watteau is familiar, does not regret the devastation made by *tasty* innovators upon the grounds laid out in the times of the Jameses and Charleses? As for old Noll, I am certain, though I have not a jot of evidence, that he cared no more for a garden than for an anthem; he would as lief have sacrificed the verdant sculpture of a yew-peacock as the time-honoured tracery of a cathedral shrine; and his crop-eared soldiery would have had as great satisfaction in bivouacking in the parterres of a 'royal pleasaunce' as in the presence-chamber of a royal palace. It were a sorrow beyond tears to dwell on the destruction of garden-stuff in those king-killing times. Thousands, doubtless, of broad-paced terraces and trim vegetable conceits sunk in the same ruin with their mansions and their masters: and alas! modern taste has followed in the footsteps of ancient fanaticism. How many old associations have been rooted up with the knotted stumps of yew and hornbeam! And Oxford, too, in the van of reform! Beautiful as are St John's Gardens, who would not exchange them for the *very* walks and alleys along which Laud, in all the pardonable pride of collegiate lionizing, conducted his illustrious guests, Charles and Henrietta? Who does not grieve that we must now inquire in vain for the bowling-green in Christ Church, where Cranmer solaced the weariness of his last confinement? And who lately, in reading Scott's life, but must have mourned in sympathy with the poet over the destruction of 'the huge hill of leaves,' and the yew and hornbeam hedges of the 'Garden' at Kelso. . . .

My garden should lie to the south of the house; the ground gradually sloping for some short way till it falls abruptly into the dark and tangled shrubberies that all but hide the winding brook below. A broad terrace, half as wide, at least, as the house is high, should run along the whole southern length of the building, extending to the western side also, whence, over the distant country, I may catch the last red light of the setting sun. I must have some musk and noisette roses, and jasmine, to run up the mullions of my oriel window, and honeysuckles and clematis, the white, the purple, and the blue, to cluster round the top. The upper terrace should be strictly architectural, and no plants are to be harboured there, save such as twine among the balustrades, or fix themselves in the mouldering crevices of the stone. I can endure no plants in pots,—a plant in a pot is like a bird in a cage. The gourd alone throws out its vigorous tendrils, and displays its green and golden fruit from the vases that surmount the broad flight of stone steps that lead to the lower terrace; while a vase of larger dimensions and bolder sculpture at the western corner is backed by the heads of a mass of crimson, rose, and straw-coloured hollyhocks that spring up from the bank below. The lower terrace is twice the width of the one above, of the most velvety turf, laid out in an elaborate pattern of the Italian style. Here are collected the choicest flowers of the garden; the Dalmatic purple of the gentianella, the dazzling scarlet of the verbena, the fulgent lobelia, the bright yellows and rich browns of the calceolaria here luxuriate in their trimly cut parterres, and with colours as brilliant as the mosaic of an old cathedral painted window

'——Broider the ground
With rich inlay.'[1]

But you must leave this mass of gorgeous colouring and the two pretty fountains that play in their basins of native rock, while you descend the flight of steps, simpler than those of the upper terrace, and turn to the left hand, where a broad gravel walk will lead you to the kitchen-garden, through an avenue splendid in autumn with hollyhocks, dahlias, China asters, nasturtians, and African marigolds.

We will stop short of the walled garden to turn among the clipt hedges of box, and yew, and hornbeam which surround the bowling-green, and lead to a curiously formed labyrinth, in the centre of which, perched up on a triangular mound, is a fanciful old summer-house, with a gilded roof, that commands the view of the whole surrounding country. Quaint devices of all kinds are found here. Here is a sun-dial of flowers, arranged according to the time of day at which they open and close. Here are peacocks and lions in livery of Lincoln green. Here are berceaux and arbours, and covered alleys, and enclosures containing the primest of the carnations and cloves in set order, and miniature canals that carry down a stream of pure water to the fish-ponds below. Further onwards, and up the south bank, verging towards the house, are espaliers and standards of the choicest fruit-trees; here are strawberry-beds raised so as to be easy for gathering; while the round gooseberry and currant bushes, and the arched raspberries continue the formal style up the walls of the enclosed garden, whose outer sides are clothed alternately with fruit and flowers, so that the 'stranger within the house' may be satisfied, without being tantalized by the rich reserves within the gate of iron tracery of which the head gardener keeps the key.

Return to the steps of the lower terrace: what a fine slope of green pasture loses itself in the thorn, hazel, and holly thicket below, while the silver thread of the running brook here and

[1] ' Tot fuerant illic, quot habet natura, colores :
Pictaque dissimili flore nitebat humus.'—*Ovid.*

there sparkles in the light; and how happily the miniature prospect, framed by the gnarled branches of those gigantic oaks, discloses the white spire of the village church in the middle distance! While in the background the smoke, drifting athwart the base of the purple hill, gives evidence that the evening fires are just lit in the far-off town.

At the right-hand corner of the lower terrace the ground falls more abruptly away, and the descent into the lawn, which is overlooked from the high western terrace, is, by two or three steps at a time, cut out in the native rock of red sandstone, which also forms the base of the terrace itself. Rock plants of every description freely grow in the crevices of the rustic battlement which flanks the path on either side; the irregularity of the structure increases as you descend, till, on arriving on the lawn below, large rude masses lie scattered on the turf and along the foundation of the western terrace.

A profusion of the most exquisite climbing roses of endless variety here clamber up till they bloom over the very balustrade of the higher terrace, or creep over the rough stones at the foot of the descent. Here stretching to the south is the nosegay of the garden. Mignonette, 'the Frenchman's darling,' and the musk-mimulus spring out of every fissure of the sandstone; while beds of violets,

> 'That strew the green lap of the new-come Spring,'

and lilies of the valley scent the air below. Beds of heliotrope flourish around the isolated block of sandstone; the fuchsia, alone inodorous, claims a place from its elegance; and honeysuckles and clematis of all kinds trail along the ground, or twine up the stands of rustic baskets, filled with the more choice odoriferous plants of the greenhouse. The scented heath, the tuberose, and the rarer jasmines have each their place, while the sweet-briar and the wall-flower, and the clove and stock gilliflower are not too common to be neglected. To bask upon the dry sunny rock on a bright spring morning in the midst of this 'wilderness of sweets,' or on a dewy summer's eve to lean over the balustrade above, while every breath from beneath wafts up the perfumed air,

'Stealing and giving odour,'

is one of the greatest luxuries I have in life.—*The Poetry of Gardening.*[1]

THE amateur who, happening to have a sufficiency of land attached to his residence, chooses himself to take the command of two or three labourers, instead of employing a trained professional at a high salary—(*wages* might be offensive)—is of compulsion the most assiduous student of garden literature. His practice will be adapted to various ends, according as utility or ornament is the object the more desirable in his state of affairs. But his horticulture is mostly of the composite order; he cultivates a garden-of-all-work. As the celebrated cobbler 'lived in a stall —that served him for parlour and kitchen and all,' so the independent manager arranges a plot of ground so as to comprise the conveniences of orchard, kitchen-garden, shrubbery, parterre, and terrace. And a capital school it is for the men and boys who are wise enough to look after instruction while working in it. How well, too, an avenue of standard perpetual roses harmonizes with the line of a feathery asparagus bed! How little there is to displease in a rectangular strawberry-ground enclosed in a framework of brilliant low-growing flowers, with an outer fillet of box, having openings left, like the gates of a Roman camp, for the approach of the workmen and the fruit-gatherers! What pleasant strolls may be taken in a wilderness of apple, bullace, cherry, plum, filbert, and medlar-trees, with an underwood of the periwinkles, great and small, honesty, and primroses, and with one path at least skirting the edge of the fish-pond, from which a pike for dinner may always be had. His visitors enjoy the combination

'QUARTERLY REVIEW' (1851).

---

[1] This essay, together with another one by the same writer, which originally appeared in the *Quarterly Review*, 1842, was reprinted by Murray in 1852, in one of the little volumes of his 'Reading for the Rail,' under the title of 'The Flower-Garden.'

as much as himself. He asks a city friend which he will have put into his carriage—a basket of flowers or a hamper of vegetables; —and the answer is, 'Both!' To make it perfect in its way, all the spare decoration he can afford to bestow upon it should tend to make it a *winter garden*.

---

SIR
ARTHUR
HELPS
(1817-1875).

AS for our love of gardens, it is the last refuge of art in the minds and souls of many Englishmen: if we did not care for gardens, I hardly know what in the way of beauty we should care for.—*Companions of my Solitude*.

---

SIR
WILLIAM
STIRLING
MAXWELL
(1818-1878).

EMBOSOMED in a valley and an unshorn forest, and refreshed by the Tagus and the Xarama which mingle their streams beneath the palace-walls, Aranjuez has long been the Tivoli or Windsor of the princes, and the Tempe of the poets of Castile. Even now, the traveller who comes weary and adust from brown La Mancha, and from the edge of the desert, looks down on the palace, sparkling with its long white arcades and gilded vanes amongst woods and waters, may share the raptures of Garcilasso and Calderon. The island garden, though deserted by royalty and grandeeship, has yet its bright sun and rivers, its marble statues and fountains half hid in thickets; the old elms of Charles V.;[1] and cathedral-walks of hornbeam, peopled with a melodious multitude of nightingales. The fountain-pipes that once climbed unseen amongst the branches, and played from the tops of the trees,[2] have long ceased to play; others, however, are still in full force; and a few camels, parading too and fro with garden burdens, preserve an oriental custom of the place, as old as the days of Philip II. Here Velasquez attended his master in his walks, or sat retired in 'pleached bowers,' noting

[1] Beckford, 'Letters from Spain,' xvii.
[2] Lady Fanshaw, 'Memoirs,' pp. 222-3.

the fine effects of summer sunlight and silvan shade, and making many sketches of sweet garden scenes. Some of these have found their way to the Royal gallery; such as the fine view of the Avenue of the Queen, enlivened by coaches and promenaders from the palace. Another is a study of the Fountain of the Tritons, a rich piece of sculpture in white marble, sometimes attributed to the chisel of Berreguete, not unlike that which refreshed the garden of Boccaccio's immortal palace.[1] Through the bough of overarching trees, the light falls brokenly on a group of courtly figures, that might pass for the fair sisterhood and gallant following of Pampinea.—*Annals of the Artists of Spain.*

---

NOW the faults of gardening, against which my present paper is directed, all centre in this one thing—the constant subjection of the imaginative, or higher, to the sensuous, or lower, element of flower beauty. We will trace this, first, in the general arrangement of gardens and of flowers in relation to each other, and afterwards in the case of their individual culture. To begin, then, we find flower-beds habitually considered too much as mere masses of colour, instead of an assemblage of living beings. The only thought is to delight the eye by the utmost possible splendour. When we walk in our public gardens everything seems tending to distract the attention from the separate plants, and to make us look at them only with regard to their united effect. And this universal brilliancy, this striking effect of the masses, is the acknowledged chief aim of the cultivator. . . .

Has any of our readers, gifted with real love for flowers, ever walked through one of those older gardens, and observed the wide difference in its effect? I am not here speaking necessarily of the grounds of a mansion, but merely of such a garden as might often be found, some twenty years ago, attached to any good-sized house in a country town or village. Or even a little cottage-plot

[1] 'Decameron,' Giorn. III., Nov. I.

of the kind so beautifully described by Clare will to some extent illustrate my meaning:

> 'And where the marjoram once, and sage and rue,
> And balm and mint, with curled-leaf parsley grew,
> And double marigolds, and silver thyme,
> And pumpkins 'neath the window used to climb;
> And where I often, when a child, for hours
> Tried through the pales to get the tempting flowers;
> As lady's laces everlasting peas,
> True love lies bleeding, with the hearts at ease;
> And golden rods, and tansy running high,
> That o'er the pale top smiled on passer-by;
> Flowers in my time which every one would praise,
> Though thrown like weeds from gardens now-a-days.'

There might be but little attempt at colour-grouping, or at the production of effect by masses in a narrow sense. But was there any want of beauty there? And did you not feel, in looking at those flowers, how each made you love it as a friend—the Pinks and Sweet Williams, the Everlasting Peas, Valerian, Day Lily, Jacob's Ladder, and a host of others? And did you not notice how ever and again you fell upon some quaint, strange plant which has been expelled from the modern border, which seemed to touch your inmost soul, and to fill the mind, especially if in childhood, with a sense of wonder and mysterious awe? What was that plant? Could not anybody tell its name, and where it came from, and all else about it, for it must surely have an eventful history? And, with curiosity rather stimulated than satisfied by the scanty knowledge you could glean, you fell back upon the imagination, which set it down as an actor in some strange and awful tale, as that of a young man who gathered some unknown wild flowers that attracted him, and who, together with his betrothed, was poisoned by their touch. Feelings of this sort were strongly awakened in my mind in childhood by such plants as Caper Spurge, Henbane, Rue, and other more beautiful species, as the Dog's-Tooth Violet, with its spotted leaves, the common Nigella, and the pink Marsh-Mallow of the fields.

Want of general effect! Is there none in those cottage gardens,

In a Scotch Walled Garden.

where the Nasturtiums twine lovingly all the summer amongst the Jasmine, Clematis, and thickly-trellised Rose—where the towering splendour of the Hollyhocks is confronted by the broad discs of the Sunflower, and where the huge leaves, herbs, and fruit-trees of the kitchen-garden run close up on, or intermix with, the border flowers, amongst which we may meet at any time with some new or long-absent friend? Here are no masses of colour in the modern sense; but do you ever feel the want of them? Or can you turn from these simple plots, unstudied for effect, to the showy, unvaried brilliancy of the modern border, and find that you miss nothing there? Do not the plants seem comparatively wanting in interest? Do they not seem to be individually less dear, to hold you with a lighter grasp? Now what can be the reason of this? The old gardeners, we are told, thought little of beauty, and chiefly of genera and species. Why, then, should the poet find that, with all its faults, the old garden stirs him in those depths which the modern one can seldom reach? This defect is far less conspicuous in the larger hothouses and greenhouses, and I am convinced that it depends almost wholly on false principles of arrangement. I will give an illustration of this. Everybody knows the little blue annual Lobelia. It is a pretty flower, but, as the gardeners place it in their show-beds, it seems as cold and unlovable as if it was wrought of steel. Yet, should we ever think it so if we found it rising stem by stem amongst the looser grass, in such meadows as the Harebell, Milkwort, or Eyebright (Euphrasia) will often enter, or perhaps in closer tufts on open banks of gravel? I have chosen localities altogether imaginary, and am, of course, well aware that the plant's colours are too bright to associate easily with the tints of our native flowers.—*Flowers and Gardens.*

—∧∧∧—

YOU have heard it said—(and I believe there is more than fancy even in that saying, but let it pass for a fanciful one) —that flowers only flourish rightly in the garden of some one who

JOHN RUSKIN
(b. 1819).

loves them. I know you would like that to be true; you would think it a pleasant magic if you could flush your flowers into brighter bloom by a kind look upon them: nay, more, if your look had the power, not only to cheer, but to guard;—if you could bid the black blight turn away, and the knotted caterpillar spare—if you could bid the dew fall upon them in the drought, and say to the south wind in frost—'Come, thou south, and breathe upon my garden that the spices of it may flow out.' This you would think a great thing? And do you think it not a greater thing, that all this (and how much more than this!) you *can* do, for fairer flowers than these—flowers that could bless you for having blessed them, and will love you for having loved them; —flowers that have thoughts like yours, and lives like yours; and which, once saved, you save for ever! Is this only a little power? Far among the moorlands and the rocks,—far in the darkness of the terrible streets,—these feeble florets are lying, with all their fresh leaves torn, and their stems broken: will you never go down to them, nor set them in order in their little fragrant beds, nor fence them, in their trembling, from the fierce wind? Shall morning follow morning for you, but not for them; and the dawn rise, to watch, far away, those frantic Dances of Death; but no dawn rise to breathe upon those living banks of wild violet, and woodbine and rose; nor call to you, through your casement—call (not giving you the name of the English poet's lady, but the name of Dante's great Matilda, who, on the edge of happy Lethe, stood, wreathing flowers with flowers), saying:

> 'Come into the garden, Maud,
>  For the black bat, night, has flown,
>  And the woodbine spices are wafted abroad,
>  And the musk of the roses blown'?

Will you not go down among them? Among those sweet living things whose new courage, sprung from the earth with the deep colour of heaven upon it, is starting up in strength of goodly spire; and whose purity, washed from the dust, is opening, bud by bud, into the flower of promise;—and still they turn to you, and for you, 'The Larkspur listens—I hear, I hear! And the Lily whispers—I wait.'—*Sesame and Lilies.* (*Of Queen's Gardens.*)

—⁂—

'*The English Sainte Beuve,*' *who, with George Meredith and Walter Pater,* **MATTHEW**
*forms the Triad of 'puissant voices' in the literature of the passing generation,* **ARNOLD**
*as he himself called Carlyle, Emerson and Newman, of his own earlier day.* (1823-1888).

THE College (Marlborough) was the old inn, but I did not know that this inn was the old home of the Hertford family, a house built by Inigo Jones, and in a style I particularly like and admire. The old garden, bowling-green, sward, and yew-trees still subsist, and give an air to the place of age and of style beyond anything that Harrow or Rugby can show.[1]—*Letter to his mother, November* 12, 1871.

*Cobham, Surrey,* will find me. The cottage we have got there is called *Pain's Hill Cottage.* The country is beautiful—more beautiful even than the Chilterns, because it has heather and pines, while the trees of other kinds, in the valley of the Mole, where we are, are really magnificent. We are planting and improving about our cottage, as if it were our own, and we had a hundred years to live there; its great merit is that it must have had nearly one hundred years of life already and is surrounded by great old trees—not the raw new sort of villa one has generally to take if one wants a small house near London.

It is a hoar frost, and you should see the squirrels scampering about the lawn for the nuts we strew there. We have also a jackdaw who visits us and is becoming very tame. But my delight at present is in the blackbirds and thrushes, who abound,

[1] Arnold makes no mention of the Mound situated in 'the wilderness'—perhaps the largest of its kind in England. 'Such a mound (as at Wressel, mentioned by Leland) still exists at the Castle Inn at Marlborough, not ascended by steps or degrees, but by a winding path, covered with ancient yew-trees.'—*Loudon.*

and sing indefatigably. Now I must take a turn round the place and then work at my Goethe.—*December* 1877.

And I do very much enjoy the life at home, with half an hour in the garden every morning, and two hours in the lanes every afternoon. The aconites are coming out, and as for the primroses they are all over the place. I have been repairing the ravages made by the elm-tree's fall, and really with cupressuses and thujas the gap has lost its horror already, and will be quite filled up in a year or two.—1882.

The colour has come at last, and the horse-chestnuts and poplars are a sight. I go about the garden—I cannot come in to work—examine the acorns on the Turkey Oak, with their curly-haired cups, which I had never noticed before; they are very effective. Then I give Flu, who is driving to Lady Ellesmere, a Duchesse pear to take to her, who says she shall carry it to her gardener to show him how much finer pears are grown at the Cottage than at Burwood. Then I go to pick up some Spanish chestnuts. At last I come in to work.—*To Miss Arnold, October* 29, 1886.

You can imagine the relief with which I have been going about the garden this morning and planting. Numbers of summer flowers—the red salvia, for instance—are blooming. The birds are happy in the open weather, and the sweet robins keep following Collis and me about as we open the ground to plant rhododendrons.—*Letter to his eldest daughter, November* 13, 1886. (*Letters of Matthew Arnold, by G. W. E. Russell.*)

—∿∿∿—

**WILLIAM MORRIS** (1834-1896).

OUR suburban gardeners in London, for instance, oftenest wind about their little bit of gravel walk and grass plot in ridiculous imitation of an ugly big garden of the landscape-gardening style, and then with a strange perversity fill up the spaces with the most formal plants they can get; whereas the merest common-sense should have taught them to lay out their morsel of ground in the simplest way, to fence it as orderly as might be, one part from the other—if it be big enough for that—and the whole from the road, and then to fill up the flower-growing space with things that are free and interesting in their growth, leaving Nature to do the desired complexity, which she will certainly not fail to do, if we do not desert her for the florist, who, I must say, has made it harder work than it should be to get the best of flowers. . . .

As to colour in gardens. Flowers in masses are mighty strong colour, and if not used with a great deal of caution are very destructive to pleasure in gardening. On the whole, I think the best and safest plan is to mix up your flowers, and rather eschew great masses of colour—in combination, I mean. But there are some flowers—inventions of men, *i.e.* florists—which are bad colour altogether, and not to be used at all. Scarlet geraniums, for instance, or the yellow calceolaria, which, indeed, are not uncommonly grown together profusely, in order, I suppose, to show that even flowers can be thoroughly ugly.

And now to sum up as to a garden. Large or small, it should look both orderly and rich. It should be well fenced from the outside world. It should by no means imitate either the wilfulness or the wildness of Nature, but should look like a thing never to be seen except near a house. It should, in fact, look like a part of the house. It follows from this that no private pleasure-garden should be very big, and a public garden should be divided and made to look like so many flower-closes in a meadow, or a wood, or amidst the pavement.

It will be a key to right thinking about gardens if you will consider in what kind of places a garden is most desired. In a very beautiful country, especially if it be mountainous, we can do without it well enough; whereas in a flat and dull country we crave after it, and there it is often the very making of the homestead. While in great towns, gardens, both private and public, are positive necessities if the citizens are to live reasonable and healthy lives in body and mind.—*Hopes and Fears for Art.* ('*Making the Best of it.*')

## THE PRAISE OF GARDENS

**WALTER PATER (1839-1894).**

THE worship of Demeter belongs to that older religion, nearer to the earth, which some have thought they could discern behind the more definitely national mythology of Homer. She is the goddess of dark caves, and is not wholly free from monstrous form. She gave men the first fig in one place, the first poppy in another; in another she first taught the old Titans to mow. She is the mother of the vine also; and the assumed name, by which she called herself in her wanderings is Dôs—a gift; the crane, as the harbinger of rain, is her messenger among the birds. She knows the magic powers of certain plants, cut from her bosom, to bane or bless; and, under one of her epithets, herself presides over the springs, as also coming from the secret places of the earth. She is the goddess then of the fertility of the earth, in its wildness; and so far her attributes are to some degree confused with those of the Thessalian Gaia and the Phrygian Cybele. Afterwards, and it is now that her most characteristic attributes begin to concentrate themselves, she separates herself from these confused relationships, as specially the goddess of agriculture, of the fertility of the earth as furthered by human skill. She is the preserver of the seed sown in hope, under many epithets derived from the incidents of vegetation, as the simple countryman names her, out of a mind full of the various experiences of his little garden or farm. She is the most definite embodiment of all those fluctuating mystical instincts, of which Gaia, the mother of the earth's gloomier offspring, is a vaguer and mistier one. There is nothing of the confused outline, the mere shadowiness of mystical dreaming, in this most concrete human figure. No nation, less æsthetically gifted than the Greeks, could have so lightly thrown its mystical surmise and divination into images so clear and idyllic as those of the solemn goddess of the country, in whom the characteristics of the mother are expressed with so much tenderness, and the 'beauteous head' of Kore, then so fresh and peaceful.—'*The Myth of Demeter and Persephone.*'

BOCCACCIO and the Italians more usually employ the word *orto*, which has lost its Latin signification, and is a place, as we learn from the context, planted with fruit-trees and with pot-herbs. . . . But although in this story (of Madonna Dianora) Boccaccio employs the word *giardino*, instead of *orto*, I think we must imagine that magic flower garden rather as a corner—they still exist on every hillside—of orchard connected with the fields of wheat and olives below by the long tunnels of vine trellis, and dying away into them with the great tufts of lavender and rosemary and fennel on the grassy bank under the cherry trees. This piece of terraced ground along which the water—spurted from the dolphin's mouth or the sirens' breasts—runs through walled channels, refreshing impartially violets and salads, lilies and tall flowering onions, under the branches of the peach tree and the pomegranate, to where in the shade of the great pink oleander tufts, it pours out below into the big tank, for the maids to rinse their linen in the evening, and the peasants to fill their cans to water the bedded-out tomatoes and the potted clove-pinks in the shadow of the house. . . .

'VERNON LEE.'

Now this poverty of flower-beds and richness of pots made it easy and natural for the Italian garden to become, like the Moorish one, a place of mere greenery and water, a palace whose fountains plashed in sunny yards walled in with myrtle and bay, in mysterious chambers roofed over with ilex and box. And this it became. Moderately at first; a few hedges of box and cypress—exhaling its resinous breath in the sunshine—leading up to the long, flat, Tuscan house, with its tower or pillared loggia under the roof to take the air and dry linen; a few quaintly cut trees set here and there, along with the twisted mulberry tree where the family drank its wine and ate its fruit of an evening; a little grove of ilexes to the back, in whose shade you could sleep, while the cicalas buzzed at noon; some cypresses gathered together into a screen, just to separate the garden from the olive yard above; gradually perhaps a balustrade set at the end of the bowling-green, that you might see, even from a distance, the shimmery blue valley below—the pale blue distant hills; and if you had it, some antique statue, not good enough for the courtyard of the town house, set on the balustrade or against the tree; also, where water was plentiful, a little grotto scooped out under that semicircular screen of cypresses. A very modest place, but differing essentially from the orchard and kitchen-garden of the mediæval burgher; and out of which come something immense and unique—the classic Roman villa.

For your new gardens, your real Italian garden, brings in a new element—that of perspective, architecture, decoration; the trees used as building material, the lie of the land as theatre arrangements, the water as the most docile and multiform stage property. . . .

Now go where you may in the outskirts of Rome you are sure to find ruins—great aqueduct arches, temples half-standing, gigantic terrace works belonging to some baths or palace hidden beneath the earth and vegetation. Here you have naturally an element of architectural ground-plan and decoration which is easily followed: the terraces of quincunxes, the symmetrical groves, the long flights of steps, the triumphal arches, the big ponds, come, as it were, of them—obeying the order of what is below. And from underground, everywhere, issues a legion of statues, headless, armless, in all stages of mutilation, who are charitably mended and take their place, mute sentinels, white and earth-stained, at every intersecting box hedge, under every ilex grove, beneath the cypresses of each sweeping hillside avenue, wherever a tree can make a niche or a bough a canopy.
—*Limbo and other Essays.* (*Old Italian Gardens.*)

---

**ALICE MEYNELL**

FORGOTTEN by the side of some rosy palace by the Adriatic, its fountain overrun with maidenhair, its gold fish twinkling in the marble font, and grass growing gaily and wildly where it will, the garden that once was trimmest has a delight and a spirit that it could not have without precisely that past of artifice and ceremony. No prosperity except that of summer, no order that is not sweetly made light of while it is carelessly fulfilled, and all access open by way of the sunny air, so that no seeds are denied an anchorage in this port and harbour of the winds. A trim garden that is no longer trim is full of frolic. A trim garden that is still trim has a kind of comeliness as an accessory of architecture. It is, at any rate, a garden and not a landscape.

For obviously the landscape garden, called abroad the English garden, is the thing most at fault. The English garden is like ' English glass '—that is, cut glass. Both things are a kind of adulteration. Both things were eagerly admired and imitated on the Continent.

Landscape gardening, literally, would have been a good thing—the enclosure of the half-wild copse, the arbitrary capture and captivity of a space of wood, meadow, stream, and bank, and the mere harbourage of wild flowers; it would be the field with all its accidents secure from spoiling. But landscape-gardening that implies sinuous walks and futile hillocks, and those dullest of all dull things—shrubs—can never have given any genuine joy to man.

Everyone knows that 'landscape garden.' It has improbable knolls and hollows, closely and accurately fitted with a green sward on which show no daisies. The shrubs grow in groups, very round of shape, and dense to the penetration of the alert and eager glimpses of the sky. Its trees are rarely deciduous, or, if so, are of the fuller and thicker kind; it has no slender aspens, caught and mingled with the light, and alive with the wind and weather. It has chiefly evergreens of the rarer kinds, having their lower branches so near the ground as to show no stems. 'All the Psalms are good,' says Mrs Pendennis. All trees are good, but those are the least good.

See, however, how charming is a fruit-garden, or that still simpler fruit-garden, an orchard. All fruit-trees are at play with the light and at peace with the sky. There is nothing in the world more peaceful than apple-leaves with an early moon. The grass beneath them is not cropped of daisies, or fitted and clipped as if by an able dressmaker. Let the garden be a vegetable garden with fruit-trees, with gooseberry bushes to give the first buds of leaves, and let there be slender flowers all along the edges, and a concourse of standard rose-trees for the sake of gathering the roses, peas in rows and rows, with the twigs they grow upon delicate against the light; all gentle and fortunate and useful.

How has the world so long taken so much trouble to make less lovely things out of those fine materials—the blossoming earth and the fostering sky? Pity is it that the word garden should so be vulgarized by worldly gardens. It is an early word to all men, one of the earliest of words. It is an Orient word, fresh and perpetual from childhood and the Divine East. A garden of olives, a garden of cucumbers, a garden of herbs, a vineyard, a garden enclosed—all these have the gravity of use and labour, and are as remote as memory, and as familiar, secluded, and secret.

—⋀⋀⋀—

**HENRY A. BRIGHT.** ONE of the greatest ornaments to a garden is a fountain, but many fountains are curiously ineffective. A fountain is most beautiful when it leaps high into the air, and you can see it against a background of green foliage. To place a fountain among low flower-beds, and then to substitute small fancy jets that take the shape of a cup, or trickle over into a basin of gold-fish, or toy with a gilded ball, is to do all that is possible to degrade it. The real charm of a fountain is, when you come upon it in some little grassy glade of the 'pleasaunce,' where it seems as though it sought, in the strong rush of its waters, to vie with the tall boles of the forest-trees that surround it. Such was the fountain in Leigh Hunt's *Story of Rimini*, which shot up 'beneath a shade of darksome pines,'

'And 'twixt their shafts you saw the water bright,
 Which through the tops glimmered with show'ring light.'

\* \* \* \* \* \*

One of the most beautiful gardens I ever knew depended almost entirely on the arrangement of its lawns and shrubberies. It had certainly been most carefully and adroitly planned, and it had every advantage in the soft climate of the west of England. The various lawns were divided by thick shrubberies, so that you wandered on from one to the other, and always came on something new. In front of these shrubberies was a large margin of flower-border, gay with the most effective plants and annuals. At the corner of the lawn a standard *Magnolia grandiflora* of great size held up its chaliced blossoms; at another a tulip-tree was laden with hundreds of yellow flowers. Here a magnificent *Salisburia* mocked the foliage of the maiden-hair; and here an old cedar swept the grass with its large pendant branches. But the main breadth of each lawn was never destroyed, and past them you might see the reaches of a river, now in one aspect and now in another. Each view was different, and each was a fresh enjoyment and surprise.

A few years ago, and I revisited the place; the 'improver' had been at work, and had been good enough to *open up* the view. Shrubberies had disappeared, and lawns had been thrown together. The pretty peeps among the trees were gone, the long vistas had become open spaces, and you saw at a glance all that there was to be seen. Of course the herbaceous borders, which once contained numberless rare and interesting plants, had disappeared, and the lawn in front of the house was cut up into little beds of red pelargoniums, yellow calceolarias, and the rest.—*The English Flower-Garden.*

—∿∿∿—

IT is said that a garden should always be considered simply and wholly as a work of art, and should not be made to look like Nature. That is true enough. Nothing, indeed, can be in worse taste than the landscape-gardener's imitations of Nature. But there is another plan. If your garden be large enough you can let Nature have her own way in certain parts of it. This takes time, but the result is eminently delightful. For the most part o u have only to stand aside and watch. If anything at all be done it should only be a little judicious pruning—accomplished in such a way that it need not be observed—and the blending by unobtrusive gradations of the artificial with the natural. I well remember how skilfully this was done in that 'careless order'd garden' of the late Laureate, at Freshwater, in the Isle of Wight, where—

> 'Groves of pine on either hand,
> To break the blast of winter, stand;
> And farther on, the hoary Channel
> Tumbles a breaker on chalk and sand.'

And, curiously enough, the only other garden which I invariably think of in this connection is that of Tennyson's predecessor. However it may be to-day, I know that thirty years ago that which struck me most at Rydal Mount, and which appeared to me its greatest charm, was this union of the garden and the wilderness. You passed almost imperceptibly from the trim parterre to the noble wood, and from the narrow, green vista to that wide sweep of lake and mountain which made up one of the finest landscapes in England. Nor could you doubt that this unusual combination was largely the result of the poet's own care and arrangement. He had the faculty for such work. . . .

By this time I have got round to the old English flower-bed, where only perennials with an ancient ancestry are allowed to grow. Here there is always delight; and I should be sorry to exchange its sweet flowers for any number of cartloads of scentless bedding-plants, mechanically arranged and ribbon-bordered. This bed is from fifty to sixty yards long, and three or four yards in width. A thorn hedge divides it from the orchard. In spring the apple-bloom hangs over, and now we see in the background the apples themselves. The plants still in flower are the dark-blue monks hood, which is seven feet high; the spiked veronica; the meadow-sweet or queen-of-the-meadow; the lady's mantle, and the evening primrose. This last may be regarded as the characteristic plant of the season. The flowers open about seven o'clock, and as the twilight deepens, they gleam like pale lamps, and harmonise wonderfully with the colour of the sky. On this bed I read the history of the year. Here were the first snow-drops; here came the crocuses, the daffodils, the blue gentians, the columbines, the great globed peonies; and, last, the lilies and the roses.—*Country Pleasures.* (*The Chronicle of a Year, chiefly in a Garden.*)

—∿∿∿—

**ALFRED AUSTIN**
(b. 1835).

A GARDEN that one makes oneself becomes associated with one's personal history and that of one's friends, interwoven with one's tastes, preferences and character, and constitutes a sort of unwritten but withal manifest, autobiography. Show me your garden, provided it be your own, and I will tell you what you are like. It is in middle life that the finishing touches should be put to it; and then, after that, it should remain more or less in the same condition, like oneself, growing more deep of shade, and more protected from the winds. . . .

'Tell me, will you, what governed you in the laying out of the Garden that you Love?'

'What governed me was what I found here: the house, its time-consecrated architecture, its immovable boundaries, the old oak, and not it only, but all the ineradicable old timber within sight, the park, and finally, when all these were allowed for, the general fitness of things. I am quite of opinion that a garden should look as though it belonged to the house, and the house as though it were conscious of and approved the garden. In passing from one to the other, one should experience no sense of discord, but the sensations produced by the one should be continued, with a delicate difference, by the other. Terraces and balustrades, box edgings, or yew hedges, anything obviously and intentionally formal, which is imperative in the case of certain stately dwelling-houses, would surely have been out of place here. Near to the house, the garden, you will have observed, is more formal and shapely, and you never, I trust, altogether lose vague evidences of design. But absolutely symmetrical it is not, though a careless observer might imagine it to be so, and it gradually assumes

a less definite and disciplined air as it gets nearer to the tract
of orchard, meadow, and park, to which it is sunnily open
and which it commands. Thus I have obtained, I think, a
certain sense of spontaneous seclusion, without wholly shutting
myself in, or wholly shutting out everybody or everything else.
Of course, there are nooks of perfect shelter, as Goldsmith said,
for whispering lovers made; and the South Enclosure curves
and winds as it chooses, as though there were no other curve
or line in the world. Poet's Walk comes on you as a surprise;
and when you think you have seen everything, you suddenly
discover the copse kitchen-garden, which, I confess, contains
fully as many flowers as vegetables, and conducts to an orchard
whose existence you had not surmised.—*The Garden that I Love.*

---

ÉMILE ZOLA (b. 1840). SOUS ce poudroiement de flammes (du soleil) le grand jardin vivait avec une extravagance de bête heureuse, lâchée au bout du monde, loin de tout, libre du tout. C'était une débauche telle de feuillages, une marée d'herbes si débordante, qu'il était comme dérobé d'un bout à l'autre, inondé, noyé. Rien que des pentes vertes, des tiges ayant des jaillissements de fontaine, des masses moutonnantes, des rideaux de forêts hermétiquement tirés, des manteaux de plantes grimpantes traînant à terre, des volées de rameaux gigantesques s'abattant de tous côtés.

A peine pouvait-on, à la longue, reconnaitre sous cet envahissement formidable de la sève l'ancien dessin du Paradou. En face, dans une sorte de cirque immense, devait se trouver le parterre, avec ses bassins effondrés, ses rampes rompues, ses escaliers déjetés, ses statues renversées dont on apercevait les blancheurs en fond des gazons noirs. Plus loin, derrière la ligne bleue d'une nappe d'eau s'étalait un fouillis d'arbres fruitiers; plus loin encore une haute futaie enfonçait ses dessous violâtres, rayés de lumière, une forêt redevenue vierge, dont les cimes se mammelonnaient sans fin, tachées du vert jaune, du vert pâle, du vert puissant de toutes les essences. A droite, la forêt escaladait des hauteurs, plantait des petits bois de pins, se mourait en broussailles maigres, tandis que des roches nues entassaient une rampe énorme, un écroulement de montagne barrant l'horizon ; des végétations ardentes y fendaient le sol, plantes monstrueuses immobiles dans la chaleur, comme des reptiles assoupis ; un filet d'argent, un éclaboussement qui ressemblait de loin à une poussière de perles, y indiquait une chute d'eau, la source de ces eaux câlines qui longeaient si indolemment le parterre. A gauche enfin, la rivière coulait au milieu d'une vaste prairie, où elle se séparait en quatre ruisseaux, dont on suivait les caprices sous les roseaux, entre les saules, derrière les grands arbres ; à perte de vue, des pièces d'herbage élargissaient la fraîcheur des terrains bas, un paysage lavé d'une buée bleuâtre, une éclaircie de jour se fondant peu à peu dans le bleu verdi du Couchant. Le Paradou, le parterre, la forêt, les roches, les eaux, les prés, tenaient toute la largeur du ciel.

Le Paradou ! balbutia Serge ouvrant les bras comme pour serrer le jardin tout entier contre sa poitrine.

*La Faute de l'Abbé Mouret.*[1]

—∿∿∿—

THE characteristic of the old formal garden, the garden of Markham and Lawson, was its exceeding simplicity.

The primary purpose of a garden as a place of retirement and seclusion, a place for quiet thought and leisurely enjoyment was kept steadily in view. The grass and the yew-trees were trimmed close to gain their full beauty from the sunlight.

Sweet kindly flowers filled the knots and borders. Peacocks and pigeons brightened the terraces and lawns. The paths were straight and ample, the garden-house solidly built and comfortable ; everything was reasonable and unaffected. But this simple

[1] Never, perhaps, has the fecundity, the exuberance, one might almost say the debauchery, of Earth and her Gardens been so painted as in this book. We feel as if Nature were an immeasurable and impersonal Heliogabalus burying the world, convened as guests at a vast garden-banquet, beneath a mighty avalanche of flowers.

304    THE PRAISE OF GARDENS

genuine delight in nature and art became feebler as the seventeenth century grew older.

Gardening became the fashionable art, and this was the golden age for professional gardeners; but the real pleasure of it was gone. Rows of statues were introduced from the French, costly architecture superseded the simple terrace, intricate parterres were laid out from gardeners' pattern-books, and meanwhile the flowers were forgotten. It was well that all this pomp should be swept away. We do not want this extravagant statuary, these absurdities in clipped work, this aggressive prodigality. But though one would admit that in its decay the formal garden became unmanageable and absurd, the abuse is no argument against the use. An attempt has been made in this book to show the essential reasonableness of the principles of Formal Gardening, and the sanity of its method when properly handled. The long yew-hedge is clipped and shorn because we want its firm boundary lines and the plain mass of its colour; the grass bank is formed into a definite slope to attain the beauty of close-shaven turf at varied angles with the light. The broad grass walk, with its paved footpath in the centre, is cool to walk upon in summer and dry on the pavement in winter; and the flower border on either side is planted with every kind of delightful flower, so that the refinements of its colour may be enjoyed all through the summer.
—*The Formal Garden in England.*

—ⱮⱮ—

**MRS J. FRANCIS FOSTER.**

AGAIN, with our hedges and formal lines, how charmingly might we screen off lesser gardens within gardens, and we might, thus, have sweet retired places for lilies of sorts, or for roses, or for specimens of all British flowers, or one after the manner of the old '*gardina sacristæ*,' where special flowers might be grown for the decking of our churches. Passing through these we might lead to a pleasant place for the delight of the antiquarian gardener. Here we might, for instance, please ourselves by creating the reflection of a mediæval garden. Such a one as Chaucer loved to describe, saying that its beauty 'would have made any hearts light.' Such a one as that in which the 'fayre' Emilie walked up and down one May morning long ago, gathering

> 'Flowers partie white and red
> To make a subtle garland for her head.'

This garden, as we have seen, should be square of shape, it should be enclosed with walls, and with trellis work, and espaliers; within it should be grown quinces and pears, plums, cherries and apples of many kinds and also bullaces and the service-berries which, English born as they are, have been forgotten in England. Also, in this place, we must have a medlar tree like that from which the goldfinch, 'leaping prettily,' sang to the old poet, and we may plant an Agnus castus, for we read how the chief lady of the company, which came into Chaucer's dream, bore an Agnus castus branch. Plant also Holly trees and Spindle, and bushes of Broom and of Berberry, and a Rowan tree which we must have not only for beauty but also for good luck, since the old Ballads say that '*witches have no power where there is roan-tree wood.*'— *On the Art of Gardening.* 1881.

—⁂—

IN some writings on garden design, it is assumed as a truism that **WILLIAM** the landscape and naturalistic view of that design was the **ROBINSON.** invention of certain men, and a mere passing fashion, like many that have disfigured the garden. This is a serious error, as landscape beauty has existed ever since the eyes of men were first opened to the beauty of the earth, as now when from thousands of places in England beautiful landscape views are seen. It exists in wild mountain woodland, and in the forest plain, apart altogether from man's efforts, as seen in the parks of England from Alnwick to Richmond; and in either case it is too lovely a lesson to forget so long as man has any eyes to see beauty. If all the works of man in landscape planting were swept away, there would still be beautiful landscape on vast areas in many lands. There are ten thousand grassy lawns among the mountain Pines of Switzerland, where beautiful things are seen in landscape, as there are on the mountains of California and Cashmere, and, indeed, the many other woody mountain lands of the world.

Apart from the disposition of ground and its form, there is the question of the arrangement of all the beautiful things of earth—flower, shrub, or tree in right or wrong ways. Here there were always lessons to be learned: lovely colonies of Bird's-eye Primrose in the bogs of Westmoreland; little families of Gentian by the alpine streams; groups of Venetian Sumach cropping out of the hot southern rocks; groups of May on the hill, the stately groves of the lowland forest, and the Grey Willows of the marsh land. In planting in the same way we are simply learning a lesson direct from Nature, and not carrying out a mere fashion. Even the creatures of earth and air are held together beautifully —wild birds in the air, delicate brown flocks of them by the cold northern sea, as well as groups of nobler birds on the banks of the Nile and southern rivers; the cattle on a thousand hills: in no other way could their forms or colours be so well seen. And so it must ever be in the garden where natural grouping is the true and artistic way.

The gardener should follow the true artist, however modestly, in his love for things as they are, in delight in natural form and beauty of flower and tree, if we are to be free from barren geometry, and if our gardens are ever to be pictures. The gardener has not the strenuous work of eye and hand that the artist has, but he has plenty of good work to do:—to choose from ten thousand beautiful living things; to study their nature and adapt them to his soil and climate; to get the full expression of their beauty; to grow and place them well and in right relation to other things, which is a life-study in itself, in view of the great numbers of the flowers and flowering trees of the world. And as the artist's work is to see and keep for us some of the beauty of landscape, tree, or flower, so the gardener's should be to keep for us as far as may be, in the fulness of their natural beauty, the living things themselves. The artist gives us the fair image: the

## WILLIAM ROBINSON 307

gardener is the trustee of a world of fair living things, to be kept with care and knowledge in necessary subordination to human convenience, and to the conditions of his work.—*The English Flower Garden.* (*Nature in the Garden.*)

So far from its being true, that high mountain plants cannot be cultivated, there is no alpine flower that ever cheered the traveller's eye that cannot be grown in these islands. What are alpine plants? The word *alpine* is used to denote the vegetation that grows naturally on all high mountain-chains, whether they spring from tropical plains or green northern pastures. Above the cultivated land these flowers begin to occur on the fringes of the woods; they are seen in multitudes in the broad pastures with which many mountains are robed, enamelling their green, and where neither grass nor tall herbs exist; where mountains are crumbled into slopes of shattered rock by the contending forces of heat and cold; even there, amidst the glaciers, they spring from the ruined ground, as if the earth-mother had sent up her loveliest children to plead with the spirits of destruction. . . .

Alpine plants possess the charm of endless variety, and include things widely different :—tiny orchids, tree-like moss, and ferns that peep from crevices of alpine cliffs, often so small that they seem to cling to the rocks for shelter, not daring to throw forth their fronds with airy grace; bulbous plants, from Lilies to Bluebells; evergreen shrubs, perfect in leaf and blossom and fruit, yet so small that a glass would make a house for them; dwarfest creeping plants, spreading over the brows of rocks, draping them with lovely colour; Rockfoils and Stonecrops no bigger than mosses, and, like them, mantling the earth with green carpets in winter; in a word, alpine plants embrace nearly every type of the plant-life of northern lands.—*The English Flower Garden.* (*Alpine Flower and Rock Gardens.*)

**PHIL ROBINSON.** PLEASANT indeed is my Indian Garden. Here in a green colonnade stand the mysterious broad-leaved plantains with their strange spikes of fruit—there the dark mango. In a grove together the spare-leaved peepul, that sacred yet treacherous tree that drags down the humble shrine which it was placed to sanctify; the shapely tamarind, with its clouds of foliage; the graceful neem; the patulous teak, with its great leathern leaves, and the bamboos the tree-cat loves. Below them grow a wealth of roses, the lavender-blossomed durantas, the cactus grotesque in growth, the poyntzettia with its stars of scarlet, the spiky aloes, the sick-scented jessamine, and the quaint coral-trees; while over all shoots up the palm. The citron, lime, and orange-trees are beautiful alike when they load the air with the perfume of their waxen flowers, or when they are snowing their sweet petals about them, or when heavy-fruited they trail their burdened branches to rest their yellow treasure on the ground.—*In my Indian Garden.* ('*The Birds.*')

—ᨆᨆ—

**CHARLES DUDLEY WARNER.** THE man who has planted a garden feels that he has done something for the good of the world. He belongs to the producers. It is a pleasure to eat of the fruit of one's toil, if it be nothing more than a head of lettuce or an ear of corn. One cultivates a lawn even with great satisfaction; for there is nothing more beautiful than grass or turf in our latitude. The tropics may have their delight, but they have not turf: and the world without turf is a dreary desert. The original Garden of Eden could not have had such turf as one sees in England. The Teutonic races all love turf; they emigrate in the line of its growth. . . .

The principal value of a private garden is not understood. It is not to give the possessor vegetables and fruit (that can be better and cheaper done by the market-gardeners), but to teach him patience and philosophy, and the higher virtues,—hope deferred, and expectations blighted, leading directly to resignation, and sometimes to alienation. The garden thus becomes a moral agent, a test of character, as it was in the beginning. I shall keep this central truth in mind in these articles. I mean to have a moral garden, if it is not a productive one,—one that shall teach, O my brothers! O my sisters! the great lessons of life. . . .

This sitting in the sun amid evidences of a ripe year is the easiest part of gardening I have experienced. But what a combat has gone on here! What vegetable passions have run the whole gamut of ambition, selfishness, greed of place, fruition, satiety, and now rest here in the truce of exhaustion! What a battle-field, if one may look upon it so! The corn has lost its ammunition, and stacked arms in a slovenly, militia sort of style. The ground-vines are torn, trampled and withered; and the ungathered cucumbers, worthless melons, and golden squashes, lie about like the spent bombs and exploded shells of a battle-field. So the cannon-balls lay on the sandy plain before Fort Fisher, after the capture. So the great, grassy meadow at Munich, any morning during the October Fest, is strewn with empty beer-mugs. History constantly repeats itself. There is a large crop of moral reflections in my garden, which anybody is at liberty to gather who passes this way.—*My Summer in a Garden.*

---

**GABRIELE D'ANNUNZIO.**

WE walked among evergreens, among ancient box-trees, laurels, myrtles, whose wild old age had forgotten its early discipline. In a few places here and there was some trace of the symmetrical shapes carved once upon a time by the gardener's shears; and with a melancholy, not unlike his who searches on marble tombstones for the effigies of the forgotten dead, I noted carefully among the silent plants those traces of humanity not altogether obliterated. A bitter-sweet odour hung round our path, and from time to time one of us, as if wishing to weave afresh an unravelled web, would reconstruct some memory of our far-off childhood.

The hoarse song of the water came to us through a high myrtle hedge as we stood in a little meadow strewn with daffodils, and guarded by a statue of Pan green with moss. A delicious softness seemed to spring in my veins from the soft turf my feet pressed, and once again the sudden joy of living took away my breath.—
'*The Virgins of the Rocks,*' *translated by Agatha Hughes.*

—∿∿∿—

'E. V. B.'
(*Hon. Mrs Boyle*).

A GARDEN !—The word is in itself a picture, and what pictures it reveals ! All through the days of childhood the garden is our fairy-ground of sweet enchantment and innocent wonder. From the first dawn of thought, when we learned our simple lessons of Eden and its loss, and seemed to see the thornless garden, watered with clear streams, beautiful with spreading trees, and the train of un-named beasts and birds meekly passing before their spotless lord ; and then beyond, far onward to that other garden beloved by the Man of Sorrows, Gethsemane, where we could never picture the blossoming of roses or murmurous hum of summer bees, but only the sombre garden walks, and One kneeling among the olives, and dark, heavy drops upon the grass. And near to this, the Garden of the Sepulchre—in a dewy dawn-light, angel-haunted. These were our Gardens of the Soul. In later years the mists of those older, holier spots wear away as snow-wreaths in the vivid brilliance of the Gardens of Poetry. Then, dreamlike from sapphire seas arose the Gardens of the Hesperides, and we beheld the white-vestured maidens as they danced around the golden-fruited dragon-guarded tree. Then bloomed for us the gardens of Mediæval Italy. The Poets' gardens of cypress and lemon, of marble stairs and sparkling fountains, with all their moonlight mirth and sorrow ; ilex-groves of song and silver-threaded laughter ; visions of Rimini or gay Boccaccio's tales. Then did we linger where high-piping nightingales sang to the Persian Rose in the Gülistan of Saädi :—felt the pure sunlight shine in a little wilderness of roses, or the green shade that lay round the apple-trees of Andrew Marvell ; or in the

'E. V. B.'

garden of the Sensitive Plant, we followed the shadowy steps of the Lady, our souls entranced with the love of every flower she loved. They are all beautiful, these Gardens of Poetry! and through the midst of them flows the broad stream of Memory, isled with fair lilied lawns, fringed with willowy forests and whispering reeds. And not less beautiful than these ideal shades, are the gardens which live unchanged and unchanging in many a painted picture within the heart. Real, and not less ideal, is the remembrance of the gardens we have seen: seen once, it may be, and never since forgotten.

> ' Un souvenir heureux est peut-être sur terre
> Plus vrai que le bonheur.'

So, lovely as truth, crystal-clear as a poet's thought, are the earthly Edens our eyes beheld, in the years that are past. How can we forget the gardens of queenly Genoa, in the days ere yet she was discrowned? of Florence, of Rome and Albano and Tivoli? The palm-gardens of Bordighiera, where periwinkles—*fiori dei morte*—rain down their blue from the overflowing laps of ancient palms, or wander in smiles about their rugged roots; the trellised pergolas and anemonied lawns of Mortola; or those strange island-gardens, Isola Madre of Maggiore, and terraced Isola Bella? Long indeed is the lovely list. Think back into the days that were, and remember them. . . . How they live green and fresh and sweet, in the bloom and the glow of their eternal summer! For you, their skies are ever blue, their roses never fade. Winter has never silenced the plash and flow of their fountains, nor chilled the green from one leaf in their deep groves. The lemon, ripening in pale gold, still hangs ungathered against the southern terrace, where scarlet passion-flowers burn in drifted fire-spots. The peacock, sunning himself upon the stone balustrade, shakes out his emerald glories, while you loiter along the flowery borders of his kingdom; and you know that violets hide somewhere in the grass, for the very sunshine is impregnated with their perfume. Or perchance in fancy, you may tread again the narrow pathway that winds around the rocky sea-wall at Old Monaco. There, for you, the globes of red geranium reflect still, warm shadows about the names of lovers long since forgot or dead, wrought upon the tablet leaves of aloes or of cactus. There mesembrianthemums shine still, sunned over as of old with rayed discs of red and yellow, while basking lizards at your approach rustle away under the leaves. Lean over the low parapet wall and watch the waves dash in white foam against the jagged rocks below. The old cliff blooms out into cistus and spikes of purple stocks; midway the sea-birds scream and play above the little fishing-boats, tossing like fairy nut-shells on the crisp blue summer sea. From the sunny Mediterranean and that narrow strip of hanging garden, dream on into the black cypress shades of Tuscany.

In all Italy—the land of flowers, the garden of the world—there are no gardens more stately, nor any nobler cypress-trees, than at Villa d'Este of Tivoli.[1] In the spring, by the straight smooth ways under the ilexes and cypresses, all day the golden gloom is made rosy where ever and anon red Judas-trees shower down their bloom. Marble stairs lead up through terraced heights to paved walks under the Palazzo walls. There the air is faint with rich fragrance of the orange-trees. The lofty spires of ancient cypresses reach up above the topmost terrace; far below in the garden, between their dark ranks sparkle the up-springing fountains. Beyond, above the tallest cypresses, rise brown crumbling walls of the old town, piled up with open loggie and arched gates and overshadowing roofs: and high over these, great barren hills crowned with ruined fortresses and shattered keeps. To the west rolls out the ocean of the wide Campagna, undulating far away where Rome is lost in the sunset. Dream on, until you sigh with the wondrous sweetness of Rome herself in the wild wood-garden of the Vatican, where in April days ten thousand odorous cyclamen flowers, flush with crimson all the moss beneath the trees. Dream on, till you see once more the swaying of the tall pines and bathe your steps in tracts of flowery grass in the green Pamphili Doria, and watch the mystic fountain, most like the form of an inconstant spirit, like a pale blue-robed

[1] See Illustration in Appendix.

'E. V. B.'

Undine uncertain if to leave her source, trembling betwixt desire and fear.

Fain would we linger in the gardens of Portugal, under the sweet-scented camellias of Cintra—lost in golden reveries amid her rose-wreathed thickets. Strange is the remembrance of the beautiful Montserrat cathedral water-aisles, whose torrents foam down in long cascades beneath the high-arched Tree-ferns! And in Spain, like a scene in the Arabian Nights, comes back to us the old Moorish garden of Granada, with marble-lined canal and lofty arcades of trimmed yew, topped with crescents, pyramids, and crowns.[1]

[1] This beautiful rhapsody, addressed 'to the Garden-loving Reader,' formed the Prelude to the first edition of this book.

# HISTORICAL EPILOGUE

THE foregoing collection of extracts contains, perhaps, in essence a sufficient History of Gardens; but there may be readers who prefer a less broken thread of narrative, and to them is offered the following clue to the labyrinth of garden literature.

Ever since the gardening art has been anything more conscious and definite than the haphazard planting of fruit-trees, herbs and vegetables in orchards and kitchen-gardens for practical use, garden design may be said broadly to have adopted one of two forms or styles, each capable of infinite variation and modification in treatment, and each liable at times to trespass upon the territory and overlap the limits, of the other.

One of these styles has been distinguished by such various names as Architectural, Classical, Formal, Regular, Rectangular, Symmetrical and Geometrical; or has been called Italian, French, or Dutch, according to the country of its origin. As the terms denote, the exponents of this style chose for model and inspiration the art of the architect, who designed, or 'built' the garden in harmony with the plan of the house, of which it was a sort of open-air extension; for detail and decoration it laid under contribution the art of sculpture, in the form of clipped hedges and trees (known as 'topiarian work'), statuary, vases and fountains.

The second school endeavoured to follow Nature more closely, believing that, with this aim in view, the sister art of painting was a surer guide, and has been variously called the Natural, Irregular, Landscape, Romantic, English or Chinese School; these two nations having had most influence in its creation or development.

This later school in its designs 'lays out' or 'composes' its gardens as a painter his landscapes, and employs so far as possible the irregular curves of Nature and her dispositions of rock, wood and water, rather than straight lines and geometrical curves; but in the hands of mannerists these irregular windings and serpentisings often become as arbitrary, unnatural and monotonous as the more intentional regularity of the architect.[1]

Broadly it may be said that the 'landscape-garden' in its purity resembled a park, and that the landscape-gardener was a creator of park scenery; but it is clear that the division into two styles is only for the purposes of rough classification, and that between the two are innumerable gradations and shades. Gardens may be and have been made of the greatest beauty, which would resist all attempts to force them into any æsthetic categories; while no more definite plan of design, 'laying out' or 'composition' may have been followed than dictated by the instinct of beauty, taste and the love of Nature and Art.

In an historical account of gardens the precedents are in favour of beginning with the Garden of Eden, which undoubtedly claims priority in time; but until we know whether Major Seton Karr,

[1] It may be interesting to note a few of the many names that have from time to time been put forward as claimants to the honour of initiating, prophecying or suggesting the principle of the Modern, Natural or Landscape Garden :—
1. Homer's Grotto of Calypso; Œlian's Vale of Tempe (Böttiger).
2. Nero in Tacitus (Loudon).
3. Petrarch's 'Vaucluse.'
4. Tasso's Garden of Armida (Eustace).
5. Christopher Wren (father of the Architect), inventor of the serpentine river.
6. 'Bacon the prophet, Milton the Herald' (W. Mason).
7. Milton's Paradise (Dr J. Warton and Horace Walpole).
8. Sir Henry Wotton (G. W. Johnson).
9. Huet, Bishop of Avranches.
10. Dufresny (Gabriel Thouin).
11. Hogarth's 'Line of Beauty.'
12. William Kent.
13. Pope in the *Guardian*, and at Twickenham.
14. Addison in the *Spectator*.
15. The English (Gray).
16. The Chinese (Geo. Mason and W. Chambers).

# HISTORICAL EPILOGUE 317

dissatisfied with the opinions of Bishop Huet and others on the 'Situation of Paradise,' has succeeded in his attempt to identify its precise position at the heads of the four great rivers of Africa,[1] we must be satisfied with Milton's imaginative description in 'Paradise Lost.'

Possibly it may eventually be proved that Eden is identical with the 'Gardens of the Hesperides' near Mount Atlas; although these gardens, again, stripped of poetic fruit and foliage, have been declared to be only disused stone quarries at Berenice (Bengaze) affording fine soil and shelter for luxuriant fruit-trees.[2]

Milton, it is interesting to note, has so carefully 'trimmed' and 'hedged' his garden, as to have been claimed in turns by the partisans of either school as representing its views.

A set of quotations is necessary to enable the reader to judge whether Horace Walpole is right in seeing only Nature therein, or Walter Bagehot in asserting you could draw a map of it.

> Of Eden, where delicious Paradise,
> Now nearer, crowns with her enclosure green
> As with a rural mound, the champain head
> Of a steep wilderness; whose hairy sides
> With thicket overgrown, grotesque and wild,
> Access denied; and overhead up-grew
> Insuperable height of loftiest shade,
> Cedar and pine and fir, and branching palm,
> A sylvan scene! and, as the ranks ascend
> Shade above shade, *a woody theatre
> Of stateliest view.* Yet higher than their tops
> The verdurous wall of Paradise up-sprung:
> . . . In this pleasant soil
> His far more pleasant garden God ordained.
>
> . . . . . . .
>
> Flowers worthy of Paradise, *which not nice art
> In beds and curious knots*, but Nature boon
> Pour'd forth profuse on hill and dale and plain.
>
> . . . . . . .

---

[1] See Mr W. Marshall Adams's letter to *The Times* on 'The New Search for Eden.' November 23, 1898.

[2] Lieut. Beechey's Travels in Cyrene, 1828, and *Gardener's Magazine*, vol. iv. p. 398 (Loudon).

## THE PRAISE OF GARDENS

> A happy rural seat of various view :
> Groves, whose rich trees wept odorous gums and balm ;
> Betwixt them lawns or level downs, and flocks
> Grazing the tender herb.
> Another side, umbrageous grots and caves
> Of cool recess, o'er which the mantling vine
> Lays forth her purple grape, and gently creeps
> Luxuriant: meanwhile murm'ring waters fall
> Down the slope hills, dispers'd or in a lake,
> That to the fringed bank with myrtle crown'd
> Her crystal mirror holds, unite their streams.
> —*Paradise Lost*, Book IV.

The earliest historical gardens are those of ancient Egypt, of which a description from the pen of Sir J. Gardner Wilkinson has been quoted in the text, and Mr Percy Newberry now seems to be convinced that the illustration reproduced from Rosellini is the design of the gardener Nekht for the Great Temple at Karnak.[1]

Besides the Monuments and Herodotus's mention of the sacred groves and gardens of Ammon and Osiris in Egypt as of extraordinary beauty, we have little authentic record.

Those who will penetrate into the mystery of the Hanging Gardens of Babylon further than is disclosed by Diodorus Siculus,[2] may dip into the learned Dr Falconer's 'Historical View of the Gardens of Antiquity.'[3] The Hill Amron-Ibn-Ali is the supposed site of the 'Horti Pensiles.' Some may have their imagination of the subject quickened by the sight of the stupendous columns and cypresses in Martin's pictures of the 'Destruction of Babylon' and the 'Fall of Nineveh,'[4] or by De Brosse's description of the terraced gardens of Isola Bella—perhaps the nearest comparison to be found in Europe:—

"Imagine a quantity of arcades formed in the centre of a lake, supporting a conical-shaped hill, cut on four sides, covered with

---

[1] See *ante* pages 1-3.   [2] See *ante* page 12.
[3] See also Dr Sickler's Introduction to his 'Geschichte der Obst Cultur,' 1802.
[4] See, too, a fine fanciful sketch by A. Castaigne in *Century Magazine* for June 1898.

# HISTORICAL EPILOGUE 319

thirty-six terraces, one above the other, nine on each side, and one of the sides covered with buildings. Each of these terraces is hung with pallisades of jasmine, orange-trees or pomegranates."

Besides being a mystical poet, King Solomon was a very practical gardener and botanist, and as we know that his garden was quadrangular and surrounded by a high wall, it may be surmised that he favoured the formal style. Josephus gives him credit for being the first to plant the cedar in Judæa, and 'the humble hyssop in the wall' did not escape his notice any more than the more heavily scented rose, lily, camphire, spikenard, saffron and cinnamon; it is rumoured Solomon's pools still exist,[1] but had they been in Europe, instead of the unchanging East, there is little doubt they would long ago have been thrown into a lake.

The ancient Persian garden or park (Paradise) seems to have undergone little change in form from the days of Xenophon, through those of the later travellers Chardin and Tavernier in the seventeenth century, down to our own time;[2] and for the 'roses and raptures' which you may find missing in their actual gardens, you must appeal to the imaginative ones of Hafiz, Saadi and Omar Khayyam.[3] Compare, for instance, Lord Curzon's description of the gardens of Shiraz with the utterances of the poets:—

'From the outside, a square or oblong enclosure is visible, enclosed by a high mud wall, over the top of which appears a dense bouquet of trees. The interior is thickly planted with these, or as Herbert phrased it, with lofty pyramidal cypresses, broad spreading *chenawrs*, tough elm, straight ash, knotty pines, fragrant masticks, kingly oaks, sweet myrtles, useful maples. They are planted down the sides of long alleys, admitting of no view but a vista, the surrounding plots being a jungle of

[1] 'Maundrell's Travels.'   [2] See *ante* pp. 4 and 126.
[3] One wonders if 'Come into the Garden, Maud' with all its flower personification was inspired by Jami's 'Come into the Garden, for without thy care or mine, all is ready for pleasure. Since the rose has removed the veil from before her cheek, the narcissus has become all eyes to gaze upon her.'

bushes and shrubs. Water courses along in channels or is conducted into tanks. Sometimes these gardens rise in terraces to a pavilion at the summit, whose reflection in the pool below is regarded as a triumph of landscape gardening. There are no neat walks, or shaped flower-beds, or stretches of sward. All is tangled and untrimmed. Such beauty as arises from shade and the purling of water is all that the Persian requires.'[1]

Of the ancient Greek gardens the sum of opinion from the scant authority at hand is that they were little more than olive groves or orchards. Pliny ascribes to Epicurus, the 'Philosopher of the Garden,' the introduction of the Pleasure Garden within the walls of Athens, between the Cephissus and the Ilissus; and if it was not Formal, it was certainly Classic and Academic. It is a little difficult to reconcile this account with Plutarch's statement that a century earlier the General Cimon first reformed the Academy from savagery by conveying streams of water to it, and planting it with groves of the olive plane and elm trees; unless we suppose Epicurus to have possessed the first *private* garden in Athens.

These trees were cut down in the siege of Athens by Sulla, as the trees of the Bois de Boulogne were sacrificed at the siege of the modern Athens. From Aristophanes we have this picture of an Athenian bourgeois's ideal of 'cabbage planting':—

> 'If my lot be join'd with thine—
> To plant in lengthen'd ranks the vine,
> To graft the fig tree's tender shoots,
> To pluck the vineyard's purpling fruits;
> And olive-trees in many a row
> Around our farm shall circling grow.'[2]

Passing to Roman gardens, Livy (as early as B.C. 534) mentions the garden of Tarquinius Superbus. Forgetful of the stern simplicity of old Cato the Censor and his injunction to each Roman citizen to cultivate flowers in his enclosure as a source of elegance and moral culture, we find in Imperial days that

[1] 'Persia,' by Hon. G. N. Curzon.
[2] 'The Acharnians' (Mitchell's Translation).

# HISTORICAL EPILOGUE 321

even the stoic Seneca indulged in garden magnificence strangely out of keeping with the ascetic philosophy he professed.

Other famous Roman gardens were those of Scipio; Lucullus's, on the promontory of Misenum (perhaps on the site of his so-called existing villa near Baiae, in the Bay of Naples), where Martial declares his preference for the wild country over the prevailing fashion of roses and clipped box-trees amongst myrtles and planes:—

> Baiana nostri villa, Basse, Faustini
> Non otiosis ordinata myrtetis
> Viduaque platano, tonsilique buxeto,
> Ingrata lati spatia detinet campi
> Sed rure vero, barbaroque lætatur.

On the Quirinal Hill lay the gardens of Sallust, afterwards merged into the Negroni, Ludovisi and Barberini gardens;[1] Cicero's villa at Arpinum is constantly referred to: but best known of all, from the owner's descriptions, are the villas of Varro and of Pliny the Consul. The latter's Laurentine villa on the Tiber, near Paterno, now called 'San Lorenzo' and his Tusculan villa, now Frascati, situate in the natural amphitheatre of the Apennines, are so fully detailed in his letters that learned archæologists, Scamozzi, Félibien (1699), Schinkel and Castell (1728) have essayed to reconstruct the plan of them.[2] But even more interesting than the gardens of Pliny are the excavations at Pompeii showing the plan and design of the inner city gardens, and the wall paintings at Herculaneum. In one of the latter the trellises, pergolas, statuary and fountains might have emanated from Mollet or Boyceau in the sixteenth or seventeenth century; and so striking is the likeness, that Horace Walpole expressed his opinion that 'nothing is wanting but a parterre to make a garden in the reign of Trajan serve for the description of one in the reign of King William III.'; and in the Inner Garden

[1] See De Brosse's 'Life of Sallust'; also *ante* p. 160.
[2] In Loudon's 'History of Gardening' may be seen reproductions on a small scale of the plans of Pliny's two villas from R. Castell's 'Villas of the Ancients.' See also *ante* p. 15 *et seq.*

to the house of Aulus Vettius, even the parterre (on a domestic scale) is not wanting. 'Pompeii,' writes Taine, 'is an ancient Saint-Germain or Fontainebleau; one sees the abyss separating the two worlds.'[1]

In the Garden of Vettius the marble basins, statues, etc., are all set up in their original places, from which some have never moved, and the beds are laid out on the old lines, following the indications in the wall paintings: for instance, the cones of basket work overgrown with creepers and ivy to be seen at various points in the garden are copied from one of the frescoes. Charles Estienne's 'De re Hortensi Libellus' throws no light upon these dome-shaped cages. The marble heads in the centre of the picture on ivy-carved stelæ are those of Dionysius with Ariadne, and Silenus with a Bacchante, back to back. The fountains on either side of the foreground are bronze boys holding geese, with water flowing from the beaks, and the fresco behind the columns represents makers of the garlands, the art to which Athenæus devotes so many pages.

Another feature of Roman gardens copied in mediæval days was the mount, called λόφος by Plutarch, no doubt raised to command a view of the surrounding country.[2]

During the dark ages the early Christian fathers and the

[1] 'Voyage en Italie.'
[2] A few authorities and references (other than these in the text) to ancient Greek and Roman gardens:—
Dr Falconer's 'Historical View of the Gardens of Antiquity,' 1785.
C. A. Böttiger's 'Racemazionen zur Garten Kunst der Alten.'
Félibien, Plans et Descriptions des maisons de Campagne de Pline le Consul, 1699.
Trinkhusii Dissertatio de Hortis et Villis Ciceronis.
C. Stephanus, 'De re Hortensi Libellus,' 1536.
Daines Barrington, 'Archæologia,' 1782.
Ælian's 'Various History.'
R. Rapinus, Hortorum Lib. IV., with Appendix,—'De Universa Culturæ Hortensis Disciplina, 'Utrecht, 1672, a most valuable dissertation: also the Paris Edition of 1780,' with a History of Gardens by Gabriel Brotier.
Scamozzi, 'Discorsi sopra l'Antichita di Roma,' 1582.
Stengel's Hortorum, Florum et Arborum Historia, 1650.

Inner Garden of the House of Aulus Vettius, recently excavated at Pompeii.

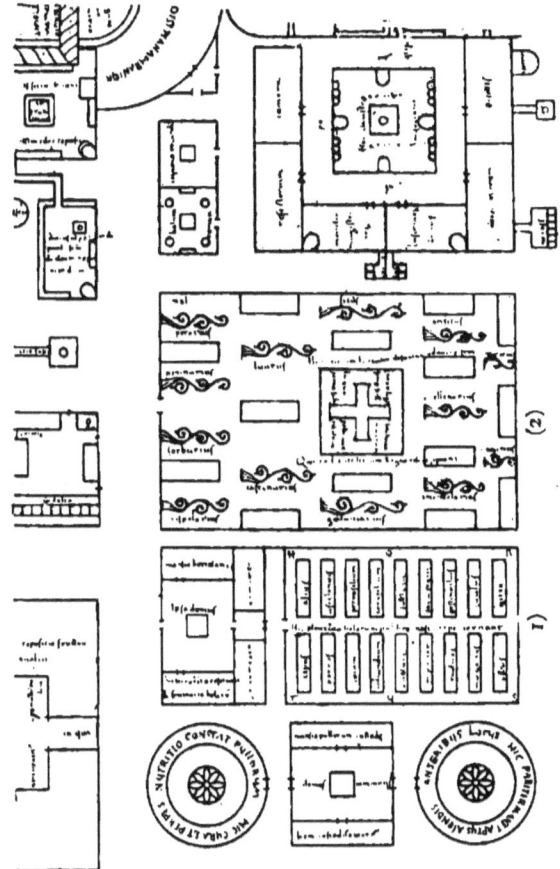

Plan of the Abbey of St Gall, by a Monk of the Ninth Century, showing (1) on left, kitchen-garden divided into 18 beds, with the Latin names of vegetables, and in the centre (2) the Cemetery and Orchard, with the Fruit trees trained between the Graves.

HISTORICAL EPILOGUE 327

monks alone preserved the arts of culture as of horticulture; in the fourth century St Jerome describes St Anthony's mountain garden; and Castell points out how several early monasteries and abbeys follow the lines and distribution of Roman villas—courts surrounded with porticoes, and containing basins with fountains—terraces upon arcades and garden oratories.

The Abbey of Icolmhill was founded in the Hebrides between 500 and 600 A.D., and from works like the 'Polypticon' of the Abbot Irminon, written between 800 and 900 A.D., we know that gardens, orchards and arboreta were attached to the monasteries of St Remy, St' Bertin and Corbie, and consisted of a plot of ground enclosed by a wall, a hedge or trellis, and devoted to the cultivation of vegetables, fruits, herbs and roots.

Miss Amherst also recites the garden accounts of Norwich Priory and Abingdon Abbey, and gives a plan of Bicester Priory.[1]

In the 'Ordinatio Hortorum' of the Abbey of Corbie, the garden is divided into four parts, and directions are given for its weeding, by the Hortulan friar sending in the 'Sarculatores' or hoers, to cleanse the *areæ* and *plantationes*.[2]

The plan of the kitchen and fruit garden of the Abbey of St Gall (on the Lake of Constance) by a monk of the ninth century, bald and uninteresting as it looks, contains much of the garden and other history of its time, bringing us into touch with Charlemagne, who himself was a constant and popular visitor here, and known as 'Noster Carolus' amongst the monks.

The plan is supposed to be by Abbot Eginhardus, Prefect of the Royal Buildings under Charlemagne, whose daughter Imma he had married, and after her death adopted a monastic life.

The kitchen garden is a parallelogram of eighteen beds, on each of which is written in Latin the name of the vegetable it contains, all of which (with the exception of carrots) are enumer-

[1] 'History of English Gardening.'
[2] The word Hortus, derived perhaps from χορτος, as it were 'Cortis' or 'Curtis,' means a garden in the Middle Ages as well as with the Latins. In the grounds of the Abbey of *Prum*, the gardens were divided into *Areæ* and *Agri*, and into *Lecti*. (M. B. Guérard, 'Commentary on the Polyptikon.')

ated in Charlemagne's *Capitulare de Villis*, as ordained to be cultivated within his dominions.

The fruit trees in the cemetery are planted around the graves of the friars, and between the monuments. The flower, *i.e.* herb or physic garden, is on the other side of the house (not shown in this half of the plan) appropriately near the doctors' quarters in the N.E. angle of the monastery: this contains sixteen beds of herbs and flowers also identical with those named in the Capitulary. As the monks were bound by their vows to live upon pulse, vegetables and fruit gathered by themselves, the importance of these gardens in the monastic economy was considerable.[1] A more detailed account of the contents of the Garden at this date is given in the poem 'Hortulus' by Walafridus Strabo (afterwards abbot of the monastery) dedicated in A.D. 849 to the then abbot, Grimald.[2]

'The gardens in the early part of the Norman Dynasty were certainly not different from what we now term orchards. Comparatively few fruit trees or esculent plants were known in England till even the latter centuries. But near the castles (as at Conway) and monasteries, a small enclosure was reserved for the ladies or for the abbot, which was surrounded by lofty walls, sometimes decorated with paintings, and filled with roses and other fragrant plants.'[3]

Brithnod, the first Abbot of Ely, A.D. 1107, was celebrated for his skill in horticulture, and laid out very extensive gardens and orchards;[4] and Neckam, in the same century, rhetorically catalogues the fruit, flowers and vegetables which should adorn 'a noble garden.'[5]

For the best descriptions in English of mediæval gardens we must consult Chaucer and Lydgate, or the 'King's Quhair,' by

[1] See the late Professor Willis's paper published in *Archæological Journal* vol. v., with the facsimile of the original plan and a modernised and anglicised form.
[2] Strabi Fuldensis 'Hortulus' per Venerabilem Bedam, Nuremberg, 1512.
[3] Dallaway's 'Supplementary Anecdotes to Gardening in England.'
[4] G. W. Johnson, 'History of English Gardening.'
[5] See *ante* p. 30.

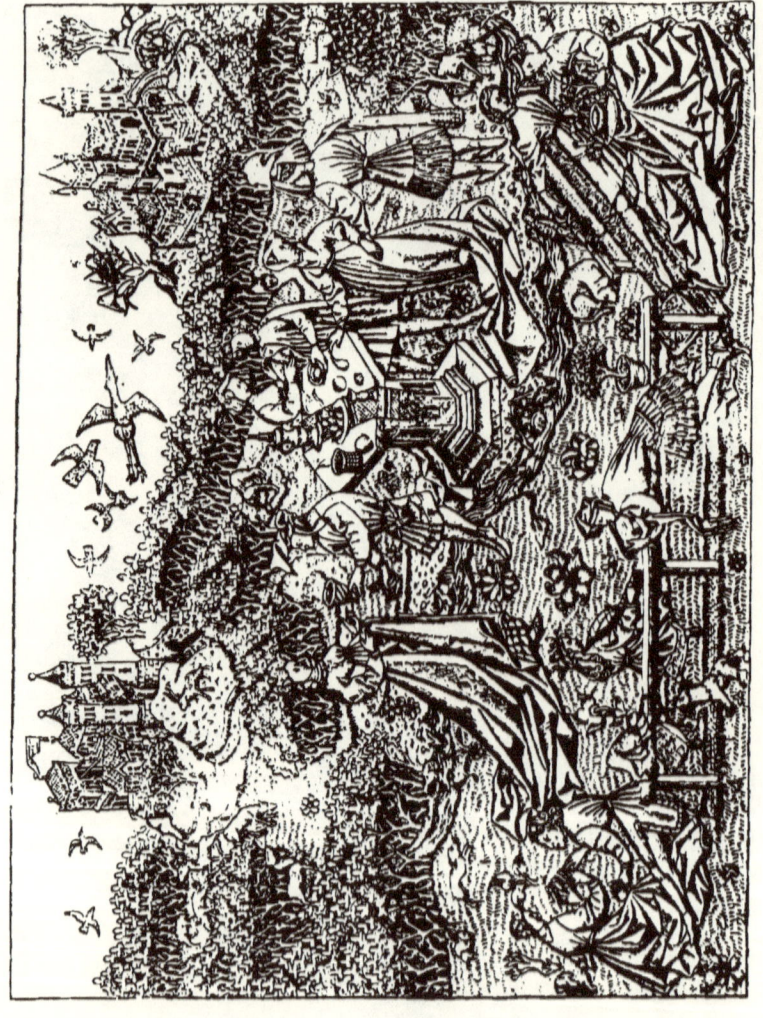

'The Garden of Love,' from the earliest known Flemish engraving (*circa* 1450).

the poet-king, James I. of Scotland, who from his prison in Windsor Castle spies

'A Garden fair; and in the Corners set
An Herbere greene, with Wandis long and small
Railit about.'

The 'wands' or railings, as a division of the beds before the use of box, may also be seen, painted green and white, the Tudor colours, in the backgrounds of Holbein's pictures of Will Somers and Jane the Fool. Chaucer's garden in 'Troilus and Cresseide,' also preserves this feature and the sanded alleys:

This Yerde[1] was large, and railed al the aleyes
And shadowed wel with blos'omy bowis grene,
And benchid newe, and sondid all the weyes.

The mediæval garden from the illumination of the 'Roman de la Rose' is shown both in Miss Amherst's 'History' and in the 'Formal Garden in England,'[2] and valuable illustrations are to be found in the 'Songe de Poliphile' and the illuminations of a French MS. of the late fifteenth-century 'Le Rustican des Profits Ruraux' by Croissant, and in the Psalter of Edwin in Trinity College, Cambridge, is given the private garden of one of the canons.[3]

Less familiar is the pleasure garden here copied from the earliest known Flemish engraving (about 1450) called the 'Garden of Love,' in which the occupants of the garden are depicted as engaged in all sorts of diversions, love-making, feasting, playing cards and music. The beasts of the field and birds of the air, monkeys and parrots even, are revelling amid perspectiveless scenery of conventialised trefoil-trees and running water, and large detached flowers are strewn upon the grass in the fore-

[1] Yerde or Yard (surviving in the Pond Yard at Hampton Court) was the earlier form of the word Garden, both being of the same etymology (the Anglo-Saxon 'geard') and signifying an enclosure—the Scotch form 'Garth' comes half-way between the two—and other forms of the word are innumerable. In Holland's Pliny we find *hort-yard* for orchard.
[2] By Reginald Blomfield and Inigo Thomas.
[3] See *Archæological Journal*, vol. iv. p. 160.

ground, suggesting the art of the goldsmith rather than of the gardener.[1]

Dr Andrew Boorde (whom the Dictionary of National Biography no longer allows to be the original 'Merry Andrew') in his 'Dyetary of Health' will have attached to a mansion a 'fayre garden, repleted wyth herbes of aromatyck and redolent savours, with a poole or two for fysche'; and the 'Mesnagier de Paris' gives a long list of all the herbs and plants which ought to be cultivated in the garden.

But the design of the garden, rather than its contents, is our theme, and we must consult the work of the French architect, Androuet du Cerceau, 'Les plus Excellents Bastiments de France,' for bird's-eye views and plans of the gardens of the 'Thuileries,' Montargis, the Châteaux of Blois and Gaillon, and many others.[2]

The gardens of St. Germain-en-Laye built for Henry II., running down to the Seine in a series of terraces under which were grottoes in rock and shell-work, and figures disporting themselves in the waters, were considered one of the marvels of the age.

The grotto has always played an important rôle in the history of gardens from the mythical one of Calypso to those of Palissy enamelled over with creeping things in pottery, and the be-spa'd and be-mirrored creation of Pope at Twickenham.[3]

To come back to England in the days of Henry VIII. The best known Tudor gardens were Nonesuch near Ewell in Surrey described by Hentzner;[4] Theobalds, of which we have a picture from the Parliamentary Survey of 1650, to which date we may assume it to have been undisturbed;[5] and greatest of all, Hampton Court. They are characterised by moats and walls, while the

[1] I am indebted to Mr Sidney Colvin for drawing my attention to Professor Max Lehr's monograph on this print, and to the latter for permission to reproduce his collotype.

[2] See *ante* p. 51.   [3] See *ante* pp. 45-50 and 143.   [4] See *ante* p. 73.

[5] 'In the Greate Garden are nine large compleate squares or knotts lyinge upon a levell in y^e middle of y^e said Garden, whereof one is sett forth with box borders in y^e likeness of y^e Kinges armes, one other plott is planted with choice flowers; the other 7 knotts are all grass knotts, handsomely turfed in the intervalls or little walkes. . . . a Quicksette hedge of White Thorne

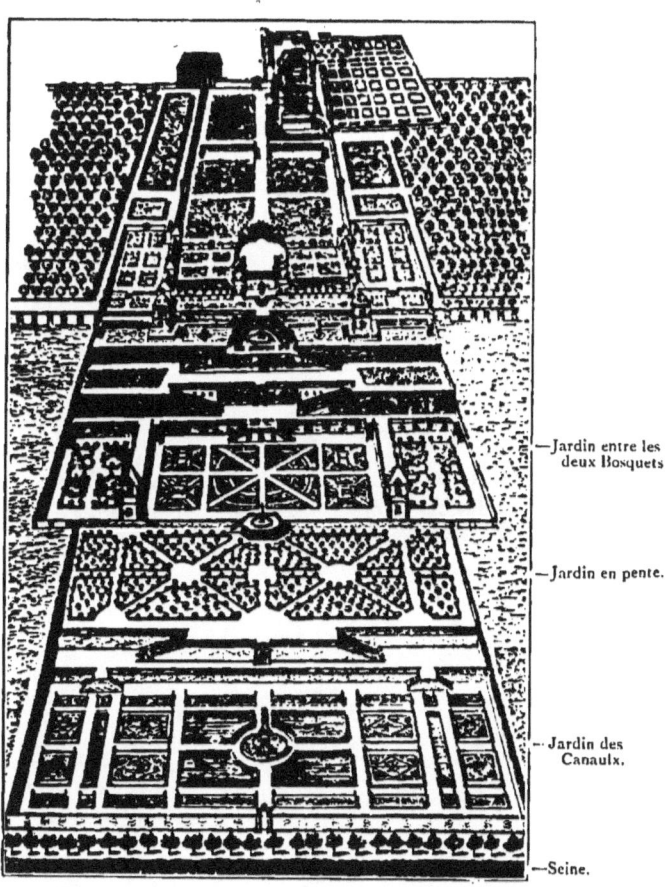

The terraced Gardens of Saint-Germain-en-Laye, 1523.
From Braun's 'Civitates Orbis Terrarum,' 1572-1618.

The Tudor 'Pond Yard' or Garden, Hampton Court, in its present state.

# HISTORICAL EPILOGUE 337

'knotted' beds are railed with painted wands (the royal colours being green and white) or surrounded with low fences of trellis-work. Cavendish in his life of Wolsey sings :—

> 'My Garden sweet, enclosed with walles strong
> Embanked with benches to sytt and take my rest
> The knots so enknotted, it cannot be exprest,
> With arbors and alyes so pleasant and so dulce.'

Mounts at the corners, galleries, dials, cabinets of verdure, columns and pyramids of marble, topiarian work and fish-ponds complete the details.

Skelton, a Tudor poet, paints the following picture of a garden of his day :—

> 'With alys ensanded about in compas
> The bankis enturfid with singular solas,
> Enrailed with rosers, and vinis engrapi'd.'[1]

The gardens of Hampton Court covered altogether 2000 acres and consisted of the Mount Garden, the King's *Newe* Garden (now called the Privy Garden) with gravel paths, raised mounds, sun-dials, and railed beds—and the Pond yard or Garden (now alone remaining, and the subject of our illustration) which retains something of its ancient Tudor aspect, being still divided into its original rectangular enclosures by low brick walls overgrown with creepers, in the corners of which may be detected the bases of the stone piers that supported the heraldic beasts 'bearing vanes and shields with the King's arms and badges.'[2]

In a drawing by Antonius Wynngarde in the Bodleian Library

and privett cutt into a handsome fashion—at every angle a faire cherrie tree, and a 'Ciprus' in the middle of the knotts—also a Marble fountaine.

'The Privie Garden has a Quadrangle or square squadron Quicksett hedge 9 feet high, with four round Arbours and seats at each corner and two Doorways to each Arbour, between which a Roman T pointing to 3 paire of Staires and a Mulberry walk.' (Shortened from the original MS. in Record Office, transcribed by Miss Amherst.)

[1] Skelton's 'Garlande of Laurell.'
[2] Ernest Law, 'History of Hampton Court.'

these heraldic beasts are the most conspicuous feature, bristling over the whole garden.[1]

As an introduction to the Elizabethan garden we must return to Italy, which, in gardening as in literature, at this time exercised so potent an influence over our ancestors.

The mediæval Italian gardens are founded upon the Roman villas evolving into fortified castles or monasteries, of which many of them occupy the sites. Meason traces the relationship in the later use of one of Lucullus's villas.

One of the oldest is Bramante's Vatican garden, on the site of the present Library of the Vatican. In 1549 the same architect laid out the *Villa d'Este* at Tivoli for the Cardinal Hippolito d'Este, the friend of Ariosto, upon the site of the Emperor Hadrian's villa. A view is here given of the Villa d'Este as it appeared about 1765, 'darkly grav'd by Piranesi's hand,' in which some of the many cypresses said to have been planted by Michael Angelo are conspicuous. 'Terrace rises upon terrace and water rushes down an artificial rock, spreading in a beautiful manner as it descends.'[2]

The terraces rendered necessary by the hilliness of the ground, with flights of steps leading to the different levels; the piazzas for shade and air; avenues and plantations of olive, vine, and myrtle; fountains, statuary, urns, and vases; these are the decorative elements of the later stately architectural Italian Gardens with their fine perspectives.[3]

[1] The Inventory of ' Beestes in freeston barynge shyldes with the kynges armes and the Queeny's,' is thus entered in the Chapel House Accounts, transcribed by Mr Law:—'foure dragones, seyx lyones, five grewhoundes, five harttes, foure unicornes, serving to stand about the ponddes in the pond yard;' and the 'paynting of 180 postes with white and greene in oyle, and sixteen brazin dials for the newe garden,' is also chronicled.

[2] Wood's 'Letters of an Architect.'

[3] Much ridicule has been levelled at the Italian Gardens for being only a means of walking up and down stairs in the open air; but a witty writer has retorted that the Italian finds but little pleasure in the melancholy monotony of an English Park, and least of all in a large extent of level lawn; and that if you tell him that in this he was to contemplate Nature *dressed*, he would probably reply that he saw in it only Nature *shaved*.

The Villa d'Este, Tivoli, by Piranesi, 1765.

## HISTORICAL EPILOGUE 341

The villas Ludovisi, Medici, Doria Pamphili, the gardens of the Quirinal and others may be studied in Giovanni Battista Falda's copper-plates of Roman gardens. The gardens of the villa Albani, outside the Porta Salaria, planned by the great Cardinal-Antiquary, Alessandro Albani, the patron and friend of Winckelmann, are taken by Taine as the text for an eloquent æsthetic sermon upon the art and arrangement loved by the "grand seigneur homme de cour" of Italy :—

'No liberty is left to nature, all is artificial. The water leaps out in jets and plumes, and has no bed save vases and urns. The lawns are hemmed in by enormous hedges taller than a man, thick as walls, and forming geometrical triangles of which the apexes all point to one centre. In the foreground stretches a compact alley of small cypresses planted in a row.

'You ascend from one garden to another by large stone staircases like those at Versailles. The flower-beds are enclosed in small box frames; they compose designs and resemble well-bordered carpets in a regular medley of gradated colours. This villa is a wreck, as it were the fossil skeleton of a life that lasted two centuries, whose chief pleasure was conversation amid beautiful surroundings, with the customs of Salon and Ante-chamber.'[1]

---

[1] The following are some of the chief authorities on Italian villas and Gardens:—
Pietro Crescenzi, 'Opus Ruralium Commodorum,' Bk. viii., 1471.
Angeli Politiani, 'Rusticus,' 1486.
M. Bussato, 'Giardino d'Agricoltura,' Venetia, 1612.
I. B. Ferrarius, 'de Florum Cultura,' Rome, 1633.
Israell Silvestro, 'Alcune vedute di Giardini e Fontane di Roma e di Tivoli,' Paris, 1646.
Melchior Kysell, 'Recueil des Jardins Italiens,' Augsburg, 1682.
G. B. Falda, 'Li Giardini di Roma,' 1670.
Evelyn's Diary.
R. Castell's 'Villas of the Ancients,' 1728.
L. Vanvitelli, 'Disegni del Reale Palazzo di Caserta,' 1756.
Piranesi's 'Vedute di Roma,' 1765.
De Brosse's Letters.
Eustace's 'Classical Tour through Italy.'
Beckford's 'Letters from Italy.'

## THE PRAISE OF GARDENS

Thus much upon Italian gardens will serve as prelude to the Elizabethan garden, which, like the literature of the day, was cosmopolitan and eclectic—a happy fusion of the early Tudor garden with the styles of Italy and France, borrowing from the former its terraces and fountains, and from the latter its parterres, alleys, berceaux and labyrinths. Its design is summed up in the famous Essay of Bacon, the crown and flower of garden literature, which contains the elements of all styles and schools—of the architect's, the painter's, the natural and wild garden alike.

One typical Elizabethan garden was Theobalds, the garden of Lord Treasurer Burleigh (of which there is a plan by Thorpe in the Soane Museum), described by Mandelslo in 1640 as a large square, with its walls covered with Phillyrea, a *jet d'eau* in the centre, a parterre, with walks planted on the sides with espaliers, and others 'arched over': a mount called the Mount of Venus is in the midst of a labyrinth or maize. The walks 'arched over' are due to the art of the 'pleacher,' a word derived from the French 'plesser' to weave (from the woven or plaited boughs), and of constant occurrence in Shakespeare.

Other gardens were Hatfield described by Hentzner,[1] Holland House, Kensington, with much of its original plan still existing; and the Earl of Pembroke's garden at Wilton (before the days of the Palladian Bridge), here shown as originally designed by Isaac de Caus, son of the old Solomon de Caus, from whom we have the plan and description of the Schloss garden at Heidelberg.[2]

The euphuistic praise of Wilton by John Taylor, the 'Water

W. S. Rose's 'Letters from the North of Italy.'
Sir R. C. Hoare's 'Classical Tour.'
Joseph Forsyth's 'Remarks on Italy,' 1802.
G. L. Meason's 'Landscape Architecture of Italy,' 1828.
R. Duppa's 'Observations and Opinions on the Continent.'
Wood's 'Letters of an Architect,' 1828.
Taine's 'Voyage en Italie' and 'Philosophie de l' Art.'
Leader Scott's 'Ruccellai Gardens.'
Charles A. Platt's 'Italian Gardens,' 1894.
[1] *ante* p. 73.
[2] 'Hortus Palatinus Heidelbergae exstructus,' 1620 (translated in Loudon).

'Hortus Penbrochianus,' from Le Jardin de Wilton, by Isaac de Caus, 1640.

# HISTORICAL EPILOGUE 345

Poet,' has already been given[1]—although the 'intricacy' of its 'setting' hardly seems to equal the 'twisting, turnings and windings' of the poet's rhetorical conceits; and if the symbolical three arbours standing in a triangle cannot be detected, the walks one within another like 'the rind of an onion' are certainly visible.

According to the letter-press with the copper-plates, the garden was 1000 feet long by 400 feet broad, and was divided into three long squares or parallelograms. The first from the house contained four platts embroidered, each with a fountain in the midst, marble statues, platts of flowers, and a little 'terrass.' The second comprised two groves or woods, with the River Nadar running through them under a bridge, the breadth of the Great Walk. In the groves were two white marble statues, 8 feet high, of Bacchus and Flora; and at the sides two covered arbours, 300 feet long, and alleys. In the third division were two ponds with fountains, and two columns in the middle, the water causing two crowns to revolve. Then came a green 'Compartment,' the walks planted with cherry-trees, and in the middle a great Oval with an antique Statue of a Gladiator in brass; at the sides were three arbours with 'twining Galleryes.'

At the end of the Great Walk stood a stone portico with pilasters and niches containing white marble figures, and a 'terrass' with sea-monsters upon the steps casting water from top to bottom; and above the portico was a 'reserve' of water for the grotto.

Of Elizabethan writers not before quoted Sir Hugh Platt of Lincoln's Inn, Gentleman, 'the most ingenious husbandman of the age he lived in,'[2] should be remembered as the author of 'The Jewel House of Art and Nature,' 'The Paradise of Flora' and 'The Garden of Eden.' He was an advocate for complete individuality of action in 'shaping or fashioning a Garden'—and considered that 'every Drawer or Embroiderer, nay (almost)

[1] *Ante* p. 87.
[2] Tracts on practical Agriculture and Gardening, to which is added a complete Chronological Catalogue of English Authors on Agriculture, Gardening, etc., by Richard Weston, London, 1769, 8vo.

each Dancing-master, may pretend to such niceties, how long, broad or high, the Beds, Hedges, or Borders should be contrived, in regard they call for very small Invention and less learning;'—but he takes much trouble to explain, in anticipation of modern Window-gardening, how 'a faire Gallery, great chamber or other lodging, may be inwardly garnished with sweet herbs and flowers, yea, and fruit—and how to make apt frames for letting down flower-pots with a pulley from your chamber-window, and flower-boxes of lead, or bordes well pitched within, and planted with Rosemary 'running up the transums or movels of your windowes.'

The illustration from the 'Hortus Floridus' by Crispin de Pass shows more in detail the pleached Galleries supported by sculptured columns, and the beds cut up into quaint geometrical snippets strewn upon a sea of sand, and 'set with fine flowers, but thin and sparingly'; a Book of Designs of a similar character by a Flemish Artist, de Vries,[1] plays more variations upon the same theme.

The name of Rembert Dodonæus [2] associated with Clusius and Crispin de Pass, recalls the long list of Herbals which appeared in connection with the Physic Gardens of Europe. The translation of Peter Treveris's 'Grete Herball' was the first published in English, in 1568. But William Turner's 'Herball,' which he claims to have written thirty years before, makes its author rather than Gerard 'the Father of the English Herbal.'[3] Dodoens-Lyte's 'Niewe Herball' appeared in 1578, and finally John Gerarde, the most renowned of all, published in London his 'Herball,' of which a reduced facsimile of the title-page is given. Gerarde was born in 1545, educated as a surgeon, and for twenty years superintended the Garden of Lord Burleigh, to whom the Herbal is dedicated

[1] I. Vredeman de Vries, 'Hortorum Viridariorumque Elegantes Formae.' Antwerp, 1583.

[2] 1517-1586 Physician to the Emperor Maximilian II., Professor of Physic at Leyden, and author of 'Sterpium Historiæ Pemptades' upon which Lyte and Gerard founded their Herbals.

[3] Dean of Wells, and M.D.; First Book, Black Letter, small fo., 1551; 2nd Book, Cologne 1562. Turner had physic gardens at Cologne and later at Wells and Kew—(Preface addressed to Queen Elizabeth).

An Engraving of a garden by Crispin de Pass, from the 'Hortus Floridus,' by Dodonæus, Clusius and himself, Arnheim, 1614.

The Title-Page of Gerarde's 'Herball,' 1st edition, 1597, folio.

# HISTORICAL EPILOGUE 351

in 1597. In his youth he had taken a voyage to the Baltic, and on his return lived in Holborn where he possessed a large physic garden, of which in 1596 he published a catalogue (the earliest in English), and this garden is perhaps the one delineated at the foot of the title-page. He also drew up a letter for Lord Burleigh recommending that a physic garden should be established at Cambridge with himself at its head, 'to encourage the faculty of simpling.'

The Herbal was, so to speak, the *Catalogue Raisonné* of the physic gardens, public and private, which, on the revival of learning, were instituted one after another throughout Europe. Until recently the earliest physic or botanical garden was supposed to be that founded at Venice in 1334 by the Surgeon Gualtieri,[1] if it was not preceded by the one of Matthäus Sylvaticus at Salerno; but Herr H. Benrath, in his interesting introduction to the official guide to the Hamburg Garden Exhibition,[2] states that the *Rathsapothekengarten* (Municipal Physic Garden) in that city is much older than the Apothecary's shop known to have been situated on the Ness in 1316; proving that a Public 'Garden of Simples' existed prior to the period usually quoted.[3]

---

[1] Hazlitt's 'Gleanings in Old Garden Literature.'
[2] Rudolf Mosse, Hamburg, 1897.
[3] See 'Sprengel's Antiquitates Botanicæ,' 1798, and 'Historia Rei Herbariæ,' 1808 ('Geschichte der Botanik').

The chronological order of the foundation of the various public physic gardens seems to be as follows :—

1545. At Padua, springing from Bonaside's private Garden of Simples founded in 1533.

1544. At Pisa, begun by Cosmo de Medici, with Ghinus and Cæsalpinus for first two directors.

1547. At Bologna founded by Lucas Ghinus, from whom Dr Turner acquired the knowledge enabling him to admonish Fuchsius (the godfather of the Fuchsia) of 'certeine erroures' (see Preface to his 'New Herball').

1560 Gesner's at Zurich; 1570 Paris; 1577 Leyden, under direction of Clusius; Petrus Paaw published 'Hortus Publicus Academicæ Lugduno-Batavæ,' 1601, with plan of the garden. 1580 Leipsic; 1598 Montpelier, by Henry IV., famous for its circular form of which De Serres gives an engraving.

1610, The Jardin des Plantes, Paris, by Louis XIII. Oxford had to wait till

Other Elizabethans besides Bacon had imaginative and prophetic glimpses of the modern or landscape garden—the worthy Ambassador (sent to *lie* abroad for the good of his country) and Provost of Eton, Sir Henry Wotton noted 'a certain contrariety between building and gardening; for as fabricks should be regular, so gardens should be irregular, or at least cast into a very wild regularity'[1]—and Sir Philip Sidney in his 'Arcadia' brings his hero to a 'well-arrayed ground,' that was 'neither field, garden, nor orchard; or rather it was both field, garden and orchard.'

Here is Sidney depicted by old Isaac Oliver, the miniaturist, reposing in the Garden at Penshurst, which he has immortalised, with its 'pleached' gallery in the distance; famous once, as Evelyn says in his 'Diary,' for the noble Conversation which was wont to meet in its Gardens; such conversation, as we know from Clarendon in more troubled days, the 'flowing' and gracious Falkland attracted round him in his garden-retreat at Great Tew, near Oxford,—a 'College situated in a purer Air; so that his house was a University in a less volume.'

And now, in the words of Sidney, let us turn to our 'sweet enemy, France,' whose hands for more than a century were destined to sway the sceptre of garden sovereignty.

1632, when Henry Danvers, Earl of Danby, gave five acres on the Cherwell, with Jacob Bobart from Brunswick as Superintendent, whose descendants (says Loudon) are still in Oxford. In 1673 the Apothecaries founded theirs at Chelsea, of which Miller, author of the Gardener's Dictionary, was the most famous Director during half a century (see Field and Semple's 'Memoirs'). Tradescant's garden at Lambeth was famous, and his collection left to Ashmole was the foundation of the Ashmolean Museum: but except the catalogue, Tradescant has left no writings (see G. W. Johnson and Loudon).

[1] The following interesting marginal note is from a copy of Wotton's 'Elements of Architecture' by Christopher Wren, Chaplain to Charles I., Dean of Windsor and father of the Architect: 'For disposing the current of a river to a mightie length in a little space I invented the serpentine, a form admirably conveying the current in circular and yet contrary motions upon one and the same level, with walks and retirements betweene, to the advantage of all purposes, either of gardenings, plantings or banquetings. In brief it is to reduce the current of a mile's length into the compass of an orchard' (see *Gardener's Magazine*, vol. iii. p. 480).

André le Nôtre : after Carlo Maratti.

# HISTORICAL EPILOGUE 357

Charles Estienne or Stephens, a member of the family of France's first and greatest printers, was also one of the first of her scholars and garden-lovers; and by his little book, 'De re hortensi libellus,' a sort of grammar and syntax of the garden-art, and his larger and more practical work in collaboration with Liébault, the 'Prœdium Rusticum' or 'Maison Rustique,'[1] showed that for him the well-known printing emblem of his family had a literal as well as symbolic meaning.[2]

This work prepared the way for Olivier de Serres, 'the Father of Agriculture,' and his 'Théâtre d'Agriculture,' (its title showing the tendency of the Gaul to seek the dramatic even in the pastoral;) wherein Claude Mollet, the King's gardener, is commended for his invention of his famous 'Parterres de Broderies,' of which specimens are given. Mollet was the ancestor of several generations of great Gardeners, who produced between them the 'Théâtre des Plans et Jardinages.'

Francis I., who died in 1547, in building his Palace of Fontainebleau had introduced into the Garden some of the features of Italian Gardens. Of Androuet du Cerceau we have already spoken, and Richelieu's Gardens at Rueil were so magnificent as to make Evelyn doubt 'whether Italy has any exceeding them for varieties of pleasure.'[3]

And now we reach perhaps the greatest name in the whole History of Gardens; a name which is a synonym for the highest magnificence in Formal or Architectural Gardening, and like all greatness has to bear the burden of the faults of feeble imitation.

At a first glance the accompanying portrait might pass for that of the Grand Monarch himself, but it is only that of his head gardener, André Le Nôtre. We have Saint Simon's word for it [4] that he was a man of great simplicity, honesty and integrity, whose only thought was to aid Nature at *the lowest cost*. In spite of his endeavours to be natural and keep down expense, Versailles Gardens are

---
[1] See *ante* pp. 43-45.
[2] That of a gardener grafting on an olive tree with the motto: *Rami franguntur ut insererer*.
[3] See *ante* pp. 51, and 104-107.   [4] See *ante* pp. 102-3.

commonly cited as the acme of the artificial, and absorbed from first to last some eight millions of pounds, its fountains at one time having cost £3000 to set working for half an hour.[1]

But it was not all Le Nôtre's fault: his master had the knack of constantly changing his mind about the designs. Of Le Nôtre's naiveté of manners and familiarity with his royal Master and the Pope amusing stories are told. Le Nôtre was educated as an Architect, and is said to have found his earliest garden inspiration at Rueil. His first actual experience in rural design was obtained at Vaux le Villars (now Vaux Praslin) and the result so delighted the King, that he made him Comptroller General of Buildings and Gardens. For Madame Maintenon he worked at her Convent Garden at Noisy-le Roi, where he formed the Grand Canal out of a marsh.

A perspective view of Versailles is here given, showing the extent and plan on a minute scale, from an engraving by Perelle.

Let not the visitor to Versailles at the present day imagine that he is gazing upon Le Nôtre's creation—there is not so much of Le Nôtre left there, as there is of Phidias in the Parthenon at Athens. If the reader doubt this, let him turn to M. Ph. Gille's historical account of the Gardens,[2] or better still to Gautier's 'comparative' Retrospect in his 'Tableaux de Siège,'—the last book he published. There he will read one by one the devastations of Reformers, Restorers, and Modernisers, no doubt all men of taste and 'improvers' according to the ideas of the time: so that what was once a whole, a great and magnificent unit, is now a defaced and disintegrated fraction.

Le Nôtre's Garden seems made to exhibit to the utmost the social characteristics of the French people of the Grand Century. They extend their houses into their gardens, which are necessarily architectural: open-air drawing and dining rooms as shown in their very nomenclature. Their groves are cut into *Salons* and *Salles de Bal*, their lawns *rasés* like their heads, and paths *bien peignés* like their periwigs; as lovers of the stage and drama, their very

[1] In their curtailed form in 1816, £200 an hour. The difference is typical.
[2] 'La France Artistique et Monumentale.'

Perspective View of the Château and Gardens of Versailles. Engraved by A. Perelle, after Israël Sylvestre, 1688 (?).

Le Théâtre d'Eau, Versailles. From an engraving by Perelle (about 1660).

# HISTORICAL EPILOGUE 363

fountains must 'play' in their *Théâtres d'Eau*, and they kill time in open-air *Circuses* and *Amphitheatres*. 'Such symmetry' we echo with Lord Byron, 'is not for solitude.'

Le Nôtre found the ground at Versailles prepared by Boyceau,[1] and the main features of his design are ; *The Fountains of Latona, The Royal Alley, The Parterre du Nord* (a Parterre of Le Nôtre's is a whole garden in itself!) ; *The Parterre du Midi*, (which still shows the sole remaining 'broderies' of Le Nôtre) : The *Bosquets* (or Groves) of which not a trace remains, *The Pyramid Fountain, The Water Alley*, and *The Water Theatre*, now altered into a great circle of turf with the *Bassin des Enfants* in the centre.

Let us go a little more into detail, humbly following the guidance of Gautier and M. Gille.

Here is a view of the *Théâtre d'Eau* as Le Nôtre designed it. Three alleys opening like a fan are cut in the 'curtain' of shaped trees, forming long perspectives bordered with yews, like the 'wings' in a theatre : three rows of fountains rise in tiers, and at the end of the alleys are statues of Jupiter on an eagle, Mars and Plutus ; fountains, too, form the 'foot-lights.' Six water 'scenes' by Vigarani, in the shape of lances, lilies and other devices are celebrated in heroic verse by C. Denis, *Fontainier du Roy*, who does honour to these watery fire-works.[2]

The *Allée d'Eau* (vulgarly called the 'Alley of Marmosets') was composed of groups of children and little genii in bronze, carrying vases, from which the water fell into marble basins.

To the *Basin of Neptune* were added under Louis XV. the Sea God with trident, Tritons and children, the work of Bouchardon, Lemoyne and Adam ; where once stood the 'Arc de Triomphe' or 'Château d'Eau Triomphale' is now a grassy waste, almost a virgin forest. The Arc was destroyed when the Park was replanted under Louis XVI. ; and at the same time the *Bosquet des Trois Fontaines* had the 144 jets of water cut off and was put under lock and key.

In the statuary of the 'Baths of Apollo,' by Girardon and

[1] Author of 'Traité du Jardinage selon les raisons de la *Nature* et de l'Art.'
[2] See also 'L'Art des Fontaines' by Jean François, 1665.

Regnaudin was a transparent compliment to 'Le Roi Soleil' reposing from his labours. 'When in the eighteenth century, Citizen Rousseau discovered Nature, English ideas invaded the Continent, and the fashion was for landscape gardens. This transformation was effected at Versailles by the plan of Hubert Robert, the designer in fashion, the " Romantique " of the moment, the painter of ruins, who, amongst other improvements, hollowed out of an enormous sham rock three grottos as a sort of umbrella to the group of Apollo and the Nymphs, and as stables for the horses of the sun; wall plants were scattered over the rocks, and water came through the fissures. The English style gained the victory over the French, and the beauties of Versailles, the marvel of the universe, became purely *historical*; its life was gone out, its character was lost.' (*Gautier*.)

The illustration after Rigaud shows the *Bains d'Apollon* before the improvements, when the gilt metal canopies still sheltered the statuary. The *Bosquet de Venus* was the scene of the famous Diamond Necklace *Rendez-vous* between the Cardinal de Rohan and Demoiselle Oliva.

The *Salle de Bal* as here given, is the least disfigured by the alterations of Hubert Robert. On this spot a royal supper was given in 1691 to the King and Queen of England; and although the steps for the spectators have disappeared and many details are changed, the shades of the courtiers might still, according to Gautier, execute the Ballets of Benserade. The *Labyrinth* was composed of a complicated net-work of alleys cutting one another at right angles or forming curves of the most puzzling character. At each turning was a fountain in rockwork on which was represented one of Æsop's fables. Of this labyrinth no appreciable trace remains.

Taine well sums up the impression left by Le Nôtre's creation:—

'The monarchical and formal gardens of Le Nôtre are the complements of the grave, pompous, and studied architecture of Mansard and Perrault; buildings and parterres are all constructed for men studious of their dignity and observers of the proprieties.'[1] 'It was,' says Gautier, 'the supreme formula of

[1] Philosophie de l'Art.

Les Bains d'Apollon, Versailles; after an engraving by J. Rigaud, c. 1730.

La Salle de Bal, Versailles: after Cottel, 1688.

# HISTORICAL EPILOGUE 369

a complete art, and the expression at its highest power of a civilisation arrived at its full expansion.'[1]

[1] For the history of the garden in France, the following works, besides those already quoted, may be consulted :—
Pierre Vallet, ' Le Jardin du Roy très chrestien Henri IV.,' 1608.
Jacques Boyceau, ' Traité de Jardinage selon les raisons de la Nature et de l'Art,' 63 plates, 1638.
André Mollet, ' Le Jardin de Plaisir,' Stockholm, 1651.
Israël de Silvestre, ' Jardins et Fontaines,' Paris, 1661.
Jean Marot's Architecture.
I. Le Pautre, Engravings of Gardens, Grottos and Fountains, c. 1670.
Adam Perelle, Collection of Engravings, 1685.
A. J. B. Le Blond, ' Engravings of Plans for Gardens,' 1685.
,, ,, ' Parterres de Broderie,' 1688.
,, ,, ' The Theory and Practice of Gardening, c. 1690.'
Translated by John James, 1728. (This book is sometimes attributed to d'Argenville, whose edition in 1739 has very valuable plates.)
' Le Labyrinthe de Versailles,' Plates of Fountains by Leclerc, 1679.
N. Langlois, ' Parterres,' 23 Plans after Le Nôtre, Le Bouteux.
L. Liger, ' Le Jardinier Fleuriste,' 1719.
J. Mariette, ' Parterres de Broderie,' etc., c. 1730.
J. F. Blondel, 'de la Distribution des Maisons de Plaisance,' 160 plates, Paris, 1737-8.
' Le Spectacle de la Nature,' Vol. II., 1735.
Galimard fils, ' Architecture de Jardins,' 68 plates, folio, 1765.
Roger Schabol, ' Dictionnaire du Jardinage,' 1767.
,, ,, ' La Théorie du Jardinage,' 1785.
Laugier, ' Essai sur l'Architecture,' 1753.
N. Morel, ' Théorie des Jardins,' 1776.
G. L. le Rouge, ' Détails des nouveaux Jardins à la mode ; 200 plates, and ' Recueil des plus beaux Jardins de l'Europe,' 1776-87.
' Promenade ou Itinéraire des Jardins d'Ermenonville,' 25 illustrations by Mérigot, Paris, 1788.
Vues Pittoresques, Plans, etc., des Principaux Jardins Anglois qui sont en France (Engravings in colour of the Trianon Gardens), 4to, c. 1785.
Description de Montmorency, 19 Engravings by Le Prieur, 1788.
A. L. Laborde, ' Descriptions des nouveaux Jardins de la France,' plates by Bourgeois, 1808-21.
J. C. Krafft, ' Plans des plus beaux Jardins,' 1810.
Gabriel Thouin, ' Plans Raisonnés des Jardins,' 50 lithographed plates, 1819.
' Essai sur la Composition et l'ornement des Jardins,' 107 plates, Paris, 1823.
Percier et Fontaine, ' Choix des plus célèbres Maisons de Plaisance,' 75 plates, Paris, 1809.

## THE PRAISE OF GARDENS

Le Nôtre was also the creator of St Cloud, where Nature had greater liberty; he made plans for the Villas Panfili and Ludovisi in Rome, and was invited to England by Charles II., where it is said he had a hand in designing St James's Park, but whether this is true or not, it is hardly necessary to say that Le Nôtre's influence extended to England. No name stands out like his, but John Rose, the best English gardener of his time, served successively the Earl of Essex at Essex House, Strand, in 1665, the Duchesses of Cleveland and Somerset, and Charles II. at St James's.

His first master sent him to Versailles to study the style of Le Nôtre, and so the French tradition was established here, and handed on to Mr London, Rose's favourite pupil and successor. Rose was painted presenting the first pineapple cultivated in England to Charles II.; and was the author of 'The English Vineyard' which first appeared in 1672, at the end of Evelyn's 'French Gardener.'

Le Nôtre's counterpart in the kitchen garden was La Quintinye,[1] the constructor of the great 'Jardin Potager' or kitchen garden, at Versailles, which exists almost unaltered to this day. Here he introduced his famous method of training fruit-trees on espaliers. The translation of La Quintinye's 'Compleat Gardener' into English by John Evelyn (or his son) brings us to the man who, in the words of Switzer, 'first taught Gardening to speak proper English,' the author of 'Sylva' and the famous 'Diary'; to whom Oxford owes the Arundel marbles, Engraving the first clear exposition, if not the invention of Mezzotint, Science the foundation of the Royal Society, and England many of her noblest trees.

Here is his portrait with the autograph inscription to La Quintinye. The Journal of his Grand Tour, as we have seen,[2] is almost that of a tour round the Grand Gardens of Europe; and he loved to read and write about gardens almost as much as to design and visit them. All through a long life of eighty-seven years, almost contemporary with Le Nôtre, John Evelyn devoted himself to the improvement of the garden by precept and

---

[1] See *ante* p. 115.  [2] *Ante* pp. 103-115.

Engraved by Swaine after Nanteüil.

## HISTORICAL EPILOGUE 373

practice. He has left us in Hortulan literature the 'Kalendarium Hortense,' a 'Discourse on Sallets,' and the scheme of a vast gardening work called 'Elysium Brittanicum,' which he did not live to complete. At Wotton in Surrey (still belonging to his descendant) he unfortunately yielded to the taste of the time and removed a mountain to fill up the Moat, and here also he contrived a Grotto which he calls a 'Pausilippo,' after the famous one near Naples. He constructed the Oval Garden at Sayes Court near Deptford, where the 'Czar of Muscovy' (Peter the Great) amused himself in 1698 by being trundled in a wheelbarrow through the holly-hedges and over the box borders; for which piece of fun Sir Christopher Wren (the Architect) and London (the Gardener) assessed the damages of a three months' tenancy at £150.

Old Sir Thomas Browne,[1] the famous Norwich Physician, treats in his 'Garden of Cyrus' of the 'Quincuncial Lozenge of the Ancients,' but inasmuch as the Quincunx had been the recognised method of planting trees (to form a grove in a square of five repeated over and over again, so that look which way you will, equal or parallel alleys are seen), he did not add much to our knowledge of garden design.

To this age too belongs the Prince of Garden Poets, Andrew Marvel, and they are to be envied who have yet to breathe the fragrance of his garden verse:

> Annihilating all that's made
> To a green thought in a green shade.[2]

A passing mention is deserved by Ralph Austen, a student of Magdalen College, Oxford, where he spent his time in gardening and raising fruit trees, and wrote the 'Spiritual use of an Orchard'; by John Rea, a practical gardener of forty years experience who laid out Lord Gerard's garden at Gerard's Bromley, and was the author of 'a rude Draught of a Rustick Garden' called 'Flora, Ceres and Pomona' (1665), wherein he states that he has seen many gardens of the new model in the hands of unskilful persons, with good walls, walks, and grass-plots, but in the most essential

[1] See *ante* pp. 94-6.   [2] *ante* p. 240.

adornments so deficient that a green meadow is a more delightful object. . . . And as all noble Fountains, Grottoes, Statues, etc. are excellent ornaments and works of Magnificence, so all such dead works in Gardens ill-done are little more than blocks in the way to interrupt the sight, but not at all to satisfie the understanding.'

While Le Nôtre's trumpet was being blown throughout Europe, a still small tune was piped in Scotland, *tenui arundine* by John Reid (gardener to Sir George Mackenzie of Rosehaugh, Aberdeenshire), who produced at Edinburgh in 1683 the earliest Scotch Gardening Book, 'the Scots Gard'ner.' The thrifty simplicity of his idea of a pleasure-garden is an agreeable contrast to the magnificence of Versailles and its imitations:—

'Pleasure-Gardens useth to be divided into walkes and plots, with a Bordure round each plot, and at the corner of each, may be a holly or some such train'd up, some Pyramidal, others Spherical, the Trees and Shrubs at the Wall well plyed and prun'd, the Green thereon cut in several Figures, the walkes layed with Gravel, and the plots within with Grass, (in several places whereof may be Flower pots) the Bordures boxed, and planted with variety of Fine Flowers orderly Intermixt, Weeded, Mow'd, Rolled, and kept all clean and handsome.'

The Dutch style of laying out gardens, introduced into England by William III. and Mary, is not unlike the French, but everything is on a smaller, almost too minute a scale; and much care is expended upon isolated details and ornaments (often trivial), such as glass balls, coloured sands and earth, flower-pots innumerable, and painted perspectives; and the garden is usually intersected with canals degenerating into ditches.

'Grassy slopes, green terraces and straight canals are more common in Holland than in any other country of the Continent, and these verdant slopes and mounds may be said to form, with their oblong canals, the characteristics of the Dutch style.' (*Loudon.*)

Typical instances on a large scale were the Gardens at Loo,

Jacobsdahl.

## HISTORICAL EPILOGUE 377

designed by Marot, the King's Architect, and the Gardens of the Count de Nassau,[1] Ryswick, Houslaerdyk and Sorgvliet.

From Dr Harris's 'Description of Loo,' (1699) we learn that 'the hedges are chiefly of Dutch elms; and the avenues of oaks, elms, and limes. The figures into which the trees and shrubs are cut, are, for the most part, pyramids. On the walls fresco paintings are introduced in various places between the trees. In the arbour walks of the queen's garden are seats, and opposite to them windows through which views can be had of the fountains, statues and other objects in the open garden. The parterres in the queen's garden are surrounded by hedges of Dutch elm about four feet high. The seats and prop work of all the arbours, and the trellis work on the fruit tree walls are painted green. All along the gravel walks, and round the middle fountain are placed orange-trees and lemon-trees in portable wooden frames and flower-pots about them.'

The copper-plates in Van der Groen's or Van Oesten's Dutch gardening books give a good idea of the Dutch Garden on a smaller scale[2]—and for an *extreme* instance of the lilliputian garden we cannot do better than quote De Amicis's description of the gardens at Broek:—

"The gardens are not less odd than the houses. They seem made for dwarfs. The paths are scarcely wide enough for the feet, the arbors can contain two very small persons standing close together, the box borders would not reach the knee of a child of four years old. Between the arbors and the tiny flower-beds there are little canals, apparently made for toy-boats, which are spanned here and there by superfluous bridges with little painted railings and columns; basins about as large as an ordinary sitz-bath contain a lilliputian boat tied by a red cord to a sky-blue post; tiny steps, paths, gates, and lattices abound, each of which can be measured with the hand, or knocked down with a blow of the fist, or jumped over with ease. Around houses and gardens stand trees cut in the shape of fans, plumes, discs, etc., with their trunks painted white and blue, and here and there appears a

[1] See Le Rouge's Designs.   [2] See also *ante* pp. 36-8.

little wooden house for a domestic animal, painted, gilded, and carved like a house in a puppet show."[1]

Hampton Court is the finest example in England of the Dutch style, modified to some extent by Le Nôtre's original plans. Beaumont, one of his pupils (who also laid out Levens, in Westmoreland, for Colonel Graham) was employed here, and in Kip's view of Hampton Court we see the Gardens in all their glory in Queen Anne's reign.

The large semi-circle of limes was planted by Charles II., enclosing 9½ acres. London (the pupil of Rose and partner of Wise) had laid out the great semi-circular parterre under William III. The only fault Queen Anne found was too much box, which she had rooted up, disliking the smell, as Defoe tells us, but it was replanted later. Evelyn notes the cradlework of hornbeam in 'Queen Mary's bower.' The style of London and Wise was said to combine the best features of the French and Dutch styles—their arbour 'an alcove arched over with trellis, excluding neither wind nor rain' existed till 1876. On the north side was the wilderness, or maze—very rectangular, bounded by tall clipped hedges, and called 'Troy Town.' Kent, under Queen Caroline (Consort of George II.) simplified the scrolls and lacework of the 'Great Parterre' by substituting plain lawns.[2]

Sir William Temple showed his love for his garden at Moor Park near Farnham by ordering his heart to be buried there in a silver box under a sun-dial. Besides writing a delightful work called 'The Gardens of Epicurus' in which he gives the palm of 'the perfectest figure of a Garden' to that of Moor Park in Hertfordshire, on the slope of a hill with two terraces, one above the other, reached by a fine flight of steps, he possessed another Garden at Sheen, in one of which his Secretary Swift was taught by the King how to cut asparagus. William was the first to replace stone walls previously used in gardens by the splendid wrought-iron gates known as '*Clair-voyées*,' on account of the uninterrupted view they permitted. Of these a fine example exists at Hampton Court. With

[1] 'Holland,' translated from the Italian by Caroline Tilton, 1880.
[2] See Ernest Law's 'History of Hampton Court.'

Bird's-eye west view of Hampton Court Gardens under Queen Anne. From Knyff's & Kip's 'Britannia Illustrata' (1706-1710) showing the great semi-circular parterre.

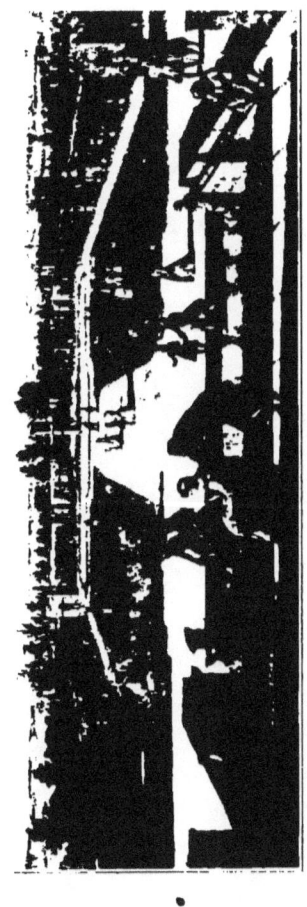

Parterre from Portico of House at Stowe, Bucks, as designed by Bridgman. (1714.) Rigaud and Baron del. et sculps., 1739.

# HISTORICAL EPILOGUE 383

all his love for the formal garden, Temple is modern enough to admit that there may be other forms, wholly irregular, that may have more beauty than any of the others, 'but they must owe it to some extraordinary dispositions of Nature in the seat, or some great race of fancy or judgment in the contrivance.' Fifty years after Temple's mention of the Chinese Gardens 'as too hard of achievement,' they were being universally copied in England and the Continent.

Our next view is Stowe in Buckinghamshire, showing the Great Parterre from the Portico, as laid out by Bridgman for Lord Cobham about 1714. Bridgman banished verdant sculpture from his garden, but still retained green architecture (observe the arches), straight alleys and palissades and began to introduce 'a little gentle disorder into the plantation of his trees and bushes.'[2] The whole garden became a sort of practical pun upon the name of its owner, Lord Temple, who seems to have had temples on the brain, and dedicated them to every possible Deity and Virtue. Stowe almost epitomises the early history of Landscape Gardening, for Kent succeeded Bridgman as its 'Improver,' and 'Capability' Brown began his career here in the humble post of kitchen gardener. Pope held up Stowe as an ideal almost unattainable, crying in ecstacy :—

> 'Time shall make it grow,
> A thing to wonder at, perhaps a "Stowe"!'

The name of Pope brings us to the borderland dividing the old garden from the new, as Pope's own verse may be said to be

[1] The following books on the Dutch Garden may be consulted :—
Beudeker's 'Germania Inferior' (*British Museum*).
Crispin de Pass 'Hortus Floridus.'
Van der Groen 'Le Jardinier des Pays Bas,' 1672.
Commelyn 'Hortus Amstelodamus,' 1697.
,, 'Belgic or Netherlandish Hesperides,' 1683.
Henrik van Oesten 'The Dutch Gardener,' 1703.
De Groot 'Les Agréments de la Campagne,' 1750.
A Rademaker, 'Holland's Arcadia' 1730.
John Ray 'Observations on a Journey through the Low Countries,'-1673.
[2] Horace Walpole.

the turning-point in literature. By his famous Number 173 of the 'Guardian' ridiculing the absurdities and excesses of 'verdant sculpture' and the cut-box system, and putting up for sale 'Adam and Eve in yew—Adam a little shaken by the fall of the Tree of Knowledge,'—by his Epistle to Lord Burlington on the Aesthetic of Gardening, and by his own example in his villa at Twickenham where he and his gardener, John Serle, planned the wonderful grotto he describes in his letters, the echo of which has alone survived, Pope is undoubtedly one of the pioneers of modern gardening. A plan is here given of the garden of five acres (never before had so small a compass produced such a revolutionary effect upon gardening!) as left at the Poet's death in 1744, by his gardener, John Serle. Thereon appears the Shell Temple, the large Mount, the two small Mounts, the Vineyard, the Obelisk in memory of his mother, the Grove, the Orangery and the Underground Passage leading to the Grotto.

We have also fourteen years later from the pen of Horace Walpole, a description of it when the property of Sir William Stanhope. 'Would you believe it, he has cut down the sacred groves themselves! In short, it was a little bit of ground of 5 acres, inclosed with three lanes and seeing nothing. Pope has twisted and twirled and rhymed and harmonised this till it appeared two or three sweet little lawns opening and opening beyond one another, and the whole surrounded with thick impenetrable woods. Sir William, by advice of his son-in-law, Mr Ellis, has hacked and hewed these groves, wriggled a winding-gravel walk through them with an edging of shrubs, in what they call the modern taste, and, in short, has desired the three lanes to walk in again—and now is forced to shut them out again by a wall, for there was not a Muse could walk there but she was spied by every country fellow that went by with a pipe in his mouth.'[1] Pope divides the literary honours of his generation with Addison who, humorist himself, in his equally famous 'Spectator' on the 'Pleasures of a Garden,' declared Nature should be humoured, instead of being coerced.

[1] Letter to Sir Horace Mann, June 20th, 1760.

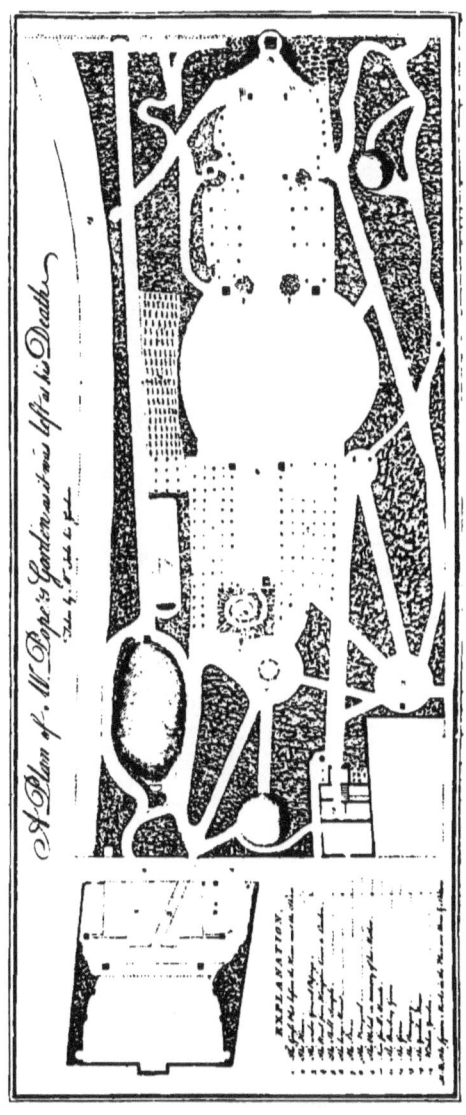

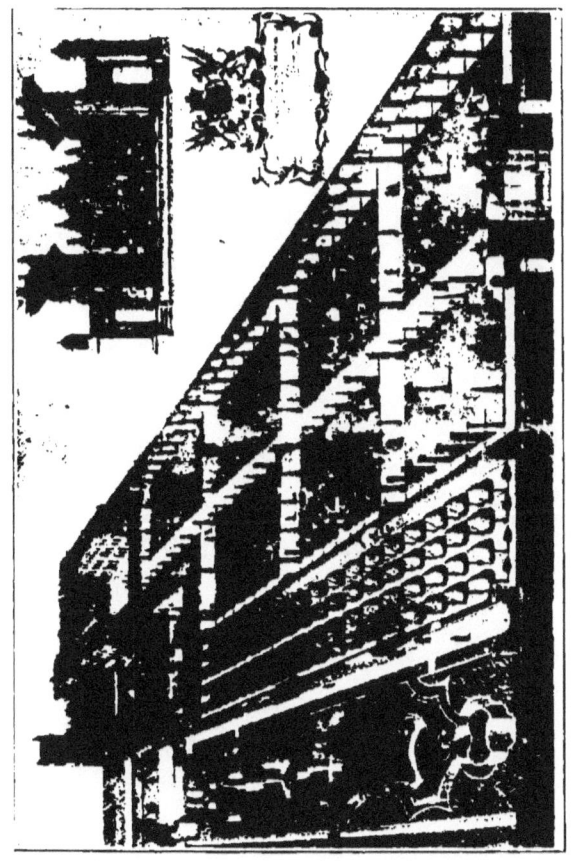

The Gardens of Trinity College, Oxford, from Williams's 'Oxonia Depicta,' 1732-3.

# HISTORICAL EPILOGUE 389

He objected to 'trees rising in cones, globes and pyramids' and thought 'an orchard in flower looked infinitely more delightful than all the little labyrinths of the most finished parterre.'

I believe Addison's garden at Bilton in Warwickshire still wears much the same aspect it bore in his own day.

Stephen Switzer in his 'Ichnographia Rustica' declares himself a partisan of Pope, and of the 'Rural' style which slowly superseded the Grand Manner of Le Nôtre; although Batty Langley tried to show the world how the Grand and Rural manners might lie down together in perfect amity.

Johnson (the Historian of Gardens) considers this book one of the Classics of Gardening. Switzer gives a discursive History of the Art up to his own day, lays down the principle that Design should be founded on variety, and is of opinion that a little regularity should be allowed near the main building and then a gradual procession from finished Art to Wild Nature.

Of the numerous bird's eye views of Gardens to be found in Kip's 'Britannia Illustrata' or Beeverel's 'Délices de la Grande Bretagne,' such as Longleat, Badminton and Chatsworth, Blomfield and Inigo Thomas's 'Formal Garden' has treated so fully, that there is no necessity to go again over the same ground.

The Colleges of Oxford and Cambridge[1] often preserved the integrity of their old-fashioned Gardens through various changes of style around them—and in Loggan's view of Wadham College in 1675 may be seen the Mount, and the Palissades or Groves looking in Horace Walpole's words, 'like Green Chests set upon Poles.' A view is given here of the Gardens of Trinity College, Oxford, on the left of which may be seen the peculiarly designed grove or labyrinth. Even so ardent a 'Landscapist' as Humphry Repton has declared that he should 'doubt the taste of any improver who could despise the congruity, ability, order and symmetry of these Gardens of Trinity.' But we have lingered long enough in the formal garden.

[1] See D. Loggan's 'Oxonia Illustrata,' 1675, 'Cantabrigia Illustrata,' Willis and Clark's History of the University of Cambridge, and the various College Histories.

The reaction in favour of the natural garden was largely assisted by the letters of the French Jesuit Missionaries describing the Chinese Emperor's gardens at Pekin.

The Père Attiret's description of the 'Garden of Gardens' was translated by Joseph Spence in 1752 and the spark kindled a flame of enthusiasm throughout Europe. Here is one of the innumerable scenes of this Panorama of Gardens, taken from a Chinese painting of the same period in the National Library in Paris.[1] The Chinese trace back the origin of their gardens to the remotest antiquity (2600 B.C.). Attiret describes the artificial hills 20 to 60 feet high with little valleys interspersed, rivers and rivulets running together through these to form lakes with pleasure-houses to the number of 200 on their banks; the rough irregular rockwork—twisting and winding paths, and bridges which also serpentised. One of the lakes was nearly five miles round, studded with islands and rocks and with infinitely varied banks.

Sir William Chambers, the King's Architect, who as a youth had lived in China, wrote an enthusiastic panegyric of their gardens, and on being appointed Superintendent of the Royal Gardens, proceeded to lay out Kew with Pagodas in the Chinese style.[2] The Chinese way of following Nature was a peculiar one, and consisted in creating mountains where they did not exist. It is true that they made these mountains to resemble 'natural' ones as closely as possible, but they were none the less artificial for all that,—then they came to the conclusion that nature abhorred a straight line, so all their paths and approaches were made to serpentine. Landscape gardening, as understood in the 18th Century, may be defined as the curved *versus* the straight line. As William Mason versified it :—

> To melt in fluent curves whate'er is straight.
> Acute or parallel . . .
>     Fair variety
> Lives only where she undulates and sports
> In many a winding train.

---
[1] See also Le Rouges' 'Recueil des Plans des plus beaux Jardins,' Paris, 1787-1790.
[2] See *ante* pp. 183-186.

'The Garden of Gardens,' Pekin, begun 1723, and pillaged in 1860.

# HISTORICAL EPILOGUE 393

Hogarth's 'Line of Beauty' was at first substituted for that of the Builders and Architects—later on, however, the curves became less manageable, and finally zig-zagged to such a degree, that a witty Frenchman, following a hint from George Mason's Essay, suggested that in order to design an English or Natural Garden all that was requisite was to intoxicate your gardener and follow his footsteps.

To supplement the Gospel of 'Nature,' Samuel Richardson, Jean Jaques Rousseau [1] and others had invented the Epistle of Sentiment or Sensibility, and so the Landscape Garden besides writhing and meandering in imitation of so-called Nature had also to display feeling, emotion, and sympathy with the varying moods and fluctuating passions of Humanity.

Lord Kames about the middle of the 18th Century wrote: 'the most perfect idea of a garden requires the several parts to be arranged so as to inspire all the different emotions that can be raised by gardening.'

Of this Emotional or Sentimental Garden—this 'Jardin Larmoyant' as the *genre* may be called—the poet Shenstone was the most successful exponent in England, by his creation of 'the Leasowes' in Shropshire; where by means of vines, weeping willows, urns, trophies, garlands, columns, mottos and inscriptions he sought to 'raise emotions' appropiate to the peculiar character of the ground, whether grand, savage, melancholy, horrid or beautiful, and to caress and cherish the corresponding human sentiments. For all Goldsmith's good-natured banter and Johnson's sarcasm, so good a judge as George Mason thought that 'of all the amateur and professional gardeners of the day the most intimate alliance with Nature was formed by Shenstone'—and his 'Unconnected Thoughts on Gardening' are still agreeable desultory reading.[2]

---

[1] Rousseau made the dawn visible to people who had never risen till noon, the landscape to eyes that had only rested hitherto upon drawing-rooms and palaces, the natural garden to men who had only walked between tonsured yews and rectilinear flower-borders.'—Taine, 'L'ancien Regime.'

[2] See *ante* pp. 167-169.

# THE PRAISE OF GARDENS

Kent was practically the originator of modern park scenery, the landscape-painter's garden; he, in the words of Walpole, being 'the first to leap the fence and show that the whole of Nature is a garden'; Bridgman by the invention of the 'Ha Ha' or sunk fence having made it possible to unite the garden with the park and the surrounding country, without any visible break.

Kent began life as a coach-painter, and by a singular revolution of the wheels of fortune found himself, under the patronage of the Earl of Burlington, an architect and landscape-painter. However monotonous Kent's 'Nature' may seem to us now, and nothing is proof against the power of fashion, there is no doubt that he dictated the style of gardening to the whole of Europe for a very long period.[1]

The great principles on which Kent worked, writes Walpole again, were 'perspective, light and shade. Groups of trees broke too uniform, or too extensive a lawn—evergreens and woods were opposed to the glare of the champaign. . . . Where objects were wanting he introduced temples, etc., but he especially excelled in the management of water. The gentle stream was taught to serpentine seemingly at its pleasure.'

He followed Nature even in her faults. In Kensington Gardens he planted *dead* trees (a genuine instance of 'laying out') but was soon laughed out of this excess. Here is a view of one of his greatest reputed triumphs—Esher, 'where Kent and Nature vied for Pelham's Love.'

To us now the design, with the house almost below the level of the ground, seems simple to baldness—but we must look at it with the eyes of 1730, accustomed to the artificialities of the French manner, and there is little doubt that the extreme reaction had something of genius in it. George Mason wrote in panegyric of Kent: 'All that has since been done by the most deservedly admired designers, by Southcote (at Wooburn Farm), Hamilton (at Pain's Hill), Lyttelton (at Hagley), Pitt (at Hayes) Shenstone (at the Leasowes), and Morris for themselves; and by Wright (Kent's successor) for others; all that has been written on

[1] See *ante* p. 140.

Esher, as laid out by Kent for Henry Pelham (1725-1735). From a drawing by Woollet (1801).

# HISTORICAL EPILOGUE 397

the subject, even the *Gardening didactic poem* and the *Didactic Essay on the Picturesque*, have proceeded from Kent.'

We may take Blenheim as another instance of Kent's success. No one better understood how to mould flat ground into gentle unevennesses, the process called by the French, 'vallonner,' and a good instance of this was his plantation at Chiswick compared with what Whately considers Bridgman's 'phlegmatic plantation' in the same garden.

'Capability' Brown, so nicknamed from his favourite habit of speaking of the 'capabilities' of the ground he had to view, is the man who, perhaps more than any other, converted the older gardens of England into parks. His method has been shortly summarised thus:—'His declivities were all softened into gentle slopes; plantations belted the estate, while clumps and single trees were sprinkled over its area.' Brown probably sat for the satirical portrait of 'Lay-Out' in Peacock's 'Crotchet Castle,'[1] and although he regarded himself as holding his own with Nature on her own ground, he was undoubtedly a very strong and very limited mannerist. He was so overcome at the result of his treatment of water at Blenheim, that he was heard murmuring to himself in gentle reproach, 'Thames, Thames, thou wilt never forgive me.'

The poet Gray, who had a fine instinct for beauty in Nature, hailed the dawn of Natural Gardening as the only Art, which the English could properly call their own. The literary counterparts of the school are George Mason's 'Essay on Design in Gardening' and Horace Walpole's still more famous Essay,[2] (which has often been quoted); and, chief of all, Thomas Whately's 'Observations on Modern Gardening.' This according to Loudon is 'the grand fundamental and standard work on English Gardening.' Whately claims for gardening that 'it has ceased to be mechanical' and become a fine art, joining utility to pleasure: no longer for the mere pleasure of the senses, it aspires to entertain the imagination—high ground creates a feeling of

[1] And perhaps for Mr Milestone in 'Headlong Hall.' See *ante* pp. 252-3.
[2] See *ante* pp. 172-8 and 203-4.

grandeur—small valleys, woods overhanging them and rivers with steep banks form a romantic disposition: grounds gently falling and rising with fine verdure suggest cheerfulness, creating little or no sentiment. But the quotation above[1] gives sufficient idea of Whately's principles. His views on the formal garden are, that in a situation of a dead flat, art is called in to aid nature, by means of bosquets, statues, vases, trees cut into arches, cascades, basins, temples, vistas and plantations, mounts and buildings of all kinds: the imagination having no scope, play must be given to the senses and flowers should be planted in beds and parterres.

After the peace of 1762 the English style of gardening passed into France and the ideas of the new school were perhaps even more successfully applied by that most susceptible nation. It has even been asserted that Dufresny was the founder of the school, and certainly the Abbé Delille's poem 'Les Jardins' both for matter and manner far surpasses its English rival by William Mason.[2] But practice is better than precept, and the example given by the Marquis de Girardin[3] at Ermenonville, near Paris, laid out under his own eye by N. Morel and the landscape-painter G. F. Meyer, exercised a wider influence than his description of it published in 1777. In this he writes very modestly of the discovery of his own mistakes as the result of experience in 'composing' the landscape. He began under the impression that all that was necessary was to substitute curves for straight lines and replace a rectangular garden by a winding one. He thought he could produce variety in a small space by 'clapping the universe between walls'; but admits that he confounded simplicity with letting loose Nature, and found he was only exchanging Nature mutilated and circumscribed for Nature *vague and confused*.

The most famous features of Ermenonville were a desert, a lake, a cascade, a grotto, and the Isle of Poplars where Rousseau was first buried, having died in the 'Philosopher's Cottage.' Besides

[1] See *ante* pp. 194-8.  [2] See *ante* pp. 182-3 and 206-8.
[3] See *ante* pp. 202 and 209-10.

View of the Principal Pavilion and 'Jeu de Bague' in the Garden of Monceau(x), as laid out by Carmontelle for the Duc de Chartres before the Revolution.

# HISTORICAL EPILOGUE 401

advising at Ermenonville, Morel was responsible for the Duc d'Aumont's Parc at Guiscard and a seat near Château Thierry. Watelet was the creator of 'Moulin Joli' and also of an 'Essai sur les Jardins.'[1]

Other historic gardens of this period were Morfontaine, Méréville, the Park of the Fermier-Général Laborde, designed by Joseph Vernet and Hubert Robert; and Maupertuis (now the Elysée) belonging to the Marquis de Montesquiou.[2] But in designing some of their chief *Jardins Anglais*, the French had the assistance of Thomas Blaikie, a Scotsman, who between 1776 and the Revolution, laid out many of the best French gardens, including Maupertuis, 'Bagatelle' in the Bois de Boulogne for the Comte d'Artois (in 1779) and alterations made in the Jardin (now Parc) Monceau(x) for the Duc de Chartres, which had been laid out by Carmontelle. Here is one view by the latter of the Chinese portion of the garden, which went through many vicissitudes, some of the original features (for instance, the pyramid from the 'Bois des Tombeaux') still surviving.

One more name brings us to an end of our list of the old school of landscape gardeners, that of Humphry Repton, the first to call himself professionally by the title. Repton's method when called on to improve a place was to prepare a description and plan of it in its existing state with his suggestions for its alteration. By an ingenious system of slides over his illustrations he was able to show a plan as it was, and as he proposed it should be.

'Amenity' Repton has very distinctly told us what he considers the requisites of perfect Landscape Gardening: viz., first 'to display the natural beauties and hide the natural defects of every situation; secondly, to give the appearance of extent and freedom by disguising or hiding the boundary; thirdly, to conceal every interference of art, however expensive, making the whole appear the production of nature only; and fourthly, to remove or conceal all objects of mere convenience or comfort if incapable of being ornamental or of becoming proper parts of the general scenery.'[3]

[1] See *ante* pp. 178-181.   [2] See *ante* pp. 199, 208-12.
[3] See *ante* pp. 218-20.

## 402   THE PRAISE OF GARDENS

Just as the Natural or 'Landscape' School was a reaction against the extreme formality or symmetry which had preceded it, so the Landscape gardeners in their turn had to fight against the opposition levelled against them by the critical group of what has been called the 'Picturesque' writers,[1] William Gilpin, Uvedale Price and Payne Knight, who steered a sort of middle course between the excesses of both the Formalists and Landscapists. To them perhaps we owe it that there is a single old-fashioned garden remaining unconverted into a park. Payne Knight in particular was a virulent opponent of Brown and Repton in prose and verse, and was satirically severe upon the desolate mansion standing

> ' 'Midst shaven lawns that far around it creep,
> In one eternal undulating sweep
> And scattered clumps that nod at one another
> Each stiffly waving to its formal brother,'

and he yearns for the moss-grown terraces, the yew and the ancient avenue 'to mark the flat insipid waving plain.'

So the prophets of 'Nature' did not finally escape the same charge of artificiality and uniformity brought against their more intentionally 'Formal' predecessors.

Price, while strongly advising that the formal garden shall be modified rather than destroyed, thought that the principles of Claude shall be followed as a safe guide. To us, now looking back, it hardly seems that a placid landscape of Claude or the more savage Salvator Rosa lend themselves to imitation or reproduction in a garden. Windham, in a letter to Repton, asks very pertinently: Does the pleasure that we receive from the view of Parks and Gardens result from their affording subjects that would appear to advantage in a picture? and answers: That places are not to be laid out with 'a view to their appearance in a picture, but to their use and the enjoyment of them in real life.'

At this point we will break off our sketch of English gardens

---

[1] Besides their writings quoted in the text (*ante* pp. 212-217), consult Gilpin's various 'Picturesque Tours' and Payne Knight's 'The Landscape' (a didactic poem) 1794.

# HISTORICAL EPILOGUE 403

to take a rapid glance at those of Germany, Spain, India and Japan.

Germany has been in the main a follower rather than a leader in garden design; but she has played an important part in spreading knowledge upon the theory, and in producing tasteful and skilful designers in the modern 'natural' style. Hirschfeld[1] in 1770 deplores the Gallomania which pervaded Germany, resulting in numerous copies of Versailles, Trianon and Marly; and later in imitations of the English taste. Solomon de Caus's plan of the Gardens at Heidelberg, published in 1620,[2] is not very different from those of other formal gardens of the period. The Episcopal Gardens at Würzburg were long reckoned the finest in Germany, first laid out in servile imitation of Versailles, and then treated in a mixed style by Mayer;[3] they are still deserving attention as the Public Gardens of the city. Krafft considered the gardens of Schwetzingen in Baden as the most splendid in Germany, and they are fully described by Dr Granville in 'In Autumn near the Rhine.'

Wörlitz and its gardens near Dessau, engage a good deal of the attention of the Prince de Ligne in his 'Coup d'œil sur les Jardins.' The same writer regards Hirschfeld (whose book is one of the leading authorities on the subject) as 'touched with Anglomania,' and Mayer, like many other German designers, learnt much of his art in England.

The 'English Garden' at Munich, the first of its kind in Germany, was laid out in 1789 under the direction of Count Rumford (the founder of the Royal Institution), by Louis Sckell, who in his day enjoyed a great reputation, and also designed an English Garden at Nymphenburg.

A few other gardens famous in Germany and Austria are :—

Schönbrunn, laid out in the French style, by the architect Fischer of Erlach, was in 1775-1780 enlarged by Steckhoven, a Dutch artist. Hadersdorf, designed by the celebrated Marshal Loudon :

[1] Théorie de l'Art des Jardins. Leipzig, 1770, 5 vols. 4to.
[2] See *ante* p. 342.
[3] Pomona Franconica, 1776, by John Mayer.

## THE PRAISE OF GARDENS

Sans-Souci at Potsdam, in the mixed style of Switzer, chiefly designed by Manger, a German architect, and Salzmann, the Royal Gardener, (see History of the Gardens, published by Nicolai): and the Gardens at Magdeburg, laid out by Linné, landscape gardener, in 1824. Hamburg has always been a garden-city and maintained its reputation in this respect by the great 'Garten-Ausstellung' held there in 1897.[1]

The earliest Spanish gardens are the creation of the Moors, and bear the Arabian stamp of their origin, half Asiatic, half African. Perhaps their design has the strongest affinity to the gardens of Persia, with their shallow waters running down the centre over coloured tiles, and their innumerable fountains, for water in one form or another is the predominant feature.

The oldest garden is at Seville, the *Alcazar*, the Moorish word for ' Royal Palace.' These gardens were laid out by Charles V., in the sixteenth century, upon old lines, the compartments being arranged in patterns of Eagles and his coat of arms: the levels vary and the plots are divided by orange-clad walls.

The *Generalife* at Granada ('Jenatu-L'arif,' meaning the Garden of the Architect, who sold the site to the Sultan in 1320), has been called 'A Villa of Waters.' The canal of the Darro flows under evergreen arches, (the subject of one of Lord Leighton's early pictures,) an open colonnade overlooks

---

[1] For other references to German Gardens, may be consulted :
Laurenbergi Petri, Horticultura, Lib II. Plans of gardens by Merian. Frankfort, 1631.
Sal. Kleiner, Vera et accurata delineatio omnium Templorum . . in urbe Viennæ, 1724-1737.
Sal. Kleiner, Maisons de Plaisance Imperiales, 33 plates.
Nuremberg Hesperides, by J. C. Volckamer, 1700, folio.
' Die Garten Kunst,' von J. F. Bloss, 28 copper plates and plans drawn by Siegel, and described by Dr. Ch. Stieglitz, 3 vols. 8vo. Leipzig, 1798.
J. C. Krafft, Plans des plus beaux Jardins Pittoresques de France, d'Angleterre et d'Allemagne, 2 vols. oblong folio, 192 plates. Paris, 1809-10.
Dr W. Beattie, ' Journal of a residence in Germany,' 1830.
Also the numerous ' Garten-Kalendär.'

# HISTORICAL EPILOGUE 405

the Alhambra and the Sultana's cypresses date back to the Moors.[1]

The gardens of the Escurial and Ildefonso in Madrid and of Aranjuez near Toledo, were laid out under Philip IV. at the beginning of the seventeenth century. The park of Aranjuez (from Ara Jovis) is several leagues in circumference, intersected by wide alleys, three or four miles long, framed of double rows of elms, with a canal running between them, and the Tagus dividing it. Velasquez has painted these gardens and their fountains, which the French under Soult converted into a wilderness, and the Duke of Wellington enjoined upon General Hill to protect.[2]

The Gardens of Hindostan are of much the same general character as those of Persia: famous especially were those of the Mogol emperors at Delhi and Bangalore: the gardens of Kalimar at Delhi were created at the beginning of the seventeenth century, at the cost of a million pounds. At Agra were the Imperial Park (Rom-Bagh); the tomb of Akbar, and the Taj-Mahal, erected by the Emperor Shah Jehan to his favourite wife. At Ahmadah was Akbar's 'Garden of Conquests,' where he collected every kind of fruit-tree cultivated in his empire: the Kajah-Mahal of Shah-Soudjah was on the Ganges; he was conquered in 1659 by his brother Aurungzeb, the last of the great Mogols, who laid out the Park of Farrah-Bagh, near Ahmehnagora, at the end of the seventeenth century, to affirm his conquest of the Deccan. These and many other Indian gardens are described by Bishop Heber in his 'Narrative of a Journey through India.' Other remarkable gardens of India are the Nashim-Bagh (Garden of Breezes), Nishât-Bagh (Garden of Delight), and Shâlamar-Bagh (Garden of

[1] See Illustration by Mr G. Elgood, *ante* p. 86.
[2] Some books of reference upon Spanish gardens are:
Gabriel Alonso de Herrera, 'Libro de Agricultura,' folio, Toledo, 1546.
'Theatrum Hispaniæ,' Amsterdam, 1660.
Ford's 'Handbook of Spain' (first edition .
Th. Gautier's 'Voyage en Espagne.'
La Gasca, 'Beautés Naturelles de l'Espagne.
Inglis's 'Spain in 1830.'

the King) at Cashmere; the Royal Gardens of Shah Leemar near Lahore, the Garden of Madura at Mysore, and the Rose Fields of Ghazepoor, near Allahabad.[1]

The Japanese derived their landscape garden originally from the Chinese, but besides imitating Nature, they endeavour to impart to their designs a symbolical character, expressing an abstract idea or sentiment such as 'Retirement,' 'Meditation' or 'Fidelity.'

Japanese Mountain Garden in the 'Shin' or 'Finished Style.'

According to Mr Conder,[2] gardening in Japan was first cultivated as an art in the regency of Ashikaga Shōgun Yoshimasha (between 1449 and 1472) in connection with tea-drinking ceremonies. As

---

[1] See *ante* pp. 40-42.
[2] For the following remarks I am mainly indebted to Mr Josiah Conder's paper on 'The Art of Landscape Gardening in Japan,' at present only accessible in the 'Transactions of the Asiatic Society of Japan,' but I hope it may before long be published independently.

## HISTORICAL EPILOGUE 407

in the Chinese gardens, hills are a fundamental feature, but the Chinese gardens abound more in small kiosks and balustraded galleries, and rockeries honeycombed with caves and grottoes—and the Chinese also employ more flowering plants than the Japanese.

Historical examples of old Japanese gardens are those of Ginkakinzi (silver Pavilion) in Kyoto, and also in old conventual establishments, which have served as models for later artists.

As described in their books the art of laying out gardens is very abstruse, fanciful and superstitious; it is made highly complicated so as to be purposely puzzling to the uninitiated.

There are three styles: 1. *Shin*, *i.e.* Finished Style; 2. *Gio*, *i.e.* Intermediate Style; 3. *Sō*, *i.e.* Free or Bold Style. The mixture of conflicting styles is carefully avoided, and the character of the proprietor and the predominating sentiment either of the natural scene or of an abstraction, such as Happiness, is considered in the composition.

One of the chief methods (the 'Distance-lowering') of laying out, was to plant large trees in the foreground and lower ones to the distance, with a view of adding to the perspective; further hills were made lower than the nearer ones and the distant water higher. Another school was in favour of 'Distance-raising.' Then there is the Garden of Artificial Hills, and space is suggested by blank spaces and obliterations. In the 'Shin' style are five principal hills of different character. Waterfalls are indispensable, in imitation of the famous Cascade in Chiang-So. Of Lakes their ideal is that called Seiko, famous for its Lotuses. Four kinds of islands are introduced into water scenery—the Elysian Isle, the Windswept Isle, the Master's Isle and the Guest's Isle.

The selection and arrangement of stones has been said to constitute the skeleton of the garden. Every stone is symbolic, and has a name according to its situation; there are whole pathways of stepping-stones and groups of stones round lanterns and water-basins.

Sand carefully raked, sometimes in patterns, is an important feature, especially in the smaller gardens. The one here given of an Inn Garden at Nara, is chiefly of sand, with large stones out of which grow shrubs scattered about; and bronze cranes. To our Western ideas there is a certain poverty and bareness about these lesser gardens. Trees are planted so as to show contrasts, and if clipped at all, it is done consistently with their general character and growth, as for instance the native pine (*matsu*). There are very strict rules as to the placing of trees, and names (such as 'view-perfecting tree,' 'tree of solitude') are given them according to their position. The flower-beds are usually in a flat area, opposite the ladies' apartments. Stone

lanterns and water-basins of various shapes are placed in appropriate positions. The garden walls are of tiles and mud alternately, and fences of split bamboos are largely used.[1]

[1] Besides Mr Conder's invaluable Essay and Kaempfer's 'History of Japan (see *ante* pp. 128-9), the following may be consulted on Japanese Gardens :— Mr F. T. Piggott's 'The Garden of Japan,' Mr Chamberlain's 'Things Japanese,' Mr Charles Holme's Essay in *The Studio*, July 1899, 'Notes on Japan' by Mr Alfred Parsons, A.R.A., and Murray's 'Handbook to Japan.'

## HISTORICAL EPILOGUE

To return to our own country. In the nineteenth century, no one better than Sir Walter Scott has held the just balance between the two rival schools, and his 'Essay on Landscape Gardening,' written in 1828, might almost be said to embody the prevailing views of to-day upon the subject. Its keynote is a wise eclecticism, the choice of the *best* that has been done in designing, laying out, 'composing' or building gardens in every age, adapted to the particular site, and its natural and architectural surroundings.

Scott's Essay seems the neutral ground upon which those desperate rivals, the Architects and Landscape Gardeners — the partizans of the Formal and of the Natural Garden—may meet half-way. For the former there is the comfort of the famous sentence, 'Nothing is more completely the child of art than a garden,' and the longer passage on the architectural garden:— 'The result was in the highest degree artificial, but it was a sight beautiful in itself—a triumph of human art over the elements, and connected as these ornamented gardens were with splendid mansions, *in the same character*, there was a symmetry and harmony betwixt the baronial palace itself, and these its natural appendages, which recommended them to the judgment as well as to the eye,'—and he can justify even 'the magnificent cascades' of Versailles. He shows the difference between the Italian and Dutch taste with its 'paltry imitations.' 'A stone hewn into a gracefully ornamented vase or urn has a value which it did not before possess, a yew hedge clipped into a fortification is only defaced. The one is a production of Art, the other a distortion of Nature.' Yet even so, he thinks that existing gardens in the Dutch taste 'would be much better subjects for our modification than for absolute destruction.' Then he shows how excellent was the ruling principle of Kent's innovation, but that Kent failed in execution from his limited view of Nature, through being 'tame and cold in spirit,' and unfamiliar with her grander scenes; thus 'his meagre and unvaried slopes were deprived of all pretension to a natural appearance'; and 'his style is not simplicity but affectation labouring to seem simple.' Scott looks forward to the day when the profession of 'landscape gardener,' which he thinks rather unhappily named, (and it is even less appropriate now than seventy years ago), would be 'more closely united with the fine arts,' and believes that 'a certain number of real landscapes, executed by men adequate to set the example of a new school, which shall reject the tame and pedantic rules of Kent and Brown, without affecting the grotesque or fantastic—who shall bring back more ornament into the garden, and introduce a bolder, wilder, and more natural character into the park, would awaken a general spirit of emulation.' Are there not such men and women at work in the garden now on these lines—painting pictures with Nature's own canvas, forms and colours? But the time has, happily, not yet come to include them in an historical sketch.

Antoine Watteau's 'Bosquet de Bacchus' is an instance of a garden that descends lineally from no school and cannot be called representative of any style, except that of Watteau himself—'le style c'est l'homme même.'

Architecture, aided by sculpture, has been taken as the type of one kind of garden design, Painting of another; may we not say of Watteau that he represents the Music of gardens? And as we see him, in his own portrait, palette in hand, standing behind his friend, Monsieur de Julienne, who holds his violoncello between his knees, with music-book upon the turf; and in the background a statue canopied by that 'tree-architecture, of which those moss-grown balustrades, terraces, statues, fountains are really accessories'; or as we gaze upon the groups in his 'Fêtes Galantes' 'half in masquerade playing the drawing-room or garden comedy of life,'[1] and seem to hear the music of lutes and viols, the murmur of falling waters and waving boughs, we feel that here at last we have realised the ideal garden, 'the chosen landscape,' the perfect fusion of Art with Nature, that

[1] Walter Pater, 'A Prince of Court Painters' (Imaginary Portraits).

'Le Bosquet de Bacchus': engraved by Cochin after Watteau.

# HISTORICAL EPILOGUE

blending and inter-penetration of all the Arts, of which Music is the archtype and symbol to the soul:

> Votre âme est un paysage choisi
> Que vont charmant masques et bergamasques
> Jouant du luth, et dansant, et quasi
> Tristes sous leurs déguisements fantasques.
>
> .    .    .    .    .    .
>
> Et leur chanson se mêle au clair de lune,
>
> Au calme clair de lune triste et beau
> Qui fait rêver les oiseaux dans les arbres
> Et sangloter d'extase les jets d'eau
> Les grands jets d'eau sveltes parmi les marbres.

FINIS.

# INDEX

(*The figures printed in the darker type are the references to the quotations from the authors*)

ADDISON, **134**, 141, 183, 384, 389
Adinaphur, garden at, 40
Adonis, gardens of, 6
Ælian, 86
Agra, gardens at, 405
Ahmadad Gardens, 405
Albanum, 20
Albury, 113
Albyterio, 45
Alcazar, 404
Alcibiades, gardens of, 18
Alcinöus, garden of, 22, 173, 242
Alcott, A. B., **260**
Aldobrandini, villa, 161
Alhambra, 405
Alison, A., 194, **221**
Althorpe, 113
Amherst, Hon. A., 327, 331
Amiel, **276**
Androuet du Cerceau, 45, **51**, 175, 332, 357
Anet, Château d', 51, 61
Annunzio, G. d', **309**
*Apothecaries' garden at Chelsea*, 352
Aranjuez, 286, 405
'Arcadia,' Sidney's, 65
Aristophanes, 320
Aristotle, **77**, 8
Arnold, T., **257**
Arnold, M., 263 n, **291**
*Ars Topiaria*, 16, 57, 246
Athens, 6, 13
Attiret, Pére, 156, 390
Audiat, 51
Audley End, 112
Aulus Vettius, Garden of, 322
Austen, R., 373
Austin, Alfred, **301**
Avignon, Petrarch's Garden near, 32

BABYLON, Hanging Gardens of, 12, 86, 94, 173, 318
Bacon, F., **67**, 141, 241, 251, 342, 352
Badminton, gardens at, 389
Bagehot, W., **317**
Bagh-e-Kilân, 41
Bagh-e Vafá, 41
Baianum, Seneca's Villa at, 20, 321
Baiae, 321
Bangalore Gardens, 405
Barberini Gardens, 321
Baudelaire, **275**
Beaugensier, 90
'Beaumont, Sir H.,' 156
Beaumont, the gardener, 378
Beauvais, Vincent de, 22
Beckford, W., **223**
Bedford, Countess of, 120
Belœil Gardens, 198-9
Belvedere Gardens, 86
Bentinck's Dutch garden, 223
*Berceaux*, 52, 342
Berlin, botanical garden at, 232
Berkeley House, 113
Bilton, Addison's garden at, 389
Biran, Maine de, **230**
Biron, Maréchal de, 175
Blaikie, the gardener, 211, 401
Blenheim, 169, 202, 267, 397
Blith, Walter, 115
Blois, gardens at, 332
Blomfield, R., **303**, 389
Boboli Gardens, 102, 224, 225
Boccaccio, **35**, 287, 295
Bois de Boulogne, 45, 320, 401
Bolingbroke, **139**
Bordeaux, gardens at, 236
Botanical Gardens, 38, 45, 57, 60, 62, 113, 351 n

# INDEX

Bouchardon, 363
*Boulingrins*, see Bowling Greens
Boutin, 199
*Bowling Greens*, as part of a garden, 80, 176
,, at Christchurch, 282
,, at Audley End, 112
,, at Marlboro', 291
,, at Piddleton, 176
,, at Wanstead, 131
Boyceau, gardener, 321, 363
Boyle, Hon. Mrs, 310
Box Hill, 112
Bradley R., 190
Bramante, 338
*Branch Work*, 126
Bridgman, 140, 176, 385, 394, 397
Bright, H. A., 298
Brithnod, 328
Broek, gardens at, 379
Brompton Park Nursery, 125
Brooke, Lady, 111
Brown, L., 169, 171 n, 211, 218, 252, 281, 383, 397
Browne, Sir T., 94, 114, 237, 373
Brunetto Latini, 33
Brussels, gardens at, 103
Bunyan, 118
Burgh, W., 141, 182
Burleigh, Lord, 62, 73, 75, 342, 346
Burlington, Lord, 140, 144, 384, 394
Burton, Robert, 33, 85
Busch, gardener, 201
Byron, 253, 363

CAMBRIDGE, Colleges, 389 n
Campbell, Lord, 247
Cannons, 132
Cantelow, Lord, 86
'Capability Brown,' 169, 171 n, 211, 218, 252, 281, 383, 397
Carlton House, 141 n, 197
Carmontelle. 401
*Cascade in* Chiang-So, 407
Casello, garden at, 54
Cashiobury, 113
Casinum, Varros' Villa at, 11
Cato, 9, 13, 19, 53, 96, 114, 320
Caus, Isaac de, 342
Caus, Solomon de, 342, 403
Cavendish, 337

Celsus, 19
Cerceau, A. du, 45, 51, 175, 332, 357
Cesio, gardens of, 55
Chabas, 1
Chambers, Sir W., 183, 211, 390
Chantilly, 102, 208
Chardin, Sir J., 126, 319
Charleton, Dr W., 8
Château—
  d'Anet, 51, 61
  d'Ecouen, 45
  de la Chenaie, 271
  de Meudon, 102
  de Madrid, 45
  de Nesle, 45
  Thierry, 401
Chatham, Earl of, 157
Chatsworth, 389
Chaucer, 328, 331
Chaulnes, 45
Chelsea Gardens, 145, 352 n
Chenaie Gardens, 271
Chenonceux, 45
Chesterfield, Lord, 144, 148
Chinese Gardens, 127, 156, 171, 176, 184, 196, 204, 211, 254, 383, 390, 401
Chiswick, 140, 196, 397
Chou-tun-I, 28
Cicero, 10, 247, 321
Cimon, 18, 320
*Citronière*, 105
Clagny, 117
Clairvaux, 32
Claremont, 140, 202
Clusius, 346
Cobbett, W., 228
Cobham Gardens, 88
  ,, Lord, 144, 169, 182, 383
Coesalpinus, 58
Colbert, 102
Collins, M., 279
Cologne, physic garden at, 346
Colonna Fra, 46
Columella, 19, 77, 114, 191
Comenius, T. A., 87
Condé, 102, 209
Constantine Arch, 105
Corbie, gardens of, 327
Cotton, Charles, 54
Cowley, A., 100, 251, 280

# INDEX 417

Cowper, W., **191**
*Cradle-walk*, 112
Crispin de Pass, 346
Croome Gardens, 169
Curzon, Lord, 127, 319
Cyrus's garden, 95
Czarsokojeselo, 201

DALLAWAY, 218
Damascus, garden of, 274
Darwin, E., **191**
Davy, Sir H., **247**
D'Annunzio, **309**
De Amicis, 377
De Brosses, **159**, 318, 321 *n*
Decker, 131
De la Quintinye, 61, **115**, 166
De Nesle, Château, 45
De Serres, 43, 44, 45, **58**, 61, 357
De Vries, 58, 346
D'Écouen, Château, 45
Defoe, **131**, 380
Delhi, Gardens at, 405
Delille, L'Abbé, 197, **206**, 247, 398
D'Este, Villa, 55, 312, 338
Deyverdun's Gardens, 204
*Dials*, 74, **79**, 151, 230, 239, 240
Diderot, **166**
" Didymus Mountaine," **77**
Disraeli, I., 91 *n*, **231**
Disraeli, B., **265**
Dodonaeus, 346
Doria Pamphili, Gardens, 341
D'Orias, Prince, 110
Douglas, Gawen, **39**
Drayton, M. **75**
Du Cerceau, 45, **51**, 175, 332, 357
Du Perac, 61
Dufresny, C., **127**, 398
Durdans, 132
Dusseldorf, Court Garden of, 259
Dutch Gardens, 36, 197, 224, 374
Dutch Garden, books on, 383

EDEN, garden of, 203, 316
Egyptian Gardens, 1
Elizabethan Gardens, 62, 342
Elyot, 19
' Enoch's Walk,' 92
Epicurus, gardens of, 4, 8, 13, 243, 320
Erasmus, **36**, 42

Ermenonville, 178, 199, 202, **209**, 398
Escurial Gardens, 86, **405**
Essex, Earl of, 113
Esher, 196, **394**
Estienne, **43**, 357
Evelyn, John, 14 *n*, 46, 91 *n*, 101 *n*, 103, 115, 116, 124, 228, 232, 251, 257, 370

FALCONER, Dr, 318
Farelli, 112
Farnese Gardens, 55
Farrah Bâgh, 405
Farnham Castle, 228
*Ferme Ornée*, 140
Ferrara Schottus, 86
Fiacre, St, 115
Fischer, of Erlach, 403
Fisherwick, 169
Fitzherbarde, **42**
*Flourishings*, 126
Fontainbleau Gardens, 60, 61, 86, 102, 107, 256, 324, 357
*Fossé* in garden, 176
Foster, Mrs J. F., **304**
Fouquet, N., 102
*Fountains* at Aranjuez, 287
,, at Haff, 103
,, at Hampton Court, 112
,, Laocoon, 105
,, at Nonsuch, 74
,, at Pagliavam, 226
,, at Versailles, 363
,, in Greek Gardens, 4
,, in Luxembourg Gardens, 108
,, in Temple Gardens, 239.
French Garden, books on, 369 *n*
Fulham, 102
Fuller, T., **98**

GAILLON, Château, 51, 332
' Garden of Love,' 331
' Garden of Gardens ' (Chinese), 390
' Gardener's Lodge,' 115
Gardens, size, 11, 69, 88, 98, 107, 145, 345
,, situation of, 196
Garth, Samuel, 196, 203
Gassendi, **90**, 91 *n*
Gautier, T., **272**, 363, 364
Genoa, 110

Gerard, Lord, garden of, 373
Gerarde, 62, 98, 231, 346
German Gardens, 230, 403
    ,,       books on, 403
*Gestatio*, in Pliny's Garden, 15
Ghazepoor Gardens, 406
Gibbon, 204
Gilbert, A., Gardener, 87
Giles, Herbert, 24, 281
Gilpin, W., 402
Ginkakinzi Gardens, 407
Girardin, Marquis de, 199, 202, 209, 398
Girardon, 363
Goethe, 213
Goldsmith, 186
Goncourt, Ed. de, 277
Googe, B., 52
Goujon, Jean, 46
Granada, gardens at, 86, 313, 404
Gray, T., 171, 397
Gray's Inn Gardens, 241
Greek Garden, 1, 320
Grilli, 45
*Grotto* at Château d'Écouen, 45
,, at Ermenonville, 398
,, at Haff, 103
,, at Rueil, 106
,, at Tuileries, 45
,, at Twickenham, 332
,, at Villa Borghese, 111
,, at Wotton, 373
,, of Calypso, 332
,, of Pausilippo, 113 *n*
Guerin, M. de, 271
Guiscard, park at, 401

HACKNES, 81
Hackney, gardens at, 111
Hadersdorf, 403
Hagley, 204, 394
Hague, 103
Hall, Bishop, 85
Hall Barn, 197
Hallam, H., 245
Ham, 113
Hamburg, 404
Hamilton, C., 140, 394
Hampton Court, 74, 88, 112, 169, 331, 332, 337, 378
Hanging Gardens of Babylon, 12, 89, 94, 173, 318

Harrison, W., 88
Hartlib, S., 102, 115
Hartrigge, 247
Hatfield Gardens, 342
Hawthorne, N., 266
Hayes Place, 157, 394
Hayley, 157, 197
Heber, Bishop, 405
Hebrew Gardens, 1
Heidelberg, 342, 403
Heine, H., 259
Helps, Sir A, 286
Hentzner, P., 73, 75, 176, 332, 342
*Herbals*, 62, 98, 346, 351
Herbert, George, 89
Herculaneum, gardens at, 173, 321
Heresbach, C., 52
Herodotus, 318
Hesperides, gardens of, 64, 94, 223, 317
Hill, T., 77
Hinton, St George, 123
Hirschfeld, 402
Hodges, Anthony, 27
*Hoeredium*, 13
Holborn Physic Garden, 351
Holland House, 342
Holland, Philemon, 14
Holmes, O. W., 270
Home, Henry, 154
Homer, 3, 22
Horne, 226
*Hort-yard*, 331 *n*
"Horti Pensiles," 318
Houghton, garden at, 172
Houslaerdyk, 379
Howell, James, 92
Huet, 122, 317
Hugo, Victor, 262, 273
Humboldt, A. von, 6, 28, 232
Hunt, Leigh, 249, 298
Hyde Park, 104

ICOLMKILL, Abbey of, 327
Ildefonso Gardens, 405
Indian Gardens, 405
Irving, Washington, 248
Isola Bella, 159, 311, 318
Italian Gardens, 338
     ,,    books on, 341

JAMES I. of Scotland, 331

# INDEX 419

James, T., 280
Japanese Gardens, 94, 128, 406-8
,, books on, 408 n
Jardine Royale of Paris, 104
*Jardin Anglais*, 312, 401, 403
,, *Larmoyant*, 393
Jerome, St, 23
Jerrold, D., 264
Johnson, Samuel, 158
Johnson, G. W., 328 n, 352 n, 389
Josephus, 95 n
Joubert, J., 220, 259 n
Julius, Pope, gardens of, 55
Juvenal, 20

KAEMPFER, 128
Kajah-Mahal Gardens, 405
Kames, Lord, 154, 208, 393
Kant, I., 191
Karnak, 3, 318
Karr, A., 268
Kelso, gardens at, 282
Kenilworth Castle, 83
Kensington Gardens, 394
Kent, William, 140, 141, 155, 170, 177, 183, 195, 196, 378, 383, 394
Kew Gardens, 228, 346 n, 390
Kinglake, A., 274
Kip, 176
Knebworth, 263 n
Knight, R. P., 214, 217, 402
*Knotted Beds*, 337
Krafft, 403

LABORDE, 199
*Labyrinth*, 50, 75, 76, 80, 117, 234
,, at Chantilly, 209
,, at Hampton Court, 378
,, at Kensington, 227
,, at Theobalds, 342
,, at Trinity College, Oxford, 389
,, at Versailles, 364
Lahore, 406
Lamartine, 255
Lamb, Charles, 238
Langley, Batty, 148, 389
Landor, W. S., 220, 242
Laneham, R., 82
*Landscape Gardens*, requisites of, 219
,, origin of, 167, 177, 315

*Landscape Gardens*, debased form of, 297
Laocoon, fountain, 105
Latini, Brunetto, 33
Laurentine, villa of Pliny, 15, 321
Law, Ernest, 337, 378 n
Lawson, W., 57, 78, 303
Le Nôtre, 61, 102, 116, 117, 122, 127, 145, 166, 199, 262, 364, 378
Leasowes, 188, 203, 393
Lebanon, 3
'Lee, Vernon,' 295
Leland, J., 57
L'Estrange, R., 38
Levens, gardens at, 378
Lewes on Goethe's Garden, 213
Liancourt, Comte de, 106
Liébault, 43, 45, 357
Lientschen, 28
Liger, 125
Ligne, Prince de, 198, 403
Linné, gardener, 404
Linnæus, 145
Lipsius, Justus, 20
Livy, 320
Long Melford, 92
Longleat, 389
London, George, 125, 133, 135, 370, 380
Longus, 25
Loo, 374, 377
Loudon, 20, 194, 211, 218, 233, 321 n, 374
Loudon, Marshal, 403
Low Laxton, 151
Lucian, 21
Lucullus, 18, 225
Ludlam's Hole, 229
Ludovisi Gardens, 160, 321, 341, 370
Luther, 39
Luxemburg Gardens, 107, 117
Lydgate, 328
Lyly, J., 64
Lyte, 346
Lyttelton, 394
Lytton, Bulwer, 263

MACHIAVELLI, 35
Madura, gardens at, 406
Magdeburg gardens, 404
Mago, 19
Magdalen College, Oxford, 373
Malmesbury, W. of, 28

Mandelslo, 126
Manger, 404
Mansfield, Lord, 202
Marie de Medici's gardens, 104, 107
Marius, garden of, 52
Markham, G., 45, 82, 115, 303
Marlborough, Duke of, 202
Marlborough College, 291
Marlia, 245
Marly Gardens, 139, 161, 403
Marot, 377
Martial, 321
Marvell, A., 240, 373
Maschal, L., 80
Mason, G., 194, 202, 393, 394, 397
Mason, W., 182, 390, 398
Matius, 16
Maundeville, 33
Maupertuis, 211, 401
Mayer, 403
Maxwell, Sir W. S., 286
*Maze*, 50, 75, 76, 80, 117, 234
,, at Chantilly, 209
,, at Hampton Court, 378
,, at Kensington, 227
,, at Theobalds, 342
,, at Trinity College, Oxford, 389
,, at Versailles, 364
Meager, L., 119
Medici Gardens, 55, 226, 341
Melmoth's Pliny, 18
Méréville, gardens at, 199, 401
Meudon, Château de, 102
Meyer, 202
Meynell, A., 296
Mickleham, 112
Mignaux Gardens, 127
Milbank, Switzer's garden at, 133
Miller, P., 145, 234, 352
Milner, George, 299
Milton, 96, 141, 175, 176, 203, 253, 317
*Moat at Wressel*, 58
Mohammad, 27
Mollet, 61, 321, 357
Monceaux, 61, 401
Montargis Gardens, 332
Montaiglon, 50
Montaigne, 53
Monte Cavallo Gardens, 55, 110
Montesquieu, 144
Montesquiou, 211

Montmorency Gardens, 45
Montpellier Physic Garden, 45
Moor Park, Herts, 120, 378
,, Farnham, 229
More, Sir T., 38, 119
Morfontaine Gardens, 209, 401
Morel, 202, 398, 401
Morine, 109
Morris, 394
Morris, W., 292
Moulin-Joli, 178, 199, 401
*Mound* at Marlborough, 291
Mount Garden at Hampton Court, 337
*Mounts*, 57, 70, 76, 79, 80
,, at Low Laxton, 151
,, at Theobalds, 126, 342
,, at Twickenham, 384
,, at Wadham College, 389
,, at Wressel, 57
,, in Roman gardens, 322
Muhammed, 40
Munich, gardens at, 403

NARA, Japan, garden at, 408
Nashîm-Bagh, 405
Nassau, Comte de, gardens, 377
Neckam, 30, 328
Negroni Gardens, 226, 321
Nekht, 3, 318
Nero, 19
Newman, Cardinal, 261
Nishât-Bagh, 405
Noisy-le-Roi Gardens, 358
Nomentanum, 20
Nonesuch, 74, 75, 88, 113, 132, 176, 194, 332
Norman Gardens, 328
Nôtre, A. Le, 61, 102, 116, 117, 122, 123, 127, 145, 166, 199, 262, 357, 364
Nymphenburg, gardens at, 403

OATLANDS, 204
*Orangery*, 134, 225
*Orbicular form of garden*, 75
Owen, 19
Oxford, Christ Church, 282
,, New College, 266
,, Magdalen College, 373
,, St John's College, 266, 281
,, Trinity College, 389
,, Wadham, 389

PAGLIAVAM, 226
Pains Hill, 140, 197, 203, 204, 394
,,    Cottage, 291
Palermo Gardens, 213
Palladio, 114
Palladius, 19, 22
Pallissy, B., 45
Pamphili Gardens, 161, 312, 370
Paradise, Persian, 4
,,    of Sardis, 5
Parc de Vaux, 102
Parkinson, J., 75
Parsons, A., 408 n
Pater, W., 9, 95 n, 294, 410 n
Pausanias, 6
*Peacocks*, 26
Peacock, T. Love, 252
Peiresc, 90, 232
Pekin, garden at, 390
Pembroke, Earl of, garden of, 87, 202, 342
Penshurst, 87, 342, 352
Pensiles, Horti, 318
Pepys, S., 124
Peresfield Gardens, 204
Persian Gardens, 1, 4, 12, 94, 127, 319
Petrarch, 31, 56
Peutexoire, Isle of, 33
Phaedrus, 6
Physic Gardens, 38, 57, 60, 62, 351
,,    ,,    at Cambridge, 351
,,    ,,    at Chelsea, 352 n
,,    ,,    at Cologne, 346
,,    ,,    at Hamburg, 351
,,    ,,    at Holborn, 317
,,    ,,    at Kew, 346
,,    ,,    at Lambeth, 352 n
,,    ,,    at Montpelier, 45
,,    ,,    at Oxford, 113, 351
,,    ,,    at Salerno, 351
,,    ,,    at Venice, 351
,,    ,,    at Wells, 346
Piddleton, 176
Pilois, 117
*Piscinae*, 113, 114, 244
Pitt, 394
Platt, Sir Hugh, 345
Plato, 5, 6
*Pleachwork*, 87, 281, 342, 352
Pliny the Younger, 15, 256, 321

Pliny the Elder, 12, 13, 63, 96, 114, 173, 320
Plutarch, 18, 320, 322
Poe, E. A., 271
Pompeii, 323
Pompey, 18
Pompylus, 8
*Pond-garden*, at Hampton Court, 331 n, 337
Poole, 27
Pope, 141, 175, 183, 253, 332, 383
Poplars, Isle of, 210
Portuguese Gardens, 313
Pratolino, grotto at, 54
Price, Sir U., 212, 214, 217, 402
*Privy garden at Hampton Court*, 337

QUAMSI, 187
*Quincunx*, 21, 95 n, 373
Quintilian, 21, 95
Quintinye, de la, 61, 115, 125, 370

RABI'S Garden at Bordeaux, 236
Rapin, René, de Hortibus, 123, 206, 236, 245, 246
Ray, J., 118
Rea, J., 373
Reid, J., 374
Renaissance Gardens, 30-61, 338
Renan, E., 279
Repton, H., 171 n, 217, 218, 252, 401
Reux Gardens, 45
Riario, gardens of, 55
Richardson, S., 393
Richelieu, 105, 109, 357
Richmond Green, 131
Robert, Hubert, 274, 364, 401
Robinson, P., 308
Robinson, R., 35
Robinson, W., 305
Roman Gardens, 1, 13, 55, 225, 296, 320, 322
,,    Cato's description of, 9
,,    Modern, 257, 296
Rosamond's Labyrinth, 75
Rose, J., 370, 378
Rousham, 140
Rousseau, 161, 202, 209, 273, 364, 393
Rueil Garden, 102, 108, 357
Rumford, Count, 403

## INDEX

Ruskin, J., 289
Ryswick Gardens, 377

St Anthony's garden, 327
,, Bernard, 32, 86
,, Bertin Gardens, 327
,, Cloud, 102, 105, 161, 370
,, Fiacre, 115
,, Gall, gardens of Abbey of, 327
,, Germain, 60, 61, 322, 332
,, James' Park, 370
,, Jerome, 23, 327
,, Martino Gardens, 209
,, Remy Gardens, 327
Saint-Hilaire, 7
Saint-Simon, 102, 139
Sainte-Beuve, 198
Sallust, 53, 321
Salzmann, 404
Sand, George, 264
Sandwich, 100
Sans-Souci, 404
Sardis, Paradise of, 5
Savage, 92
Sayes Court, 111, 373
Sceaux, 102
Schiller, 222
Schönbrunn, 403
Schopenhauer, 254
Schwetzingen, gardens of, 403
Scipio's garden, 321
Sckell, L., 403
Scott, Sir W., 229, 233, 234, 409
Seneca, 20, 323
Serle, J., 144 n, 384
Serres, de, 43, 44, 45, 58, 61, 351 n, 357
Sévigné, Madame de, 117
Sforza Gardens, 55
Shaftesbury, Earl of, 115
Sheen, Temple's garden at, 378
Shelley, 256
Shenstone, 167, 188, 204, 281, 393, 394
Shere Gardens, 228
Shalamar Bagh, 405
Shiraz, gardens of, 319
Siculus, Diodorus, 12, 318
Skelton, 337
Sidney, Sir P., 65, 202, 352
Smith, Adam, 182
Smith, Sydney, 238
Socrates, 5

Solomon, 3, 63, 237, 319
Sorgvliet, 377
South Lodge, 157
Southcote, Philip, 140, 394
Southey, 235
Spanish Gardens, 211, 226, 243, 404
,, books on, 405 n
Spence, Joseph, 156
Staël, Madame de, 230
Statues, 73
Steckhoven, 403
Stephens, Charles, 43, 357
Sterne, 165
Stidolph, 112
Stowe Garden, 140, 202, 383
Stuart Gardens, 62
*Summer Hall*, 38
,, *House*, 66, 73
*Sun Dials*, 74, 79, 151, 240
,, at Moor Park, 230
,, in Temple Gardens, 239
Sunderland, 113
*Sunk Fence* (Ha-Ha), 179
Surflet, 43
Sutton Court, 131
Swift, 133, 229, 378
Switzer, S., 133, 389, 404
Syrian Gardens, 1, 12

Tacitus, 19
Taine, 322, 341, 364
Tanks, 2
T'Ao Yuan-ming, 23, 28
Tarquinius Superbus, garden of, 320
Tasso, 55
Tatius, Achilles, 25
Tavernier, 319
Taylor, John, 87, 342
Temple Gardens, 239
Temple, Sir W., 4, 15, 75, 95 n, 119, 176, 229, 330, 378, 383
Temple, Lord, 202, 383
Temples in Gardens, 202
Tench, Sir F., 151
Tennyson's garden, 300
Terrace in Roman gardens, 16
Thalysia, 9
"The Water Poet," 87
Thebes, 1, 3
Theobalds, garden of, 75, 88, 126, 176, 332, 342

# INDEX 423

Theocritus, 9
Theophrastus, 7, 243
Thessaly, 80
*Tholus*, in Roman Garden, 11
Thomas, Inigo, 303, 389
Thoreau, H. D., 275
Thorney Abbey, 28
Thornley, George, 25
Tibault (Theobalds), 88
Tissaphernes, 18
Tivoli Gardens, 199, 311
Transtevere Gardens, 55
Treveris, 57, 346
Trianon, 210, 256, 264, 403
Trinity College, Oxford, 389
*Tsubo*, 128
Tuileries, 45, 48, 60, 61, 105, 117, 160, 332
Turkish Gardens, 86
Turner, W., 346
Tusculan, Pliny's villa, 15, 321
Tusculum, Lucullus' villa near, 18
Tusser, 115
Twickenham, Pope's garden at, 144

Ursino Gardens, 55

Vanbrugh, 140.
Varro, 11, 18, 19, 77, 114, 191, 323
Vatican, 110, 338
Vaux le Villars Garden, 358
Vegetius, 19
Vergil, Polydore, 42, 100
Vernet, J., 401
Versailles, 75, 162, 173, 196, 246, 256, 262, 273, 276, 341, 357, 403
Verulam, Lord, 67
Verville, B. de, 46
Villa Albani Gardens, 341
 ,, Aldobrandini, 161
Villa Borghesi, 110
 ,, D'Este, gardens, 297, 312, 338
Vinet, 44
Virgil, 19, 20, 55, 246
Voltaire, 148

Wadham College, 113, 389
*Walls* in gardens replaced by fossé, 176
 ,,  ,, by clairvoyées, 378
Waller, Sir W., 92, 98, 182

Walpole, Horace, 75, 95$n$, 141$n$, 156, 170, 172, 197, 200, 317, 321, 384, 394, 397
Wanstead, 131
Ware Park, 84
Warner, C. D., 308
Warwick Castle, 173 $n$
*Water*, Kent's treatment of, 178
Watelet, C. H., 178, 199, 401
Watson, Forbes, 287
Watteau, 277, 281, 410
Waverley Abbey Gardens, 229
Wells, physic garden at, 346 $n$
Wentworth Castle, 204
Weston, R., 345 $n$
Whateley, T., 140$n$, 157, 170, 193, 194, 397
Whewell, W., 258
White, G., 181
Whitehall Gardens, 73
Whitinson, 10
Wilkes, J., 186
Wilkin, 94 $n$
Wilkinson, Sir J. G., 3, 318
Wilson, J., 250
Wilton, gardens at, 87, 112, 342
Windham, W., 217
Windsor Park, 204
 ,, Garden, 331
*Winter Garden*, 136
Wise, Henry, 125, 133, 135, 233, 378
Wooburn, 197, 397
Woodstock, 75
Worcester College, 113
Wordsworth, W., 233
Worlidge, J., 129
Worlitz, 403
Wotton, Sir H., 84, 352
Wotton Gardens, 111, 114, 373
Wressel Castle, 58
Wright, 394
Würzburg, gardens at, 403

Xenophon, 4, 53, 319
*Xystus*, 16

Young, Arthur, 59, 202, 208

Zarsokojeselo Gardens, 201
Zehir ed-din Muhammed, 40
Zola, 302

2 F

www.ingramcontent.com/pod-product-compliance
Lightning Source LLC
Chambersburg PA
CBHW022137300426
44115CB00006B/224